Advancing Democracy

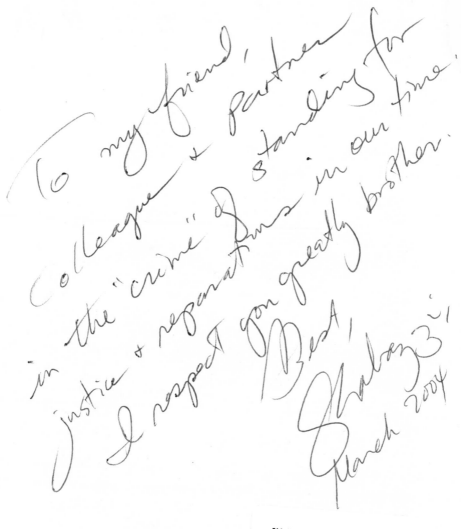

To my friend,
colleague + partner
in the "crime" of standing for
justice + reparations in our time.
I respect you greatly brother.

Best,
Shabazz
March 2004

ADVANCING

DEMOCRACY

African Americans and the
Struggle for Access and Equity
in Higher Education in Texas

AMILCAR SHABAZZ

THE UNIVERSITY OF NORTH CAROLINA PRESS

Chapel Hill and London

The paper in this book meets the guidelines for permanence and
durability of the Committee on Production Guidelines for Book
Longevity of the Council on Library Resources.

Library of Congress Cataloging-in-Publication Data
Shabazz, Amilcar.
Advancing democracy : African Americans and the struggle for
access and equity in higher education in Texas /
Amilcar Shabazz.
p. cm.
Includes bibliographical references and index.
ISBN 0-8078-2833-5 (cloth: alk. paper)
ISBN 0-8078-5505-7 (pbk.: alk. paper)
1. College integration — Texas — History. 2. African
Americans — Education (Higher) — Texas — History.
3. University of Texas at Austin — Students — History. I. Title.
LC214.22.T48 S53 2004
378.1'98'0976431 — dc21
2003012091

cloth   08 07 06 05 04   5 4 3 2 1
paper   08 07 06 05 04   5 4 3 2 1

for Leah Hebert, Winona, and Grant Saint Julian,

for Lue Metoyer, Edward and Murry Frank,

for all who inspire children onto the path of knowledge

Contents

Illustrations, Tables, Figure, and Map

Illustrations

Tables

Figure

Map

Acknowledgments

How good and how pleasant it is to give thanks and praise to the many who have helped enable me to complete this work. Almost fifteen years ago I picked up and read a book James Anderson had written about the history of African American education. I was hooked. His work inspired me to re-direct a part of my life course and to begin a process of research, analysis, writing, interpretation, and teaching, and I give him maximum respect and gratitude. I cite his work along with many other scholars in this book. To do so involves more than a professional courtesy. I want to acknowledge and honor the sacrifices of the historians who endeavored to document what was done to get us where we are. Their efforts are valuable to our present understanding and our future, if we listen carefully and act responsibly.

All of my formal higher education took place at public institutions in the state of Texas. My focus on my home state as a way to speak to the changes in American higher education as it concerns African Americans serves as a form of payback to the public education idea and to Texas itself. Specifically, I am indebted to my mentors and teachers at the University of Texas at Austin, namely John Warfield, William Darity Jr., Harry Cleaver, Tom Philpott, Douglas Kellner, and Drew McCoy. The history department at Lamar University supported me as I first journeyed into the profession and the subject of race and education. John Carroll, Adrian Anderson, Ralph Wooster, Joann Stiles, John Storey, Namaan Woodland, and Marion Holt were all exceedingly supportive as I began to see myself as a historian and in the writing of a master's thesis on the struggle for access and equity at a single institution of higher education and in publishing my first schol-arly article.

It was, however, in an oddly designed building called Agnes Arnold Hall at the University of Houston that I found a truly dynamic and challenging environment that brought out the best in me. Guadalupe San Miguel, Steven Mintz, Emilio Zamora, James Kirby Martin, Martin Melosi, John Hart, Susan Kellogg, Joseph Glathaar, Albert Miller, and Richard Blackett were remarkably generous, and each made specific contributions to my intellectual development. Linda Reed and Lawrence Hogue, in their different ways, taught me how to study African American history and culture, and I feel very privileged for all of the time they gave me. Not only was Joseph Pratt's genius the most important scholarly influence on this project, but he was — and is — the best friend and mentor a person could have both inside and outside of the academy. He is the kind of player who makes you see how great the game can be.

A rolling tide of blessings has swept over me at the University of Alabama, where I found a fitting abode in the Department of American Studies. Of all the niches in American academia, American Studies has offered a depth of purpose, a breadth of vision, and a wealth of tradition most propitious to my interests in social transformation. James Salem, Rose Gladney, Ralph Bogardus, Reid Badger, Lynne Adrian, Richard Megraw, Edward Tang, and Stacy Morgan have been superb colleagues, giving me more support than I have been able to give in return. They helped to see me through a tough period in my life as I rebounded from a serious blow to my health. Joining them in enveloping me in a community of support are my many African American Studies colleagues, especially Rhoda Johnson and Cornelius Carter. Dexter Gordon, Jerry Rosiek, and the Interdisciplinary and Interpretive Writing Group (I and I) have been marvelous friends and encouraging critics. I must also thank Andrew Sorensen and Nancy Barrett for their support, particularly for giving me some great contemplative time along the beautiful Wye River in Maryland, where I finished the last portion of the manuscript. I wish every scholar could find a place like the Aspen Institute's Wye Faculty Seminar to ponder and discuss the meaning of citizenship and the American polity.

I also owe thanks to the staffs of numerous archival libraries and special collections, namely, the Metropolitan Research Center at the Houston Public Library, the University of Houston main and downtown campuses, the Library of Congress, and the various libraries of the universities to which I made research visits. Let me especially acknowledge the Harry Ransom Humanities Research Center at the University of Texas at Austin for a productive summer as an Andrew W. Mellon Foundation fellow-in-residence. Without the help of the library staff and faculty members at the various universities this study would have been impossible to complete.

Whether for the influence they exerted on my thought about and approach to historical and cultural studies, their insightful comments on earlier drafts and their research assistance, friendship and e-mail encouragement, a meal or a place to stay, or a serendipitous encounter at a library that ended in a great tip and/or spiritual boost, I am indebted to many other good people. Let me *call out* Darlene Clark Hine, W. Marvin Dulaney, Nell Painter, Mia Bay, Wilma King, Jewel Prestage, Merline Pitre, Jacquelyn Dowd Hall, Lorenzo Thomas, William Harris, Peter Wallenstein, John Hope Franklin, Christian Davenport, Niyi Coker, Robin Kelley, Michael Fitzgerald, Maceo Dailey, Cary Wintz, Mack Jones, Imari Obadele, Dorothy Turner, Velma Roberts, Bakari Kitwana, Ajamu Nyomba, Izielen Agbon, Takunda Mojerie, Ahmed Obafemi, Chokwe Lumumba, Akinyele Umoja, Ernest Obadele Starks, Bill Kellar, and Dwight Watson. It is sometimes easy to forget friends at the victory celebration, but we look eagerly for their faces at Calvary when we stand before captious crowds. The custom of absolving folks you acknowledge for whatever shortcomings may be found in your work has become passé, but here is a toast to an old custom.

Demetria deserves the greatest thanks for her perseverance, advice, confidence, and comradeship. Diane and Lawrence Rougeaux, Leah St. Julian, and Winona Frank have been my rocks of support. Mandela, Amilcar, Gaston, Anaya, LeAndra, Fallan, Micah, Ayinde, Amara, Erica, Amiri, CJ, the youth of Kingston, Kati, Bamako, Segou, and Timbuktu, and all the children of the world inherit the challenge to go after the highest learning they can attain and to use it to advance democracy. I pray this book helps you in some way to fulfill that mission. *Pamoja Tutashinda Mbilishaka.*

Advancing Democracy

Introduction

When the incisive wit of Richard Pryor's *Bicentennial Nigger* warms my heart, I recall my hopes and dreams in 1976 as a young American who happened to be of color. I had no limits. My vision was to become the first black to be elected to the U.S. Senate from Texas, perhaps one day to become president of the United States. Of course, the reality and prevalence of racism and white supremacy did not escape me. Like Nat Turner and Dr. Martin Luther King Jr., two of my heroes, I felt I was destined to play a profound role in lifting humanity above outmoded attitudes and practices to higher ground and a better day. I worked hard all through my school years preparing: being a class representative, winning oratorical and writing contests, and reading voraciously, especially the works considered masterpieces. Then in 1976, the bicentennial of the United States, came my senior year and time to pick a university where I would further educate myself and advance toward my ambitions. From my peers, teachers, and persons who seemed to be in the know there was only one choice: the University of Texas at Austin (UT).[1]

I do not recall ever doubting whether I would be admitted to UT. My first SAT score was not promising. I retook it on a day when I was struggling

1

with contact lenses and a higher degree of test anxiety relative to my first try. The result was a lower score. Still I did not worry. I had attended a predominately white Catholic high school and had taken a college pre-paratory track of courses. My grades, except for physical education, math, and typing, had all been in the A+ to B+ range. My service activities had been extraordinary. Frankly, I did not have a well-developed sense of the competitive nature of college admissions, and I had never once heard anything about how affirmative action might help me get into UT because I was black and thereby disadvantaged. In fact, race-based affirmative action did not exist and certainly did not concern me. When my white high school chums, whom I knew I was smarter than, received their acceptance letters, I fully expected to receive mine as a matter of course. And so it ultimately arrived.

In the summer of 1977, I attended a week-long group orientation ses-sion that instructed me about the important logistical and historical infor-mation about UT, or the "Forty Acres," which refers to the original size of the Austin campus. I learned my first gang sign: the Hook 'Em Horns hand signal. I learned about the UT tower as the key campus landmark and how no one could visit the observation deck any longer after some nut went up there with high-powered rifles and shot people to death. I even learned my first Aggie jokes as I was introduced to the intense rivalry UT has with the state's older land-grant institution, Texas Agricultural and Mechanical University. I remember being told that UT had the largest endowment fund for an institution of higher education second only to Harvard, but never once was I told that people whom the state designated as Negro or black like me had only recently been allowed to attend UT. I would have to hunt and commit years of my life pursuing and engaging the hard facts of black admission to UT and the other institutions of higher education that the state of Texas had declared for whites only. I wonder how my under-graduate experience might have been different if I had been able to read what is presented in this book. I wonder how the undergraduate experi-ence of all university students might have been transformed if the role and relationship of race to higher education and democracy in U.S. and Texas history had been a mainstream part of our education.

The process by which segregated higher educational systems remade themselves to a greater or lesser extent into environments in which all citizens, regardless of racial designation, could study on a basis of equality has not been, until recently, a subject of special consideration among historians. Two reasons for the relatively undeveloped state of this field of inquiry may be hazarded. The first has to do with how historians deter-mine when events have become *historic*. Clearly there must be some tem-poral space between the historical happening and the historian's work of representing the occurrence as history. De jure desegregation, the breaking down of racially restrictive social policies and practices by resort to action in a court of law, still occurs. De facto desegregation, or the actual activity of a member of one racial group entering and becoming a part of institutions or positions or social and cultural spaces from which they once were barred, is also still taking place. For example, desegregation events such as a white or black person for the first time joining a college sorority or fraternity that had never pledged a member of the other race or the first African American becoming the president of a large, state-supported university are still a part of day-to-day current events. How does one dare treat such phenomena as a part of history rather than the sociology of a continuing, unfinished process within higher education? How can historians interpret the significance of such practices and events that directly configure their own world? Historians are clueless.

The second reason historians shy away from the subject of higher educational desegregation may have to do with the difficulty posed by subjective issues like fear, politeness, and concern for the reputations of the living or the recently departed. The ego and all of our basic human emotions often come into play more strongly with contemporary history than with the distant past. The trials of scholarly detachment are compounded when the unit of analysis is the academic historian's own shop, the place where one's living is earned or could be earned: the university. To reconstruct events that depict university life as held captive by blatant, obscene, and crude acts of ignorance, prejudice, and discrimination is not the kind of scholarship stakeholders care to partake in, least of all about their own school.

Rising against the grain, the historical literature on the desegregation of higher education has begun to make a respectable showing. E. Culpepper Clark's *Schoolhouse Door: Segregation's Last Stand at the University of Alabama* is an illuminating study of the journey toward desegregation at Alabama's flagship campus. As an administrative official at the University of Alabama, Clark studied the school that provided some of the most dramatic episodes in collegiate desegregation. His work goes beyond the "saccharin studies" and "house histories" that often characterize books on institutional change in higher education.[2]

Mark Tushnet, with *The NAACP's Legal Strategy against Segregated Education, 1925–1950* and *Making Civil Rights Law: Thurgood Marshall and the Supreme Court, 1936–1961*, greatly expands our appreciation of the complexities involved, legal and otherwise, in the struggle for citizenship rights. He shows how the fight against racial discrimination in higher education established the National Association for the Advancement of Colored People (NAACP) as a leading force in the mid-twentieth-century challenge to white supremacy, as well as the premier architect of the field of public-interest litigation known as civil rights.[3]

The kind of historical work still missing is one that weaves a critical

3

inquiry into the emergence of higher education together with an analysis of the struggle for black liberation at the state and local levels. Recently, historians have mapped a new framework for periodizing and localizing the civil rights phase of the modern black liberation struggle. No longer can the story begin with the honorable action of Mother Rosa Parks in 1955. Reassessments of the dynamic salience of the NAACP to the momentous period from before the Second World War to the Civil Rights Act of 1964 have pointed out the visible tip of an iceberg of resistance activity. It is not a matter of the NAACP doing all the work or even the most important work of the struggle. The association does, however, provide an avenue through which the heart of black resistance can be reached. Through its more or less continuous presence in areas of the South between the 1930s and the 1960s, the NAACP facilitates scrutiny of other parts of the black social quilt that sustained actions for justice, equality, and liberation. Studied carefully, the NAACP can reveal the links between churches, labor unions, fraternal and benevolent associations, organizations of professionals and business owners, newspapers and other mass communication forms, and infrapolitical contestations of a spatial or everyday sort, as well as political and cultural beliefs of a given community.[4]

A study of how white supremacy challenged black people and, in turn, how blacks challenged that ignoble system of "race" domination finds an important focal point in African Americans' struggle for higher education. James Anderson's *Education of Blacks in the South, 1860–1935* brilliantly delineates the vital importance black people in the period after slavery attached to access to the schoolhouse, to creating and maintaining centers of learning for themselves and future generations. As an integral part of the great undertaking of black enlightenment came the democratic demand of African Americans for access to institutions for their higher education.[5]

No historian has yet picked up the story where Anderson left off and carried forward the evolution of "Negro Higher Education" or, more broadly, the education of black southerners up to their rendezvous with what Manning Marable calls "liberal integrationism." The political integrationist ideology, frequently referred to in the present study as civil libertarianism, acted as the midwife to deliver the offspring of racial militancy and conciliatory interracialism: the desegregation struggle. Marable writes that the "central tenets" of this new form of black political consciousness included "the eradication of all legal barriers to blacks' gaining full access to civil society, economic exchange, and political institutions; an increase in the numbers of African Americans representing their race in both real and symbolic positions of authority within the state; [and] a strategic alliance with liberal whites, especially the national leaders of the Democratic Party, after the Great Depression." He adds that "several generations of

African-American leaders were nurtured in this secular creed and unthinkingly accepted its implications."[6] My effort here is to show how the adherents to this "secular creed," organizing under the NAACP banner, attacked the "legal barriers" that restricted access to the doors of the university. The larger aim of my historical narrative is to openly explore the "implications" that liberal integrationism had both for African Americans and for society as a whole.

Texas, of all the southern states, recommends itself for special study in the first instance because with *Sweatt* v. *Painter* it gave the nation the landmark case that launched the dismantling of racial discrimination in higher education. Of even greater importance in the choice of Texas, however, is the claim it makes to being the South's most unique and diverse state. It is the only former slave state that was once a part of Mexico and that has a substantial Mexican American population. This group never experienced legal exclusion in regard to higher education, but it did face a form of systematic discrimination despite the fact that the juridical conventions of the day declared the Mexican "Caucasian." The Tejano/a experience and the Mexican American concentration in the borderlands of the southern and western parts of the state created a Trojan horse within the fortress of white supremacy. The direct and indirect influence of the Mexican American presence in South and West Texas softened white resistance to desegregation, sped black entry into the region's colleges, and provided a valuable ally to the statewide desegregation campaign. The diversity only begins there. Texas is where the East meets the West. It looks in both directions and summons engaging comparisons of the traditionally "southern" cities of Beaumont, Texarkana, Dallas, and Houston with the more "western" or mestizo cities of Corpus Christi, El Paso, San Antonio, Amarillo, and Brownsville. Texas furnishes a revealing touchstone from which the southern story may be brought into sharper focus.[7]

The study of a single state is also an initial step toward a comparative history. With the rise of class differentiation among black Texans there emerged the most vibrant of southern campaigns to improve African American access to higher education. The unique economy of Texas, dominated after the turn of the century by the production and refining of oil, produced a deeply divided political and ideological terrain that ultimately worked against segregation in favor of national goals, such as a global image of the United States as leader of the free world. The ascendancy of the idea of human equality over white supremacy did not, however, result from federal pressure on the outside and business owners on the inside trying to bring the state out of the southern region's colonial morass and into line with national policy and the urban-industrial age, at least not in its entirety. That triumph must be found in the self-determined struggle of blacks themselves. While their choices undoubtedly reflect traces of major-

5

itarian and bourgeois class influences, this does not negate the fact that blacks chose the goals, tactics, and strategies of their struggles. Also, without African American initiative, none of the changes presented here would have occurred or mattered.

In our present time of momentous changes in higher education and the national political consensus on established desegregation strategies and racial justice policies, a study that takes aim at the histories of these important features of the American social landscape is especially warranted. How else can we know what makes racial discrimination in college admissions a "regrettable chapter" in the history of the United States? Thus, I begin with a brief overview of segregation in higher education in Texas. In the 1870s, schools were not vastly unequal. Over the next seven decades, however, Anglo-Texans established for themselves seventeen public senior colleges and continued to restrict blacks to one inadequate facility (see Table 1). Throughout this ninety-year period, blacks struggled for greater access to higher education in breath and brick. In speech and petition they demanded the creation of a new state-supported university for blacks. Refused admission to "white" colleges and universities, restricted to a single segregated college, and guided by the value of self-determination, African Americans took over the educational resources the state and custom racially identified as "for colored youth" and fought for the continuous improvement of the college at Prairie View. What they still lacked in higher education in the state they sought outside of Texas. The blacks-only inconvenience of having to leave the state to pursue advanced degrees that Texas institutions offered to all other racial groups led in the late 1930s to a campaign for state assistance in the form of tuition subsidies. Black Texans succeeded in getting the state legislature to appropriate finances for blacks who studied outside of Texas for graduate and professional education. A pragmatic, remarkably unified campaign known as the Texas University Movement followed. At first the movement rooted itself in the marrow of racial tradition, but in the 1940s, it began to embrace a new political rhetoric. The concept of opening traditionally white institutions to blacks, and vice versa, became thinkable and utterable, and around it, lawyers, schemes, and a legal campaign cohered.

As troubling as the exposure of white-domination in areas of American life might be, no intellectuals have bothered to carefully delineate the implications of a self-defined prodemocracy move to separate race from higher education. There is no single tract or collected works to hold up, but a candid and, at times, intriguing conversation can be pulled from oral and written records that document a mind at work—both for and against—launching the antiracist democratization of the university. The history of higher educational desegregation, then, is a history simulta-

Table 1. Segregated Texas Senior Colleges by Year of Creation as State-Supported Institutions and Year of Opening, 1871–1963

Institution, City	Created	Opened
Texas A&M, College Station	1871	1876
Prairie View A&M College, Prairie View	1876	1879
Sam Houston State, Huntsville	1879	1879
Southwest Texas State College, San Marcos	1881	1883
University of Texas, Austin	1881	1883
University of Texas Medical Branch, Galveston	1881	1891
North Texas State College, Denton	1899	1901
Texas Women's University, Denton	1901	1903
University of Texas Dental School, Houston	1905	1943
Texas Western College, El Paso	1913	1914
West Texas State College, Canyon	1913	1914
Arlington State College, Arlington	1917	1917
Tarleton State College, Stephenville	1917	1917
East Texas State Teachers College, Commerce	1917	1917
Sul Ross State College, Alpine	1917	1920
Stephen F. Austin State College, Nacogdoches	1917	1923
Texas College of Arts & Industries, Kingsville	1917	1925
Texas Technological College, Lubbock	1923	1925
Midwestern University, Wichita Falls	1946	1946
Texas Southern University, Houston	1947	1947
Southwestern Medical College, Dallas	1949	1949
Lamar State College of Technology, Beaumont	1949	1951
University of Houston, Houston	1961	1963

Sources: Texas Legislative Council, *Higher Education Survey*, 1953, and *Texas Almanac*, various editions

neously of a kind of legal and self-evident transformation and of a sweeping intellectual engagement and evasion.

Beginning as an attention-grabbing effort to extract concessions from white power holders who had long ignored black people's pleas for equality, the fight against segregation in Texas colleges and universities following the Second World War matured into the leading form of organized black activism. The civil libertarian thrust and the larger ideology of liberal integrationism did not assume hegemony over the black community by fiat from Thurgood Marshall, the NAACP, or Harry Truman, for that matter. Rather it was the brave example of blacks students, who, from 1949 to 1965, stepped onto white campuses in the face of white resistance that ranged from passive, to massive and legal, to illegal mob violence. These students played the decisive part in winning the hearts and minds of large numbers of blacks of all social classes and, eventually, of many white liberals to integration as the only way to ensure racial equality and justice. While the students made things happen, they drew their inspiration from myriad forces: Marshall, the NAACP, Truman, the great aims of humanity, justice, and peace that heartened soldiers and their families in the recent world war in Europe and Asia, the desire for individual advancement, torch-bearing for the race, and as many other forces as there were students who dared to cross the color line. The ultimate motor forces for the movement as a whole were twofold: to save the race and to advance the cause of democracy.

In the late 1970s, the hollowness of the integrationist ideology at its moral and intellectual core began to expose itself. When I attended UT in 1977, the school had changed in but a small way from the days of its first black undergraduates of two decades before. Black students in my generation, however, faced racism with a crumbling ideological armor. We did not know we were on the moral high road because we did not know ourselves in the context of a history as an African American people. We did not know that we were the primary heirs of the great human tradition of democratic struggle.

Moving from the Juneteenth emancipation to the 1965 Civil Rights Act, the following chapters map the intellectual, legal, and grassroots activism that helped launch a new way of thinking about race and citizenship rights in a democracy and the transformation of a segregated system of higher education. If this history helps us face the lawsuits of Jennifer Gratz, Barbara Grutter, Cheryl Hopwood, Jennifer Johnson, and Katuria Smith that challenge how we in higher education try to address racial domination's brutal effects, then let the blessings be. I hope democracy is mature enough in our part of the world to justly reconcile individual and group interests and pasts.[8]

CHAPTER ONE

As Separate as the Fingers
Higher Education in Texas from Promise to Problem,
1865–1940

Dear readers, come and walk with me on the porch of research for a little
investigation. . . . We stand today over 12 million strong. These millions
speak, sing and preach in the English language, and beginning sixty years
ago our progress has been so marvelous, having now an army of cultured
Teachers, Preachers, Lawyers, Doctors, Masters and promoters of business
enterprises. Why should we not be inspired to take courage and press forward? . . . [A]ll we ask is an equal chance in the field of endeavor and we will
build a monument of honor and love in the hearts of all mankind that shall
stand as a sure foundation for us and even unborn generations who will have
need to call us blessed.
— Andrew Webster Jackson, *A Sure Foundation* (1940)

Before black Texans had their own history, schools, churches, warriors,
martyrs, and women and men of big affairs, they had Juneteenth. It may
not have looked like much in the eyes of an arrogant world, but it was
everything black Texans had, and they each loved and cherished that day
with all their heart. On the nineteenth of June, they celebrated with their
songs of sorrow and joy, they shared the mirth that helped them to survive
the long, white-hot day of bondage, their tongues spread the lore that
sustained their folk life, and most important of all, they remembered.
Facing their past together, the know-it-alls and the know-nothings, the tall
and the short, the bright and the blighted, those whose britches seemed to
be on fire and those who could go along to get along, they all came together and remembered. Here, from that day forward, they gathered the
scattered meanings of their prehistory and put themselves to the task of
creating a new collective persona, the freedmen and the freedwomen of
the land known as the United States of America. The American soil on

which most of them had been born was, however, a land their captors had always claimed as fully theirs and theirs alone. The Euro-Texan claim to ultimate supremacy over the state and its power to control the land is what brought to the Afro-Texans's Juneteenth an enduring sense of paradox, ambiguity, and irony. Much as they would resist the prerogatives and assumptions of white power, the relative weakness of black power made negotiation a matter of necessity, and negotiate they did. To wrest from white Texans access to the higher educational resources of the state, black Texans had to negotiate a complex system of myths, authority, law, statecraft, prejudice, domination, and psychopathology. The story of how they did this is a significant and fascinating one. Telling no lies and claiming no easy victories, it is clear that the struggle for access and equity in Texas higher education is a vital part of the process of the social construction of black freedom itself.[1]

From 1866 to 1876, white Texans, against the wishes of the state's minority black population, created a dual system of public education predicated on the separation of a white race from an African or Negro race. The start of an apartheid system of racial domination in Texas began with the constitution of 1866 with its decree that the "income derived from the Public School Fund be employed exclusively for the education of white scholastic inhabitants" and "that the legislature may provide for the levying of a tax for educational purposes." The state would direct tax monies raised among people of African descent themselves exclusively toward "the maintenance of a system of public schools for Africans and their children." Political turmoil and postwar economic conditions, however, prevented the actual development statewide of any public school system.

In 1867, the Reconstruction legislature erased the language of racial segregation. The efforts of ten black representatives at the Constitutional Convention — George T. Ruby, Wiley Johnson, James McWashington, Benjamin O. Watrous, Benjamin F. Williams, Charles W. Bryant, Stephen Curtis, Mitchell Kendall, Ralph Long, and Sheppard Mullins — were a crucial part of the process that helped create public schools and take state government out of the business of maintaining race consciousness. In *The Development of Education in Texas*, Frederick Eby wrote that despite "the extreme irritation which was felt at the school system imposed by the radical régime, schools were opened; and as attendance was made compulsory many of the colored children attended, this being their first experience of public education." By 1873, however, the Texas legislature began repealing most of the Reconstruction laws, and the brief and limited episode of nonracial school access became a faint memory.[2]

In the centennial year of the American War of Independence, a racialistic and inegalitarian spirit seized the hearts of the majority of the legislators in Austin and the white majority of the state's population at large.

Where the constitution of 1869 had been silent on the matter of integrated classrooms, the 1876 constitution was quite definite: "Separate
schools shall be provided for the white and colored children, and impartial
provision shall be made for both." State government was again in the role
of preserving racial identity, and, more perniciously, it fully intended to
deny blacks the "impartial provision" of schools, as well as the "Branch
University for the instruction of the colored Youths of the State," which it
had promised them in Article 7 of the constitution ratified on 15 February
1876. Historian Alton Hornsby Jr. speculates that the integration of the
University of South Carolina, which resulted from the failure of state officials to establish any institution of higher learning exclusively for blacks,
moved Texas legislators to pass a constitutional provision creating a dual
system of higher education.[3]

Six months after Texans ratified their new, more racist state constitution, the state legislature enacted a measure creating a "State Agricultural
and Mechanical College for Colored Youths." The act gave Governor
Richard Coke the power to appoint a commission to find a site for the
college and supervise the building of its physical plant within a paltry
budget of $20,000. The state-supported school that would train the minds
of free black men and women, ironically, found a home at Alta Vista, the
1,000-acre slave plantation that became the property of Helen Marr Swear-
ingen Kirby and her husband, Jared, in 1858. In 1867, Helen Kirby, widowed shortly after the Civil War, opened Alta Vista Institute, a boarding
school for white girls. She closed the school in 1875 and reopened the
institute in Austin. The state of Texas purchased the Alta Vista Plantation
from her for $13,000, and because its lands "were exceptionally good for
farming and other agricultural purposes," it became the location for Alta
Vista Agricultural College for "colored" people.[4]

"Alta Vista," meaning the high view or landscape, did not last long
as the school's name, and the school itself almost died out with it. On
21 January 1878, the state commission concluded its work of preparing
the "colored" state college, in compliance with the federal government's
Agricultural Land Grant Act, or Morrill Act, from which Texas had benefited. It formally handed over the stewardship of the new institution to the
board of directors of the Texas A&M College, the main branch of which
was created in 1871 (but not opened until October of 1876). The A&M
directors then named Thomas S. Gathright, the president of the white
A&M college, as president of the new black A&M college, requesting that
he serve in that capacity without any additional pay. They also hired a black
man from Mississippi, Frederich W. Minor, to serve as the institution's
chief operating officer under the baneful title of principal. The title may
have caused Minor little distress; he actually constituted Alta Vista's sole
employee: chief administrator, registrar, faculty, janitor—all rolled into

11

Although the Texas state constitution of 1876 promised to create a branch of the University of Texas "for the instruction of the colored Youths of the State," legislators established a separate and unequal branch of Texas A&M. Shown in this engraving done in the 1890s is Prairie View's Kirby Hall, an old plantation house on the left, and Academic Hall on the right (Cushing Library, Texas A&M University).

one. The white president/black principal dualism, which remained in effect for more than seven decades over the objections of students and supporters of the school, signified the peculiar, subordinate place the school held within a white supremacist society. On its opening day, 11 March, a mere eight students showed up to enroll; but even they quickly fled the plantation school. Like the white A&M branch, Alta Vista only accepted men. The educational function of both the black and white agricultural schools largely involved taking young men fresh off a farm and returning them to the farm as more highly skilled or "scientific" farmers. Alta Vista's early "black students," however, as a Texas A&M historian found, "were not interested in college training which would merely return them to the drudgery of farm labor." Until 1879, the little "colored" school on the high prairie withered on the vine, until Governor Oran Roberts took up the suggestion to convert Alta Vista into a coeducational normal school for the preparation of teachers for "colored" schoolchildren. Under the new name of Prairie View State Normal and Industrial College but continuing under the control of A&M's board and the white president/black principal arrangement, the multipurpose institution began attracting students. With scholarships from the state treasury and community organizations, as well as the support of popular black political leaders like Norris Wright Cuney of Galveston, Prairie View grew slowly into a major institution of postsecondary education in Texas.[5]

Cuney, like many blacks of his day, did not rush to endorse the machinations of the white supremacists setting up Prairie View. After Cuney visited Austin in the 1870s, word spread that he had given his support to legislation establishing a state school exclusively for "colored" deaf, dumb, and blind youth. Answering the rumor in his characteristic style of burning

12

forthrightness, Cuney said he opposed segregation in no uncertain terms. Cuney stated that "had the memorial" to establish a special state school for the hearing and visually impaired "been drawn to read that the State should make provision for all her unfortunates, I should certainly have endorsed it, but I do not seek special legislation for the Negro." He assailed the fact that in Texas only two public institutions showed any eagerness about admitting persons of African descent: the penitentiary and the lunatic asylum. The state-supported institutions of higher learning and the asylum for the hearing and visually impaired were all closed to blacks, he bemoaned. He went on to articulate a clear argument against a dual system of higher education that had to wait over three-quarters of a century before it reappeared before the Supreme Court:

> It is a sad travesty upon humanity and justice that the State of Texas accepted gifts of public lands for the endowment of an Agricultural and Mechanical College for the benefit of the whole people, and bars a large proportion of her population because they were born black. . . . No, I do not ask for social equality for my race. That is a matter no law can touch. Men associate with men they find congenial, but in matters of education and State charity there certainly should be no distinction. There is a clause in our State constitution separating the schools. This brands the colored race as an inferior one.[6]

Ultimately, albeit reluctantly, Cuney became a supporter of the separate-but-unequal Prairie View. He helped many persons to get scholarships to attend the school, and his daughter, Maud, later taught there, as well as headed the music department of the Deaf, Dumb, and Blind Institute for Colored Youth in Austin. Both Cuney and his daughter, and black Texans in general, lived in an age of compromises that typically were unfairly cut against black equality. Nonetheless, for every sacrifice of principle, every indignity withstood, they also fought for ground. In 1883, when a Galveston businessman gave the city $200,000 to build a public high school, Cuney, the first African American elected to the city council, demanded that the grant be accepted only if Ball High did not exclude black children. His principled but unsuccessful stand against segregated education and Jim Crow laws faded into the background of Cuney's pragmatic maneuvering as a politician. Historian Merline Pitre argues that Cuney "was too busy climbing [ladders for political offices] to devote much of his attention to racial matters." However fair this assessment of Cuney may be, it is clear that accommodation of and rebellion against racial oppression characterized and shaped the lives of black Texans from the most privileged strata to the least.[7]

In the 1880s, when the state perfected its plans to create the University of Texas at Austin as an institution of the first class for white youths, blacks,

13

including Cuney, protested government officials' failure to abide by the state constitution and a constitutionally mandated popular vote in 1882 that affirmed that the state would create in Austin a branch of the University of Texas (UT) exclusively for black students. Black educational leaders consistently reproached the legislature's biased way of administering the state's dual system of education through the end of the nineteenth century and into the twentieth. Despite their protests, the Texas legislature did not deem it "practicable" to establish a "colored branch" of the University of Texas until it faced the possibility of having black students integrate its flagship university in the middle of the twentieth century.[8]

Texas blacks' struggle for equal education acquired the reputation of being the most progressive of any state in the postemancipation South. "During the last three decades of the nineteenth century," one historian has noted, "Texas made greater progress in reducing Negro illiteracy than any other state. . . . Until about 1880 Texas retained her primacy in Negro education, but by 1900 the state had lost this lead" in all areas except the number of black high schools. Moreover, "whites had little sincere interest in furthering the education of the Negroes."[9] Thus, a large measure of the relative advance in black education must be accorded to the actions of blacks themselves.[10]

A combination of factors enabled black education to get a strong start in Texas. The leadership of public servants like Matthew Gaines and Norris Wright Cuney was a key factor, but the military, through the Freedmen's Bureau, also played a positive role. Brigadier General Joseph Kiddoo "formalized and expanded the Negroes' school system" by combining funds from the volunteer groups working to educate blacks with government subsidies. The resulting higher salaries induced many of the northern benevolent agencies' schools to come under the bureau structure.[11]

Initially, most white Texans greeted the rise of black education, which to them invalidated the old order, with mistrust and hostility, which soon grew into stern, organized opposition. The evangelical fervor of teachers who came as God's soldiers of light to "save" a wicked and fallen South enraged the average white Texan. The state newspapers portrayed black freedmen and freedwomen as uneducable subhumans who needed hard work under the scrutiny of whites for their own best interests. A wave of school burnings and physical attacks and threats against teachers and students ensued. One white woman in Houston expressed with pith the mood of the period when she stated that she would sooner "put a bullet in a Negro than see him educated."[12]

In spite of Anglo-Texan antipathy, by 1867, the bureau estimated it had taught 10,000 blacks how to read and write. When the bureau withdrew from Texas on 30 June 1870, the schools were its only program of any lasting benefit to blacks. The agency failed to endow blacks with land, and its direct relief of emergency food rations, fair courts, and just labor contracts was at best a late and poor start. The more than 4,000 blacks attending bureau schools, however, was a significant step forward.[13]

Radical Republicans, for a variety of political reasons, tried to guarantee that these schools would not be closed once military rule was ended in the state. Before Texas could gain readmission to the U.S. Congress it had to promise "that the Constitution of Texas shall never be so amended or changed as to deprive any citizen or class of citizens of the United States of the school rights and privileges secured by the Constitution of said state."[14]

After President Ulysses S. Grant signed legislation on 30 March 1870 restoring civil government, the problems of instituting public education fell squarely into the arena of Texas politics and public opinion. This development immediately brought on dire consequences for the struggle for educational opportunity. Indeed, under the newly reconstructed Texas government, the "general system of public schools under a state superintendent of education" died a quick death when "popular hostility to the admission of negroes to the public schools, coupled with the inefficient management by the courts, rendered the plan in large measure a failure."[15]

By 1879, Texas created a public school system strictly segregated by race. A provision to the constitution of 1876 denied benefits from the Available School Fund to any Texas school attended by both white and Negro children. The legislature followed this step in 1884 with a revision of the public school law that reinforced the principle of segregation: "The children of the white and any colored races shall be taught in separate schools and in no case shall any school consisting partly of white and partly of colored children receive any aid from the public school fund." Texas laws, policies, and state actions that built and perpetuated a separate and unequal system of education already were solidly established by the time of the Supreme Court's 1896 *Plessy* v. *Ferguson* decree, which upheld the constitutionality of laws and practices that excluded African Americans from institutions, businesses, and services on the basis of racial designation. White Texans hailed the decision even though it was clear that there was no consensus regarding white responsibility to the equality part of *Plessy*'s "separate but equal" ruling. While for white Texans *Plessy* gave national sanction to state and local white supremacist policies, for blacks it spurred their move toward nationalism and an ethos of self-reliance over pleas for integration, a move Texas novelist and Baptist preacher Sutton Griggs advocated in *Imperium in Imperio* (1899) and his four other novels published in the first decade of the new century.[16]

The paths black Texans took toward solving the problem of Negro education became a double-edged sword. If the educational level of blacks somehow had been held constant at its 1870 level, a major improvement in their condition would have been virtually unthinkable. The increase in the number of educated men and women, the elimination of illiteracy, and the enlargement of black people's control over the educational institutions that served them contributed to their rising standard of living, thus expanding their power to determine the political, social, cultural, and economic conditions of their communities. Yet the push for education, its becoming a basic part of the black creed, carried with it an unfortunately high degree of uncritical acceptance of the cultural values inherent in the content and structure of Eurocentric education. The foundation of this latter aspect is grounded in the plantation experience.[17]

Beckett Harrison from San Augustine, Texas, recalled from his days in slavery that "most every farm have a cullud man l'arning to preach. 'Cose dey couldn't read de Bible, but dey pay 'tention to de white preacher when he come 'round an' some of 'em done good at it. My grampa uster claim to be a preacher." The *claiming* of roles such as preacher, which implied the acquisition of a knowledge base (perhaps divine election as well), involved a mix of imitating white behavior and black creativity. Harrison added that "dey have school in de quarters an' de li'l slaves had a chance to learn how to read an' write. Dey teach 'em manners an' behavier too. Sometime dey git a broke-down white man to be de teacher. Dey try not to let de chillun come up so ign'nant. Den dey could use 'em better for dey own purpose." Here he demonstrates cognizance of the hegemonic nature of the slave education in the quarters. Harrison estimated that "it took ten or twelve year after freedom to git de black man de qualification way he could handle things." For blacks to be able to "handle things" for themselves in a Eurocentric society in less than a generation no doubt represented a great accomplishment for the freedpeople, but it came at a price that could run terribly high.[18]

Zeno John felt the price. "I uster b'long to de Odd Fellows," the elderly black Texan remembered in an interview in 1937, "I neber be l'arn' [learned] to hol' office and I couldn' qualify. I neber did go to school."[19] The Odd Fellows, a black self-help association established in New York City in 1843, became one of the earliest community organizations after emancipation that supported the institutional and moral foundation of universal schooling for the freedpeople.[20] Membership in fraternal orders like the Odd Fellows had its privileges, but with leadership came a measure of elite status and power. The rise of intraethnic social class differentiation gave an answer to the question the enslaved black boy asked of Fanny Kemble: "Missus, what for me learn to read? me have no prospects."[21] With education a black man had the prospect of being a leader among his people, a person of status, a person with the power to direct the course of affairs in the organizations, institutions, and social life of the black community, at least as much as the white power structure would allow. "If you want to lead, you must read" was the saying that captured the prevailing attitude. Moreover, given that the power structure could allow the black elite broad latitude, leadership had its privileges. The point at which white power holders imposed limits generally came whenever expenditures rose above what they deemed necessary or whenever a rebellious attitude of some kind appeared to circulate among black people.

The educated black elite seldom sought a radical departure from white society and culture, and when they did it was truly a radical development. At the elite's most fervent and aggressive point in Texas history, its principal aim centered on getting more of what was needed to *be like white people* rather than anything else. Henry Lewis, born at Pine Island in north central Jefferson County, Texas, about two decades before emancipation, saw the dilemma of enslavement, liberation, and culture in plain terms: "Us all wanter git free and us talk 'bout it in de quarters 'mongst usse'fs, but we ain't say nuttin' 'bout it w'ere de w'ite could hear us. W'en freedom come, some stay on de ol' place a long time, and some go off. Some was scared to leave. You know dey was jis' slaves and warn't civilize'. Some ain't nebber git civilize' yit."[22] As it was in Africa, Asia, and Latin America, the schoolhouse in the United States was socially constructed into a key instrument for *civilizing* its internally colonized subjects.[23]

Black schools also became the site of significant activity that ran counter to the hegemony of white authorities. They helped to nurture, groom, and equip a cadre of leaders who challenged the caste relations and the colonial system that constrained their opportunity for social and material advancement. In Texas, a key organization of educated black men and women arose in the form of the Colored Teachers State Association of Texas (CTSAT). A dozen men, including L. C. Anderson, principal of Prairie View Normal School, and David Abner, noted educator and fraternalist, met and founded the association in 1884. For eighty-two years it continuously operated to unite black educators across denomination and from all over the vast expanse of the Lone Star State. Prairie View's principals and chief administrators wielded considerable influence over educational, social, and political matters through the CTSAT. It also served as a watchdog to protect the interest of publicly supported black higher education.

The CTSAT's advocacy function extended in at least two different, perhaps contradictory, directions: first, it reminded state officials of Prairie View's importance and worked to maintain and develop the institution; and second, it tried to keep before the public the constitutional promise of a first-class university for African Americans. From one generation to the next, CTSAT sought to fulfill its credo: "Best in Education for Every Negro Child — Best Working Conditions for Every Negro Teacher." Indeed, it was in the CTSAT that black intellectual warriors against white supremacy planted the seeds of the modern civil rights movement in Texas.[24]

17

In 1900, CTSAT members debated the industrial education idea. Booker
T. Washington's Tuskegee model ruled at Prairie View, challenged the
liberal arts orientation of the state's private black colleges, and was spread-
ing its influence across the state's common schools. Booker T. Washington
in his Atlanta Exposition Address of 1895 had expressed the idea that "in
all things that are purely social we can be as separate as the fingers, yet one
in the hand in all things essential to mutual progress." Washington categorized education as a "purely social" matter where African Americans
preferred to be away from whites. Thanks to his separatist position and the
effectiveness with which his Texas-born second in command, Emmett Jay
Scott, spread the news of the Tuskegee Institute's success with its industrial
training program, Washington became very popular with many black and
white Texans. A CTSAT committee, however, reported that the idea that
black minds were best suited for practical training was "unjust, illogical,
spurious, and antagonistic to American peace and prosperity, and entirely
out of step with the soundest philosophy of the age." Launched in 1896,
the association's petition drive for a bona fide liberal arts college curriculum at Prairie View brought results in 1901 when Texas A&M approved the
addition of college-level courses. By the 1920s, the CTSAT's sustained opposition to the Tuskegee model's limited social vision had contributed to
the galvanizing of a Texas version of the New Negro. In the 1930s, New
Negroes would launch a direct attack on the segregated order. In the years
following emancipation, educated blacks in the CTSAT played a decisive
role in shifting the worldview of black Texans away from an unfulfilled
separate equality agenda back to dreams of a racially integrated society.[25]

As for the outlook of white Texans, the pleas and arguments of the
CTSAT principally fell on deaf ears and closed minds. Eby argued that
"while there still remained some opposition on the part of many white
people, the leaders of the state recognized the wisdom of educating colored people." Of course "reasonable people" knew that educating blacks
served many useful ends, but white state leaders most wanted black schools
to instill labor discipline, as well as a peculiar, subordinate sense of *place*
within southern society, and to fulfill these ends as cheaply as possible.
Prairie View's biennial appropriation remained inadequate, the black UT
question was ignored, and the New Negro was greeted with indifference
and sometimes scorn. By the First World War the higher education of
blacks had journeyed from a constitutional promise to a clear and manifest
problem. Eby himself expressed surprise that Texas, which ranked seventh
in size of black population — 690,049 in 1910 — had a total of a mere 129
black college students in 1914. He noted that black college enrollment in
Texas had risen to more than 600 for the 1921–22 academic year, and he
attributed the marked increase to "the same causes which have operated
in institutions for white students: higher wages after the war furnishing

more with the means for higher culture, the broadening of the curricula in offering more industrial training, Federal aid in assisting ex-soldiers, and the acceptance of the work of negro colleges for teachers' certificates." The fivefold increase in black college students in Texas suggests the flowering of a black renaissance, but it also highlighted the problematic nature of the state's dual higher education system.[26]

Owing in part to the influence of progressivism, which emphasized the evaluations of experts, so-called Negro education in the early twentieth century inspired a great many studies, surveys, and reports, complete with recommendations for improvement. Although the major studies generally reflected the biases of the experts who authored them and the governmental or philanthropic agencies that commissioned them, black leaders and intellectuals often participated in and influenced these studies. Thomas Jesse Jones, in his *Negro Education: A Study of the Private and Higher Schools for Colored People in the United States* (1917), produced a massive national survey that stimulated a heightened level of concern among state education officials, resulting in some minor changes in educational policy in Texas.[27]

After receiving a subvention from John Rockefeller's General Education Board (GEB) in 1919, a first for Texas, the legislature established a Division of Negro Education (DNE) within the State Department of Education. The DNE opened a new, progressive thrust on behalf of the state government in the field of Negro education.[28] It advocated industrial education for the black masses and gathered facts in its execution of the state's first survey of Negro schools in 1921.[29]

In 1924, Texas governor Pat M. Neff announced the completion of a comprehensive survey of the state's system of public education, which the state published the next year in eight separate volumes. In accord with the segregationist spirit of the times, several volumes of the *Texas Educational Survey Report* contained a separate subsection that treated "Negro education." On the basis of scientific testing of black school-age children, the survey commission reached the conclusion that "the mental ability of the negro . . . indicate[s] on the whole, that they would be able to profit by increased educational opportunity." In addition to offering proof of the educability of blacks, the writers of the *Survey* appealed to the white ruling class's sense of its own self-interest for their arguments for improving "negro" education. Particularly, the commission stressed that better schools could improve Negroes' lifestyles and their health — mental and physical. Given the fact of the "interwoven" nature of black-white economic and geographic life, it would be of "mutual gain" and would free both races "to a certain extent from the danger of epidemics." Allowing blacks to live in conditions that made them more susceptible to disease caused greater absenteeism from work, lower productivity, and, in the case of communicable diseases, cross-race exposure to whatever illnesses blacks carried. Additionally, the self-interest argument emphasized the ability of schools to reduce the so-called criminal-mindedness of blacks.[30]

Using data from southern states that educated children separately in white and black schools, the *Survey* ranked Texas fourth after Missouri, Oklahoma, and West Virginia in having the lowest percentages of "negro" illiterates; moreover, in 1920, approximately 70 percent of black Texans lived in rural communities working as landowners (23,519), tenant farmers (54,945), or farm laborers (91,000). Texas ranked ahead of all other states surveyed except for Maryland and Oklahoma in expenditures for teachers' salaries and in narrowing the dollar gap between white and black teachers' pay. On average, white teachers in Texas received slightly more than double what black teachers earned. Maryland and Oklahoma, on the other hand, paid a little less than double, while South Carolina, the worst case, paid white teachers almost ten times more than black teachers. Likewise, Texas paid higher average annual teachers' salaries to blacks and invested more in the physical plants of black schools in per capita terms than all other states besides Oklahoma and Maryland. Texas ranked second among the states surveyed in the percentage of black scholastics enrolled: 87 percent of black school-aged children (classified as between the ages of six and fourteen) were enrolled, compared to 91 percent of white children. Only Oklahoma did better, with 88 percent black enrollment versus 87 percent white enrollment.[31]

The Texas Educational Survey Commission also brought to Texas Leo Favrot, a field agent of the General Education Board, who had primary responsibility for producing most of the *Survey*'s reports on Negro education. Favrot's assessment of the Negro part of Texas's dual education system was thoroughly consistent with the designs of the GEB:[32]

> The Prairie View Normal and Industrial School is the only State supported college for negroes in Texas. It should develop several other lines of work, such as painting, brick-laying, and the like, of less than college grade. It should develop more two-year courses above high school for those who find it impossible to continue in the four-year collegiate courses. Above all, it should be equipped to do better teacher training. The library needs more generous support, more cows are needed, and a more adequate training school should be provided. In short, the standard of support, in general, is too low. The general spirit of the institution and the conduct of its students are very creditable. Plans should be laid now for the early provision of professional education for negroes in such lines as law and medicine.[33]

Favrot, moreover, determined that Willette Rutherford Banks "was the man to carry out the Board's program at Prairie View," and his recommendation secured Banks the Prairie View principalship. His recommendation of "early provision" of professional education for blacks, however, went unheeded for more than two decades.[34]

Another widely circulated study, Arthur Klein's *Survey of Negro Colleges and Universities*, published in 1929, also had the general effect of highlighting certain problem areas and of affirming the need for black higher learning. Klein, as did the 1925 state survey, called upon black colleges to modernize their classical liberal arts curriculums by making them more in line with their white counterparts. Above all else, he noted the need for teacher training, followed by agricultural, industrial, and vocational education. "National social and economic life demands the training of many more negro professional and technical leaders," Klein wrote. "This is also a question of higher education." He stressed that "to safeguard the health of the colored people and of their neighbors," it was vital that the relative size of the black profession-managerial class match the rate of increase of the general black population. This class was best able "to instruct" the masses "in hygiene, sanitation, and in the measures necessary to ward off disease."[35]

If read with genuine concern, Klein's study might have alerted Texas officials to their culpability for the dismally low numbers or nonexistence of black physicians, surgeons, dentists, architects, engineers, designers, inventors, pharmacists, and other professionals. State leaders chose instead to ignore his findings. Prairie View did not institute a division of graduate study until 1937, when black activists pressured the state legislature and the A&M board to do so.[36]

Black Texans received little help from state government officials and fellow white educators, who made no pretense of friendship or liberalism on race. Nevertheless, blacks, with the few whites they could find, did organize interracial committees and conferences. The significance of interracial gatherings on education lay more in the way they helped to galvanize black educators and political activists and spurred them to clarify problems and goals than in stimulating actual corrective action. In 1930, the first Prairie View Educational Conference inaugurated the most important series of symposia on black life of the decade. The annual meeting satisfied a variety of purposes. As a collaborative project between the State Department of Higher Education and Prairie View, it became one of Principal Banks's favorite ways of leveraging his college into a more favorable relationship with the state government and a more central and authoritative position on Negro affairs and of enhancing the school's image before philanthropic boards, accrediting associations, and the community at large.[37]

The first conference on the outstanding problems of Negro education in Texas posed that before the "problem" of black education could "be intelligently attacked it must be thoroughly studied in almost all of its ramifications and viewed from several points of vantage."[38] The conference sought to present an authentic portrait of how the dual educational system functioned for blacks in Texas; to more widely disseminate the "significant information and facts released by the Texas Survey, U.S. Government studies, Reports of the Department of Education, and other sources"; and to stimulate "educational planning."[39] Henry Allen Bullock, professor of sociology at Prairie View and editor and director of research for educational conferences, conducted prodigious scientific research on an array of topics concerning the social status of black Texans and put a considerable amount of energy and genius into publicly showcasing and disseminating the results. From the first conference, Bullock published a slim monograph, "The Survey of Education for Negroes in Texas."[40] Principal Banks, in later years, proudly announced that conference bulletins and studies were in libraries all across the country and as far away as Europe, Japan, and China.[41]

Each year, the conference grew into a larger and more diverse, biracial gathering. Banks and Bullock expected the inaugural conference to draw about 75 people, but 138 attended. By 1936, Bullock reported that the number of registered conferees had increased to 574 persons, with a total attendance of about 1,500. Of those who registered that year, 11 percent were white, an increase of 24 percent from the 1934 conference.[42]

The most important conference on the question of black higher education in the state, the eighth conference, in 1937, had as its subject "The Availability of Public Education for Negroes in Texas." Banks opened the gathering with praise for the work and cooperation of all involved in the educational conference "movement." He acknowledged a national study of black educational access that Ambrose Caliver had conducted a few years earlier and said that the present meeting aimed to do specifically for Texas what Caliver had done for the country. Professor D. B. Taylor, the State Department of Education's white supervisor of Negro education, introduced the conference's purpose and scope. He listed eight purposes, which included as goals "to discover some of the basic facts concerning Negro Colleges of the State" and "to present possible steps for making public education more available for Negroes in Texas." Regarding the availability of higher education for blacks in Texas, conference organizers collected information on college personnel, "projects carried on by colleges in behalf of communities," and "sources of support." They used as their primary sources the biennial reports of the State Department of Education and the State Board of Education, bulletins of the U.S. Office of Education, and the answers college presidents gave to questionnaires they had distributed.[43]

Bullock, who followed Taylor in the morning session, presented the findings of his research and an analysis of the "availability" of public education. He cited Caliver's 1932 study of black secondary education and his 1935 study of black rural education as having suggested the benefits of a broader investigation. "Whether education is being made available or not," Bullock argued, "depends upon the degree to which the masses of our population are being reached by educational influences with a rate equivalent to the rapidity with which new demands are being made by national change." The Prairie View sociologist identified as the major current of national change the "shift from a handicraft to a machine economy" and the attendant increase in occupational "specialization" and the overriding emphasis on "profit accumulation." Thus, the crux of the problem centered on closing the gap between the imperatives of modernity and the status of black education.[44]

After presenting various demographic changes in the Texas Negro population between 1850 and 1930, Bullock posed that blacks showed an increasing demand for public education that necessitated corresponding "increases in educational facilities, involving changes in physical equipment, personnel and organization." In a matter-of-fact style, he highlighted the gross inequality of the dual system of education. The statistical measure of black-white educational inequality, by 1937, came as no secret but appeared in sources as common as the *Dallas Morning News*'s biennial *Texas Almanac*. In drawing comparisons between blacks and whites, Bullock attempted to illustrate how black schools would never be able to accomplish the fundamental goals of public education. Underfinancing, not separation from whites, thwarted black schools from producing efficient workers, responsible consumers, and educated citizens. Bullock made it plain: "The ultimate factor in the availability of public education is an element of financial support." A "racial factor," however, dictated the amount of property, equipment, per-pupil expenditure, and teachers' salaries black schools received, and in all cases blacks did not receive what they needed.[45]

Frederick H. Eby, UT's well-known history of education professor, followed Bullock, presenting last at the morning session. Eby's *Development of Education in Texas*, published in 1925, defined the subject for almost three decades.[46] After a lighthearted opening, Eby attempted to compress into a thirty-minute talk a copious amount of information about the public education idea in early Texas history, party politics and school legislation between 1871 and 1936, changes in popular attitudes, and, finally, the relationship between state government leadership, public education, and blacks. Eby held that white supremacists in the Constitutional Convention of 1875 "who feared the domination in many counties of the Negro people" did not support the education of blacks and, consequently, they "bound up the constitutional article on education with many clauses."

Through the leadership of governors like Oran M. Roberts and James Ferguson, stated Eby, "the public school systems today are unshackled." He intended his concluding remarks to warm the hearts of his audience: "There is only one thing that has not been fulfilled. There is in the constitution of Texas a university for Negroes established at Austin. It has never been established."[47]

Eby did not miscalculate. In the afternoon, panelists discussed the black UT issue at a session titled "What Steps are Necessary in Order to Increase the Availability and Effectiveness of Education for Negroes in Texas?" Gordon Worley of the State Department of Education chaired the panel of black educational leaders. When CTSAT president I. Q. Hurdle's turn came to speak, he kept his comments brief and to the point. He began by uttering half of the political slogan the CTSAT had adopted over a decade before: "The Best in Education for Every Negro Child."[48] After Hurdle stated a basic principle of CTSAT philosophy, that "the teacher who does not love people is a failure in the beginning," he then briefly described the organization and the program of action its executive committee had adopted. He also called for support for one of the association's most important and enduring campaign since its establishment in 1884. "House Bill No. 678 was introduced February 23, 1937," he observed. "It is our hope that every citizen will urge passage of this bill ... [which] will lead to partial provisions for higher education for colored in Texas until the university for Negroes in Texas be established, according to the constitution of Texas."[49] Hurdle ended with a prophetic message: "We are not far from the time when we shall have the University for Negroes in Texas, if we work together building a stronghold of citizenship development by loyal cooperation."[50]

The process of "loyal cooperation" to create the university that Hurdle labored for already had begun to achieve a high level of organization a year earlier in the founding of the Texas State Conference of NAACP Branches. The new state conference, however, stood on the shoulders of the CTSAT and the black intelligentsia, who came into their own in Texas in the Jazz Age. An educated black elite not only had begun to articulate the educational needs of black Texans but also had sowed "civil rights" ideas into the black freedom struggle. The struggle for full citizenship rights, equality under the law, and inclusion in the American political economy and social body marks a particular phase of black political and discursive practices. It does not sum up the entirety of black exertions in behalf of their liberation. Historically, the way to black liberation has been characterized by many roads, of which the campaign for civil rights represented only one, even if the most influential, path.[51]

In Texas, the civil rights movement remained in an embryonic form until the 1920s. Late in that decade, a more or less tightly knit group of black lawyers and leaders, with financial and moral support from many local blacks and organizational backing from the NAACP, galvanized into a small but effective force against the legal exclusion of black voters from the Democratic primary election. They took the lawsuit as their weapon and filed four cases that reached the U.S. Supreme Court: *Nixon v. Herndon* (1927), *Nixon v. Condon* (1932), *Grovey v. Townsend* (1935), and *Smith v. Allwright* (1944). In *Smith* the Supreme Court struck down the Texas Democratic white primary as unconstitutional. The strategic, organizational, and financial nerve centers of the legal campaign were located in Houston and Dallas, but blacks from El Paso to Port Arthur also played an instrumental part in the work that spanned two decades.[52]

Although the NAACP became the decisive organizational factor in the fight for full franchise rights, the campaign itself represented a much broader black revolt. Historian Darlene Clark Hine has found that "by the mid-thirties, an increasing number of aroused Texas black citizens, most of whom were middle-class entrepreneurs and professionals, became caught up in the struggle against the white primary."[53] Indeed, black professional men and women, educators, and entrepreneurs were in the thick of the fight for the vote.[54] Moreover, by the 1930s, black women and men who held college degrees tended to be the state's most important "race" leaders. Table 2 shows the rise in the number of black Texans in professional-managerial class occupations between 1900 and 1940. As a portion of the black population, however, only black women increased their percentage. From representing less than 2 percent of employed black women in 1910, their number in the professions more than doubled to nearly 5 percent by 1940. Black men in the professions began and ended the period representing 2 percent of employed black men in the state.[55]

As the small, black professional-managerial class in Texas became more organized, its leaders consistently focused their limited political capital on greater access to higher education. They saw their work as producing something meaningful for themselves, their children, and the future of the race. The New Negro intellectuals pressed on three fronts in regard to what they perceived as their race's need for higher education in Texas. First, they continued the fight for a Negro branch or counterpart of the University of Texas at Austin. Second, they advocated greater financial support for the development of the Negro branch of Texas A&M College that already existed at Prairie View. Third, they lobbied the state to support blacks who sought professional and graduate education not available to them in the state. In 1934, a venerable New Negro named Richard T. Hamilton opened this third front in the campaign to expand black higher educational opportunity.[56]

Born on 31 March 1869 in Montgomery, Alabama, Hamilton graduated with valedictory honors from Alabama State Normal School in 1890. He left the Deep South for Washington, D.C., took a clerical position in the

Table 2. Texas Blacks in Professional-Managerial Class (PMC) Occupations by Gender, 1900–1940

Census Year	1900	1910	1920	1930	1940
PMC black males	2,693	2,897	3,349	5,255	4,705
Total black males	117,181	219,644	227,377	265,660	218,967
Percentage of total	0.02	0.01	0.015	0.02	0.02
PMC black females	1,199	2,085	3,284	5,031	5,679
Total black females	67,709	139,247	103,946	124,095	119,504
Percentage of total	0.018	0.015	0.03	0.04	0.048
Total in PMC	3,892	4,982	6,633	10,286	10,384

Source: Twelfth through Sixteenth Censuses of the United States

Department of Interior, and began studying medicine at Howard University, where in 1893 he obtained his M.D. degree. He moved to Dallas in 1901.[57] Propelled by the human determination to be free, Hamilton led a five-year-long campaign for graduate education assistance as chairman of the Committee on Civics and Public Welfare of the Dallas Negro Chamber of Commerce (DNCC). In 1926, key members of Dallas's black professional-managerial class had founded the DNCC as a way of promoting black enterprise and elevating the standard of living of the city's black population. However, by the early 1930s, the DNCC was dormant. Dallas was not a friendly place for any kind of work aimed at black advancement, especially when it threatened the racial status quo.[58]

In 1932, the spark that revitalized the organization and ultimately acted as the catalytic force behind a new wave of the black freedom struggle in Texas was Antonio Maceo Smith. Albon Holsey, the executive secretary of the Negro Business League of Oklahoma City, wrote a letter of introduction for Smith to Hamilton, recommending that the DNCC hire him to be its executive secretary. The DNCC took Holsey's advice.[59]

Smith, who left his hometown of Texarkana to study at Fisk University and went on to earn his master's degree in business administration at New York University, like Hamilton, saw himself as a New Negro. Exposed to the Black Renaissance at its epicenter in Harlem in the 1920s, the Texas native briefly published a weekly newspaper and established his own business, the Harlem Advertising Agency.[60]

In 1929, after his father's death, Smith returned home. In Dallas, he went into the insurance business and became the city editor of the black weekly, the *Dallas Express*. In addition, through his organizing work he became a leading figure in Dallas's Negro Business League, the NAACP, and other black groups in the city and across the state. Through the dynamic energy Smith injected into the DNCC and elsewhere, specific projects like Hamilton's educational equalization work gained an effective organizational base, an extensive network of support, and, perhaps most important, a rising mood of optimism. He could be seen as the Marcus Garvey of Texas.[61]

Historically, moving the Texas legislature to spend money on black social or educational needs had proven to be a Herculean — more often a Sisyphean — task. Hamilton conceived that the campaign for state support of black out-of-state graduate education work needed allies, black and white. In 1934, he secured the support of the CTSAT. In 1935, he turned to the Texas Commission on Inter-racial Cooperation (TCIC) for white support. Founded in 1922, the TCIC brought together reform-minded whites under the program of the larger Commission on Inter-racial Cooperation (CIC), which by the middle of the decade was the largest southern-based organization promoting interracial communication.[62] At a meeting held at Prairie View on 6–7 December 1935, the TCIC unanimously adopted a resolution that Hamilton submitted to the group. It concluded with the following:

> Whereas, in lieu of establishing separate universities for the Negro race wherein such courses may be pursued, a number of Southern States, including Oklahoma, Missouri, West Virginia, and Maryland have made provisions under certain conditions, to give aid to Negro students who are denied permission to enter the state universities on account of race, and who desire to enter the professions or to take post-graduate work, by paying their tuition and their transportation to recognized institutions outside the state wherein they are admitted, therefore Be it resolved, that the Texas Commission on Inter-racial Cooperation be, and is hereby requested to sponsor an enactment by the Texas Legislature similar to the existing law in the State of Oklahoma.[63]

On 11 March 1936, Hamilton sent letters of inquiry to the Department of Education of each of the four states identified in the resolution. He sought detailed information regarding the kind and number of scholarships they had given, the requirements and procedures they used, the amount of money spent, and any printed matter they may have produced on their programs. He received responses from every state except Oklahoma.[64] In 1937, Hamilton hired a lobbyist to help him prepare a draft bill and secure a legislator that would introduce the measure. For $200, the lobbyist prepared a legislative proposal and, in the artful language of governmental prose patterned after the U.S. Constitution, it made no mention of race. Representative Lonnie Smith of Tarrant County became the sponsor of House Bill No. 678 for out-of-state scholarship aid.[65]

Hamilton knew he faced an uphill battle. Even after the legislature created the Division of Graduate Study at Prairie View, which offered a master's degree in education, he remained hopeful that a lily-white Texas legislature would still do the right thing and pass H.B. No. 678.[66] As soon as Smith got the bill drafted, Hamilton sent a copy of it, along with supporting information, to President Harry Y. Benedict of the University of Texas. Benedict answered that the student aid bill was "the best and most inexpensive way to attain a result that should be desired."[67] On 1 March, Hamilton wrote Benedict to thank him for his "kind letter" and asked his permission to use it in his lobbying efforts. He attached to his letter clippings of editorials and articles favorable to the bill from the *Dispatch*, the *Express*, and the *Times Herald*, all Dallas newspapers. The editor of the *Dispatch* opined that "good argument is given for the appeal to the legislature for funds for the education of qualified Negroes in the professions." The editor reported that the lack of opportunities for blacks to pursue advanced degrees led to a situation where the state's six Negro colleges were "largely staffed by Northern Negroes, unfamiliar with the problems and the customs of the South." Furthermore, Texas faced a "genuine shortage in the number of Negro doctors, dentists, and lawyers." He also maintained that new additions to professional ranks could also "assume leadership among their own people," which "would make for better racial relations." Apparently, the editor had little apprehension of the possibility that out-of-state experiences, most likely at northern universities, might turn black Texans against their native "southern" customs.[68]

The *Dallas Express* article showed Hamilton also trying to milk Lone Star State particularism. It reported that Hamilton wrote to Representative Harry N. Graves on the bill, stressing the idea of a regional mismatch between the folkways of the state's black college educators and those of their students and other persons at the college and its environs. Texas needed "educated southern Negroes" in the professions and the classrooms, according to Hamilton, "because Negroes who were raised in the east do not understand the situation in the south and often come to this area and embarrass themselves as well as southern Negroes." He went on to state that 97 percent of the faculty in the six black colleges in Texas were "not native Texans" and that "not infrequently the teachers can't adjust themselves to Texas customs and traditions." As a consequence, Hamilton said, "complications ensue."[69]

An editorial in the *Dallas Times Herald* offered another perspective. Calling the requested annual appropriation of $15,000 a "small" sum, it held that "by enacting this bill, the legislature would give the colored race its due." It added that "in some places where discrimination exists, the Negroes have resorted to litigation to gain entry into white colleges and universities, but the colored race in this state is not following such a policy." Only through just such a policy, however, would the state legislature be shocked into action regarding black higher education.[70]

As for House Bill No. 678, the legislature dragged its feet for more than two years. Despite the wise counsel of a university president, newspaper editors, leaders from the Negro Chambers of Commerce, the TCIC, and the Colored Teachers State Association of Texas, the legislature delayed passage of the bill. Even after Hamilton led a DNCC-CTSAT-TCIC delegation to meet with Governor James Allred and won his "whole-hearted support" for the measure, nothing occurred. Hamilton tried to think of what else could be done to get legislative action. In the formal language of the bill, it called for an emergency to be declared in appropriating funds to aid Texas students who had to leave the state. Something had to be done to create a state of emergency. With the chips down, the critical hour demanded a bluff.[71]

Leaders of the student aid bill campaign, which had come to include NAACP activists, decided to show state officials that blacks meant to have access to graduate and professional education even if it required them to integrate the state's precious University of Texas. In October 1838, George L. Allen of Austin, district manager of Excelsior Life Insurance Company, became the test case for the demonstration effort. Ironically, Allen chose to enroll in UT through its extension division, which was the byproduct of the progressive impulse in Texas higher education. Historians Robert Calvert and Larry Hill explain that the extension division, established in 1909, had a mandate to train Americans on a "practical, nonelitist" basis to be responsible citizens in a participatory democracy.[72] Allen enrolled in an evening extension class titled "Business Psychology and Salesmanship." Having registered over the telephone, he went to the first meeting of the class fully expecting to be turned away.[73] "The only wrench in the whole machine," Allen mused in an interview more than forty years later, "was that they admitted me."[74]

Allen's "wrench" did not clog the sputtering, machinelike operation of white supremacy for long. Thomas H. Shelby, head of the Department of Extension, sent Allen a letter informing him that his enrollment at the university had been canceled. C. P. Brewer, the instructor of the extension course, also met with Allen to tell him he could not return to the class because of his race. Allen protested the decision to terminate his registration, but officials made it clear that he would not be allowed back into the class.[75]

Allen served his role and faded from the scene. Hamilton and his comrades tried to convert the episode into a fillip for movement in the legislature. On 12 December 1938, however, Hamilton received the boost he needed with the Supreme Court's decision in *Missouri, ex rel. Gaines* v.

Canada, Registrar of the University of Missouri, et al. Initiated in 1935, this case involved Lloyd Gaines, a twenty-four-year-old graduate of Lincoln University who sought to attend the law school of the whites-only state university. The court ruled that Gaines "was entitled to be admitted to the law school of the State University in the absence of other and proper provision for his legal training within the state."[76]

Soon after the Court's decision, Gaines mysteriously disappeared. The state of Missouri complied with the ruling and set up a "makeshift" law school at Lincoln University. The Texas legislature now had its state of emergency. But should it pass the out-of-state education assistance bill? The *Gaines* case resulted from a black man who refused to go out of state for his professional training. Would not some black Texans also opt to stay in the state, despite out-of-state assistance? The weight of history clearly marched on the side of a black UT. Given the Court's ruling, should not the state move straightaway to erect the institution the state constitution promised almost fifty years earlier?[77]

In a letter to the People's Forum published in the *Dallas Times Herald* soon after the *Gaines* decision, Hamilton offered solutions to the "professional training problem of Negroes." He explained that "in view of present needs and pending extension of the educational curriculum and establishing of professional schools for Negroes in Texas, Negroes are willing to accept a substitute. The more practical substitute is scholarship aid in standard out-of-state institutions where Negroes are admitted." Hamilton supported the creation of a separate-but-equal university for blacks, but he also stressed that any "provision made for Negroes must measure favorably with those provided for whites." As such a development would take a considerable amount of time, Hamilton recommended passage of the student aid bill, which would satisfy present needs and "return rich dividends to the state in all elements that make for a contributing, constructive, grateful and loyal Negro citizenship."[78]

The political winds inside the state legislature began to shift in favor of the renumbered House Bill No. 255, but with a reduction in the proposed appropriation. The original proposal called for $15,000 a year, but a front-page *Dallas Express* article of 22 April 1939 reported that the legislature now proposed "an allotment of $10,000 per annum for the entire state." Noting that "Maryland, which has a much smaller Negro population has already appropriated $35,000, and the state of Virginia, $30,000," the article cited a TCIC report that more than 450 students had left the state for graduate education at their own expense. The article warned that "the inadequacy of this expected appropriation has already caused speculation throughout the state over the probability that a number of Negro graduate students, who will not be covered by this small scholarship appropriation, will make strenuous efforts to enter A&M College and Texas University to do their graduate and professional work."[79]

Although no prospects for lawsuits to desegregate Texas A&M and the University of Texas existed, word had begun circulating that such a step marked the new direction in the movement for black educational and civil rights. Letters from black students seeking admission to UT, dated from 15 January to 6 March 1939, suggest the likelihood of extensive black concern over policy on higher education. Grandvel A. Jackson, a graduate of Samuel Huston College in Austin, sought admission to the Department of Law and Government. Judge Goss, a graduate of Texas College in Tyler with one summer of graduate work at the University of Michigan, desired master's level work in physical education not offered at Prairie View. Joseph H. Hayes, a native of San Antonio and a soon-to-be graduate of Morehouse College in Atlanta, applied for entry at the university's medical school in Galveston. Samuel J. Murphy, a graduate of Wiley College in Marshall, Texas, with an M.A. degree from the University of Southern California, found that he could not afford to attend the University of Cincinnati, where he was pursuing studies in higher education administration (as he had also done briefly at Columbia University). "If what I have heard is true," wrote Murphy, "I can enroll in your University and live with my relatives in the city." He asked that if he could not, could he have an out-of-state scholarship to continue his Ph.D. work. Neither university administrators nor state legislators could keep their heads in the sand any longer.[80]

The legislature approved House Bill No. 255 in June 1939, and Governor James Allred signed it into law the next month. They set the available funds for out-of-state aid at $25,000 for each year of the biennial appropriation. Allred appointed deans from UT, Texas A&M, and Sam Houston State Teachers College to oversee the disbursement of scholarship funds. A little over a month after enactment, they had received sixty applications and doled out forty-five awards. The *Dallas Express* warned black students to claim the grants or risk having the program terminated for lack of interest. A limit on grant aid per student had been set at $200, but medical and law students could receive up to $300. Award recipients studied in the following areas: seventeen in medicine; four each in pharmacy, dentistry, and social work; five in doctoral studies in the sciences, fourteen in master of science programs, and one student each in law, optometry, library science, music, and costume design. By the end of 1939, 53 students had received assistance out of 180 who had applied. At $11,415.40, the state had expended less than half of the annual amount reserved for the purpose of helping black students acquire the graduate education that white Texans could receive inside their native state.[81]

Richard Hamilton could reflect with a degree of satisfaction on what he had helped accomplish. "From the very outset," wrote the scholar of African American folklore J. Mason Brewer about Hamilton, "he has, in spite of his lucrative practice found time to give the welfare of his race deep study. He has given the public the benefit of this study from the platform and through the columns of the leading newspapers of the city and state."[82] Brewer included two of Hamilton's poems in his *Heralding Dawn*, "the first anthology of Negro verse published in Texas."[83] Hamilton's poem "A Negro's Prayer" speaks best to the ideas and feelings of an intellectual who at seventy achieved a small but important victory in the fight for black freedom and equality. Before the "Lord God of Hosts," he asked, "What more must Afric's sons endure / For manhood rights — to have secure / The blessings of sweet liberty?" Hamilton recounted the "years of unrequited toil," noting how blacks fought bravely in the American Civil War and in foreign wars in the defense of "country, human rights and law," but then he questioned how much longer before they are given "an even chance" in the land of their birth.[84]

Hamilton's work for an "even chance" spirited all the organizations involved and at the same time prepared black activists to face the momentous decade of the 1940s, in which the world would become engulfed in another major war on European shores. In later years, Henry Allen Bullock, an eyewitness to and a participant in the intellectual attack on segregated higher education in the 1930s, summarized the lesson experience had taught the new black professional-managerial class and, to an appreciable extent, the general black population in Texas: "Prior to 1940, there was an attitude of indifference on the part of the public. Since that time, feeble efforts have been made to improve Negro education. Signs of these efforts, however weak they are, have been shown in capital investment, income, and the faculty of Negro public colleges. These improvements came in response to Negro pressures. Such changes as we can expect in the future will depend upon the extent to which this pressure is increased."[85]

Increased pressure did come in the 1940s, but it won changes in the state's separate and unequal social structure and public educational system only after blacks further clarified for themselves the fundamental goals and direction of their struggle. With black professional-managerial class leaders taking the driver's seat, they steered the black freedom struggle toward status goals such as access to institutions of higher learning. They left the welfare goals — the direct, material advancement of black people in terms of more jobs and pay, better working and living conditions — to another day and time. That does not mean that black Texans were passive or less politically sophisticated than they might have been. The new black elite class assumed the leadership of the black freedom struggle, bringing its class aspirations and adopting techniques of resistance to white supremacy with which it felt most comfortable. As early as the mid-1930s, the idea of resorting to the courts, not for *better* segregation through the equalization of the state's segregated educational system but for full-blown desegregation of white colleges and universities, had begun to gain currency among a critical mass of black intellectuals. Through the fight against the white university, black leaders forged a powerful consensus. Building on the old consensus that advocated the creation of the black constitutional university, it forsook the promise of 1876 in search of a new promise. As always, what blacks received was not the promise but compromises, and still more problems.

CHAPTER TWO

The All-Out War for Democracy in Education
Ideological Struggle and the Texas University Movement

The NAACP needs to lead out in all programs of advancement of Negroes in
Texas. . . . I was glad to see in the News Letter that the Legal Committee was
doing something about this, "EQUAL BUT separate EDUCATIONAL OPPORTU-
NITIES." That's right, nothing can be equal if it is separate.
— Lulu B. White to Thurgood Marshall, 11 December 1946

Even if Sweatt enters the University of Texas, we will not want to get rid of
Texas State University for Negroes[;] the Texas Constitution decrees separation provided it is equal, why shouldn't we make them carry out the Constitution and equalize Texas State University in toto with the University of Texas?
— Carter Wesley, "Ram's Horn," *The Informer*, 2 July 1949

After 1940, higher education policy and racial politics in the United States
began to collide, and from their collision came one of the most significant
fronts in the battle for black democratic rights and the dismantling of
America's version of apartheid. Texas became the site of the first direct
legal challenge to the constitutionality of *Plessy* v. *Ferguson* and thereby
provided the context for the transition from a legal strategy centered on
separate-but-equal schools to a frontal assault on the legitimacy of racially
segregated education as such. The legal arguments of Thurgood Marshall
in key education cases in the 1940s, along with Truman administration
studies and pronouncements on racial segregation, began preparing the
Supreme Court to bring the idea of desegregation into the vocabulary of
national affairs in its landmark 1954 *Brown* v. *Board of Education* decision,
which banned the segregation of blacks in schools. Before the Court pronounced Jim Crow legally dead, however, the long journey from *Plessy* to
Brown had to turn an important corner in Texas.[1]

Outside the courtrooms, beyond the briefs and oral arguments, a drama unfolded that shared points of common purpose with the juridical contest, but in other respects it was a quite different ordeal. Black Texans were divided in their response to desegregation. Their divisions matched the four major social philosophies that the Howard University economist Abram Harris identified in the 1930s: interracial conciliation, militant race consciousness, civil libertarianism, and class consciousness.[2] The way they related to the making of new civil rights law constitutes a significant, even if perplexing, story. The depth and complexity of desegregation emanates not so much from the clash of competing ideological positions. Although the story has its share of conflict, it is the way various black worldviews grew and struggled together against a common enemy that is most striking and enigmatic. In a time of rising expectations and uncertainty about the future that the war against European and Japanese fascism engendered, black Texans sensed the time was ripe to assert themselves in behalf of their own best interests. But exactly what were their best interests? In the fight for equality of opportunity in higher education, blacks reanalyzed the history of their struggle to define a place in society for themselves. In the 1940s, a new generation discovered a mission: the eradication of segregation.[3]

Willette Rutherford Banks, principal of Prairie View Normal and Industrial College, represented the interracial conciliation position par excellence.[4] A country boy from the northeastern Georgia hill country of Hartwell, Banks was twenty when, in 1901, he enrolled at Atlanta University. Starting with only an eighth grade education, he graduated with a bachelor's degree eight years later, and the president of the university recommended him for a teaching position at Fort Valley Normal and Industrial Institute. Beginning with his years at Atlanta University and throughout the rest of his life, historian George R. Woolfolk writes, Banks "gave his heart to [W. E. B.] Du Bois." Even so, he gave his head to Booker T. Washington. In the often surreal world of white domination, Banks adroitly harvested the goodwill of ruling-class whites. Banks did not merely accept the fact of racial separation; he embraced it as a positive good and sought, through various artful means, to get from whites all the material resources for black education that he could. He honed his administrative and leadership skills as principal of Elmore County, Alabama's Kowiliga Community School from 1912 to 1915 and as president of Texas College at Tyler from 1915 to 1926 before coming to Prairie View.[5]

In August of 1941, however, as he faced his sixtieth birthday, Banks was a deeply disappointed man. That summer the legislature rejected a proposed $168,000 appropriation for a library and books at Prairie View. Moreover, Banks saw the state slash his total budget by $3,000 from the previous biennial appropriation. His was the only state-supported college that had its funding cut that year.[6] "I feel that the situation is of such gravity," Banks stated, "that it precipitates an emergency." In response, he

35

applied to the General Education Board for a $1,000 grant to hire Leo Favrot to conduct a study of black higher education in Texas. He scuttled the project, however, when A&M College president T. O. Walton and University of Texas president Homer Rainey wrote to him, suggesting a conference of educational leaders.[7]

Banks eagerly responded to Walton's and Rainey's request. In the past, A&M, Prairie View's parent campus, had shown little concern for the immediate and pressing needs of the black normal and industrial college, to say nothing of long-range planning. Banks welcomed the interest. Allies of a sort, Banks and Rainey both belonged to the Texas Commission on Interracial Cooperation. During the summer of 1942, as soldiers of all colors and ethnic backgrounds donned American uniforms on distant shores, the leaders of public higher education in Texas, with the blessings of Governor Coke Stevenson, convened "representatives of the white and colored people of the state, to meet at the capitol in Austin, to discuss some of the problems that had arisen in connection with the education of colored children and youth." Wartime conditions and postwar prognostications imbued the seventy male and female leaders with a sense of urgency. They created an organization called the Bi-racial Commission on Negro Education in Texas (BCNET). Walton, Rainey, and L. A. Woods (state superintendent of public instruction) comprised its sponsoring committee. Prevailing norms did not permit Banks's inclusion at that level, despite his being the initiating agent of the conference.[8]

At the meeting, the forty-three white and the twenty-four black conferees authorized the formation of a steering committee and several subcommittees to assess the problems of "colored" education. B. F. Pittenger, dean of the UT School of Education, chaired the steering committee, which included three blacks: Banks, Joseph J. Rhoads, president of Bishop College in Marshall, Texas, and Richard Hamilton, the Dallas physician who led the charge for the out-of-state tuition subsidy program. Duties were delegated, and the work of surveying what to do with the Negro in higher education commenced.

In April 1944, the BCNET released its ninety-five-page study, *The Senior Colleges for Negroes in Texas*. Forthrightly, the report declared two issues at the heart of the state's educational troubles: the lack of graduate and professional education for blacks and inadequate funding for Prairie View. The state of Texas, in other words, was subverting the doctrine of "separate but equal." Inequality in educational opportunity between white and black youth affected the status of black Texans economically, culturally, and educationally. The BCNET cautioned, however, that "only the surface of the problem of Negro education will have been scratched" once the equalization of education is achieved. Quoting from the work of the native Texan and University of Chicago–trained social anthropologist Ina Corinne Brown, the study contended, "The real problem is that of the Negro's freedom to incorporate in his own life and conduct the values and goals of American life." It explained further, "Until the Negro is free to accept for himself the same goals as the rest of the population, the integration and solidarity of the Nation are only partially achieved."[9]

The Bi-racial Commission did not endorse the elimination of all lines of demarcation between the races. Paraphrasing Brown, the commission added that the "Negro in America wants to be regarded as an American rather than a Negro, and to be so treated. The desire of the Negro for a larger participation in American life does not necessarily include amalgamation and an increase in race mixture, but it does include the removal of barriers of social mobility and free competition and the giving of Negroes an opportunity to make their way as individuals without the limitations now imposed by the status of a minority group." The commission held that blacks wanted to stay to themselves in sexual and marital activities but, as Booker T. Washington said a half century before, to mix in the competitive capitalist free market.[10]

Far from questioning the validity of white supremacy, the commission took it as a given. It acknowledged that "the crux of the problem of admitting Negro youth to the graduate and professional schools supported by the state for white students is the traditional policy of segregation." Placing Texas policy solidly in the context of southern mores and custom, it noted that black students were barred from flagship state universities in Virginia, Missouri, and Maryland, with the exception of a single black at Maryland's law school. "Admission of Negroes to existing state universities for whites is not acceptable as a solution to the problem of providing opportunity for graduate and professional study for Negroes, on two counts," the study explained. The two counts were "(1) public opinion would not permit such institutions to be open to Negroes at the present time; and (2) even if Negroes were admitted they would not be happy in the conditions in which they would find themselves."[11]

Polite language and phrasing in the report, like "at the present time," with its suggestion of future possibilities, conceal the probable course of events and the virulent attitudes that forbade institutional inclusiveness at the University of Texas. A few months before the publication of the BCNET study, UT regent Orville Bullington was forthright and assertive about the matter. "The Board," he wrote in a letter to the eminent folklore scholar John A. Lomax, "has already been discussing this negro situation, in viewof [sic] the decision of the Supreme Court in the Missouri case." After mentioning that the state legislature had voted for an appropriation for out-of-state tuition assistance "for any negroes who happen to apply for entrance to any of our state colleges," Bullington professed that he did "not know whether any of [the appropriation] has been used or not." But irrespective

37

of what blacks were doing for graduate education, the regent declared that "there [was] not the slightest danger of any negro attending the University of Texas as long as the present Board are [*sic*] on the throne." Bullington went on to boast, "We city-slicked Washington on our Navy contract, by nullifying the provision in the contract which would have permitted negroes to attend the University, under the guise of being Naval students. As you know, every contract that comes out of Washington contains a provision, the substance of which is that there can be no discrimination against any person on account of race, color, religion, etc." Bullington told Lomax that he did not want him to publish his views of the board's position on segregation at UT, but he did ask him to tell his friends that there was not "the slightest danger of any negro attending the University of Texas, regardless of what Franklin D, Eleanor, or the Supreme Court says, so long as you have a Board of Regents with as much intestinal fortitude as the present one has."[12]

Black Texans identified Bullington and his like-minded peers on the UT board of regents as prime examples of "American Hitlers," their open enemies on the homefront even as the battles and holocausts in Europe and the Pacific raged. How bitter the irony of southern life for black Texans? In his home state, Dorie Miller, the sable son of Texas soil who became America's first hero of the Second World War for his "extraordinary courage" at Pearl Harbor, was no hero at all to the "Hitlers" on the UT board of regents. To Bullington and his kind, Miller represented nothing more than another low-down "negro" "in the guise" of a Naval student and fully deserved every "city-slick" tactic that they could imagine to keep his likes out of *their* white university.[13]

If public opinion and the "intestinal fortitude" of the "Hitlers" on the UT board of regents would not permit desegregation, what then was the solution to the *problem* of giving blacks the same opportunities for advanced education? The BCNET study contemplated four alternatives. First, the state could continue its policy of providing tuition subsidies for out-of-state graduate and professional study. The report offered a detailed discussion of the subsidy program as it functioned during the two biennial budgets of the legislature, 1939–41 and 1941–43. During this period, the legislature appropriated $100,000 ($25,000 annually), which was paid out in scholarships for varying amounts to 393 students out of 872 who applied for aid. More than a fourth of those assisted did graduate study in education, 16.3 percent went to professional schools, and 14 percent did advanced studies in the social sciences, 11 percent in the vocations, and the remaining third in fields such as languages, music, science, library science, mathematics, and nursing. The program for which Hamilton worked so tirelessly helped hundreds of blacks who otherwise would have been entirely on their own. But the Supreme Court's ruling in *Gaines* v.

University of Missouri rendered this remedy unconstitutional. It did not satisfy the mandate the "separate but equal" doctrine placed on each state. The BCNET thus concurred with the opinion expressed in a *Dallas Morning News* editorial that described the out-of-state scholarship provision as "a rather ridiculous side-stepping of an obligation . . . upon the state."[14]

The second alternative suffered from the same liability as the first. The idea arose at the Southern Governors Conference: the best manner in which the southern states could comply with the *Gaines* decision would be to create one outstanding medical school, one law school, one graduate school, and the like at logical locations in the southern region. These centers of advanced learning would be reserved for blacks, and with all of the states sending their black students there and with ongoing interstate support, they would acquire prestige and be comparable to the schools for whites. *Gaines*, however, required that equivalent educational opportunities exist *within* a segregated state, not the South as a whole; if these opportunities did not exist within a segregated state, the "separate but equal" doctrine would be null and void. The development of a regional program for graduate and professional training thus failed to satisfy the ruling of the Supreme Court. Besides the legal difficulty, the study noted that "little progress ha[d] been made in line with this proposal." Only in Virginia had a governor gone so far as to recommend that his state enter into a contractual relationship with Meharry Medical College in Nashville, Tennessee, to serve as the Jim Crow campus for Virginia blacks who sought a medical education.[15]

The third alternative was to erect a new state university for Negroes with the necessary facilities and faculty to be of "equal rank and quality" to those of the University of Texas. Elsewhere in the South, the state legislature established the major state university for whites and the state's black college in the same city. In North Carolina this meant that a cooperative plan of sharing the library and faculties of the white university with the black sister school could alleviate immediate disparities. The BCNET study observed that faculty members from "all the Negro colleges except Prairie View" gave "considerable support" to the idea of establishing a Negro branch of the University of Texas in Austin. The division in black opinion pitted Rhoads against Banks, a variant of the civil libertarian position against the interracial conciliator. The study indicated that Rhoads's plan might be part of the "ultimate pattern," but it doubted that the Texas legislature would seriously consider building a black state university in Austin until the final alternative was "more fully explored."[16]

The BCNET suggested that the option "most likely to provide an immediate solution to the problem of meeting the obligation of providing adequate facilities for graduate and professional education of Negroes in Texas" was to expand Prairie View, as the legislature of the state of Missouri had done to Lincoln University. Missouri discontinued its out-of-state tuition subsidies and hastily enlarged Lincoln to the point that it offered makeshift graduate and professional training in areas to which blacks applied. Likewise, the BCNET held that Texas could have separate-but-equal education by developing Prairie View's nonvocational fields (namely, the arts, humanities, and basic sciences), paying adequate salaries to hold good teachers, and building a library.

The problem of a library was, by far, the most distressing. Prairie View had no building exclusively devoted to serving as a library. Moreover, if each student and faculty member checked out six books from the existing multipurpose facility, not a single volume would remain on the shelves. Until the legislature altered such dire conditions, Prairie View could never become a first-class state university, let alone a center of graduate and professional education. Given the reality at Prairie View, the study emphasized that "an adequate plant is not only essential to a strong graduate program; it is a prerequisite to pride, confidence, and loyalty in a constituency. The State has made no appropriation for a new building at Prairie View since 1925; such plant improvement as has been made was accomplished by penurious hoarding of local funds and by gifts from philanthropic foundations."[17]

Undoubtedly, much of the study's emphasis on the status of Prairie View reflects the influence of Banks. The principal was a hard-nosed and practical man; if he was an accommodationist, a gradualist, or an opportunist, he was so, at least in his own mind, for the advancement of Prairie View *and* his own ego. It was his dream to create "separate but equal education for blacks," and as Woolfolk explains in Banks's defense, "he intuitively, if not fully intellectually, understood the barriers to substantive cultural change among the masses." Like Booker T. Washington, however, Banks let his sense of white power and his pragmatism blind him to new possibilities that stood for the taking just beyond the "for whites only" screen. So firmly planted in the Jim Crow order, he severely restricted black resistance to white control. Banks was a victim of the changing times. The historical moment for interracial conciliation had come and gone.[18]

Joseph J. Rhoads, on the other hand, began to sing a song of redemption. Seeking to widen the spectrum of political action, he was utterly uninterested in getting the State of Texas to make something respectable out of Prairie View. His goal of a black University of Texas emanated from a civil libertarian reading of the Texas constitution. The law stated that blacks had a right to a black university, and he intended on seeing the law enforced. In 1928, the Colored State Teachers Association of Texas elected him to become its forty-first president. As the tenth college president to serve in that capacity, he immediately succeeded W. R. Banks at the end of his year in office. Rhoads had obtained his baccalaureate degree at

Bishop before earning a master's degree at Yale University and doing advanced work at the University of Michigan. Although he had more formal education than Banks, he always seemed to be in the shadow of the Georgian, who was nine years his senior. Rhoads's position ultimately shifted away from the demand for a black UT in the direction of desegregation of UT. As much as any single person, he helped move black Texans toward desegregation.[19]

As for Richard Hamilton, his tenure on the BCNET ended while the survey work was getting under way. His eyesight, which had been weak throughout his life, was now almost completely gone, and in 1944 he moved to his native state of Alabama to live out the remainder of his life. He left behind a distinguished legacy even if he did not militantly confront the white establishment by seeking an immediate elimination of racial segregation in higher education. Many social scientists who studied the American race question in the 1940s would have categorized Hamilton as a "gradualist," an "accommodationist," or a "racial diplomat." In black vernacular, Hamilton might have been called an "Uncle Tom," a "sellout," or an "Oreo cookie." The use of such labels, however, is only possible in the absence of an informed appreciation of his historical context. Hamilton pressed both for increased funding for Prairie View and for a black branch of the University of Texas, possibly to be located in Dallas. The BCNET filled his position on the steering committee with a Houston surgeon, H. E. Lee. The impact of Hamilton's departure, coming at a time of growing racial solidarity among black Texans, was not felt so strongly at the time. In a few years, however, when ideological divisions emerged over the question of which way forward for the Texas University Movement, the leadership of the venerated and sagacious elder was missed.[20]

Of course, no one individual was responsible for the practical struggle that Rhoads and his contemporaries called the "University Movement." Some of the state's most important black community organizations, often formed and led by members of the community's newly emergent professional-managerial class, cared passionately about education. Group leaders worked to influence political outcomes despite the fact that blacks were effectively disenfranchised and marginalized. Table 3 shows the numbers of black Texans in professional occupations in 1940. They represented barely 1 percent of the 924,391 blacks the census of that year enumerated as living in the state. Rather than make them a negligible force, the relative scarcity of black professional men and women magnified their status in both the black community and the larger society.[21]

Black professionals were more important members of society than their roles or income-level would dictate for the average white professional. Within their subjective space, moreover, their small numbers and the hardship it took to achieve their class status infused them with a sense of special

41

Table 3. Black Male and Female Professionals in Texas, 1940

Occupation	Total	Male	Female
Teachers and college faculty	6,747	1,819	4,928
Clergy	1,780	1,780	0
Nurses, professional	228	0	228
Artists, musicians, and art and music teachers	183	0	183
Physicians and surgeons	160	160	0
Dentists	81	81	0
Pharmacists	48	—	—
Librarians	36	0	36
Social and welfare workers	33	0	33
Lawyers and judges	23	22	1
Authors, editors, and journalists	21	16	5
Engineers and surveyors	5	5	0
Architects, designers, and draftsmen	3	3	0
All professions	9,300	3,886	5,414

Sources: Brophy, "Black Texan," 101, 113; McDaniel, *History of the Teachers State Association of Texas*, 146.

importance and mission. Few felt comfortable merely emulating the example their white peers set. The racial reality compelled a different approach to life, at least for the African Americans who sacrificed and contributed to the war for democracy in education and the other spheres of social life. Teachers and college educators were the most numerous strata of the black petty bourgeoisie, and they chiefly demonstrated their interest in the prospects of higher education for blacks through the Colored Teachers State Association of Texas, from which came the Texas Commission on Democracy in Education (CODE) in November 1941.[22]

Other professionals and business leaders became politically active through organizations like the Lone Star Medical Society, the Negro Chamber of Commerce, the State Progressive Voters League, and the NAACP. Many of the leaders of these organizations (nineteen initially) came together through the work of Dallas businessman A. Maceo Smith to form the Texas Council of Negro Organizations (TCNO) in 1942. Smith got black Texans to form a united front in response to Governor Coke Stevenson's call for a biracial commission on Negro education. The work of Smith and others also received invaluable support from the black press, notably Carter Wesley's *Informer* chain of weekly newspapers. Based in Houston, Wesley's printed word stretched across the states of Texas and Louisiana. Wesley was crucial to the spread of propaganda and information among the black masses as related to antisegregation lawsuits in particular and the fight against white supremacy in general. He was also instrumental in the raising of the large sums of money it took to litigate civil rights cases.[23]

Of all the many groups, institutions, and leaders, the NAACP would lead black Texans from the goal of separate equality to desegregation. In 1940, however, the NAACP begrudgingly accepted racial separation as a fact of life in the South. Its political and litigative approach did not directly challenge the "separate but equal" dictum. The great mastermind of its legal work, Charles Hamilton Houston, in his "Statement on the University Cases" before the NAACP national conference in 1940, asserted that "[w]e are essentially fighting for America, to eliminate the waste of duplications of public facilities, to establish common public honesty by stripping the farce away from the phrase 'separate but equal.' We are challenging America to make democracy work." He cautioned that "the victory [was] going to come slowly. Nobody need expect any blitzkrieg. Prejudice does not cave in; it fights to the last ditch, and has more lives than the proverbial cat. All we lawyers can do is open the door and get Negroes into position to exercise their rights. The final push must come from the citizens themselves."[24]

Houston was content to leave the "final push" to black people, which was not the case for the staunch integrationists in the NAACP like its national secretary, Walter White. In his address to the 1941 NAACP national conference in Houston, the first time the association had ever held its annual meeting in a Deep South state, White attacked Jim Crow higher education: "Then there has been the continuation of our struggle against discrimination in graduate training, and we herewith serve notice on the tax-supported institutions of the State of Texas that we hope we may get around to them; so you might as well prepare now."[25] He then interrupted his speech to introduce Lucille Bluford to the audience. Bluford was the plaintiff in a lawsuit to integrate the University of Missouri's School of Journalism. She was a minor celebrity at the conference, but a month later the state courts dismissed her suit, giving school officials time to present its plan to commence graduate education in journalism at the all-black Lincoln University. Charles Houston, Bluford's lawyer, was unable to prove that this plan did not meet the equality standard since the University of Missouri eliminated its journalism school, ostensibly because of a wartime enrollment decline.[26] The NAACP, nevertheless, hailed Bluford as on the cutting edge of the fight for black democratic rights. Her image and the rhetoric of leaders like White was so influential that the NAACP youth section adopted the resolution: "Whereas, there exists in the United States certain inequalities regarding educational facilities between Negroes and Whites and whereas, these inequalities not only tend, but do make for a weakening of democracy, therefore be it resolved that we do all in our power to make for uniform educational opportunities for everyone regardless of race, creed or color."[27] After all was said and done, however, more was said than done. Blacks in southern states like Texas were not yet prepared to pursue vigorously a direct challenge to segregated education.

On 9 April 1945, A. Maceo Smith wrote to inform Thurgood Marshall that the executive committee of NAACP branches in Texas had requested Resident Counsel W. J. Durham "to prepare an opinion on the possibility for legal action in connection with equalizing educational opportunities for Negroes in Texas." He sent Marshall a copy of Durham's opinion for him and Judge William Hastie to review. He added, "The Texas Conference is now ready for action and we want to go about it in the same manner that we handled the Texas Primary Case."[28] The voting rights victory won a great deal of credibility for the NAACP in Texas and buoyed the hopes of its members for the NAACP's legal strategy against white supremacy.[29] Major branch leaders were ready for legal action at a time when lawsuits to equalize the salaries of black and white teachers began achieving desired results. Also, state officials seemed to be taking steps toward implementing the BCNET's recommendations. In January 1945, Texas A&M's regents proclaimed they would make a first-class university out of Prairie View. In May, the legislature passed a bill renaming the college Prairie View University but also voted down a measure that would have allowed Prairie View to draw from the Permanent University Fund, which remained exclusively reserved for UT and Texas A&M. Fine words and fancy name changes looked good in principle, but to black observers the dollar sign remained the bottom line.[30]

The shift in the political terrain from interracial conciliation to civil libertarianism may be traced in various developments through the 1940s. Although it does not completely explain the complicated process of change concerning legal strategies and ideological struggles, the protracted political feud between NAACP leaders Lulu B. White and Thurgood Marshall on one side, and Carter Wesley on the other offers an illuminating representation of the changing times. Merline Pitre has provided a good introduction to the "continuous warfare" that arose between White and Wesley.[31] Additionally, Mark Tushnet has pointed out that this fight extended to the national office of the NAACP. He credits the Wesley-Marshall exchange in letters on legal strategy as responsible for Marshall and the national staff's clean break with Charles Houston's original equalization-based legal strategy in favor of a direct assault on segregated education.[32] Both authors rightly impute a critical historical significance to the equalization-versus-desegregation debate. Pitre limits her focus to the Houston area, and Tushnet accepts Marshall's side rather uncritically and restricts his analysis to the legal and organizational aspects of the struggle. A close reading of the debate reveals deep fissures within the black professional-managerial class and the larger black community vis-à-vis the direction and purposes of their struggle. In that reading, the story of a social change movement in the making and its malcontents emerges.

The confrontation between the NAACP and Carter Wesley underscores the new ideological setting of 1940. From the end of Reconstruction to the 1930s, if an official party line can be said to have existed among black folk, especially its upper classes, then interracial conciliation surely represented the line. Radical dissenters from the canon no doubt existed, but the political faith to which most blacks publicly professed an allegiance remained the one the interracial conciliator presented. With no great tumult, the party line had simply faded from existence by the 1930s. The unabated string of lynchings, of whitecappings, of injustices of so many kinds simply led blacks to lose interest in an ideology that delivered nothing and freed them from none of their social afflictions. To wit, the Commission on Inter-racial Cooperation went out with a whimper. Blacks, as well as their sympathizers from other races and cultures, came to desire a more assertive type of social action in the South.[33] Black leaders who had patiently worked inside the CIC or who searched elsewhere for less conservative southern whites to join with in struggle for a racially democratic "New South" were able to take heart.

Carter Wesley represented one such soldier for black rights. In letters to the NAACP's New York headquarters, Wesley kept Thurgood Marshall and the other national leaders of the NAACP informed about the work of southern black leaders, even though he felt they were "not interested in what is being done down here[;] you think we are all Uncle Toms."[34] Nonetheless, from the call of Gordon B. Hancock, a dean at Virginia Union University, for southern Negroes to conference at Durham, North Carolina, in October 1942, to the formal creation of the Southern Regional Council (SRC) in 1944, Wesley participated in the wartime challenge of black southerners to "that element of the white South who express themselves as desirous of a New Deal for the Negroes."[35] He saw the movement that culminated in the SRC as a covenant "to give equal opportunities to Negroes." It successfully attracted the financial support of the Rosenwald Fund and the American Missionary Association, which wanted more effective "direct action" than the CIC or black colleges seemed capable of taking to eradicate the caste system in American race relations. Cultivating the goodwill of whites and slowly making a Negro elite educated in the ways of Western civilization had done little to undermine Jim Crowism and to create an antiracist, integrated South. To Wesley, blacks had to organize whites into a strong southern movement to create "equal opportunity" in education, jobs, voting rights, and social mobility. In his brand of militant race consciousness, he saw the general line of march toward full Negro emancipation as the movement for equality in the first instance, and the breakdown of segregation after that wherever possible. As long as the southern movement did not become "another old hen's group like the Interracial Commission was," Wesley committed to it his full support.[36]

A product of the activity that founded the SRC, the Southern Negro Conference for Equalization of Educational Opportunities (SNC-EEO) held its first annual meeting in May 1945 and elected Carter Wesley its president. Other officers included C. A. Scott of Atlanta and Lucy Harth Smith of Lexington as vice presidents; Reid E. Jackson of Southern University in Scotlandville, Louisiana, as secretary; and R. B. Atwood of Kentucky State College in Frankfort as treasurer. Horace Mann Bond of Fort Valley State College agreed to serve as director of research, and thirteen others permitted their names to be listed as SNC-EEO commission members: Henry A. Bullock and E. M. Norris of Texas (Prairie View); A. W. Dent and Lucius L. Jones of Louisiana; Lawrence A. Davis of Arkansas; Roscoe Dunjee of Oklahoma; G. Blyden Jackson and Frank L. Stanley of Kentucky; Edward Bishop, Percy Greene, and S. D. Redmond of Mississippi; and R. O'Hara Lanier of Virginia. They launched the group with high hopes for its success. Its first task was raising the enormous sum of $100,000 to support the antidiscriminatory legal work of a Southwide legal committee composed of Marshall, Alexander P. Tureaud of Louisiana, A. T. Walden of Georgia, Arthur Davis Shores of Alabama, and W. J. Durham of Texas.[37]

In the wink of an eye, Wesley's hopes floundered. The legal committee never got organized. Wesley scheduled the group to meet the day after the SNC-EEO's first annual meeting in Memphis, but it was called off when Marshall claimed he could not make travel arrangements to be there. Tureaud offered to host a meeting in New Orleans in June, but it came to no avail. That month, however, Marshall sent out a memorandum to A. Maceo Smith and other officers of the NAACP State Conference of Branches, sparking, at least in Wesley's eyes, the impression that the NAACP wanted to be the vanguard leader in the fight for equalization of educational opportunities in the South and had opted to "preempt" all comers to the field of battle. Wesley responded that if the NAACP was going to "take over" all the work, he would "present the matter to the Southern Conference and give them a chance to dump it in your lap."[38] Marshall answered Wesley that the NAACP headquarters had for some time periodically sent memos to the branches to urge them to study local problems in preparation for litigation or some other NAACP-directed activity. Marshall promised that no legal action would be undertaken without first contacting Wesley and others but underscored that the NAACP had gotten into the fight to see it to the finish: "As you know, I have been in full accord with the Southern Negro Conference and its objectives and have been and am still anxious and willing to work with you. However, I do not understand that the NAACP was to abandon its fight for equalization of educational opportunities."[39]

This exchange was the first indication of a rift developing between Wesley and the NAACP, particularly Marshall. It was not over a difference in approach or principle, however. Through their work together on the legal challenge to the white Democratic primary, a personal closeness grew between Wesley and Marshall. By 1943, Marshall would greet the Houston publisher in his letters with "Dear Carter" and on occasion "My dear buffle-headed friend."[40] Likewise, Wesley wrote to the New York attorney using colorful and jocular terms such as "Hi Toots" and "chucklehead" and might even curse him with no malice intended: "You just are a long, lank 'Nigger.' "[41] Given their relationship and their mutual sense of the other's importance to the cause of racial justice, neither man relished a course toward conflict.

In late July, Wesley went to New York for a meeting of black publishers. While there, he and Marshall met and discussed the campaign for educational equalization. Marshall summarized the points of the discussion in a letter to Wesley in August:

> It is my understanding that we agreed that in states where the N.A.A.C.P. was sufficiently active to handle cases to equalize educational opportunities that these cases would be handled by the N.A.A.C.P. and the Southern Negro Conference for Equalization of Educational Opportunities would handle cases in places where the N.A.A.C.P. was not sufficiently active. . . . [I]t was believed that the [SNC-EEO] could lend aid in all of these cases, and should not under any circumstances disband. . . . I for one am not kidding when I say that we want and need, not only the cooperation of your organization but also your continued personal cooperation.[42]

Pacific relations between Wesley and Marshall, as well as the SNC-EEO and the NAACP, resumed through the fall and into the spring of 1946, when Marshall filed a lawsuit against UT's racially discriminatory admissions policy. The case of Heman Sweatt brought unity and enthusiasm to the University Movement, but beneath the surface, Marshall and the NAACP still harbored suspicion toward Wesley and the SNC-EEO. When the SNC-EEO held its second annual meeting in New Orleans at the Booker T. Washington High School on 13 April 1946, despite Wesley's open-faced manner of dealing with the NAACP, Marshall felt it necessary to ask Daniel Ellis Byrd, executive secretary of the New Orleans NAACP branch, and A. P. Tureaud to attend the conference as representatives of the NAACP. He asked them to send him "a confidential and full report of what happens at the meeting, which will be between the two of us."[43] Marshall's fear of rivalry with the SNC-EEO contrasted sharply with conference members' repeated statements of full support for the NAACP's educational equalization work. The Southern Conference also began encountering a difficult time getting itself organized.

With suspicion in the air, the fire of trouble blazed nearby, and it first flared in Wesley's hometown of Houston. On 3 September 1946, Smith and Wesley sent out an open letter to people on a statewide mailing list announcing that the TCNO had voted to launch its effort for educational equality through a branch of the SNC-EEO "known as the Texas Negro Conference on Equalization of Education" (TNCEE), which would hold its first meeting at Houston's Emancipation Park.[44] For almost two decades before this letter went out, Lulu White and her husband, Julius, had been allies with Wesley as part of the city's family of leading black activists. The Smith-Wesley letter, however, prompted bitter words from the Houston branch's executive secretary against Wesley. In the margin and on the back of the letter, she implored Walter White to "read this d—— thing." She argued that Texas did not need a TNCEE; the work of the NAACP needed help enough. Moreover, the existence of the TCNO, which she never supported, already cluttered the field. "If the NAACP is spearheading this case," White wrote, "why have any other organization to compromise over?" She answered her own question saying, "Maceo is bound to have an organization to accept the segregated college for Negroes." Linking Wesley and Smith with a plot in support of a black university, she complained, "I may be wrong Walter, but this is nothing but a *sell out*."[45] Walter White reacted myopically and completely supported her position.

In a memorandum to Marshall, Walter White informed the special counsel that the TNCEE had organized "to devise [a] means of effecting a compromise in the Herman [*sic*] Sweat [*sic*] case." Nowhere in the Smith-Wesley letter does it speak of working for a compromise in the *Sweatt* case, but they did call for establishing the TNCEE to "cooperate with the NAACP in its fight for entrance into the University of Texas." The national secretary either did not read the Smith-Wesley letter carefully or deliberately misrepresented its content to Marshall. Misrepresentation is the most likely possibility given that he took quotes from the letter in every particular, except the "compromise" issue. Furthermore, Walter White informed Marshall that "Lula wants our go ahead signal to fight this outfit [the TNCEE] with every possible weapon and also the Texas Conference [*sic*] of Negro Organizations, apparently another A. Maceo Smith operation, to accept 'equal but separate educational facilities.' Lula wants me to call her back this afternoon to tell her our decision. . . . What do you think?" White sent a telegram to Lulu White notifying her that, at the suggestion of Thurgood Marshall, he had written Wesley and Smith "affirming our position of opposition to any form of segregation." The war was on.[46]

On 25 October 1946, Marshall fired off a letter to Wesley marked "Personal," emphasizing that he considered the communication strictly between the two of them, saying, "For once, I am serious." Marshall expressed worry over the program of the TNCEE. He regretted he had not written to Wesley sooner, but he had been recuperating from an illness since July. Marshall complained that either the TNCEE duplicated the work of the NAACP in Texas or it constituted a "competing organization." If the group truly committed itself to working "on cases in the segregated field of education," then to Marshall, such work conflicted and competed with the "principles" of the NAACP. Invoking the story of the woman who said she was just "a little pregnant," Marshall explained to Wesley that there could be no acceptance of "a little segregation," not even in the short run. "The N.A.A.C.P.'s State Conference in Texas is opposed to segregation in any form," he continued. The TNCEE, on the other hand, "is going to try to get as much as possible under the segregated system. The Negroes in Texas will most certainly end up in two divided camps, and I do not believe it is possible to be in both camps at the same time." Marshall's only evidence for the mutual exclusivity of the two positions on segregation was a story about people who try to carry a bucket of water on each shoulder, ending up "with both buckets and water parked on the middle of their skulls." Marshall also called upon Wesley to rethink the purpose of the TNCEE in that the opposition could view it "as a counter-move and as a compromise answer to the problem." He portrayed Wesley as "clamoring for a segregated school" of law for Negroes and reminded him that "every segregated elementary school, every segregated high school and every segregated college unit is a monument to the perpetuation of segregation. It is one thing to 'take' segregation that is forced upon you and it is another thing to ask for segregation."[47]

Of more pressing concern to Wesley than Marshall's avuncular letter, however, were the public attacks at his flank coming from Lulu White. She had been railing against Wesley and others she suspected of collaborating with state government leaders in the creation of a segregated black university. Less than a week before the hearing in which Judge Roy Archer promised he would issue a mandamus compelling the admission of Sweatt to UT if no law school had been created for him, White wrote to Marshall and urgently repeated her opposition to Wesley. "The NAACP needs to lead out in all programs of advancement of Negroes in Texas," she affirmed. "I was glad to see in the News Letter that the Legal Committee was doing something about this, 'EQUAL BUT separate EDUCATIONAL OPPORTUNITIES.' That's right, nothing can be equal if it is separate."[48]

White had the simplest of reasons to hope that Archer would rule in Sweatt's favor: the state had not established a Negro law school equal to the one Negroes were banned from in Austin. Targeting Wesley for her bit-

To the consternation of Texas activists like Carter Wesley, NAACP's top executives (seated, left to right), administrator Roy Wilkins, executive secretary Walter White, and special counsel Thurgood Marshall, tried to maintain hegemony over the Texas campaign for equal educational opportunity (*Crisis*, July 1950, 445).

terest criticism, however, seemed a strange choice given that he had editorialized on 7 December that if Judge Archer was "a jurist of integrity and follows through on his June decision," he could do nothing else but order the desegregation of the UT School of Law. Wesley castigated members of the governor's biracial commission on education as accomplices with Governor Stevenson in perpetrating a "hoax" on black Texans and Judge Archer. He published a front-page indictment of W. R. Banks, retired principal of Prairie View, and Dr. M. L. Edwards for "doing the dirty work in this swindle" by helping to set up a makeshift law school in Houston. These broadsides had not been Wesley's first attacks on interracial conciliators; but despite his record of vigilance against those who compromised in favor of separate equality, White continued to scandalize him as a sellout unfaithful to the NAACP.[49]

Wesley did not suffer White's attacks with grace. Although on 14 December he defended White and the NAACP against the charge that communists had come to dominate the Houston branch, a week later he threw

White in with the "'red' white people" who had replaced "respectable 'high class' Negro board members."[50] Wesley jabbed at White with a red smear and followed with solid left and right punches. He attacked White for endorsing a conception of the NAACP as having the prerogative to preempt any other form of organizing among black Texans that proposed to fight on fronts where the NAACP refused to be involved. The knockout blow charged that White had chosen to work to undermine the unity and solidarity that black leaders in Texas had been forging since 1941. Wesley's pugilistic work in the pages of his papers pushed White to the point of resignation. She disclosed that her Achilles heel, her vow to "honor and obey" her husband, Julius, had been struck.[51]

Julius White, a most fascinating, if shadowy, figure in the freedom movement of blacks in Texas, had the reputation for being a man with a "truculent" temperament and the means to get physical with anyone he felt had disrespected him or his wife. Lulu White felt resourceful enough to fight her own battles until the internecine warfare with Wesley got heated to a point that Julius could take no more.[52]

On 29 December, Lula White placed a collect telephone call to Walter White reporting to him that "Julius insists that she resign because Carter Wesley and Maceo Smith are making the fight a personal one against her." The national secretary, dismayed that he had to hear "the whole story at our expense," counseled her not to resign "under fire," and urged her to send him a "temperate statement of facts" so that the national board could determine if there were grounds upon which to "take appropriate action."[53] With support from Walter White, Thurgood Marshall, and other NAACP leaders at the national level, the board of the local branch took courage and refused Lulu White's resignation. Considerably deflated, she stayed on as executive secretary even as Wesley continued to batter her in his editorials. In June of 1949, she finally left office saying that she could no longer "say 'pay Wesley no mind, he has to sell his paper.'"[54]

In the 1940s, a word like "sexism" did not roll off the tongues of men like Carter Wesley, or even women like Lulu White. From the vantage of five decades removed, however, the equality a black woman like White exercised in "a man's world" is striking. Although he was convinced "Lulu is full of prunes" on the question of strategy in the fight for educational equality, Wesley readily admitted that she had excellent skills as an NAACP organizer. Any sentimental regrets he felt were not about White, however, but about her husband. In December of 1946, Wesley wrote President John Jay Jones of the Texas State Conference of Branches:

> I never had any doubts about your understanding of my position, or any other intelligent leader of Negroes in Texas misunderstanding my position. Lulu's attitude nonplussed me, but I knew she just didn't know what she was

talking about and didn't get too excited. . . . Only a few of them got the real significance of Lulu's resignation Tuesday night. Lulu wouldn't run away from the fight, but Julius, her husband, is very sensitive to publicity about his wife. He can't appreciate the fact that when his wife is in a public office she is always subject to criticism, as is any other public official. So the crux of the thing really is that Julius wants Lulu out of the whole mess. Julius is a square-shooter, and I am really sorry that the thing came out for his sake. I imagine if I ever talk to anybody about this thing, it will be to Lulu and Julius together, but other than that I am content to have the thing stay now as an issue.[55]

Lulu White and Carter Wesley might have generated a healthy debate about the equalization versus desegregation strategy, but they failed to do so, and their failure begins with White. From the point she personalized Wesley's position and inveighed against him in emotionally charged terms like "sell-out" and "traitor to the race" working for segregation, she substituted calumny for calculated argument. Wesley, in turn, resorted to the same tactics to destroy her standing. The charge of communism in black Houston meant roughly the same thing as calling *her* a sell out. Where she vilified Wesley as the running dog of whites who wished to manipulate and control blacks in their segregated, bourgeois world order, Wesley responded by calling her the running dog (knowingly or unwittingly) of "red" whites who sought to control blacks in an integrated, proletarian political order. The exchange between Wesley and Marshall had somewhat more substance, but frequently it also lapsed into sideline issues.

In advance of the deadline in Judge Archer's courtroom on 17 December, the NAACP organized a statewide mass meeting at Dorie Miller Auditorium in black East Austin. The executive committee of the Texas NAACP also scheduled a meeting for the day after the hearing to take place at Samuel Huston College, inviting Wesley and his colleague in the TNCEE, Dr. Waldo Howard, to attend so that the "confused situation" between Wesley (TNCEE-TNCO) and Marshall (NAACP) could be settled. Wesley attended the mass meeting and the hearing in Archer's court. However, when Archer had done his work of ruling in behalf of white supremacy, the publisher left and returned to Houston. Wesley later claimed to have heard that Lulu White opposed his appearing before the committee and would attack his presence there. Although Wesley saw no sense in staying overnight for the meeting, it might have been more colorful if he had. In a review of the Texas case, Marshall stated as plain as ever the legal strategy of the NAACP regarding higher education equalization. All cases were being processed on the basis of the *Gaines* decision and the Fourteenth Amendment to the U.S. Constitution. Furthermore, the NAACP did not see where the creation of Jim Crow schools compromised its legal position. "The development of public sentiment" made it necessary to attack such schools and show them no quarter. Marshall even "endorsed the technique of 'picketing'" so-called makeshift schools to discourage blacks from attending such institutions.[56]

In his reply to a letter from Marshall regretting his absence at the Austin meeting, Wesley reexamined the history of his involvement in the Texas University Movement and his approach to the battle for winning improvements in the opportunities for black higher education in Texas. His approach treated the matter of equalizing education as a "total problem" rather than an isolated issue of integrating a single black student into UT. He infused his argument to Marshall with strong language in behalf of the rights of local people over the processes of struggle that most immediately affected their future. "I make this jibe at you," Wesley quipped, "if you spent half of the energy trying to get up the other suits that need to be filed in Texas for entrance into the University of Texas that you are spending in trying to cut off some possible rivalry of the Texas Conference on Equalization, you, we and everybody else would be a hell of a lot better off."[57]

Marshall's reply to Wesley took up many tangential issues, while Walter White, who also sent a reply, recast Wesley's letter into a personal condemnation of the special counsel as all out for himself. Wesley's criticisms of selfishness, however, were mainly against the association, not Marshall. Both letters were silent on Wesley's charge that the NAACP demanded exclusive control over the Texas University Movement.[58]

In separate letters to Walter White and Marshall, Wesley tried to get an answer from the NAACP as to why it was bent on trying to "kill off" the TNCEE and taking a "narrow view and a narrow attitude."[59] White bowed out of the controversy, snapping to Marshall, "Don't Texans ever write short letters?" He requested from Marshall an opinion as to some action the national board might take in response to the "trouble" in Texas.[60] Marshall composed a letter, but Roy Wilkins, the editor of the NAACP's *Crisis* magazine and assistant to White, pulled it because it was too "hot." He drafted a cooler version of the letter, but Marshall rejected it, asking that he "please put this into English." Marshall took another day to complete a different, longer letter, in which he refrained from suggesting that Wesley supported the erection of monuments to Jim Crow education. He answered Wesley's main question by referring him to his letter of 25 October 1946.[61] Such a referral only served to lead Wesley to find proof of his charge that Marshall intended to make "an attack upon [his] integrity."[62] On 13 January, Marshall wrote that he would cease trying to answer Wesley as he had concluded that "nothing can be gained from this continued exchange of correspondence."[63]

The Marshall-Wesley exchange, however, was not over. On 17 January, Wesley tendered his written resignation from the local, state, and national NAACP, citing as his reasons that the NAACP had become "a source and means of malicious and entirely unjustifiable slander against me in my area" and had "recklessly taken a course to split the leadership of Texas." The next day, he pressed Marshall to "show forth proof" that he was "seeking segregation" and "a compromise of the Sweatt case." Marshall felt "duty bound" to send him a hair-splitting rehash of his arguments that failed to prove Wesley was a traitor to his race.[64] Wesley responded with a letter charging Marshall with evading the issue. James Nabrit, co-counsel with Marshall on the *Sweatt* case and a longtime friend of Wesley, called on the men to "battle this thing out between yourselves, compose your differ-ences and again join in this fight," but the two men continued to drift apart.[65] In February, Marshall wrote Wesley a short note sniping at an article he had written. Wesley was mostly taken aback by Marshall's manner of address: "I notice that it has drifted to 'Mr. Wesley.'" He accepted the new formal terms of address, and their correspondence ceased for seven months.[66]

During the hiatus in Wesley-Marshall communication, Marshall came to some significant insights regarding the Texas University Movement and related cases in Louisiana, South Carolina, and Oklahoma on which he served as co-counsel or adviser. For the first time, he began acknowledging that the "cases against state universities . . . are brand new types of legal action striking at segregation per se." Moreover, in a memorandum to Gloster B. Current calling for closer coordination of NAACP legal work with local branches and the branch department, Marshall, ever the great story-teller, offered an interesting comparative observation:

> In Texas, as a result of the intensive work by the State Conference and others, there is hardly a Negro in Texas today who is not convinced that segregation is not only bad, but cannot be tolerated. It is likewise evident that this senti-ment does not exist in any other southern state where we are operating. I remember, for example, that several months ago we had a meeting in Austin, Texas; I made the statement that the NAACP was sick and tired of separate but equal and would fight to the last ditch to remove all segregation and the applause of the white and Negro people in the audience was terrific. A week thereafter I made the same statement in Charleston, S.C., at a regional meet-ing, on three different occasions, including twice in a working session and once at the mass meeting, and there was absolutely no applause, but rather a look of apprehension on the faces of most of our delegates.[67]

He noted that blacks (including many NAACP members) in states outside of the South — namely, Illinois, Ohio, Michigan, Pennsylvania, Kansas, and New Jersey — approved of their children attending "completely segregated schools." Marshall offered no reasons for why, in his estimation, Texas blacks marched ahead of the rest of black America in their readiness to embrace desegregation, but he emphasized the need for "complete support of all the Negroes" in those states having antisegregation legal action. Texas, site of the NAACP's most noteworthy case of this kind, represented a crucial object lesson for the masses of black folks across the entire country. "All out" war on segregation rendered counterproductive Wesley's two-line approach of fighting for equal opportunity both in separate facilities and through integration. For desegregation efforts to succeed, the NAACP felt, all Jim Crow schools had to be condemned without pity. For the sake of good propaganda, of winning the hearts and minds of the people to integrated education as the only assurance of equality, Marshall demanded unequivocal support of his legal work. It did not matter how long the realization of the goal might take; he was committed forthrightly to a head-on collision with the legal foundations of segregation. The honesty or accuracy of his assessment of how black Texans felt about his new direction also did not seem to matter to Marshall. He felt his way to be the only way the race could be saved, whether the race liked it or not. In his view, blacks who failed to appreciate the cause he led were like children who refused to take their medicine, and the choice was the medicine or death.

Two different examples may be presented to show how Marshall misjudged black Texans and their reaction to the contrasting positions of Wesley and Marshall. Over a year after the critical exchange developed between Marshall and Wesley, Marshall related to Carl Murphy, editor of the Baltimore *Afro-American*, that "as a result of Carter Wesley's attack on us, I am certain that he has lost circulation instead of gaining it, and all of the people I have talked to, many times without revealing my identity, offer unanimous support for our all-out attack on segregation in Texas." Figures from Ayer and Son's *Directory of Newspapers and Periodicals* indicate that the years between 1944 and 1948 were banner years for Wesley. In those years, the total circulation of the papers under his control, at a minimum, reached between 40,000 and 50,000 people per week. The numbers declined after 1948, with the sharpest drop coming in 1953. There is no evidence in the circulation rates, nor in the pages of his newspapers or his correspondence, to suggest that the criticisms Wesley launched against the NAACP in 1946 led to any drop in circulation.

Polling data also indicated Marshall's miscalculation of reality. The *Texas Poll*, established in 1940, began surveying public opinion regarding civil rights in 1946, especially in the areas of voting rights and education. In 1947, through its quota-sampling technique, the poll's findings contrasted sharply with Marshall's assertions. Blacks were in favor, eight to five, of the creation of a separate University of Texas for their race rather than entering UT. Whites supported the separate university option twenty-five to one over integration.[68] The complete results of the poll are represented in Figure 1.

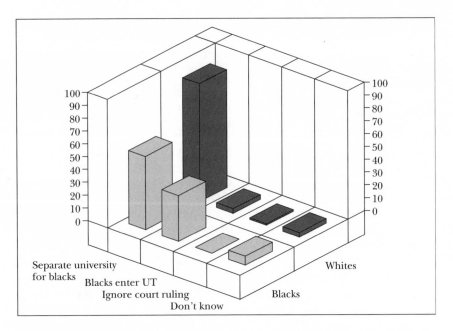

Figure 1. Results of *Texas Poll*, Report No. 132, 26 January 1947. *Question*: "Under a Supreme Court ruling, Texas is faced with the problem of either setting up a first-class university for Negroes or allowing them to enter The University of Texas. What do you think ought to be done?" *Source*: Scott, "Twenty-Five Years of Opinion on Integration in Texas," 158

Clearly, Marshall overstated the support among black Texans for his "new" position on university litigation and sacrificed the truth to serve personal and organizational purposes. Emboldened to chart a new course, the special counsel put together a case that repudiated and denigrated the possibility that a separate law school for blacks could ever be equal to the established one set up for whites. In the brief filed in Sweatt's behalf after he refused to attend the Houston law school on the grounds that it was inadequate, Marshall stressed the inherently discriminatory nature of a separate law school.[69] Moreover, when the trial began before Judge Archer in May 1947, Sweatt's attorneys (Marshall, Nabrit, Durham, and C. B. Bunkley), produced a "surprise witness." They called Robert Redfield, professor and chairman of the Department of Anthropology at the University of Chicago, to take the stand as an expert witness on the effects of racial segregation on education. Also described as an "eminent sociologist" and a lawyer who "for twenty years had given special attention to racial differences in education," Redfield was the living symbol of a growing number of social scientists who since the 1920s had begun to attack the intellectual underpinnings of white supremacy as a social doctrine. Influenced by Bronislaw Malinowski (the Polish-born scholar who brought anthropologists off the "verandas" of colonial administrators and into the lives, living spaces, and folk cultures of colonized peoples in the "primitive" and "peripheral" societies of the global market system), Redfield was more a civil libertarian ally than an author with a distinguished publication record on the subject of segregation in the American South. He substituted well enough for white scholars like Hortense Powdermaker and John Dollard who had produced such a record. His testimony did not center on the ramifications that racial separation in education had on the personalities or ego states of blacks. Instead, he drew attention to the way in which racial separation perpetuated a "mythical conception of differences" that restricted the field of participation both across cultural or racial lines and within a specific cultural or racial group. "Segregation," Redfield stated, "tends to intensify suspicion and distrust" between and within all categories of American citizens.[70]

Marshall's case, weaving together Redfield's testimony, with references to Gunnar Myrdal's *American Dilemma*, the reports of President Harry Truman's Committee on Civil Rights, articles from the *Journal of Negro Education*, and testimony from Dean Charles H. Thompson of Howard University, did little to sway Archer and white Texans. Nevertheless, the use of experts to document the inequality of the dual system of education and its negative social consequences grew into a major part of the legal strategy of direct assault on segregated education.

While Sweatt's case went up the appellate process, the NAACP legal staff grew anxious to test out the new direct-assault approach at other levels of the dual school system. Local people in Texas communities like Hearne, LaGrange, Texarkana, and Wichita Falls, on the move against oppression and discrimination in the public schools provided to blacks, offered the NAACP the test cases it sought. A few of these cases that developed in the late 1940s will be explored in Chapter 3, but one case involving a challenge to segregation at the secondary school level deserves consideration here. It is a prime example of local blacks growing tired of appeals to the consciences and the hearts of whites and, through a surge of racial militancy, experimenting with the civil libertarian remedy of legal action.

In Hearne, a Negro Citizens Committee (NCC) could not accept that in a town where the scholastic population of black to white pupils was 712 to 650, facilities for blacks (including proposed development) did not exceed $300,000, although facilities for whites were valued in excess of $3 million. The committee's petition arose from the smoke and ashes of a fire on 9 December 1945, when the Negro primary school burned to the ground and severely damaged the adjacent high school. The Hearne Independent School District (ISD) approved a replacement facility financed from a bond issue and federal aid, but when "school authorities proce[e]ded to throw up an unsightly, inadequate makeshift plant constructed mainly of prisoner-of-war barracks given them by the Federal government," protest was immediate.[71] The NCC's petition noted that the teacher-student ratio for whites was 27:1 but for blacks it was 60:1 and concluded, "[I]n the light of the present world picture we believe that Democracy should begin at home and its practices extended to all citizens to share and share alike. Therefore we submit this petition to your honorable body in the hope that you reconsider your present plans and provide equal instructional facilities for Negro students with those provided for whites."[72]

On 14 August 1947, A. Maceo Smith seized upon the case and quickly sent a copy of the petition to Lulu White, noting that the Hearne case might be "our next 'battleground.' "[73] Special counsel Marshall and regional NAACP counsel W. J. Durham, however, had problems with the local citizen's request for equalization instead of integration. Marshall had a new version of the petition written without the request for equalization and in its place a demand for the school board to end its discriminatory policies without stating how it could remedy the situation. On 15 September 1947, C. G. Jennings, one of the NCC members who embraced the integrationist revision, took his thirteen-year-old stepdaughter, Doris Fay, to Hearne High School for whites and attempted to enroll her. The district superintendent, R. M. Hix, told him that he would not enroll the girl. Jennings, with Durham and Marshall for attorneys, filed suit in behalf of his daughter. In support of Doris Fay and in protest of conditions at the black school, 300 black students launched a boycott of classes on 17 September, which lasted several days.[74]

As the *Jennings* suit developed, Marshall attempted to elicit the help of George I. Sanchez of the University of Texas's Latin American Education and Intergroup Relations. Sanchez had been involved in the Orange County, California, case *Mendez* v. *Westminster School District*, in which the Supreme Court had ruled unconstitutional the segregation of Mexican students. In a 6 July 1948 letter to Marshall, Sanchez expressed his doubt that the affidavits of expert witnesses used in that case would be of any assistance to Marshall "since those affidavits are pointed specifically towards a denial of the pedagogical soundness of segregation that is based on the 'language handicap' excuse." Sanchez pointed out that the case's general "plan of attack" could be of use.[75]

Judge Ben Rice, with no regard for argument against the "separate but equal" doctrine itself, issued a declaratory judgment in the case on 1 September 1948. He gave district officials until the opening of the schools a few weeks later to furnish equal facilities, but the district did nothing at all close to equalizing the schools. Hearne parents like Mrs. Carrie Mack grew despondent. On 19 October, Smith wrote to assure her that the NAACP was "not nearly through with the Hearne case." From the standpoint of the national staff, however, the Hearne case was a dead letter. It did not get off on the right foot, and Smith never got educational experts to come and survey the school situation there. On 5 May 1949, Smith gave Mack the brush off, saying that NAACP attorneys remained undecided as to whether to file a new lawsuit or contempt proceedings based on Judge Rice's original ruling, which they all deemed to be too "weak" to get the school board to do anything. Black children in Hearne were left behind.[76]

NAACP failures, like that at Hearne, confirmed for black Texans the definite limitations of the civil libertarian strategy. Suing whites carried risks of physical and economic recriminations for what many blacks saw as perhaps a noble, but utterly impractical and inflammatory, strategy. Mark Tushnet offers a different view. Rather reductively, he argues that because "there were at least a few lawyers who were available for facilities suits," Marshall and other NAACP lawyers "could be reasonably confident that, when no such suits were brought, the black community taken as a whole did in fact prefer the direct attack to equalization litigation." Without any justification, he says that Wesley, "the most vocal advocate of facilities litigation," was "presumably" available to represent blacks who did not desire the integration approach. Although Wesley was a lawyer "with significant experience in constitutional litigation," he was a newspaper publisher by choice. In the late 1930s, when he started to create his chain of papers, he consciously made himself unavailable for such legal work, except indirectly as an armchair lawyer. In establishing the SNC-EEO (and the TNCEE on a statewide basis), Wesley hoped to organize a Southwide network of lawyers committed to a two-line approach, but this never materialized thanks in large part to the NAACP covertly undermining his efforts. Tushnet is wrong, however, not merely because of fallacious reasoning but on a factual level as well. He misrepresents the Hearne case as a "facilities" case, when it was an unsuccessful direct-attack case. He misrepresents Wesley as solely an advocate of facilities litigation, when he was a better champion of desegregation than equalization litigation. For reasons he never completely divulged — perhaps a product of NAACP domination of the legal field in the 1940s but more likely a result of Marshall influencing his position — Wesley let the SNC-EEO and the TNCEE die a quiet death. He resigned from the NAACP and withdrew to his role as a publisher and opinion maker. Finally, Tushnet is flatly in error in his argument that "the fact that Wesley did not mobilize any communities for facilities cases suggests that he did not speak for a significant portion of the black community anywhere in the country." Leaving aside his making a straw man out of Wesley to "prove" that Marshall and the legal whips in New York fully represented the masses of black folks in the United States, the evidence shows that Wesley did back the postwar grassroots movement for separate equality in public education. Lawsuits did not figure prominently as a means or an end; rather, the movement sought tangible improvements to the schools of patient, long-suffering black communities. Wesley did not start every petition and protest action for separate educational equality, but the influence of his newspaper chain and his contact with key leaders can be identified in many equalization struggles across the state.[77]

The upper Gulf Coast oil producing and refining boomtown of Beaumont provides a good example of the representativeness of Wesley's position and his role vis-à-vis the spontaneous movement for separate equality in education. In the bloody summer of 1943, Beaumont, like forty-six other American cities that year, became a racial battleground.[78] The scars of the tragedy were still fresh when the Negro Goodwill Council (NGC) went into action to increase the opportunity for vocational, adult, and college education for blacks. As the city's white junior college grew (doubling its enrollment in 1946 over the previous year) into Lamar State College of Technology, black leaders asked for their Negro equivalent. Boycotts and petition campaigns in protest of deplorable primary and secondary school conditions already had commenced during World War II. The NGC and other black groups applied pressure in a variety of ways and contemplated a facilities equalization suit. One of Beaumont's school districts attempted to satisfy blacks in 1947 with the construction of a new, brick high school known as Charlton-Pollard (named for two local black pioneer educators) and the George Washington Carver Elementary School. The other district erected a new building in 1952, Hebert High School, named for a local black benefactor of education.

The NGC did not compete with the local NAACP. Public work in behalf of social reform or human rights for blacks could scarcely be done in the name of the NAACP in Beaumont, especially in the years immediately after the riot of 1943. Most whites considered the organization too provocative. For a southerner to publicly identify herself as a member of the NAACP was to threaten her employment or business dealings with the average white person in the South. It could also invite white distrust and harassment. Black leaders created the NGC as a united front of blacks across the spectrum of ideologies that had a name that would sound safe and respectable. The improvements in facilities the NGC wrested from the white power holders did not produce a dual system that was equal, but it did bring a change that most blacks hailed as meaningful and considered long overdue. Wesley's connection to the spontaneous upsurge in black agitation came in the person of Aaron Jefferson. A grocer and a charter member of the Beaumont branch of the NAACP when it resurfaced in 1930, Jefferson also worked as Wesley's point man for the *Informer* in the Golden Triangle area of Beaumont, Port Arthur, and Orange. He gathered the news from the tricity area, reported it to Wesley, and helped distribute the paper's state edition. Through the paper, Wesley circulated information on developments occurring elsewhere but also gave blacks the chance to read about their own problems and see themselves as change agents when they took steps to address those problems. When the NGC sent a delegation to Austin to meet regarding their educational concerns with Governor Beauford Jester, the event fulfilled the ideas Wesley sought to provide with an organized structure in the TNCEE. Beaumont's black leaders tried to stall or defeat any bills being passed to upgrade Lamar Union Junior College into a four-year state-supported college without some assurance that blacks, in exchange for their support, would get something in return. John Gray, president of the junior college, promised the NGC separate facilities, and a year later a black branch of Lamar "was instituted at Charlton-Pollard High School during the evenings." Twenty years behind what whites had, the school nonetheless gave area blacks a starting point. Wesley provided the work in Beaumont and in other cities with mass exposure, legitimacy, and critical feedback. Coupled with his support of desegregation, his separate equality agitation won consistent support as a method of addressing educational inequality from Beaumont's black Texans throughout the 1940s.[79]

Contrary to Marshall's view and Tushnet's shallow defense of the same, all black Texans did not stand pat for desegregation. Black people in Beaumont and elsewhere did not struggle for abstract ideas from anyone's head but for concrete, material changes in their quality of life. Those who waded into the troubled waters of the emerging civil rights movement always had the familiar harbors of interracial conciliation or militant "do-for-self" race consciousness to which they could return. Marshall knew the significance of the ideological challenge Wesley posed. Somehow he felt he had to neutralize the publisher in his own region. Marshall had to negotiate a complex ideological terrain and win a solid number of black Texans behind the direction he sought to take the University Movement. It would be no easy task. Undaunted neither by Wesley nor the cofounder of the NAACP, W. E. B. Du Bois, who was back on the staff of the association as director of special research, Marshall took on the same attitude as Walter White, Roy Wilkins, and others in the NAACP hierarchy that the association had a monopoly on certain areas of the budding civil rights struggle. Civil rights litigation, especially in the realm of Negro education, would be the exclusive domain of the NAACP and its Legal Defense and Educational Fund, also known as the LDF or Inc. Fund. Marshall would no more allow black Texans to file school equalization lawsuits outside of the NAACP's control than he would accept Du Bois's salary being taken out of the LDF's coffers. Nor would he permit the old man's efforts to organize a Pan-

African Congress or to press the cause of the colonized world before the United Nations to overshadow his legal attack on Jim Crow inside the United States.[80]

Publicly, Marshall ignored Wesley's steady stream of editorials against the "strutting," limelight-seeking NAACP from February to August 1947, when the *Informer* carried a front-page editorial titled "We Query the NAACP."[81] On 5 September, Marshall struck back at the Texas State Conference of NAACP Branches convention at Denison. He answered Wesley's editorial with a masterful piece of sarcasm, black folk wit, legal acumen, historical analysis, American idealism, base propaganda, malignant name-calling, and outright deceit. In searing language, he suggested that Wesley and other blacks who accepted the Texas State University for Negroes (TSUN), which the state moved to create in answer to Sweatt's lawsuit, were "selling the race down the river." Many blacks could listen to Marshall's moving oratory and hope that his ideas would prevail. The next day, however, they still had to send their children to schools that desperately needed improvements. Marshall's complaint that black Texans had been pursuing separate equality for eighty years and had "not obtained the semblance of equality" must have rung hollow in their ears. What now would the NAACP have them do? Boycott the monuments to Jim Crow and keep their children in ignorance until the NAACP and the Supreme Court got white schools opened to blacks? And if black children were to continue in segregated schools until the NAACP changed the law and the law changed social policy and practice, then what would it hurt to struggle to materially improve those schools now? Marshall contended that equality could only come within a unitary, integrated school system; any work to improve black schools would only blunt the point that segregation was "illegal as well as immoral."[82]

Wesley responded to Marshall's Denison address with fury. In reply, Marshall wrote Louis Martin, the publisher of the *Chicago Defender*, complaining how, since the Denison address, Wesley had been having "a field day in his paper." He also told Martin he had concluded that the time had come for him "to quit trying the 'get along'" with Wesley. The NAACP special counsel prepared to mount a national attack against the Texas-based newspaperman.[83] On that same day, however, Marshall sent a letter to Wesley asking him to "concentrate on constructive criticism rather than on destructive criticism," noting his immunity to Wesley's rebuffs since he had come to develop a "skin closely resembling that of a walrus." Marshall also got a little rough with Wesley. Solely because of the NAACP's "forthright attack on segregation," he boasted, "the whole State of Texas is scurrying around appropriating millions of dollars" all "in an effort to counteract the suit." In the meantime, complained Marshall, "you and your paper haven't accomplished a darn thing toward getting a stick of wood for a building, a book, or a chair or anything else for the education of Negroes in Texas. Oh, yes, you say that you are for the *Sweatt* case. But your continued diatribe against the lawyers in the Association that are fighting this case belie your very high sounding statement." Marshall also asked Wesley to admit that his criticisms of the NAACP's handling of the *Hearne* case stemmed from the fact that the people in Hearne chose the NAACP "and not your paper organization to handle their case." Marshall described Wesley as crying "like a baby" over the Denison attack and as having "the same degree of maturity as a young kid who takes his baseball and bat away from the game because they won't let him pitch." He ended his letter doubtful that Wesley would change his ways but needing "to satisfy my own self that I have made every effort to present to you logic and reason in support of our position."[84]

Marshall's letter reopened communication with Wesley. After his first letter and Wesley's reply, their discourse changed abruptly to a more positive tone, with Marshall affirming that he was near a point of understanding the Houstonian. By the end of October, the two men had returned to addressing each other on a first-name basis and both diligently avoided inflammatory rhetoric. Also, Marshall sent the publisher a copy of the brief the legal staff had prepared to send to the court of civil appeals requesting a rehearing in the *Sweatt* case. The only new twist in the renewed correspondence was Wesley's attempt to harmonize his position with the second section of the NAACP's "new" two-line strategy. Marshall argued that in elementary and secondary school cases the NAACP would fight inequality with lawsuits that made "the general prayer that the court restrain and enjoin the defendant school board from denying to the Negro the equal facilities furnished to the white student."[85] Marshall delineated two key differences in this approach from the straight equalization approach. In his procedure, before blacks would bring suit, they would first attempt to enroll their children at a white school; and, second, they would make no plea for equalizing segregated facilities. Wesley interpreted this as precisely his position: "I can't see for the life of me where you really state any distinction or difference in what you now say is the second section of the NAACP program, and the position I have taken regarding the matter all along."[86]

Wesley did not object to blacks attempting to enter white schools, provided that the NAACP did not make it the prerequisite of all legal action. He also accepted the Fourteenth Amendment as the foundation of litigation as long as state statutes demanding "impartial provision" could be invoked when necessary to get the most out of local school authorities who refused the option of admitting blacks into the white schools. The differences could be seen as minor, but from an absolutist standpoint within the postwar world's "rights revolution," an unscalable mountain stood between Marshall and Wesley.[87]

THE TEXAS UNIVERSITY MOVEMENT

The rapprochement that seemed at hand proved elusive. Wesley published another "blast" against Marshall and the NAACP and distributed copies to other newspaper editors, namely Louis Martin of the *Chicago Defender* and Carl Murphy of the Baltimore *Afro-American*. Marshall assumed Wesley would not "write up the NAACP" while they were engaged "in an effort to arrive at a clear understanding" and rebuild "mutual trust." Wesley, however, repudiated the charges of "bad faith" and resumed a combative posture in a letter to Marshall on 11 December. Marshall replied with a final sign-off letter on 16 December, after which the correspondence between the two men ended. As for Thurgood Marshall and the NAACP, the lines of demarcation between progressive and reactionary black politics had been drawn. Armageddon had commenced, and one either marched with Uncle Sam or shuffled along with Uncle Tom. That such rhetoric amounted to utter nonsense did not go unnoticed by black Texans. The critical consciousness Wesley directed at the NAACP and its all-out war on Jim Crow may have been a secret source of the association's success. By dispelling the illusion of mass acceptance of the new dogma of the NAACP, Wesley may have held back black and white conservatives from a more feral reaction to the association's challenge to legalized white supremacy. The articles he published engendered a healthy public conversation and revealed the complex political interior of the Texas University Movement.[88]

As for the political interior of the NAACP, the Wesley-Marshall fracas of the late 1940s was a sort of rerun of the 1934 Du Bois–NAACP brouhaha over Du Bois's January-to-May editorials in the *Crisis*. David Levering Lewis has likened Du Bois's separatist writings that year — articles such as "Segregation" and "Counsels of Despair" — both to a "concussion grenade" and to a "heuristic exercise" that drove the NAACP hierarchy with a bit of good old-fashioned drama to give its founding member the boot as editor-in-chief of its official organ. Ten years later, he was invited back into the fold, but by 1948 he again became too much trouble to the NAACP of White, Wilkins, and Marshall, and in September he was no longer director of special research. Carter Wesley, who always had identified himself as a disciple of Du Bois and explained that his life membership in the NAACP was paid when it was under the leadership of Du Bois and James Weldon Johnson, published Du Bois's explanation of his departure on the front page of the *Informer*. "The NAACP," wrote Du Bois, "has taken no stand nor laid down any program with regard to Africa. I have repeatedly urged this since my return but I have neither the help, funds, nor authority to accomplish much." On 7 December, less than three months after his ejection from the NAACP, Du Bois came to Houston and spoke at the one-year-old TSUN. The available sources are silent on his visit, but it is easy to imagine that the two warriors for democracy and against the hegemonic backwardness of the NAACP had a good time together.[89]

Just as Du Bois carried on the fight, Wesley continued to advocate separate equality simultaneous with the fight against racial discrimination. Although he used his newspapers as chief weapons, occasionally he participated in face-to-face public debates such as one organized in 1949 on the question: "Are there any circumstances under which separate but equal educational facilities should ever be accepted by Negroes?" Heman Sweatt and Arthur Mandell, an activist left-wing white lawyer, took the negative position. Wesley and the prominent Houston businessman and race leader Charles A. Shaw argued the affirmative. Sweatt proposed a full-scale boycott of the public school system, a total refusal to use the segregated schools until state policy makers eradicated the dual system. In response, Wesley pledged his allegiance to the desegregation cause but countered Sweatt's immediatism by asking, "How will the Negroes produce the Sweatt's of tomorrow?" Education, he averred, was at once a right, a social process, and a societal product. Blacks did not have mere citizenship rights to an equal education; they also, as members of civil society, consumed and produced education "for life." If blacks forced their way onto white campuses overnight, would they find the pedagogical, administrative, and collegial contexts prepared to educate them? Wesley knew that while some blacks could successfully manipulate whatever contexts they faced, many others might not. If Texans woke up the next morning and suddenly found themselves going to racially integrated schools, in his mind, there would still be a valid mission for black institutions of higher education. Wesley was convinced that black schools, with competent, autonomous administration and improved funding, could make a greater contribution to society than they had already done in producing Heman Sweatts, J. Mason Brewers, A. Maceo Smiths, Lulu Whites, and many other Texas "Race Builders," as A. W. Jackson called them in his book *A Sure Foundation*. Neither side "won" the debate. Although a broad segment of black Texans, including Wesley, genuinely supported Sweatt's bid to attend the University of Texas, few took seriously his suggestion of an all-out boycott of segregated schools. A number of young Texans, however, did join his crusade. Prior to a Supreme Court decision ordering UT to admit Sweatt, there emerged in Texas a small but consequential wave of twentieth-century neo-abolitionists.[90]

CHAPTER THREE

Lift the Seventy-Five-Year-Old Color Ban and Raise UT's Standards
University Students for Democracy before *Sweatt*

W. Astor Kirk is trying to force an issue. . . . Does this colored man want to study courses in government and political science, or does he want social equality with the white students? . . . From one who used to sit out in front of the Old Main Bldg & pet your beautiful collie, Please don't change your mind this year anyway.
— Luciel Decker to UT president, 9 January 1950

Money and numbers are the language of politics, and the Texas NAACP expanded rapidly in both categories with victory in the *Smith* Democratic primary case. As never before in its history, the association suddenly became a player in the raucous arena of Texas politics. Statewide in 1945, the NAACP had more than a hundred branches with some 23,000 members. In Houston, during the late 1930s only a few hundred members paid their membership dues; but by 1943, the membership roll had soared to 5,679, and by 1945 it had doubled to over 12,000 members. Propagandists and organizers like Carter Wesley and Lulu B. White, as well as wartime influences — of jobs and mass politicization — fueled this growth. In many ways it was a golden age.[1]

Golden ages are only worth their place in time by the extent of social change accomplished in such eras. The Texas NAACP wanted to deal Jim Crow a mortal blow, but first it had to raise money, and second, it had to find someone willing to sue the state for practicing caste discrimination. Carter Wesley helped the NAACP address the first need after he collected over $7,000 for a lawsuit. The question of the right plaintiff for the legal battle with segregation was the next order of business.[2]

Heman Sweatt, Henry Eman Doyle, and the Rites of Passage

At a gathering of Houston's best and brightest at the Wesley Chapel AME Church, a young letter carrier and emerging NAACP activist, Heman Sweatt, listened intently as Houston branch leader Lulu White, a graduate of Prairie View, asked for a volunteer to file a lawsuit to gain admission to the University of Texas. A hush fell over the meeting. The other brothers and sisters present looked strangely at White and then searched the faces of their peers. No one wanted to be the sacrificial lamb; no one was prepared to endure the hardships such litigation would undoubtedly wreak. Sweatt finally broke the icy silence. In a soft but certain voice, he stood up and said he would do it. White was overjoyed and arranged for Sweatt to meet with NAACP attorneys, who assessed that he was a good applicant. It was high noon at the University of Texas.[3]

Sweatt's bid to enter the University of Texas Law School rejected the rationale of the Bi-racial Commission on Negro Education in Texas (BCNET) study, or, at the very least, it indicated that here was a black student who wanted to attend a law school in his home state so ardently that he was prepared to be in an unhappy situation to do so. On 26 February 1946, his application to attend UT was carefully choreographed as part of a meeting that the Texas State Conference of NAACP Branches set up with UT president Theophilus Painter. R. A. Hester, president of the Progressive Voters League of Texas, headed the committee and was joined by his fellow Dallas citizens Reverend C. D. Knight and Dr. B. E. Howell, together with Houstonians Lulu White, James H. Jemison, C. F. Richardson Jr., and Sweatt; and St. Philip's College president Artemisia Bowden, Euretta K. Fairchild, and Reverend E. J. Wilson of San Antonio. Painter had Vice President J. C. Dolley, Scott Gaines (UT board of regents attorney for land matters), and registrar E. J. Matthews on hand for the meeting. Hester opened by asking what steps Painter had taken to provide blacks with equivalent graduate and professional school opportunities relative to the twelve-point program he released to the press on 20 January. Painter reported that virtually no progress had been made and asked Hester and his group to give him suggestions. Hester replied: "We are not here to discuss or try to solve the race problem. The Negro citizens of Texas are seriously interested and concerned about provisions for them in the graduate and professional schools. We want to know what the committee has done. What is available now. Not tomorrow, next week or next month. We need training for our returning GIs and our children who must compete with others in their own state for jobs with inferior education."[4] The committee did, however, recommend to Painter that Prairie View be severed from the control of Texas A&M and be upgraded to a status equal to its white counterpart. Second, it called for a black graduate and professional school to be created at a large urban area. When the university officials hedged, citing the lack of funds, White reminded them of the more than $10 million in additional appropriations coming to UT and Texas A&M and suggested that the state should use that money instead to institute a black graduate and professional school center. Matthews sarcastically questioned White: "What would you have us do, close down the white schools for a year?" White answered him, "That would not be a bad idea. It would give us an opportunity to catch up with you in training."[5] Painter then shifted the discussion to the prospect of making some kind of a start by the coming fall semester. Hester then tossed the ball to Sweatt, and on cue he sent the meeting into an entirely different direction.

With all the courteousness of a southern gentleman, the thirty-three-year-old, bespectacled Sweatt asked for permission to speak. He asserted that he had a right to legal training and the state had the duty and the money to see to it that he got such training. Taking tuition assistance to go to a law school outside of Texas and waiting for some unspecified time when the state of Texas would erect a black law school was unacceptable. He pulled out a transcript from Wiley College, from which he had graduated in 1934, and asked to be admitted to the UT law school. Painter had a ticking time bomb in the UT tower, but he took it calmly. He acknowledged Sweatt's request and said he would seek a ruling from Texas attorney general Grover Sellers as to what the law required. He doubted, however, that Sweatt would be admitted because the university was bound by the laws of Texas requiring the separation of the races. Matthews reacted by professing his love for black folks and that he held no more "than the normal amount of prejudice against Negroes." In the spirit of love, he warned Sweatt that he would roll back great strides that the state government had undertaken to advance black higher education.[6]

Matthews was trying to intimidate the wrong group of Negroes. It did not see Prairie View's name change as anything substantive. Moreover, the state's announcement on 1 June 1945 that Prairie View would some day offer courses of study in law, medicine, engineering, pharmacy, journalism, and other professional fields did nothing to satisfy the immediate demand for legal instruction that Sweatt presented. Whites like Matthews and Painter, on the other hand, did not like Negroes telling them to hurry up. A very real potential existed for state government officials to halt all efforts to improve black higher education if they perceived that blacks would refuse to attend the segregated graduate and professional programs they proposed to establish. Matthews was not making an idle threat. The UT meeting amounted to a notification of white authorities of black Texans' preparedness to take legal action.

Notwithstanding the threat of litigation, the new wave of black assertiveness, and the democratic and antiracist rhetoric of the recently ended war,

UT officials found no difficulty in refusing Sweatt admission solely on the basis of race. Painter wrote Attorney General Sellers that Sweatt was "duly qualified [for admission to the UT School of Law] . . . except for the fact that he is a Negro," and asked for his opinion. Sellers stated on 16 March that Sweatt must not be admitted to UT but that a single instructor in law at Prairie View would answer his demand of equal educational opportunity.[7] Painter complied with the opinion, and by June he found himself in the 126th District Court in Austin on charges that he had violated Sweatt's constitutionally protected civil rights. The Texas A&M board of regents proffered that it would create a law school for blacks at once; consequently, Judge Roy Archer ruled against Sweatt. A&M fulfilled its claim with a makeshift solution. It hired two black lawyers to hold classes in their own offices in Houston and call it a law school. No blacks dignified the cracker-jack facility with as much as an application.[8] The Texas legislature next began to work out the transformation of the twenty-year-old Houston College for Negroes into the Texas State University for Negroes, but in the meantime it enlisted law professors at UT to establish a better makeshift arrangement than what the Aggies had proposed. Professors, the most junior in rank, would hold class in the basement of a building south of the UT campus on Thirteenth Street, a block from the state capitol. On 10 March 1947, when the teachers appeared for class, they found no black students present. In September, however, Henry Eman Doyle became its first Jim Crow enrollee.[9]

Dean McCormick of the UT School of Law expected Doyle in the spring term, but mysteriously he did not show up. After calling him to a meeting to ask if he had been intimidated from attending the makeshift law school, Doyle had to assure his white interrogators that only business matters had kept him away. For black Texans, Doyle and Sweatt thus became the physical embodiment of the terms of a critically important political and theoretical debate. Within the black community Sweatt *and* Doyle both could be respected. Each embraced the time-honored black value of self-improvement through education. Each man wanted to study law. Black institutions like Howard University had produced great lawyers like Thurgood Marshall, just as white institutions like Harvard University had produced great lawyers like Marshall's teacher, Charles H. Houston. Likewise, both schools produced their share of not-so-great lawyers. The East Thirteenth Street law school of Texas State University for Negroes was undoubtedly no Howard or Harvard, but it could be seen as a start. In spite of the deficiencies of his school, Doyle might still make a good lawyer. Sweatt, on the other hand, might attend a better school and not become as good a lawyer as Doyle. Both men received both admiration and criticism in black communities across the state.

The public debate, however, transported the contemplation of educa-

69

tional values to a political level. On this terrain, Doyle and Sweatt could be represented as racial villains and traitors, as well as saints and heroes. Setting up the ideological terrain of the debate over equalization versus desegregation, the *Houston Defender* on 9 March 1946 quoted John W. Davis, president of West Virginia State College: "Negro education postulates doctrines of minimization of personality, social and economic mediocrity, and second class citizenship. The remaining task for it is to die. The aim of all segregated institutions should be to work themselves out of a job."[10] Inflammatory statements of this kind increased in the mid-1940s, invoking a mish-mash of theories and research from the social sciences in an effort to demonize black schools as inherently inferior and breeding grounds of mediocrity. By this mode of representation, Sweatt appeared as a sort of messiah while Doyle's attendance at a segregated institution constituted an act of self-negation, Samboism, and complicity in his own psychosocial subordination. Beneath the mythic images, however, Doyle appeared as a climber, an oppressed man of African descent, trying to get out of the bucket of despair and powerlessness through the system of education available to him. He graduated from Anderson High School and Samuel Huston College in Austin and then worked as a teacher, a principal at an elementary school, and an instructor at his collegiate alma mater. He took a summer course at Columbia University, studied law through the Extension School at La Salle University, and broadened his horizons through travel, such as a trip to Europe to the Boy Scout World Jamboree as scoutmaster of an Austin troop. He also ran a grocery store but sold it to enter the "makeshift" law school.

Doyle explained his feelings about being the sole student at the Texas State University for Negroes law school to a reporter for the UT student newspaper: "It's just like having a steaming plate of chicken on a box in the back yard. I'd rather have it in the house here, but chicken is chicken, and it's better in the back yard than not at all." He was reported to have been "well satisfied" with the school's one-to-five student-teacher ratio but that he looked "forward to the day when segregation will be a thing of the past." In regard to Sweatt's decision to boycott the basement law school, Doyle pleaded for his personal freedom to choose a different course. His situation offers a striking contrast to a momentous event that would take place almost a decade later involving Rosa Parks and blacks in the capitol city of another southern state. "If I filed suit against the Austin Transit Company because they would not permit me to sit in a seat designated for white people," he remarked, "I couldn't very well expect all my friends to stop riding the buses here until the case was settled." Sweatt, Marshall, Lulu White, and other "true believers" did expect such a response. Such a united black stance, however, never came to be. The very idea of desegregating the South through the method of public litigation, let alone the tactic of an all-out boycott, was so novel that the ordinary Texan simply did not feel obliged to disrupt her or his life — albeit a Jim Crow life — for what seemed a futile protest.[11]

Years later, as Attorney Doyle, the man who would eat his fried chicken on a box in the back yard if those were the terms white supremacy decreed, surprised those who thought he was a docile, "resigned" Negro when he brought suit on behalf of Attorney A. W. Plummer to desegregate the cafeteria at the Harris County Courthouse. He secured a desegregation order from a federal judge, but on 12 April 1956, a "scuffle broke out" when Plummer, two other attorneys (Francis Williams and Robert D. Ford), *Informer* reporter Nina McGowan, and Lillie Marie Alonzo tried to eat their chicken dinners inside the cafeteria. Doyle represented the group in the proceedings that followed and also shored up his pro-integration credentials when he and two other Houston attorneys on 26 December 1956 filed the lawsuit that eventually led to the token desegregation of the Houston city schools, the largest Jim Crow school system in the United States.[12]

Texans may not have been willing to boycott the state's dual system, but a brave handful was ready to cross the color line and demonstrate that Sweatt was not a lone star. Only smatterings of information are available about some of the students who sought admission to schools that prohibited them from attending solely on the grounds of race. A year after Sweatt applied to UT, Ben Davis wrote President Painter, identifying himself as a "Negro Student" who wanted a medical education but could not afford to leave the state to study. He indicated that he did not "desire any publicity" but that he and more than thirty other youths that he knew of shared the common problem of being long on will and an ability to learn but short on opportunity. Dr. A. Julian Lee, chair of the biology department at Samuel Huston College, had administered to them the Carnegie Medical aptitude test and the graduate record examination, and he and his colleagues had their scores and their transcripts in hand. All they needed was a medical school in their home state to which to apply. Painter answered: "I am writing to tell you what you probably already know": that the Texas Senate had approved Governor Beauford Jester's choices for the board of directors for the TSUN and that, by law, the problem of graduate and professional education for blacks rested in their hands. He asked Davis to direct his inquiries to the chairman of the board, Craig F. Cullinan. Davis and his peers would, however, find no answers with the TSUN board.[13]

James Hemanway "Little Doc" Morton behind the Scenes

Samuel Huston College students — with the encouragement and guidance of James Hemanway Morton, their chemistry professor and president of the Austin NAACP branch after 1945 — kept the pressure on UT and finally provided from their ranks the student who would make the first crack in the wall of segregation in Texas higher education. That student was Herman A. Barnett, and his appointment with destiny came in 1949. Morton taught Barnett more than the wonders of atoms, molecules, and the periodic table; he gave him valuable lessons in self-pride, black unity, and organizing for social change. "Little Doc" Morton never became the physician he dreamed of becoming as a boy growing up in Owensville, Indiana, in the first decades of the twentieth century. He graduated from Indiana University in 1927 and straight away started searching for employment to support his family. His search brought him to Wiley College in Marshall, Texas. The crushing weight of the Great Depression dried up whatever lingering ideas he harbored of going to medical school. He did, however, obtain a master's degree at the University of Chicago in 1935. In the late 1930s, he stepped onto the political scene, first in Marshall and Harrison County.

Starting with his fraternity, Kappa Alpha Psi, Morton went to churches and public events and talked to folks. Before long, he had helped to stir up area youth and sparked a movement. Rallies attracted "hordes of young males and females [who] swarmed the [Wiley] campus listening to student leaders sound off on literally every subject from the chains of slavery to the NAACP Freedom Movement." He left his ebony tower in the summer of 1944 and traveled across Texas as the state organizer for the Texas Progressive Voters League agitating for blacks to pay their poll tax and vote for their interests. By the fall, his political savvy landed him an appointment as an examiner for the Tenth District of the Fair Employment Practices Commission, but in his official work of investigating a complaint against a pipeline company in Harvey, Louisiana, it was his streetwise savvy that helped him escape a trip to the hospital or the morgue. After that incident, he settled in Austin and embarked on a distinguished career as a citizen-scholar. He expressed his civic work through his leadership of the Austin NAACP branch and his academic work through his involvement with the National Committee on Atomic Energy, numerous honorary and professional societies, and, most important, in the lives of the students he helped shape. Three of those students became Texas's frontline challengers to racist policies in higher education: Heman Sweatt and W. Astor Kirk, whom Morton knew from his tenure at Wiley, and Herman Barnett, his star pupil at Samuel Huston College.[14]

The Texas University Movement entered a new phase after Governor Jester signed the Stewart-Moffett Bill into law, which created TSUN on 3 March 1947. On paper it fulfilled the original goal of the Texas University Movement: the creation of the constitutional university for blacks that would be the equivalent of the white university in Austin. Jester's enactment of the Stewart-Moffett Bill marked a point of climax for a struggle that had its roots in Reconstruction Texas and galvanized as a social movement in the New Deal era and wartime era of black militancy of the early 1940s. The black UT arrived too late; however, a new tact had already emerged. The NAACP, and its point man, Heman Sweatt, had redirected the University Movement toward the abolition of segregation in higher education, with a particular focus on the state's one bona fide law school. A new beginning in the movement called for new fronts in the head-to-head fight against segregation, and Austin was the natural site for the first challenges.

Kirk, Givens, and a March in Austin

Dallas and Houston were without question the hubs of intellectual, material, informational, and economical resources that powered the Texas University Movement. When black Texans launched the Sweatt case, NAACP organizational work in Austin languished. In April 1946, NAACP state organizer Juanita Craft, whose organizational skills perhaps surpassed those of Lulu White and A. Maceo Smith, announced to *Crisis* editor Roy Wilkins that under her direction the Austin branch had started a process of revival. She informed him that the Tillotson College chapter was "doing a nice job" of revitalizing and that the Samuel Huston College chapter had been "revamped." These student members worked together with the city's "adult body," which had officers that Craft dubbed "unfinancial." On the strength of the *Sweatt* case, she predicted she would be able to organize a large branch in short order. She noted, as well, that she had interviewed a committee of white students from the University of Texas and that they promised to bring at least one hundred persons to the mass meeting on the *Sweatt* case, planned for 5 May.

By the end of the year, Austin had a viable NAACP branch with James Morton as its president. Under his leadership, supported by Craft, the branch established several committees, including one for legal redress and another for lobbying the Texas legislature. The executive committee picked Arthur DeWitty, a local community activist and the Austin editor of the *Houston Informer*, to serve as its chief lobbyist at the capitol. The committee also gave a group of law students at UT consideration, but "there was not much favorable opinion expressed in regard to this resource."[15] Although hailed initially as a great triumph, the involvement of UT students in the NAACP's all-out war against segregation also gave Morton and other NAACP leaders more than a few headaches. No sooner had almost twenty campus organizations come together to form a UT chapter of the association than it became embroiled in a political battle between liberals, socialists, and communists. Despite its internal contradictions, the group did raise funds and consciousness and could be counted on to organize credible numbers of whites to mass meetings and protest marches. Moreover, some of the student leaders had good relations with prominent liberal faculty and staff members. However, the successful effort of certain white leaders to obtain a special charter making the campus formation autonomous of the local adult branch and the state conference of branches irked veteran leaders of the Texas University Movement.[16]

W. Astor Kirk, a professor of political science at Tillotson College, provided another Austin-based challenge to segregation in Texas higher education. He was a recent addition to the faculty of the college when he put himself forward as a candidate for a companion suit to Sweatt's in 1947. As a former student of Morton's, he graduated magna cum laude from Wiley College in December 1946 and went on to earn a master's degree in political science in June 1947 at Howard University. The young professor eagerly desired to obtain his terminal degree, especially if he could do so in his native state, where he had already started his teaching career and planted residential and social roots. He applied by mail to UT on 5 December 1947. Painter answered him on 21 January 1948 that the same UT faculty members "who now give graduate work to students in The University of Texas will be available for your instruction" at the Negro Law School where Doyle and his two other classmates matriculated. Kirk, uninterested in joining the three-student makeshift school, enlisted Morton's help in putting his case before A. Maceo Smith and the Texas State Conference of NAACP Branches.

Smith found "the merits of the application [of Kirk to be] convincing," but it seldom took much to convince Smith, as long as others had to do the work.[17] He called upon the Austin branch financially to sponsor the case through 1948, when the state conference could include it in its budget. Marshall also agreed that the case should be filed, but attorney W. J. Durham demurred. He prepared and filed the complaint, investigated all the facts of the case, and turned the matter over to Ulysses S. Tate upon his taking office as NAACP's regional attorney. Durham advised against filing the case from the start, but Marshall, who interviewed Kirk personally, overruled him. The resident counsel complained that the case had attracted their support for "publicity" reasons rather than based on its strategic merits to the University Movement as a whole. He argued that it would be "very easy for the University of Texas to set up a school covering the courses Mr. Kirk wanted. But I am here to follow instructions."[18]

Durham's opinion proved accurate since very little ever came of the case. Kirk rejected classes at the Thirteenth Street Basement School, and since TSUN had no doctoral degree to offer him in his field, he requested regular admission to UT. In March 1948 he filed suit in the Travis County District Court, but by mutual consent the attorneys postponed the case pending a final ruling in *Sweatt* v. *Painter*. Kirk's aborted case thus won nothing for the desegregation cause, except, perhaps, a small bit in the war for additional public support. It did, however, thrust Kirk into the lime-light and instantly made him a player in Texas's fledgling civil rights move-ment. Many other blacks as well as whites filed applications contrary to the state universities' race-based admission policies between 1947 and 1950. The Texas University Movement embraced such actions (with the excep-tion of Everett Givens's separate equality suit after UT refused to provide him with a refresher course in dentistry), but not every applicant desired the adulation and the censure Sweatt and Kirk took on.[19]

Austin continued as a key pressure point for the Texas civil rights strug-gle and the University Movement in still another way. Movement leaders reasoned that a bolder, more dramatic initiative had to occur to keep alive hope in Sweatt's drawn out legal battle. On 18 February 1949, the "Presi-dent and moving spirit" of the Texas Council of Negro Organizations, Dr. Joseph J. Rhoads of Bishop College, called together the leaders of thirty-one statewide organizations. He charged the group with the task of draft-ing a "program of action for an attack on discrimination and segregation in the state from every conceivable angle."[20] He also brought word that stu-dents at Bishop and Wiley in Marshall had suggested and stood ready to execute a new tactic: a mass demonstration at UT and the state capitol. Morton, chair of the TCNO's lobbying committee, knew he could interest some seniors at Samuel Huston College and that Kirk could do the same at Tillotson. NAACP brass A. Maceo Smith, secretary of the State Conference of Branches; U. S. Tate, southwestern regional counsel; and Donald Jones, regional NAACP field secretary, agreed that such an action would provide a needed boost in the drive to open UT to black students. The NAACP, no stranger to marches, endorsed the action. It would be the first time black students attempted collectively to apply to a white university or stage a demonstration at a state capitol. Over the next three months, students and state leaders finalized plans for the Austin demonstration and brought on board students from Jarvis Christian College. They set the date for 27 April. A week beforehand, the Houston branch of the NAACP informed the Asso-ciated Press that thirty-seven blacks would attempt to enroll in three dif-ferent branches of the University of Texas: the graduate school in Austin, the dental school in Houston, and the medical school in Galveston. In Austin, Morton was elusive when a reporter from UT's *Daily Texan* asked him about whether a large group of black students would march on the Forty Acres. "There will possibly be someone on the campus Wednesday," Morton stated, "but I don't know for sure."[21]

When the appointed day came, there was more than *someone*. A reporter from the *Austin Statesman*, a bevy of photographers, and white student supporters met some three dozen blacks described as "quiet" and "well-dressed." The students and their NAACP organizers, advisers, and lawyers converged on the campus of Tillotson College and met in a closed session before boarding a bus that took them to UT. Virginia Forbes of the *Statesman* noted their arrival at the Littlefield Fountain and their orderly march, two abreast, up the South Mall "past statues of Robert E. Lee and Jefferson Davis to the Main Building." Their procession ended at the office of admissions in the Main Building. As the students spilled into the room from the corridor, Kirk approached Max Fichtenbaum, assistant registrar, saying, "We have some students here from senior colleges who would like to make application for graduate work." Fichtenbaum answered that they had come to the wrong place and should instead file their applications in Houston at Texas State University for Negroes. "That's the law in Texas," he added. Attorney Tate queried the office worker further asking him to give the students application blanks and to note that they wished to do work at the medical and dental schools. Fichtenbaum stood his ground, repeating that whether UT provides the courses or not the students would still have to file their applications at TSUN. With that, the group marched out of the building and off the campus as quietly as they came.[22]

The students' actions spoke louder than words, but their placards also carried their message in words. Some of their posters read: "Lift the 75-year-old color ban and raise the standards of the University of Texas"; "Regional Education is Unconstitutional"; and " 'Separate and Equal' Education is Mockery." Other signs had lengthy comments on the connections between their action and struggles in Tennessee and elsewhere in the South, on the inability of a "modern state" to "long endure" under conditions of segregated higher education, on how the dual system of graduate and professional education was too expensive for Texas, and on how it would take the state another hundred years to build a comparable university for blacks. White student supporters carried placards saying "Civil Rights are Everyone's Rights" and others demanding equal educational opportunities, equal job opportunities, and equal justice in the courts.

After a brief lunch at Tillotson, the delegation resumed its march, with placards in hand, to the state capitol. Some seventy-five picketers silently filled part of the gallery overlooking the state senate pit. As they held their posters, cameras clicked, bulbs flashed, and the tempers of certain senators exploded. The sergeant-at-arms on duty approached the picketing students and told them they would have to stack their signs outside the senate gallery. W. Astor Kirk answered, "We'll follow your rules, of course." Kirk may have known very well that it was against the rules to display posters inside the gallery beforehand. Forbes reported in an article in the evening edition of the *Statesman*, written before the action at the capitol, that "there was an indication that the group might picket the Capital [*sic*]. The attorney general's office was approached earlier this week by Negro

Students from across the state staged a historic march for equal educational opportunity on the University of Texas campus and at the Texas state capitol in Austin on 27 April 1949 to show that Sweatt's fight had broad support (Center for American History, University of Texas, Austin, CN No. 01466).

leaders seeking information on state picketing laws." It is doubtful Kirk and the NAACP organizers made an innocent mistake. From start to finish, the NAACP and the students intended that the Austin action would be as strong and visible a statement as they could possibly make.[23]

The protest visit to the capitol received no official recognition from either the senate or the house. Governor Jester did, however, permit nine representatives of the picketers to come into his office for an informal audience. He also allowed the entourage of photographers and reporters inside. With his large, oblong desk acting as a barrier between him and his Negro visitors, Jester sat and explained that he had sympathy for their plea for better educational facilities for their race and that he wanted to hear their concerns. Students David Williams and Sheffield Quarles acted as spokespersons for the group. Wearing a white suit with a polka-dot tie and with one hand in his jacket pocket, Williams stepped up and put his fist to rest on the governor's desk. He "told the governor that Negroes [were] not looking for sympathy, but as citizens of the U.S. and as native Texans [were] ask[ing for] what [was] rightfully theirs." They called attention to a petition, left at the governor's office earlier in the day, that indicated that they represented from 300 to 1,000 seniors in accredited colleges for Negroes who sought to "extend their preparation for profession [*sic*] service to their under-privileged race." Jester assured the group that he would turn their letter over to the proper authorities and took the opportunity to tell them some of the steps he had taken to build separate-but-equal facilities for them. Quarles and Williams objected that the creation of new institutions set aside for blacks exclusively could never furnish a true solution because of the problem of a "time lag."

Jester retorted that "time is not the whole answer" and advised the group that its time was up. Jester's encounter with the black college students did nothing to alter his course from support of the southern governor's regional compact for graduate and professional education of blacks up to his last days in office. On 11 July 1949, five days after the Texas legislature ended the longest session in its history, Jester died of a heart attack. The hand that signed into law measures that revamped the funding and administration of the state's school system (the Gilmer-Aiken laws) approved laws modernizing the state prison system, enacted an antilynching law, created the Board for Texas State Hospitals and Special Schools, and accepted the first biennial budget that reached a billion dollars lay stilled. But despite these momentous changes, the problems of black higher education remained.

The new chief executive of the state, the erstwhile Lieutenant Governor Allan Shivers, soon would prove to be a formidable enemy of the agenda of the Texas University Movement, as well as the larger civil rights cause of the black freedom struggle. In comparison, Jester would seem less conservative than his successor, but such an assessment must be scrutinized against the fact that he faced a civil rights movement in its infancy as it had just begun to cohere and assert a new politics centered on integration. If Jester had lived to face the challenges Shivers did, or if he better understood the young men and women like Quarles, Williams, and Kirk that addressed him in his office, he may have reacted as bitterly to civil rights advocates that came to his office door as Shivers later did.[24]

Besides sending a signal to Jester, Shivers, and the 51st Legislature, the graduate and professional school applications filed in April of 1949 had one unusual outcome. Herman A. Barnett became the first person of color to be voluntarily admitted to the University of Texas Medical Branch at Galveston. This turn of events resulted from at least two factors. First, the hierarchy at UT had weakened its resolve to maintain racial purity at all costs. Efforts to launch a black medical school in Houston were going nowhere, and no educator worthy of the name could pretend otherwise.

Second, Barnett was a student who demanded a medical education in his native state, and he held qualifications outstanding not for a Negro but across the board. In May, Jester put it to the UT board of regents that if TSUN did not have a medical school ready by 1 September, the medical branch for whites at Galveston would have to admit "Negro students with proper scholastic averages." UT admitted Barnett in the fall of 1949, but in a last-ditch measure to preserve segregation, he was formally listed as a TSUN student and told that his degree would bear the name Texas State University for Negroes Medical Branch.[25]

Herman Barnett and the Contract Experiment

On 18 August 1949, Herman Barnett received a reply to his application to the University of Texas Medical Branch (UTMB) at Galveston. President Painter informed him that the Committee of Admissions had evaluated his records and determined that he was "well qualified to enter a medical school and have met all the technical requirements." The biologist-turned-university-president told the twenty-one-year-old veteran of the Second World War that he had informed the officials of Texas State University for Negroes of the findings of the UT Admissions Committee and then vaguely indicated to Barnett that he could apply at TSUN but would receive his medical training at "an existing medical school in the State . . . until such time as they [TSUN] can recruit a staff, equip the school and begin operation on their own." Why Painter could not say directly what he meant typifies the dissembling and disingenuous nature of a racist mind. The "existing medical school in the State" to which he referred was the same one Barnett applied to and no other. He said TSUN was "now making" an "arrangement" with a medical school, which state officials had established more than a year before.[26]

In the fall of 1947, when TSUN first began operation, the board of directors of the new school and the board of regents of UT launched a collaborative effort to settle the problem of equalization of educational opportunity at the graduate and professional levels. Their collaboration resulted in contracts, the first of which they signed and dated 24 January 1948. The chair of the TSUN board, Craig F. Cullinan, and the chair of the UT board, D. K. Woodward Jr., agreed that UT would, where possible, furnish graduate instruction on a segregated basis to qualified black students who registered at TSUN for graduate courses not available there. The contract period extended from 2 February to 31 August 1948; but university officials subsequently renewed the contract for additional terms. Thus, in 1949, when Painter wrote Barnett, TSUN and UT had in place a contractual agreement; the basic infrastructure of a partnership between the two

Herman Barnett, the first black Texan to enter and graduate from the University of Texas Medical Branch, also became the first African American to serve on the Texas State Board of Medical Examiners, as well as to be elected president of the board of trustees of the Houston Independent School District. He is also memorialized in the distinguished professorship UTMB established in his name in 1997 (Blocker History of Medicine Collections, Moody Medical Library, University of Texas at Austin).

schools for the expressed purpose of avoiding the full-blown desegregation of the state's graduate and professional programs already existed.

Despite the actions of the Austin administration, the medical branch at
Galveston jealously protected its autonomy from the main campus and
would not willingly submit to being a guinea pig simply because Painter
said it should. Although the plan to admit Barnett was a bitter pill to
swallow, ultimately the medical school accepted it. Why they made the
decision to do so remains a bit of a mystery, but UTMB's prior involvement
in the problem of medical education for blacks suggests that the Galveston
campus got pulled into the vortex of segregationists in Austin trying desperately to maintain a dying system.

In 1946, Painter broached the idea of a black medical school being
opened in Houston and asked officials at the Galveston campus to help
him work out the details of a plan that he could present to the regents and
the state legislature. Vice President Chauncey Depew Leake, UTMB's chief
executive officer, sent Painter his estimate of the cost of turning Houston
Negro Hospital into a medical school. Leake figured that to attach a medical school to the hospital would require a minimum of $154,000, not
including the cost of the actual operation of the hospital. The hospital, the
first establishment of its kind in the city when it opened on 19 June 1926,
had benefited from a magnanimous donation of $80,000 from Joseph
Stephen Cullinan, Texaco founder and father of TSUN board chairman
Craig Cullinan.[27]

Leake emphasized that "the costs of medical education are greater than
any other form of university effort" and would become more expensive "as
standards continue to improve." Maintaining segregation at the medical
school level would allow no quick, makeshift solution and would not be
cheap.[28] Nevertheless, in the summer of 1949 the Fifty-first Legislature
appropriated $175,000 for the creation of a Negro Medical School and put
the problem in the hands of TSUN's board of directors. On 13 July, Chairman Craig Cullinan wrote Painter a sarcastic letter quoting from a resolution the TSUN board had passed the night before. The resolution cited that
"our information is that [Painter] has advised the Legislature that we could
satisfactorily operate a Medical School the first year of the biennium for
that amount of money[;] we desire information from him as to the details
of how it can be done between now and the opening of the school year on
September 1, 1949, with that amount of money, since we do not have any
equipment or qualified teaching personnel."[29] Painter postured before the
state legislature as the wizard with a crystal ball and magic wand who, in an
instant, could transform the base metal of a historically neglected system of
public higher education for Negroes into a golden treasure substantially
equal to the university system over which he presided. He bumbled into the
role of grand warlock over the dual higher education system because he

81

wanted to assure that the legislature would take no steps that might impinge on UT's reputation or appropriations. Having witnessed the dumping of his predecessor, Homer Rainey, he understood the fatal effect of neglecting the wishes of his superiors — the regents and state government officials — and essentially became their number one yes-man. However, when Painter's actions affected TSUN, he put the board members of the black college on the spot.[30]

Cullinan did not appreciate decisions that would place additional burdens on TSUN without a commensurate amount of financial and technical support. He invited Painter to meet with his board or send the details in writing of how a bona fide Negro medical school could be set up in a month and a half. He also noted that information had reached his board "that the University of Texas will have at least one qualified applicant for admission to your Medical School." It is amazing that Cullinan had this information only a month after Barnett submitted his application and before Barnett received notification of admission. Perhaps Cullinan had the better crystal ball after all.[31]

Herman Barnett, the man in the middle of the orbs of both Cullinan and Painter, apparently had some powerful magic of his own. He grew up in Lockhart, Texas, where his preparation for life had few, if any, lessons about the ending of the social degradation of blacks. Instead he lived, ate, prayed, played, perhaps everything but dreamed, in a black-and-white, caste-bound context. The young, gifted, and black Texan dreamed of flying airplanes, of being a fighter pilot. With few black aviators to model himself after, still he dreamed. As Barnett watched the Second World War engulf the United States, he reasoned that if he had to serve in its defense he would try to do so as much on his terms as possible. Then news that the U.S. military had begun training select blacks at the Tuskegee Institute to become airmen gave him an opportunity he had to seize.[32]

Straight out of high school, Barnett presented himself for the required tests. Fortunately, his short and lean stature did not become a liability. The air force demanded brains more so than brawn. Although many of the men Barnett competed against already had graduated or at least attended college, his excellent scores on the qualifying exams secured him a place at the world's only training school exclusively for black pilots. Barnett soon discovered that getting into the cadet school represented the least of his difficulties; staying in and completing the training to become a pilot would be the real test. Enemies of the Tuskegee airman experiment in the military and political milieu did not want to see any African Americans trained as pilots. He persevered, however, and even managed to have some fun; in the process, he acquired a reputation for "buzzing" the all-female campus of Spelman College in Atlanta, Georgia. Although the air force forbade it and college officials did not like it, a Tuskegee airman flying at low altitude over the campus thrilled the students. The Black Eagles became instant celebrities. Among their own folk they were seen as the crème de la crème of the U.S. military.[33]

As much as Barnett may have wished to remain an aviator, when the war ended so did all hope of being a professional pilot. The Tuskegee experience endowed him with greater confidence and an even keener sense of ambition. Nevertheless, he decided the time had come to move on from army life. One of his instructors described him as a "natural born flyer, but no soldier." The young prodigy had a problem with following orders. Thus, he mustered out to his native state still a teenager with the rest of his life before him. Barnett enrolled in Samuel Huston College in Austin, a good school and the closest one to his family home in Lockhart.[34]

With a genius for science and math, Barnett quickly adopted J. H. Morton as his tutor and mentor. Likewise, Morton took to his young prodigy and, in time, harbored the hope that he might become his son-in-law. He even may have projected onto Barnett the medical career he dreamed of but never realized. In Austin, Barnett, who lived in the home of a local minister and his wife, found himself vigorously pursuing his studies in a time when his peers and teachers, like Morton, grew increasingly impatient with the strictures of a segregated society. As Barnett neared completion of his work at Huston, the desegregation movement informed him that Texas needed him to strike down segregation at UTMB. Like Sweatt, he would refuse to attend a hurriedly created makeshift medical school, and this pleased all-or-nothing integrationists in the University Movement. Barnett agreed to become the next court challenge. The only problem he had is that he did not want to have to wait three years or more for a lawsuit to work its way up to the Supreme Court, as was the case with Sweatt. Also, he had no money to hire attorneys. Carter Wesley, the Sweatt Victory Fund, and the Lone Star State Medical and Pharmaceutical Association, a professional association of black doctors and pharmacists, pledged to raise money for Barnett to file suit if UTMB denied him admission on account of race. Dr. J. L. Dickey, president of the Lone Star State Medical Association, stated the case plainly: "We are tired of going a thousand miles to a medical school; we ought to go in Texas, and I don't mean to a segregated medical school, but to the one already operating in the state." Stepping in high cotton with the state's brightest, wealthiest, and most highfalutin Negroes, Barnett decided to be their test case. He participated with his peers in the protest action on the UT campus and at the state legislature on 27 April, hoping throughout that his qualifications and a favorable ruling in Sweatt's case would make it unnecessary for him to file a lawsuit.[35]

A diligent student, Barnett completed Sam Huston's course of study for his baccalaureate degree in 1948 with high honors. Subsequently, he took the entrance exams for medical school and applied for admission to the

University of Chicago and Meharry, the developing regional medical college for blacks in Tennessee. Upon examining his record and test scores, Chicago and Meharry accepted him, but UT stalled. Barnett hoped fervently that he could remain and study in his home state, privately relishing the opportunity to show the world that just as members of the Negro race could make great aviators, they could also make great doctors, if given equal educational opportunity. Barnett got his chance. No sooner did Painter's letter arrive at Barnett's permanent home address in Lockhart than word spread from Texas to the NAACP national headquarters in New York City. The vagaries associated with his status as a TSUN student who would matriculate at UT *by contract* did not damper the NAACP's enthusiasm or jubilation. Henry Lee Moon, NAACP director of public relations, sent out a press release dated 26 August, with the heading "NAACP Hails First Break in U. of Texas Jim Crow." The release quoted the association's Southwest regional secretary Donald Jones, who said that Barnett's admission was a "major step in the fight of Negro students for the equal educational opportunities which are their Constitutional right." It occurred, moreover, without the necessity of another lawsuit.[36]

Carter Wesley gave the story front-page treatment with a streamer above the *Houston Informer* masthead boldly proclaiming that UT had admitted its first Negro student. Arthur DeWitty, the Austin correspondent who wrote the story, praised Samuel Huston College's Department of Science and Mathematics, which Morton chaired, and called Barnett's admission a "moral victory." He also noted that creating a "makeshift Medical School" could not be done "because of the nature of the class room work that has to be done with all the necessary facilities in the way of laboratory equipment" and mentioned the existence of a contract between TSUN and UT. "All Negro applicants who qualify in any field regardless to whether or not the facilities are at the Negro University at Houston," the Austin activist rather blithely observed, "will be channeled through that Institution." For DeWitty, the "number one problem" came down to the preparation of black undergraduates "to meet the competition on all fronts and with all students." If the Negro College fails here," he continued, "then our going will be very difficult in the future."[37]

However much becoming a celebrity may have swelled Barnett's ego, he did not let his notoriety interfere with his schoolwork. Immediately, he had to relocate to Galveston and get ready to begin his training to become a medical doctor. After completing all the necessary arrangements for enrollment at TSUN, Barnett moved in with a prominent Galveston educator and his family on 31st Street, a short distance from the medical school. For Barnett, the distinction of being the first black man to attend a formerly all-white, publicly supported medical school in a southern state rapidly became less an honor than a cross to bear, a sacred responsibility to fulfill. He had to do well and show that he deserved the distinction.

After saying his morning prayers asking God for strength and guidance, Barnett prepared himself to face the many questions, evil eyes, and dilemmas his first day at UTMB would bring. Financially, Barnett was ready. TSUN president Ralph O'Hara Lanier gave Barnett's financial needs utmost consideration, especially in clearing the way for him to receive the books and equipment he needed. The school agreed to reimburse the UT Medical Branch and then bill the Veterans Administration (VA). The VA's response to this procedure would later become a problem.

Barnett's chief worry was whether his white peers and teachers would accept him and, if so, on what terms. Upon arriving for class, Barnett encountered a policy of internal segregation and discrimination but nothing greater than he could bear. Instructor's forced Barnett to sit outside the classroom, making him have to listen to lectures and view slide presentations awkwardly from a distance. No teacher expressed any great interest or support for Barnett and did nothing to lessen his isolation. When the time came to pair up with a partner for laboratory assignments, a white student voluntarily asked Barnett to work with him. Chauncey Leake, in his recollection of Barnett's admission to UTMB in an interview nearly three decades after the event, accorded himself a progressive attitude: "I took the position right away that anybody applying to the School would be admitted if that person had the intellectual qualifications. . . . So, a man showed up. His name was Ross [*sic*] Barnett. He was a Negro and he *certainly* was well-qualified. Okay, and he comes. Well, I was nervous the first day, but I went with him into the cafeteria and as soon as a couple of boys said to come over and sit with them, I knew everything was alright."[38] Officially, the state of Texas and UTMB labeled Barnett a TSUN contract student subject to internal segregation. Leake's story suggests, however, that the young black man did not experience unrelenting racist mistreatment and isolation every minute of his school day. Barnett in no way felt inferior among the whites and was not above taking on a superior attitude around black *and* white subordinates. A straightforward, no-nonsense person, when it came time for business, he could be very demanding. His wife, the Spelman- and Yale-educated Wylma White Barnett of Beaumont, recalled how black custodial workers approached her at UTMB and John Sealy Hospital, where her husband did his residency, with comments about Barnett. He was their champion, and he made them proud of their race, but they begged her to make him "change his attitude." The strain of being the first Negro, the only Negro in his position, contributed to estranging him from regular folk.[39]

Barnett dealt with the lingering discriminations of segregation mainly as a private matter. On 19 November, after several weeks at UTMB, he wrote Morton a short letter saying that "things have progressed at such a normal pace that there was no need for earlier reports. In fact my every resource will be taxed to find even one unfavorable incident." He promised to give him "a detailed verbal report" of everything that had taken place when he came to Austin for the Thanksgiving holidays. "Tell Messieurs [Donald] Jones, [Ulysses] Tate and [Maceo] Smith that I am so sorry that they won't be able to build a case around me," he teased. "[T]here just won't be any grounds." Undoubtedly Barnett had abundant "grounds" for litigation and protest action, but that was not his way. His determination centered on obtaining his goal—a UT medical degree. He would let nothing over-shadow that pursuit.[40]

Barnett completed the four-year degree program of the University of Texas School of Medicine and became its first black graduate. UTMB had enrolled him as a regular student in his second year. The school altered his status after the VA refused to recognize the UT-TSUN contractual agree-ment and disallowed GI Bill tuition and expenses, other than "subsistence funds," for Barnett's 1949–50 and 1950–51 school terms. Tate, as NAACP regional special counsel and Barnett's attorney, sent Painter a letter on 28 September 1950, pointing out that because of the contract student arrangement his client was being subjected to "a position of doubt and embarrassment as to his rights under the Veteran's Administration, and is threatened with serious financial loss. . . . Further, Mr. Barnett's present status as a medical student in Texas places him under an emotional stress which is detrimental to him." The threat of a lawsuit and the loss of federal GI Bill monies for every black veteran it admitted on a contract basis acted in concert to convince UT officials to abandon its bizarre contract scheme. On 12 October, D. Bailey Calvin, dean of student and curricular affairs at UTMB, related the news to Barnett that his academic status had changed[41]: "I have received notice from the secretary of the Board of Regents of the University of Texas to the effect that the contractural [*sic*] relationships with the Texas State University for Negroes, Houston, Texas, for medical education no longer obtain, but rather that you are now to be enrolled as a regular student."[42] TSUN never opened the medical school Painter con-vinced the state legislature to appropriate funds to establish. Thus, in 1953, when the medical branch of UT awarded Barnett his degree at its commencement exercises with a standing ovation, the TSUN-UT contract era, which his application inaugurated, had come to a complete and cere-monial end. The Texas-trained doctor remained in Galveston and did his residency in surgery, one of the medical world's elite fields of special-ization. No fanfare or banner headlines accompanied Barnett's gradua-tion, although the event represented the first time that the state of Texas had allowed an African American to demonstrate his capability by attending and graduating from an erstwhile white institution of higher learning.[43]

Barnett's desire to maintain a low profile and avoid newspaper headlines notwithstanding, he found himself in the 18 July 1953 edition of the *Informer*. A headline that streamed below the masthead reported not his graduating medical school but read: "Will the Brutal Beating of Dr. Barnett Be Whitewashed?" On 12 July, state highway patrolman John Connor stopped Barnett for speeding at a hundred miles per hour en route to Galveston. The twenty-five-year-old intern sometimes drove his car like an airplane, "hightailing it" across the back roads of Texas while he enjoyed music from a 45-rpm phonograph he wired up. Connor did not like what he saw. He ordered Barnett out of the car, handcuffed him, and beat him unconscious. When he came to, he lay bloody in a squad car headed to Jefferson Davis Ross, the local justice of the peace. One of the officers asked Barnett who he was, and he answered that he was an intern at John Sealy Hospital. Upon hearing this, Connor grew enraged: "You're a damned liar!" No Negro had ever attended UTMB, much less worked a white man's job at the hospital. Barnett's ring with the university's seal suggested theft. The officer removed the ring and inspected the markings engraved inside, which read: "HAB, MD." Rather than giving the officers cause to look at the black doctor in a more favorable light, the truth sent them into a rage and they again pistol-whipped Barnett. Their savage beating knocked him out. After he was arraigned, the judge and the officers agreed that Barnett should be taken to nearby Texas City Hospital. Fortunately for Barnett, a UTMB student who worked at the hospital recognized him. At three o'clock in the morning the intern called Leake and said, "You'd better come over here."

As soon as Leake arrived, he knew what he had to do. "Oh, this is terrible," he began to wail. "This is an awful situation, he [Barnett] has to come back with me into our hospital, he can't stay." Leake got Barnett discharged to his care, and he admitted him for multiple lacerations of the skull at John Sealy Hospital in Galveston. Thomas Dent, an attorney, told Wesley that the police had brutalized Barnett not only near the town of Alvin when they arrested him but a second time as well. Dent also said that he had asked the Federal Bureau of Investigation to probe whether police had violated the doctor's civil rights. Wesley visited Barnett and later described his head as "looking like a sieve from the big holes knocked in it . . . and his eye blackened and swollen."

Although Wesley gave the story prominent coverage, he observed that Galveston whites and even members of the Negro elite in Texas had "rigged up" an "Iron Curtain" to "silence the story of the alleged beating of Dr. Herman A. Barnett." Police officials of the island city investigated the incident but would not comment on it. UTMB officials distanced themselves and became "mum on the matter." Leake, who tried to keep anyone from seeing his special patient, stated to the *Informer* that the medical school and hospital had "nothing to do with the Barnett affair," since Barnett had not been on hospital business at the time of his arrest and battery. On the other hand, Leake stated that he had been "giving the young intern advice . . . whether or not . . . an 'issue' should be made of the alleged beating." His "advice" was that to make a to-do over the police brutality would amount to nothing more than a racket and that he should drop the matter. Leake offered to pay the fine, and Barnett agreed to such a resolution. "A peculiar thing," Barnett lamented to Leake however, "my father had given me a ruby ring, but ever since that business in Texas City I don't have the ruby ring."

As for the Hitchcock justice of the peace before whom Barnett was arraigned for speeding, resisting arrest, and assault on a police officer, he went on record stating that "if the policemen whipped Dr. Barnett, he deserved it." In this, Justice Ross sided with Connor's official version of the incident, that Barnett had attacked him with a knife, but when Conner was asked for the reputed weapon, he could not produce it. Later, however, Ross himself turned up with an "old rusty knife," which he claimed he found when he visited the scene of Barnett's arrest. The highly unusual case became even more bizarre when a white student filed charges of assault against Ross. Three or four months later, the small town justice was admitted to UTMB's psychiatric hospital. Leake, who reviewed all admissions, spotted Ross's name. When he checked the listing of the patient's valuables and clothing, "there was the ruby ring." He recalled, "I took the ruby ring and it had . . . Barnett's initials in it, so I put it in my pocket and gave it to [him]. Then I went to the Justice of the Peace and said: 'Your Honor, when you came into this hospital you had a ruby ring and when you leave, you don't take that ring with you.' He looked at me," but Barnett "really made good. He was the first certified Negro surgeon in Texas and he was great!" Barnett undoubtedly shared Leake's enthusiasm about being the first Texas-certified black surgeon. He also appeared to be more interested in getting on with his life than in becoming a cause célèbre for the Texas civil rights movement.

It may have been that Barnett did not care for being a political icon, but he also may not have thought enough of the Texas civil rights movement to stake his livelihood and future on its capacity to effect change. Although a gifted and talented individual, Barnett did not come from a privileged family and faced his personal and financial challenges almost entirely on his own. Most of Galveston's black elite, such as Dent, his lawyer, and

Professor Leon Augustus Morgan, the island's leading black educator who let him have free room and board in his spacious house on 31st Street, embraced and supported Barnett materially and morally for what he symbolized and for the kind of character he exuded. The factual record does not reveal whether the island's black vanguard wanted him to make a case of his brutal mistreatment and would pay for the litigation. Even if they had, it is questionable that he would have gone against Leake's advice and made an "issue" of the police assault and miscarriage of justice. The incident allowed Wesley the hot month of July to agitate and educate around the issue of police brutality, but the opportunity to organize against the barbaric practice would have to await another day, another victim. The whipping of Barnett was whitewashed.[44]

Interestingly, the NAACP did not enter the picture. In the black community, Wesley directed his queries to "leading Houston physicians" and the public at large about what they would do about the attack on Barnett. He questioned the immediate past president of the Houston Medical Forum, Dr. Perry W. Beal, whether the group would call for a complete investigation or complain to "high officials." He received the answer that it should be looked into but was given no indication that the group had demanded federal authorities to do so. Dr. E. B. Perry, an officer in the Lone Star Medical Association, responded that "the uncalled-for incident was so horrible that I'm afraid to put my thoughts in writing." Likewise, Dr. J. C. Madison regarded Barnett's plight as an "unfortunate thing," and Dr. Charles Pemberton stated he had not had enough time to form an opinion about the matter. Wesley condemned the "brass" for "playing ostrich" and burying their heads in the sand. He called upon the general black community to recognize that the beating of Barnett "was a beating of the Negro group." The attack led him to draw the conclusion "that the best, the finest, the most highly advanced in the group are in greatest jeopardy of being brutally treated at the hands of 'the law.' " However factually inaccurate he was as to what strata of the community suffered the most police brutality, Wesley had a point that, for blacks, the police was no respecter of education or class.

The educated, black professional-managerial elite may have become the most cautious and conservative strata of black society in the face of Barnett's attack and Wesley's counsel, but still more blacks followed Barnett's lead. The year after Barnett's admission, another veteran, J. H. Pendleton Jr. of Houston, entered the medical school on a contract basis; in 1952, three blacks, Frank Bryant Jr. and Robert L. Hilliard of San Antonio and Edward W. Guinn of Fort Worth, enrolled; and in 1954, the school admitted its first African American woman, Mae Frances McMillan of Houston. UTMB took an absolute position to desegregate itself.[45]

W. Astor Kirk Claims His "Forty Acres"

The Austin campus of the University of Texas regained its position as a focal point of the desegregation movement in 1950. While Barnett quietly began his second semester at UTMB, two events put the spotlight on UT. First, W. Astor Kirk resumed his attempt to enter UT's graduate school, this time based upon the contract system of internal segregation that Barnett had pioneered at the medical school. Second, Heman Sweatt's lawsuit against the university became a national news item as it came before the U.S. Supreme Court.

Kirk, who undertook his struggle for admission to UT in 1947 only to have UT offer him segregated classes at the makeshift Negro Law School, applied again on 3 May 1949. He received a letter the next day from Painter notifying him that his application and supporting attachments had been forwarded to TSUN. If the two universities agreed that UT would temporarily offer graduate work to Negroes in government, then he would become the Austin campus's first nonextension contract student. For reasons not altogether clear, however, the necessary arrangements between UT and TSUN did not materialize for Kirk in time for him to begin classes in the fall semester, as happened for Barnett. Apparently, TSUN's President Lanier requested of the TSUN board of directors the authority to develop a doctoral program for Kirk as well as to recommend he be admitted to UT on a contract basis in the meantime, but by 11 November, Lanier's requests had not been granted. Finally, by January of 1950, TSUN and UT established a contractual agreement that allowed UT to accept Kirk for graduate work. Lanier dispatched H. Hadley Hartshorn, director of admissions, and S. E. Warren, dean of the TSUN graduate school, to Austin for a meeting with A. P. Brogan, dean of the UT graduate school, "to work out . . . the final steps and procedures for processing Mr. Kirk's application." The last stumbling block, at least for Kirk, concerned whether his contract status meant he would attend classes with whites, as had more or less happened with Barnett, or whether UT would offer him the same segregated classroom situation of two years before.[46]

While behind closed doors UT inched closer to voluntarily admitting its first black student, Painter assured the white public that UT had no intentions of permitting Negroes to attend classes with Caucasians. Luciel Decker of Port Arthur, Texas, a young UT student, wrote Painter after learning from an article in the *Houston Chronicle* that the university had admitted Kirk. "I merely want you to know," she implored, "that I hope you don't change your mind about segregating the negro students who may attend the University on a contract basis." Decker's belief that the decision to segregate Kirk or not rested with Painter is not unusual; to the average student, the president is in charge of the university. The determinant role of regents and state government officials, especially Attorney General Price Daniel, on matters such as Kirk's presence at UT remained less apparent to the casual observer. What is striking about Decker's letter, however, is her sense that some administrative wavering about Kirk might have been going on behind the scene. She explained, "I believe W. Astor Kirk is trying to force an issue like Sweat [*sic*] did." In response to a newspaper article reporting that Kirk might not accept segregated instruction at UT, Decker caustically asked, "Does this colored man want to study courses in government and political science, or does he want social equality with the white students? Inaugurate the courses at the negro university in Houston and I bet he wouldn't enter any more than Sweat entered the law school."[47]

In restrained language, Painter answered Decker that under the UT-TSUN contract "we are obligated to give [graduate] work on a segregated basis." Painter went on to inform her that UT had arranged to instruct Kirk in a room off campus and noted that he would have access to the university library, which "for a long time" had been opened to Negroes. "I shall be interested," wrote Painter intimating a common bond of concern with Decker, "in seeing whether or not Mr. Kirk goes through with his work."[48]

On January 24, Brogan wrote Painter that Kirk "had unusually good grades in government through a Master's degree at Howard University." He assured the president that Kirk had applied to the university in good faith and sincerely wanted to study courses in government that could not "reasonably be given at Texas State University." Painter then instructed UT registrar Captain H. Y. McCown to write Kirk and meet with him to "arrange the necessary preliminary details" of his becoming UT's first (nonextension course) contract student. Kirk did not divulge to university and state government officials that he would not accept segregated accommodations. But, apparently, he harbored the hope that UT might permit him to attend classes as a regular student. In the weeks before this official contact from the university, Kirk had put the question of his being segregated from white students before various organizations in the black community.[49]

Members of the Omega Psi Phi fraternity (Qs) of Tillotson College pleaded with Painter to offer Kirk classes on a nonsegregated basis. "We believe that the time has come for the unconditional acceptance of Negro graduate students at the University of Texas," wrote the Qs, adding, "We do not believe it is in the best interest of the University of Texas, or of the people of Texas to accept Negro graduate students on a basis that will reflect upon the dignity, reputation, and respect of the University of Texas, and the people of our great state." "Therefore," they concluded their appeal, "we respectfully urge that Professor Kirk be accepted in the Graduate School of the University of Texas on the same terms and under the same conditions as all other graduate students."[50]

Painter paid no attention to the fraternity's plea and on 2 February, he had UT vice president James C. Dolley inform Kirk of the separate arrangements that the university would make to accommodate him as a student. The wily government professor, however, played his cards up to the final moment. He replied that he had registered for two courses in public administration and expected to attend these classes at the time listed in the course schedule. Kirk informed Dolley, "I am prepared to report for class at the hours that these classes are regularly scheduled," stating the issue as more a problem of scheduling than an outright refusal to participate in a segregated set up. Meanwhile, UT made all its final preparations to provide Kirk with the same offer it made him nearly three years before, which he refused. Comptroller C. D. Simmons secured the collaboration of the university YMCA: for a monthly fee of twenty-five dollars, he got YMCA general secretary W. A. "Block" Smith to let UT lease a room for six hours a week. Also, six university faculty members agreed to teach "contract Negro students" in the separate classroom.[51]

On 6 February, Kirk went to his special classroom at the YMCA, where he met Charles Timm, his government instructor. After less than an hour of discussing with Timm the course and the racial restrictions the administration imposed on him, Kirk left the room and issued a statement to reporters who waited to see how his first day of class as a UT contract student had gone. Kirk informed them that he could not accept the segregated arrangements UT presented to him and that he would quit unless the university reversed its policy at once. He then walked over to Dolley's office and expressed to him what he had told the press. He also "declared [his] willingness to accept separation in the regular classes on the University campus." The next day, he delivered a letter to Dolley in which he reaffirmed his "willingness to accept separation in the regularly scheduled classes on the campus of the University of Texas." McCown replied to his letter on 9 February, telling Kirk that the laws of Texas did not permit the university to admit him as a "regular student."[52]

Kirk answered McCown's perfunctory letter with strong words. He stated that he regarded the issue of whether existing state law required separation of black and white students on the graduate level in state universities as "an open question." In the interest of "a cooperative solution of the present problem," he averred, "I acquiesced in the University's view that existing state law does require such separation. But I insisted then, and I still insist now, that separation can be effectively applied in the classrooms on the campus of the university." Kirk knew he needed to argue why he opposed off-campus segregation. "If existing state law requires separation," he explained, "it does not require adoption of a mode of separation deliberately calculated to embarrass the person to whom it is proffered—a mode, mind you, that makes the University look ridiculous in the eyes of the rest of the nation and the world." Kirk would accept assignment to a chair in an anteroom or on a railed-off row several feet away from white students in a regular class but found a separate classroom intolerable and embarrassing. Internal segregation of the sort he could accept had resulted in G. W. McLaurin's suit against the University of Oklahoma, which the Supreme Court had before it along with the *Sweatt* case. Untroubled by abstract and legalistic problems, Kirk implicitly referenced Barnett's arrangement to bolster his argument. "I cannot accept as conclusive the University's construction of the contract which it maintains with the Houston institution," he wrote, adding that "it is a matter of public record that where the contract is currently being implemented, its application is along lines different from those which the University categorically affirms as mandatory." Kirk also questioned how UT-TSUN could permit him unfettered access to the university library but deny him admission to the regular classroom under any conditions whatsoever. Finally, the chair of Tillotson's Department of Government ended with a moral: "It is just such attitudes of intractableness that incline individuals with legitimate grievances to invoke the assistance of federal authority."[53]

UT had TSUN reimburse Kirk for the money he had paid for his tuition and fees. On 2 March, TSUN issued a check for twenty-six dollars, thus ending the Kirk affair. Kirk's activism against segregation in Austin continued with the successful effort he led involving African American access to the city's public libraries and nearby state parks. In 1954, however, Kirk stepped into a controversy over compromising remarks attributed to him regarding the policy of Texas state officials in response to the *Brown* decision. After that incident, he faded from active involvement in the antisegregation movement and restricted himself to a more academic role. UT, however, had not heard the last of the government professor. In the 1960s, Kirk did attend and earn his Ph.D. there. More than a decade before that personal triumph, however, UT failed to provide Kirk with either the internally segregated educational opportunity Oklahoma University gave to George McLaurin or the kind UTMB furnished to Barnett. The decision to keep the Austin campus for whites only, on the face of it, appeared inconsistent and a step backward from the direction state officials took in the case of Barnett. The flagship status of Austin's Forty Acres and the fact that the state was locked in battle against Sweatt's admission to the law school undoubtedly served to mitigate any compromise with the forces of desegregation.[54]

Whatever the imperatives that inhibited Painter from relaxing his stance on segregation, student opinion at UT did not parallel the administration's rigidity. In March of 1950, a student referendum emerged regarding the question "Should the university lift its ban on Negro students?" Two days before the election, the five-member student court called the poll off. "Anti-referendum forces" convinced the court that however the vote went,

93

the result would be a net disservice to the university. Most of the students endorsing the ban "would give the Russians another chance to howl at the U.S.," while a majority vote "to lift the ban would bring a lot of howling Texans down on the university's neck." The latter possibility no doubt concerned Painter, and it is likely that he compelled the student court to cancel the referendum. The attorney general's office also did not want to risk UT students voting to drop the color bar on the eve of its going before the Supreme Court to present oral argument in favor of maintaining the ban. Better to suppress democracy than to defy segregation.[55]

Modernity stood against the status quo in race relations. The power holders in Texas, nonetheless, made every last ditch effort to save the state's racial essence; but like the lad's actions in the story of the emperor's new clothes, theirs only made more obvious the unessential nature of segregated education. The legal campaign against segregation stripped off all the layers of self-delusion and forced Texans to see the naked truth: Texas was a white man's state and its institutions reflected that fact. If such a proposition no longer remained conscionable in an ethnically diverse, racially tolerant, and democratically organized post-Nazi world order, then the state's public institutions had to change. Massive resistance did not delay change in Texas; elite resistance did. But even the power holders in the Texas economy and higher educational bureaucracy could not keep the wall of segregation from crumbling. Ultimately, black students across the state demanded and eventually won places in white universities. Active resistance to segregation grew from ground fertilized by the de jure challenges, the ideological struggles that crystallized among black Texans in the 1940s, and the brave, if sometime halting steps of the trailblazers — Sweatt, Doyle, Barnett, Givens, Kirk, and the interracial marchers of 1949. With a growing number of students on the front lines, the Texas University Movement changed directions and with it the future of the state.

CHAPTER FOUR

This Is White Civilization's Last Stand
University Desegregation before *Brown*

DISCUSS your plans with this office before you move into a fight. We have the KNOW HOW to help you. Do not go off before you are ready. But do not stand still. We can help you get ready[;] we will help you do the job right. Some will say that you cannot do it, but the facts prove that we can. We have done it and the white community has shown a readiness to advance with us.
— Ulysses S. Tate to NAACP branch officers, 1 August 1952

Bringing law to the side of desegregation represented a landmark achievement, but it was also an empty glove without the flesh and blood experience of the individuals who crossed the line to make the legal victory a lived reality. The women and men who breathed life into the social, legal, and political debates that arose from the *Sweatt* case and enacted their historic role as "firsts," reacted to their experiences in many different ways. Likewise, students, teachers, and administrators at black-only, as well as black-excluding, universities responded in various ways to the challenges and changes to their campus traditions when desegregation finally occurred. Jim Crow's death had grave consequences for his alter ego, "Joe Cracker." Desegregation also meant that the state's erstwhile black institutions of higher education were no longer exclusively "for Negroes." Within the citadels of historically black higher education, desegregation threw the common stock of presuppositions about the white race up for grabs. Segregation's official demise at the ebony and ivory towers of learned society mightily assisted the unshackling of the southern mind. Blackness and whiteness ceased to appear as mutually exclusive, diametrically opposed categories of humanity existing in a hierarchically ordered relation to each other. Black and white Texans had to have an equality of rights and access to higher education, but what would equality mean and what difference would it make if change grafted itself to existing traditions? Democracy required the dismantling of racial hierarchy yet gave no clues about how to do so democratically.[1]

The black Texans who mobilized to achieve white recognition of equal rights and justice in higher education encountered considerable dangers and traps along the way. Desegregation at the "token" level occurred in Texas in three stages. The first period extended from 1949, almost a year before the Supreme Court's decision in *Sweatt* v. *Painter*, to 1954, the year of the court's decision in *Brown* v. *Board of Education*. Next came the immediate post-*Brown* period, which climaxed with the grand posturing of one of the worst race-mongering governors in modern Texas history, Allan Shivers. The final period spanned the late 1950s to the middle of the 1960s. The salient activities that helped characterize and shape each of these periods were, respectively, litigation and legislation, propaganda and pacification, resistance and reconciliation. Although the process of change developed with remarkable similarity across the state, its pace varied greatly by location. Such variations reveal local differences in the specific historical social arrangements of a particular town or city, especially as concerned configurations of power shaped by race, religion, and class. Desegregating Texas higher education illuminates much about negotiating complex and varied cultural and political terrain.

In the first phase of Texas collegiate desegregation, the Supreme Court's 1950 watershed decision acted as the catalyst to change the racially based admission practices of fourteen institutions of higher education. Initially, black students won admission to graduate and professional programs at the University of Texas beginning in 1949 at its Galveston medical school and in 1950 at the Austin campus. Subsequently, a few seminaries and denominational colleges set a proper Christian example and began admitting black applicants. Some of these limited desegregation to their graduate theology departments, while others opened all their branches and programs to blacks. Several junior colleges quietly moved toward desegregation as well. Collegiate desegregation spread across the state, but East Texas colleges put up fierce opposition.

The rock of separatist resistance first appeared in Texarkana, Wichita Falls, and Kilgore. The battles against admitting blacks to the colleges in these East Texas cities led to the organization of the White Citizens' Council movement in the state. Then came *Brown*. In the pre-*Brown* period, resistance to desegregation of higher education was minimal and primarily confined to the courtroom and the boardroom. Of course, desegregation was also minimal and the initial phases of the process were largely orchestrated behind closed doors by rights-seeking blacks and white elites. Yet something vastly more important occurred than what the small, token numbers of blacks stepping onto ground formerly reserved for whites

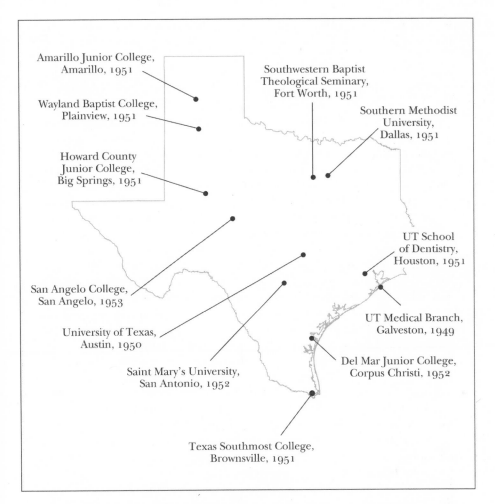

Amarillo Junior College,
Amarillo, 1951

Wayland Baptist College,
Plainview, 1951

Howard County
Junior College,
Big Springs, 1951

Southwestern Baptist
Theological Seminary,
Fort Worth, 1951

Southern Methodist
University,
Dallas, 1951

UT School
of Dentistry,
Houston, 1951

San Angelo College,
San Angelo, 1953

University of Texas,
Austin, 1950

UT Medical Branch,
Galveston, 1949

Saint Mary's University,
San Antonio, 1952

Del Mar Junior College,
Corpus Christi, 1952

Texas Southmost College,
Brownsville, 1951

Texas Universities and Colleges that Initiated Desegregation before the U.S. Supreme
Court's *Brown* Decision, 17 May 1956

suggests. A most significant set of social experiments took place on fourteen Texas campuses between 1949 and 1954; they directly challenged
government, religious, and educational leaders to consider social realities
and questions that most never dared to ponder. Moreover, leading black
Texans began to recognize through Sweatt's protracted fight and eventual
victory that desegregation was a means to a larger end: social equality with
whites in a unitary society, not a separate equality. They came to see the
path of separate development as having reached a dead end. For each
institution that African Americans desegregated, they claimed additional

ground for a new vision of social equality that now looked to be within their grasp.[2]

Price Daniel and the Price of Fighting *Sweatt*

Of course, only the attitudes of nine Supreme Court justices mattered most to Sweatt's immediate fate. Originally scheduled for January 1950, oral arguments came instead in April. The case put Texas in the national spotlight as the great defender of the lost cause. Attorney General Price Daniel represented the state's prosegregation position and howled right back at critics of Texas's higher education policy. He asked for the backing of the attorneys general of the southern states that practiced segregation. Marking his undated letter "URGENT — PERSONAL," he informed each attorney general that the *Sweatt* v. *Painter* case "is as important to your state as it is to Texas." He called for a minimum of six states to file a joint brief or for individual attorneys general to file briefs in support of the state of Texas. Daniel explained that he did not desire for them to take the side of Texas in any of the factual issues in the case but asked that they stress the point "that separate schools are constitutionally within the police power of the States so long as they are substantially equal." Daniel, pondering the historical significance of the moment, quoted from a letter in which Attorney General Harry McMullan of North Carolina stated that he was of the "opinion that this case [*Sweatt* v. *Painter*] is the most important decision to the Southern States that has been before the Supreme Court since the Dred Scott decision." Daniel also quoted McMullan as holding that a decree in favor of Sweatt would "be calamitous to the cause of public education and I am afraid that racial conflict of the most unfortunate character would result."[3]

Daniel hoped that his fellow attorneys general of the South would support his position. Eleven of the eighteen segregating states (including the District of Columbia) backed him in an amicus curiae brief. Alabama was the only Deep South state to dissent, and its decision not to support the white supremacist position sparked the ire of Eugene "Bull" Connor, Birmingham's commissioner of public safety. Failing to get the support of Governor James E. "Big Jim" Folsom and "Folsom progressive" attorney general Albert Carmichael, Daniel wrote Connor asking him to do what he could to get his state into the fold. Connor, in turn, called upon the Alabama Bar Association to file a brief stating that "our State administration fails to protect the interests of Alabama's people." Writing Francis Hare, president of the Alabama State Bar on 10 January 1950, he noted that attorneys general in several southern states had "joined the Honorable Price Daniel, the Attorney General of Texas, in defending the principle of Texas before the Supreme Court of the United States. Alabama has refused to join. I think nothing is more important since the Civil War than this to the welfare of our people, both white and black. I am sure you realize the danger of riot and bloodshed, even in peaceful Alabama, if the races are thrown together by a mandate of law from Washington."[4]

The amicus brief of Dixie's attorneys general represented the solid South as giving Negroes equal educational opportunities out of a deep-seated wish to maintain the separation of the races. It asserted that "the furnishing of equal educational privileges to all through separate schools does not involve discrimination." Moreover, "the continued constitutionality of the separate system," it argued, "furnishes an incentive to Southern States to provide more and better schools, especially in higher education, as the only way in which separation can be maintained for peace, harmony, and the general welfare." Thus, to create greater access to quality education for Negroes, the Court should uphold the legitimacy of segregation and use the threat of selective integration to achieve the greatest good for the greatest number of Negroes. The Court's declaring segregation unconstitutional would take away the carrot and the stick and invite violence and social chaos. On the other hand, "if admittance to a separate grade school or university for whites is obtained by individual Negroes because of unequal facilities for their own race, it will be understood by those at fault." In an ahistorical flourish, the brief claimed that "Southern people" knew "that Negroes are entitled to equal educational opportunities, and they will share without conflict or resentment the result of any failure on their own part to provide equality."[5]

As Daniel ascended the steps of the Supreme Court for oral argument, letters and telegrams such as concerned citizen W. R. Hughes's must have given him a sense of sacred obligation as well as a heavy burden of expectation. "This is White Civilization['s] last stand," read Hughes's telegram, the "hand of Texas and South is on your shoulders." Daniel knew his duty to his state required him to uphold segregation. To perform that duty he assigned his chief assistant, Joe Greenhill, to cover the legal history of the Fourteenth Amendment while he concentrated on expounding the police power position.[6]

Daniel warned against any external interference with southern custom and dismissed the sociological theories about the pernicious effects of racial segregation by observing that institutionalized white supremacy in the form of Jim Crow laws had nothing to do with bolstering white egos or abusing black self-esteem. Segregation existed as an extension of police power; it grew out the natural requirements of law and order. "Some people have feelings that make for conflict when the races associate too closely," Daniel remarked.[7]

The amicus brief of his peers offered an even bleaker admonition: "The

99

Southern States trust that this Court will not strike down their power to keep peace, order, and support of their public schools by maintaining separate facilities." "If the States are shorn of this police power and physical conflict takes place," warned the attorneys general, then "the States are left with no alternative but to close their schools to prevent violence." The South's position had able legal representation in Price Daniel; his only problem was that the region had no legal position.[8]

Winning *Sweatt*

Thurgood Marshall countered Daniel's "frantic battle to have discriminatory racial practices upheld by law" with an impressive set of supporting briefs and his own inimitable, to-the-point style of legal argument. Beside the support of U.S. attorney general J. Howard McGrath and solicitor general Phillip B. Perlman on behalf of Harry Truman's Justice Department, the NAACP received friends of the court briefs from diverse sources such as the Congress of Industrial Organizations, the American Veterans Committee, the American Jewish Congress, along with the Anti-Defamation League of B'nai B'rith, and the Committee of Law Teachers Against Segregation in Legal Education. The latter group represented an important piece of organizing on Marshall's part.[9]

The convening of the Committee of Law Teachers, which was composed of 205 deans and professors from the country's leading law schools, reportedly constituted the first time in U.S. history that so many legal minds had united to intervene in a case. Lambasting the law school of Texas State University for Negroes as a "mockery of legal education and of equal protection of the laws," their brief launched three salvos against segregation. First, they charged that segregation "perverts and distorts the healthy development of human personality." Second, from their study of U.S. legal history, they concluded that the Fourteenth Amendment's equal protection clause had to be "thoroughly understood to mean identical, and not separate rights," especially in education. Third, they pointed out that while the Truman government distributed the message of a united America through a book by General Bedell Smith, a former U.S. ambassador to Russia, which featured pictures of desegregated schoolrooms, the *Sweatt* case might require "we send a postscript that there is a special exception for young men studying their Constitution of the United States in the State of Texas." All three points underscored the key arguments Marshall put to the Court.[10]

Supporting Sweatt's right to attend the white law school, the Southern Conference Education Fund, Inc. (SCEF) tried to help discredit the picture of imminent race war over a decision unfavorable to segregation. Eighteen southern lawyers associated with SCEF, including Ben N. Ramey and Arthur J. Mandell of Houston, attacked the doctrine of "separate but equal" as unconstitutional and injurious to both blacks and whites. The attorneys contended that the harmfulness of segregated legal education appeared in the "tension between lawyer and client" when the "attitude ingrained" in a white lawyer trained at a white law school carried over into his or her work on behalf of a Negro client, which must, at times, occur. SCEF got some headlines and riled southern white supremacists, but its lawyers failed to get the NAACP or the Supreme Court to accept its brief. Also, none of the black attorneys in Texas, especially Durham or Wesley, signed onto the brief. Marshall and other top brass in the New York office took little notice of SCEF's activities, although key NAACP-connected attorneys A. P. Tureaud of New Orleans and Arthur D. Shores of Birmingham did join the eighteen signers.[11]

None of the pro-integration briefs, however, confronted the central issue that Daniel and his peers raised, namely, the issue of segregation as a means of maintaining racial peace. In oral argument and later in the press, Marshall dismissed the specter of violent outbreak resulting from a decision striking down segregation: "Our rights cannot be conditioned by a threat of what a few unlawful people will do." He also countered that all of Dixieland's doomsayers had come out with their hellfire and damnation prognostications when the "white primary" cases were before the courts, yet no incidents of violence resulted from the decisions of the Supreme Court in *Smith* vs. *Allwright*. "Negroes are not only voting freely in Texas," Marshall asserted, "but are part and parcel of the political machine as though this had been going on for a hundred years." Although his point here had validity, more than anything else Marshall offered proof positive that he was no stranger to the realm of overstatement.[12]

Tom Clark, a native Texan, a former U.S. attorney general, and a Truman appointee to the Court in 1949, in a memorandum to the conference of the Court on the *Sweatt* and *McLaurin* cases, debunked the picture of an outbreak of horrifying lawlessness following a reversal of the cases. In Clark's opinion, the attorneys general in their amici curiae statements offered "highly exaggerated" assessments. He excluded from this criticism Oklahoma, whose attorney general "was frank enough to admit" that if the Court limited the ramifications of a desegregation order to graduate schools, no ugly incidents would follow. Clark called upon his brethren to reverse *Sweatt* but not to overrule *Plessy*. He cited several reasons for his opinion that the "separate but equal" doctrine should be abandoned at the graduate level but not in the lower grades: "I see no reason why we should not concern ourselves here with the equality of education rather than social recognition. These are, after all, education cases. And it is entirely possible that Negroes in segregated grammar schools being taught arithmetic, spelling, geography, etc., would receive skills in these elementary subjects equivalent to those of segregated white students, assuming equality in the texts, teachers, and facilities."[13] A round of discussion followed Clark's memorandum. Justice Harold Burton's clerks dismissed the possibility of affirming the lower courts' decisions as requiring an act of "plain sophistry." Other possible dispositions involved reversal with various answers to the constitutional question, from upholding *Plessy* to making a broad pronouncement against it. Justice Clark's clerk proposed a "compromise" course.[14]

While the Court pondered the arguments for and against desegregation, black Texans continued to press the envelope. Texas State University for Negroes received an unknown number of applications and inquiries from black students requesting graduate and professional degree programs it did not offer. Having received numerous applications in the spring of 1950, TSUN made several recommendations to the Austin campus of so-called Negro contract students. In response, Painter pressed the TSUN board for progress in its creation of graduate-level Jim Crow schooling. On 1 May, he wrote TSUN board vice president W. R. Banks to inform him that UTMB's sole TSUN contract student, Herman Barnett, was "doing good work and there has been no difficulty regarding him at all." "All of us however," he continued, "are quite anxious to see established in connection with your institution a medical branch, for we feel that it would have a very wholesome and upgrading effect in the whole area of Negro education." Of course, with the passage of each semester, Painter's ability to keep UT "wholesome" and lily-white increasingly became tied to the extent to which black Texans could find advanced educational opportunities at TSUN and to the degree such segregated programs satisfied their needs and expectations. Reluctantly, the UT board of regents gave up on the possibilities of a black medical school being established in Houston or of a southern regional school coming to the rescue of the Galveston campus. As for saving the Austin campus, the regents put their hopes in a favorable decision of the Court.[15]

The moment of truth finally arrived on 5 June 1950. Chief Justice Fred Vinson presented the opinion of a unanimous Court: the University of Texas School of Law had to admit Heman Sweatt. A cunning compromise, the decision gave Sweatt what he sued for, yet it did not strike down Texas's beloved right to segregate. In agreement with Sweatt, the opinion read, "We cannot find substantial equality in the educational opportunities offered white and Negro law students by the State." Emphasizing so-called intangible factors, Vinson added, "[W]hat is more important, the University of Texas Law School possesses to a far greater degree those qualities which are incapable of objective measurement but which make for greatness in a law school." In deference to the segregating states, however, the justices

Standing tall with the bespectacled Heman Sweatt are (left to right) his wife, Constantine Mitchell Sweatt, father, James L. Sweatt, and mother, Ella Rose Perry Sweatt. In June of 1950, the Supreme Court ruled that the University of Texas Law School had to admit Heman Sweatt. After two frustrating years as a student facing exceptionally hostile conditions that broke up his marriage and affected his mental health, he dropped out. Other students who benefited from his case, however, did obtain degrees at UT and other schools previously closed to African Americans (Center for American History, University of Texas at Austin, CN No. 01839).

added that they need not "reach petitioner's contention that *Plessy* v. *Ferguson* should be reexamined in the light of contemporary knowledge respecting the purposes of the Fourteenth Amendment and the effects of racial segregation." The Supreme Court deferred judgment day on whether separate schooling denied blacks equal protection of the laws, but for black civil libertarians in Texas, the *Sweatt* decision occasioned a great awakening.[16]

Advancing Democracy, Engaging Resistance

At the head of the momentum of the University Movement was J. J. Rhoads. As chair of the Texas Commission on Democracy in Education (TCODE), the Bishop College president commissioned (and perhaps wrote) a booklet that extolled Sweatt's "frontal attack on separate equality," which TCODE sent to public libraries throughout the state. Titled *Advancing the Cause of Democracy in Education* (1951), the booklet contained a verbatim reproduction of the Supreme Court's opinion that ordered UT to admit Sweatt to its law school. It also contained pictures of the celebrated plaintiff and an aerial view of the UT campus and the U.S. Supreme Court building. It also reported that the successful case demonstrated that "the wall of obstruction to the progress of democracy in public education in Texas and the South is crumbling. Having been established on the vicious presumption of racial superiority, its false foundation is giving away, and its ultimate collapse is inevitable."[17]

TCODE's manifesto recapped Sweatt's legal fight, analyzed how Marshall and the other "able" attorneys "seized the opportunity to convert his case into a frontal attack on segregation," emphasized how tangible and intangible factors combined to prevent the possibility of equality in a dual educational framework, and noted as "highly improbable that Texas will attempt to comply" with the Court's definition of equality. The document further predicted that "Little Sweatts" would not be kept out of UT simply because the state spent more money on the School of Law at TSUN nor would the " 'growing crop' of Barnetts" transfer from the Galveston medical school to TSUN if it undertook the segregated training of doctors. Projecting the struggle to increase blacks' access to the state's institutions of higher education as irreversible, Rhoads's tract also added a poignant warning about democratization and the high cost it could exact on the movement's symbolic leader:

> If . . . we should localize our national hero by divorcing the support of his neighbors from that of others of his admiring Americans; if we should individualize him by divorcing his personal academic engagements at Austin

104

from his larger unfinished adventure in the interest of his underprivileged race; if we should embarrass him and his cause by forcing him to "take sides" between divided friends and supporters, we shall dissipate the larger values of his partial "victory" and lose him as an inspiring national symbol of progress in democracy and equality.[18]

Consistent with the vision in the TCODE statement, on 4 July 1950, Rhoads convened the Texas Council of Negro Organizations "to take immediate steps to extend the field of its attack on legalized segregation." He listed education as number one on the list but added transportation, housing, military service, health, and political rights as additional areas of priority. Representing forty-five affiliated organizations from across Texas, the eighty delegates voted unanimously in favor of resolutions condemning segregation. The TCNO held a victory dinner in the gymnasium of the Moorland YMCA in honor of Heman Sweatt. Afterward, council delegates gathered for their final event, a public mass meeting at Saint John Baptist Church. The warm evening air, the music, and the preliminary oratory had the crowd more than enthused to hear Marshall deliver the word from NAACP headquarters. Just a few days before arriving in Dallas, Marshall had called together his staff, the collaborating attorneys, and the lawyers from interested parties that had filed amicus briefs or otherwise backed the association's cases. They studied the ramifications of the decisions in the 1950 trilogy of cases in relation to the fight to abolish segregation and reached the conclusion that all future legal work had to be done on the basis of challenging the constitutionality of the "separate but equal" doctrine. Southwestern regional counsel U. Simpson Tate and everyone else had to be clear that the days of accepting improvements in black schools or the creation of new black schools could no longer be tolerated or accepted. School cases in Hearne, LaGrange, Dallas, Lubbock, and Euless had all ended in such a compromise answer or had been dismissed. Likewise, pending suits for black admission to the state parks, a Houston suit for admission to the whites-only municipal golf courses, and lawsuits against separate and unequal grammar schools in Winnsboro and the junior college and high school in Texarkana might go the same self-defeating way unless the lawyers unified the community and took a resolute stand before local officials and courts, a stand in favor of desegregation and nothing but.[19]

The civil libertarians who gathered in Dallas, the embryo of the modern civil rights movement in Texas, did not constitute the only social force to try to become better organized and more influential in the wake of the *Sweatt* decision. Old-time white supremacists of the rural sort interpreted UT's desegregation as a clear sign of what lay ahead and now understood that the NAACP's allure to the blacks in their midst had one intention:

social equality, which would never do. Not surprisingly, in Texarkana only two days after the TCNO's meeting in Dallas, the Knights of the Ku Klux Klan launched a membership drive. Roaming the streets with application forms to sign up new members, they distributed propaganda pamphlets titled "Why You Should Become a Klansman." They used the generic literature produced in Atlanta, Georgia, which invited all white, Protestant, gentile, native-born Americans "who want to keep America American" to pay the $10 fee and join the movement. About a week later, twenty-five black-owned homes in the Exline Park area of South Dallas were bombed. No group took credit for the deed, and the crime went unsolved after the unsuccessful prosecution of one Mexican American man.[20]

The rise of overt and covert Klan activity in Texas seemed to fulfill the prediction of the *Atlanta Constitution and Journal,* which held that the high court's opinions in the desegregation cases would lend encouragement to the Klan and posed "grave problems for the South" in the days ahead. Georgia governor Herman Talmadge shouted defiantly: "As long as I am Governor, Negroes will not be admitted to white schools. The line is drawn. The threats that have been held over the head of the South for four years are now pointed like a dagger ready to be plunged into the very heart of Southern tradition." U.S. representative Ben H. Guill, a Texas Republican House member, added to Talmadge's racist, demagogic rhetoric a partisan and anticommunist jab. "As long as Texans continue to support in office their worst enemies, the Socialists who call themselves Democrats," he fumed, "they can expect to be stabbed in the back repeatedly as a reward for their misplaced loyalty."[21]

Such ominous signs of rising incivility among white Texans and southerners in general may have appeared as the opening acts of the racial discord Attorney General Daniel predicted before the Supreme Court, but his office and the Texas legislature itself did little to prepare for or address the trouble that had begun to brew. Although Daniel advised Painter to enroll Sweatt in the white law school, he still refused to accept the Court's unanimous decision and chose to seek a rehearing. He claimed that facts regarding the new law school for Negroes were not in the record before the Court. Moreover, he said, "even if a full hearing of the evidence does not convince the court that the new school is now substantially equal, it is believed that the evidence would show that it can in time become substantially equal and therefore meet the state's responsibilities to its Negro citizens who desire to study law."[22]

After its recess, the Court acted on his plea in October. It rejected Daniel's argument and refused to review its decision in the *Sweatt* case, thus stripping Texas officials of their last legal means of hedging and dodging. Despite the Supreme Court's clear opinion on the matter, Texas and other segregating states continued to resist a full-blown dropping of the color line in graduate and professional school admissions. An uneven step forward, step back, process emerged. At Greensboro, North Carolina, segregationists received the support of a federal judge who ruled that an all-black law school satisfied the test of substantial equality with the University of North Carolina's law school for whites. The black litigant appealed the decision to the Supreme Court. In Louisiana, on the other hand, black citizen Roy S. Wilson won a court-ordered admission to the state's law school. Carroll G. Jones, state representative from Lincoln parish, answered the verdict with the suggestion that the legislature close the law school of Louisiana State University rather than let a black man into the school. The legislature did not follow his idea, but an extremist mood in reaction to desegregation of higher education had begun to register itself in pronounced terms throughout the South.[23]

One gauge of the political temperature of Texas reactionaries were the letters that Daniel's office received on the desegregation issue. Throughout the litigation process, the attorney general earned the praise and admiration of opinion-makers and ordinary white Texans alike. In 1947, one correspondent who supported his efforts sent him a detailed letter proposing a "super state" university for blacks in Texarkana, the center of the black population of Texas, Arkansas, Oklahoma, and Louisiana. He exhorted Daniel to stand strong against Eleanor Roosevelt's "nigger baby," the NAACP. That same year, "a white Democrat while I breathe" of Dallas offered Daniel the suggestion that he use deportation law to get rid of Heman Sweatt, "our $3,000,000.00 Negro" who claims to be smart enough as to need university training and demands that he be "tolerated" in the schools "for the whites." In February of 1948, George W. Hawkes, editor of the *Arlington Citizen*, commended Daniel for his handling of the *Sweatt* case and his advocacy of the right of individual states to resolve the matter of black higher education. To these and other letters, which all opposed desegregation, Daniel replied with gratefulness for their support.[24]

After the Supreme Court ruled against the state's prosegregation argument, letters came in expressing grave concern and questioning Daniel's conviction on behalf of white supremacy and separatism. In June of 1950, letters came in like that of Mrs. A. R. Kavanaugh, an Austin septuagenarian and "daughter of the South," who avowed that she held "no grudge for negroes" but believed it less troublesome for blacks to have "equal educational facilities — provided on a segregation basis." Since Sweatt would not enroll until September, she wondered why the black law school in Houston could not be made equal to the University of Texas in the next few months so as to keep him out of UT. "If one negro is admitted to the University of Texas, there will be many negroes apply[ing] for admission and that will cause trouble I fear." Mrs. Edith Robeson of Fort Worth wrote Daniel with a trembling hand. "Excuse this writing I realy am nervous [*sic*]," she scrawled from her sickbed. "[T]he idea of one nigger over powering the whole of Texas, we are plenty mad about it." She demanded that he, as her elected official, stop the blacks or face being tossed out of office in favor of officials the voters could trust to keep the schools of Texas from being "rouined [*sic*]." In the face of "this nigger business," she complained, "you are just soft period." Expressing grave disapproval of the Truman administration, she called on Daniel and Governor Shivers "to do something to save the white people." Cotton ginner and Hereford cattle breeder E. M. Brady of Hearne informed Daniel that he had no idea "how the white men feel about" the "negro problem." "We don't care what it cost lets give them school equal of our own"; do anything, Brady implored, but do not "mix" our young people. From the tiny town of Lorena, near Waco, with a population of only a few hundred people, rural mail carrier Herbert B. Harlow protested that state officials seemed "only concerned over the tideland issue," but the majority of the white and black people he delivered mail to "had rather see every oil well in Texas capped than see one black negro enrol [*sic*] in our State University." He asked Daniel what he planned to do, or, he jabbed, are "we going to take it lying down." Harlow thanked Daniel for his past stand and told him that he was praying that he would be "the 'Moses' of today, to lead us out of such a serious position," for "if this negro question isnt [*sic*] quieted down we will have a race war in the near future." No letter came too off the beam for Daniel to courteously reply that he would do all he legally could to uphold segregation.[25]

One letter, however, slung some mud at Daniel. Attorney Charles Howell of Beaumont, a regular editorialist in several of the state's newspapers, sent Daniel an open letter questioning his judgments and actions on several particulars. A staunch supporter of Daniel in his early work against the "Communist inspired Sweatt suit," Howell became irate that "two days after the decision [in the *Sweatt* case] was rendered and before the same could be received in Texas and read and carefully studied and thoroughly analyzed, and before a motion for rehearing was filed and acted upon, and therefore, long before the judgment could become final, negroes had been admitted to classes of the summer school at the University." He queried Daniel about why blacks appeared at the UT registrar's office the morning after the announcement of the Court's ruling; why university officials permitted blacks to enroll in graduate programs when the decision pertained only to the law school; and why he had not already filed a motion for rehearing. Howell's questions, largely based on inaccurate suppositions, cast Daniel in a soft, do-nothing role in relation to Texas's sovereign right to discriminate against its black subjects. The enrollment of blacks such as John Saunders Chase and Horace Lincoln Heath at UT (discussed below) should have destroyed Daniel's future in Texas politics. The *Texas Poll* in March of 1950 reported no change from its 1947 survey in attitudes regarding blacks entering the University of Texas. Nine out of ten whites still preferred for blacks to attend their own university rather than enter UT. Daniel, however, remained popular thanks to the "white horse" called "tidelands."[26]

In the tidelands battle, both the state attorney general and Governor Allan Shivers had a perfect issue to deflect public attention away from desegregation and through which to represent themselves as champions of state's rights government. In 1937, a controversy had arisen over whether states like Texas or the federal government owned the submerged lands off its coast. The issue came to a head when, on the same day it made its ruling in *Sweatt*, the Supreme Court, in a 4–3 split decision, asserted that the U.S. government had "paramount rights" to oil and gas revenues generated by offshore lands. Also, the tidelands issue, which disrupted Democratic Party dominance in the 1952 presidential election because Shivers supported Republican presidential hopeful Dwight D. Eisenhower, drove a serious wedge between Daniel and Shivers. Daniel took an all-or-nothing position on the state's claims, and Shivers agreed with Texas congressmen Sam Rayburn and Lyndon Johnson on a compromise that would have involved Texas sharing the revenues with the federal government. The controversy remained unsettled until 1953, when Eisenhower signed a quit-claim bill that overruled the Court's 1950 decision. Thus, as state officials beat the drums of defiance in the tidelands brouhaha and chanted the mantra of state's rights over federalism, the desegregation of higher education proceeded at a slow but definite pace across the state. In every case, the judgment call on when and how to respond to the challenge of desegregation fell in the laps of specific college board members and administrators. The state attorney general, the governor, the federal and state legislators all steered clear of the issue as best they could until the Court's ruling in *Brown*.[27]

Through the Door *Sweatt* Opened

While white state officials avoided significant engagement of the ruling in *Sweatt*, many blacks reveled in it. Despite the fact that *Plessy* remained the law of the land, many would-be black professional men and women acted as if it had been discarded as surely as Prohibition had been repealed. The morning after the *Sweatt* decision, several blacks went to the registrar's office at UT, and their applications went beyond law school admission. UT staff advised those applicants who sought entry into programs provided at TSUN to apply at the Houston campus. Two black students, however, received notice that they could enroll for summer classes as regular students. They, along with another applicant, had presented Painter with a "Negro situation" over a month before the Supreme Court ruling in the 1950 desegregation cases. John Saunders Chase desired to pursue a master's degree in architecture, and Horace Lincoln Heath sought admittance to the Ph.D. program in government, to which a few months earlier Kirk had been admitted but declined to attend on a segregated, contract basis. Painter knew what to do with Heath. Dean A. P. Brogan would make the arrangements for teaching staff, and Comptroller Simmonds would make the arrangements for classroom space at the YMCA, followed by the UT registrar, Captain McCown, notifying Heath when and where to report for separate instruction. Architecture required laboratory sections that could not be offered at the YMCA. Painter noted to himself that if Attorney General Daniel would advise him "in writing" to admit Chase to the campus for his laboratory classes, Painter would do so, otherwise, "we refuse to admit."[28]

The case of Mrs. Curtis McPhail Collins, the third applicant for graduate instruction offered at UT but unavailable at TSUN or Prairie View, presented Painter with an additional problem. An examination of her undergraduate transcripts revealed that she did not possess the minimum twelve semester hours in suitable library science courses necessary for admission to do graduate work at UT's Library School. Students applying with deficiencies in prerequisite course work had been a commonplace problem that the university had customarily answered by admitting students "on condition that the undergraduate courses be satisfactorily completed during the first summer session in residence." In Collins's case, however, that meant taking desegregation an additional step beyond what the UT-TSUN contract allowed. Consequently, on 30 May, Painter advised TSUN president Lanier that Collins should complete the necessary training in library science at TSUN or some other accredited institution. Lacking the additional schoolwork, she remained ineligible to do graduate work in library science at UT.[29]

Daniel's opinion that the *Sweatt* decision required UT to admit all qualified black Texans to its School of Law and to any other graduate or professional degree program it offered but that Prairie View and TSUN did not revised the university's admissions policy in an immediate but limited way. Collins remained ineligible for admission, while Chase and Heath instantly became regular students and avoided Painter's plan to accept them as contract and internally segregated students. The admission of the two black men, as Marshall predicted, resulted in no acts of violence and did not launch an ugly parade of unspeakable horrors. Educated southern white men, according to their own peculiar logic, showed some tolerance for integration as long as it involved mature, southern-bred adults. Chase and Heath were not minors, nor were the students with whom they would attend classes. Chase, a twenty-five-year-old native Texan, who in May of

1948 had attained a baccalaureate degree in architecture at Virginia's Hampton Institute and with plans that summer to marry a black woman, fit the necessary profile of a safe candidate to let into UT. At fifty years of age, Heath, a Wacoan, presented an even better prospect, except, ironically, for his having studied at Colby College in Waterville, Maine, and his having earned a master's degree from the Ivy League's University of Pennsylvania. Southern white traditionalists did not trust "nigras" with too much northern exposure.

Both Chase and Heath had applied to TSUN months earlier following the contract procedure. President Lanier recommended Chase for segregated admission on 20 April and Heath on 11 May, and, accordingly, UT accepted them both. In Chase's case, however, before taking graduate classes, he had to complete undergraduate courses in design, advanced composition, and architectural history and submit "evidence of ability in reinforced concrete and steel construction." These requirements resulted from an interview between Chase and Hugh McMath, director of the School of Architecture, who determined that Chase had deficiencies arising from inadequacies in the curriculum at Hampton Institute, a nonaccredited institution. UT did nothing irregular in setting up such prerequisites for Chase. Routinely, white students who presented transcripts that the admissions committee determined lacked specific course work it deemed essential for success in the graduate program, first had to take undergraduate classes. The *Sweatt* and *McLaurin* decisions striking down segregated arrangements in graduate and professional education and Daniel's opinion directing UT to comply with the Court's order led to the admission of Chase and Heath as regular students.[30]

J. H. Morton and W. D. McClennan, both faculty members at Samuel Huston College, also applied for admission to become students at UT during the summer of 1950. The administration at first rejected McClennan's application but then reversed its decision and held his and Morton's applications to do advanced work in mathematics "under consideration." Officials ultimately admitted McClennan, but Morton's application died on the vine, perhaps due to his having been identified as a "political" applicant. Other blacks entered in the second summer session. The first African American women to attend UT, Emma L. Harrison, pursued a doctorate in education, and L. June Brewer, pursued the doctorate in English.[31]

Patterns of regional socialization, gender, marital status, and age mattered greatly in a world where social contact between blacks and whites at a level of equality had been against the law, or against custom, which often had more force than the law. Since the Reconstruction era's brief hour in the sun almost three-quarters of a century before, whites believed that coeducation of the races would bring contact among minors, especially between black boys and white girls that might extend from the classroom

to the bedroom, and nothing remained more anathema to white supremacists than the black male–white female miscegenation bugaboo. As long as
desegregation went no further than the graduate and professional levels
involving older students well-schooled on the boundaries of appropriate
social interaction between the races, whites could comfort themselves that
no "moral" outrages would occur. So confident had Chase's instructors
felt about his intentions to pursue his higher education and not social
equality with whites that he received an unusual welcome. On his first day
as UT's first full-fledged black student, he stood up as McMath introduced
him to his fourteen white classmates "and then sat down in an unsegre-
gated seat." After class, the low-key veteran of the Second World War
informed curious news reporters that "everything went fine, everybody
was swell."[32]

With news of the warm reception, McMath received a number of disap-
proving letters and official censure. A wire service reporting McMath's
welcome and his comment that Chase was "just one of the boys" incited
John Pence Jr. of Houston to write that "while there is apparently nothing
that can be done about the enrollment of these people in our University,
we question the advisability of greeting them with open arms. I don't seem
to remember any such cordial reception being showered on any of the
people who entered the University when I was there." Pence ended his
letter saying that, on behalf of an unspecified collective, "we feel that you
are entitled to know how some of us in Houston feel about this matter.
Frankly, we don't like it and hope that with proper handling the whole
thing will die a natural death."[33]

Another letter writer, a "former Texan," told McMath that if he extended a Negro the welcome the newspapers reported, "shame on you."
The director of UT's School of Architecture, who proved to be a friend and
mentor to Chase throughout his attending UT, never retreated from his
initial openness. When he interviewed Chase in May he suggested to him
the possibility that the Court's decision in *Sweatt* might compel UT to admit
him as a regular student. Chase, wearing the mask that blacks learned to
wear to disguise or hide their true feelings, approached his meeting with
McMath without revealing any great awareness of the civil rights case and
prepared to take correspondence courses or study wherever and under
whatever circumstances he could. Later, he realized that McMath had a
genuine interest in seeing him do well and achieve his goal of a master's
degree in architecture. Other whites he met were not so supportive.

Chase never experienced any overtly racist behavior from UT students
or faculty, but, as he put it, "other things happened that were worse." He
drew an analogy to sitting on an airplane with open seating. As the passen-
gers boarded they would see the open seat next to you, look at your color,

and move on to take a seat somewhere else until the seat next to yours was the last seat available. Such ostracism, being treated as a leper, could scar you, Chase observed, in much more devastating and enduring ways than straight-out racial animosity. Moreover, being known as the plaintiff who forced the school to open its doors to blacks must have compounded Sweatt's sense of alienation. "Had the Supreme Court case been *Chase* v. *Painter*" instead of *Sweatt* v. *Painter*, Chase stated, "then I might not have made it through. I think he bore that pressure, that he would be stopped — I really believe that — and they stopped him, they stopped him."[34]

Although beset with "a lot of mental anguish" of his own at UT, Chase was not stopped. He married the year he entered UT, and, unlike Sweatt's, his marriage lasted beyond his graduate work at UT. His marital status was, of course, an important issue. Attuned to the paranoid white male mind-set, a local Austin newspaper noted about Chase: "Single, he plans to marry in August." Despite Chase's success at UT and that of other black students, and despite their not threatening white supremacy with the criminally prosecutable outrage of miscegenation, state and university officials continued to plan a future course that maintained segregation in higher education, even at the graduate and professional levels.[35]

Chase's background is both different from and similar to other blacks who broke the color line in Texas higher education. His father, a graduate of Morgan College, taught school for a while but left teaching for a better-paying job at the post office. His mother, also a college graduate, chose the better-paying work of maid over teaching. Born on 23 January 1925, Chase received his early education from all-black Stanton Elementary and Wiley H. Bates High School in Annapolis, Maryland. At Bates, he was influenced by his drafting and industrial arts teacher, Professor Marchand, who gave him the word "architect" for what he described as his desired occupation and guided him in that direction. Following in the footsteps of his older sister, Chase attended Hampton Institute, but the draft interrupted his education in 1944 for two and a half years of service, which included duty in the South Pacific. Afterward, Hampton helped place him in a job in Philadelphia, but he grew dissatisfied with northern segregation. He sought another placement and landed a job in Austin teaching at the Crescent Institute, which was owned and operated by a Hampton graduate and provided adult education to black veterans. He also taught at Anderson High School while his architectural firm, Chase and Buckley Modern Designers, from an office on East Eleventh Street, together with the Lott Lumber Company, built black Austin. He desired graduate training so that he could design more than homes and small buildings for African Americans. He wanted to help design and build the modern world.[36]

Limiting Desegregation at UT

While Chase dreamed of being a UT-trained and certified architect determining the form and function of the structures of the future, segregationists busied themselves with maintaining the already obsolete structures of the past. TSUN's contract with UT became the framework for limiting the speed and extent of desegregation in Texas higher education. A year after the *Sweatt* decision, board vice chairman W. R. Banks informed Painter that "it was definitely decided" that TSUN would provide, on an "equal basis," bachelor's and master's degrees in major subjects in the arts and sciences, in education, and in business, as well as professional degree programs in law and pharmacy. "Dr. Lanier has been requested to build his faculty and secure supplies and equipment to support this training program," Banks dryly reported. Painter, for his part, assured Banks, Lanier, and other TSUN officials that UT had no intention of "competing" with the black university or the A&M college for black graduate students. The law school would admit blacks because the Supreme Court ruled that it had to, but, as for other fields of study, it would admit qualified blacks only to programs neither Prairie View nor TSUN listed in its catalog. UT admissions staff strictly adhered to such a policy, but occasionally contradictions arose. Although TSUN's catalog stated that it offered a master's degree and courses required for a teaching certificate in special education, applicants to the program found reality to be different. When blacks, mostly special education teachers, began to apply directly to UT, they explained the situation to Captain McCown, who in turn informed President Painter. Instructed to contact Lanier, McCown reached the TSUN president by telephone on 11 April 1951 and finally received official word that UT should not admit blacks to the university even though TSUN did not yet have a full program in special education.

A verbal reply to Painter, however, would not be sufficient. On 7 July, he wrote Lanier asking for "an official letter so that our records of cooperation will be clear." He explained that "it is not the desire of the University of Texas to compete with your institution in the graduate field, and therefore, we have consistently refused admission to the University when the work sought was being offered either at your institution or at Prairie View University. In the present case, it is important that we have from you an official statement with regard to the above matter. If you do not offer a Master's Degree in Special Education, obviously the University of Texas should receive the Negro students who are applying for this work." Lanier responded that TSUN had just reached the point where it would offer one course in the present summer session. He said that there were plans to offer a larger program the coming academic year and a full program in the Texas Education Agency–recognized area of special education by the summer of 1952. Lanier asked Painter to refer all applications back to TSUN and noted that Chairman Banks had endorsed his position. As for the many students UT had rejected in the 1950–51 academic year and his lack of timely response, Lanier explained that "we had planned to consummate our plans this present summer session, but we were waiting on our budget before going through with our plans." Obviously, Lanier did no planning at all for the blacks who desired what TSUN could not provide but UT could. What he did offer was the opportunity for black students who could not wait for TSUN to accommodate them to apply for financial help to Banks, who also chaired the Out-of-State Aid Committee. "Some teachers," Lanier told Painter, "due to the uncertainty of our offerings in this area, have been granted Out-of-State Aid to study Special Education this summer."[37]

The efforts of President Lanier and Trustee Banks to block blacks from entering UT's graduate school did not extend across the board. TSUN's programs in education, however, constituted in their minds a major priority area. Student demands for immediate provision in other fields that TSUN listed in its catalog but remained only in the planning stage left Lanier in a quandary. Stephen L. Carraway's application to do graduate work in clinical psychology, a program that did not exist at TSUN, left Lanier two choices: refer him to UT or to the Out-of-State Aid Committee. Lanier may have wanted to put Carraway on hold or send him out of Texas, but he acquiesced to referring him to UT after H. E. Wright, head of the Department of Psychology; S. E. Warren, acting dean of the graduate school; and Dean H. Hadley Hartshorn informed him that budget reductions for the 1951–53 biennium left them unable to provide a full course of study in the field Carraway requested. UT records do not indicate whether it admitted Carraway.[38]

Despite occasional contradictions and minor controversies arising from UT's limited desegregation policy, blacks entered various graduate-level departments and professional schools and successfully matriculated with white students. In all, between 5 June and 2 October 1950, thirty-two blacks applied for admission to UT. The group consisted of twenty-five men and seven women applying to sixteen different departments for degrees on the baccalaureate, master's, and doctoral levels. UT officials accepted twenty-two and refused ten of the applications. They rejected five of the applications because their degree programs of choice already existed at TSUN or Prairie View, three because they applied for work at the undergraduate level, and two because their academic qualifications did not meet university requirements. The applicants accepted to UT, many with impeccable academic records, enrolled in law or graduate programs not offered at either of the black colleges.

UT's first 22 black students out of a total student body of over 12,000 faced a considerable degree of hostility. George Washington Jr. of Dallas, one of the six black men who entered the law school in the fall term, described the racial atmosphere in the fall of 1950 as "icy and uncomfortable." One night, in the first week of the term, Ku Klux Klansmen erected a burning cross in front of the law school building. The Klan meant for Sweatt, Washington, and all others to know that white supremacy continued as the true law of the land. As Sweatt left the law library after studying late, he walked to his car in the glow of a fiery spectacle. The jeers and taunts of the crowd assembled on the lawn crowded out of his mind much of the information he had spent hours learning. Now he had to worry about whether he would make it home in one piece. A white friend accompanied him to his car, but, with four slashed tires, his car would not be able to take him anywhere. In the days after the incident, a few white liberals offered words of consolation, but UT officials expressed no serious condemnation of the crime and Austin police never arrested the culprits. The black students downplayed the incident and went about their studies showing no outward signs of embarrassment or that their faith in the righteousness of their course had been shaken. Sweatt, in remarkable a letter to Thurgood Marshall dated 28 October 1950, portrayed the cross-burning as working to the benefit of the black students. White students, he reported, "have gone obviously out of their way to amend for any discomfort likely to have been caused us as a result of it [the Klan action]." UT's most famous student noted that he and his black peers had not been subjected to many of the commonplace forms of segregation at UT that existed elsewhere for blacks. They used the same university restrooms and water fountains whites used and sat wherever they desired in the lounges, campus eating places, and sports events that occurred at UT. In the first month of school, Sweatt received an appointment to his class's social committee and attended a "stag" party at the student union and a dance the students organized at the Austin Commodore Perry Hotel. He informed Marshall that his white classmates were "very agreeable."[39]

Sweatt would later describe himself during this period as an emotional wreck. Four years of putting his life on hold, of making his life a front-page, policy-changing legal case had taken its toll. His health had begun to fail him, and at the same time his marriage hit rock bottom and soon ended in a divorce court. A man of enormous will, he somehow felt that he could overcome the frustrations in his personal life, brave a hostile and high-pressured environment (which kept his ulcers from healing), and make passing grades at an intensely competitive law school after being out of school for more than a dozen years. He also worried incessantly over whether he had what it took to pass and whether certain members of the faculty or certain classmates were out to "get him." Ultimately, the demons of white supremacy did drive him from the school and even from the state itself. He lived out the balance of his life in Atlanta, Georgia, earning a graduate degree in social work and working for the Urban League. A shroud of public silence and shame fell over Sweatt's nervous breakdown, as his condition was called in the rare moments it was mentioned and given a name. Although Sweatt was recognized by UT Africana Studies director John Warfield and others on campus, it was not until a decade or more after his death in the 1970s that UT acknowledged its debt to Sweatt with the creation of a civil rights symposium and other honors.[40]

Comparatively, his classmate, George Washington, faced a less difficult situation. The great J. H. Morton mentored Washington, one of Huston College's stellar pupils, and recommended him to teach government classes at the college after his graduation. From the little campus sitting in UT's shadow at day's end, Washington watched Sweatt's legal fight with hope in his heart and prayers on his lips. He entered UT thanks to Sweatt's sacrifice, but without his burdens, at least to an extent. Once, during class, a student said "nigger" as casually as a Christian would call the name Jesus. Washington's jaws tightened, but he dismissed the student's choice of words as merely the product of a bad habit of speech and not a specific attempt to degrade him. However, "there were a few liberals in the room who I knew would resent it if I showed no offense," he recalled, "so I turned around and looked at the fellow with as stern a look as I could muster." He never heard another student use the word again.[41]

How heavy an inward price desegregating UT exacted on the young men and women who attended the school in the early 1950s defies easy estimation. If the black experience at UT could be compressed into a single word it would have to be "loneliness" or perhaps "estrangement." Desegregation did not mean inclusivity. Publicly, however, the black students did not broadcast their troubles and typically did all they could to represent their experience in as upbeat a manner as they could. As a result, the applications from blacks continued to come into UT and to other institutions of higher learning.[42]

The Beal Brothers and the Texas Medical Center

The big city of Houston, presumably safe from NAACP work against racial discrimination in higher education, thanks to the presence of Texas State University of Negroes, became the site of quiet, in-house desegregation. UT's outposts in the Bayou City included its Postgraduate School of Medicine and its School of Dentistry. In 1950, they functioned as units of UT's newly developing Texas Medical Center, an affiliated but autonomous part of the University of Texas. The Medical Center's centerpiece was the hospital for cancer research named for the multimillionaire bachelor Monroe Dunaway Anderson, who at his death in 1939 left $3,250,000 in money, gifts, and land for its creation. In 1950, when Anthony Wayne Beal read that the Texas Medical Center would open a postgraduate medical school where a practicing physician could take courses to remain abreast of the latest advances in medical sciences, he did not think for a second about segregation preventing him from enrolling. Born in rural Hammond, Texas, his father mastered the carpentry trade and his mother, part African and part Choctaw, kept house and raised fourteen children. In 1934, Beal graduated in a class of thirteen from Calvert Colored School, where he never saw a new textbook in twelve years of study. W. R. Banks, the keynote speaker at his graduation commencement, gave, as Beal recalled, a "strong and progressive speech" titled "Ruling the Roost." It motivated the young student to attend Prairie View, but having no success at finding a job to pay for his education, Beal transferred to Paul Quinn College. Still faced with the burden of inadequate funds, he took time off to work a while. He soon resumed his studies, however, and finally completed a bachelor of science degree in chemistry at Bishop College in 1939.[43]

The tenacious Texan next became one of the first blacks to take advantage of the out-of-state tuition assistance program that Dr. Richard Hamilton prodded the state legislature to create. He graduated from Meharry Medical College in Nashville, Tennessee, in 1943, whereupon he traveled to St. Louis to do his residency training in surgery, anesthesia, and psychiatry at the Homer G. Phillips Hospital. On 15 January 1945, Beal moved to Houston and joined his older brother Perry, who had been practicing medicine in the city since 1935. The elder brother's struggle for a medical education had been even more arduous without the tuition subsidy. Together the two Beals became a dynamic force in black Houston, especially in black medical organizations such as the Lone Star State Medical Association and the Houston Medical Forum, which pledged to support a student to sue the University of Texas for admission and tacitly supported Barnett's entering the school. Anthony Beal's activism arose out of a spirited black weltanschauung. "We were all dedicated to the fight at that time and it was a do or die," he recalled. "It was a fearless type of aggressive movement . . . a really critical time . . . from 1945, when I came to practice, . . . [the struggle for racial justice] was very aggressively pursued, fearlessly, we just let the chips fall where they may."[44]

In the 1950–51 academic school year, the "chips" fell in a classroom of the University of Texas Postgraduate School of Medicine in Houston's Texas Medical Center. Drs. Anthony and Perry Beal sat in middle-row classroom seats in Mavis P. Kelsey's course in modern therapeutics. These men had complexions of a dark black-brown hue that revealed their father's African Madagascar ancestry. The Beal brothers had come for education, not demonstration; and on those terms, Kelsey and the officials made no fuss or furor. Beal received his certificate for twenty-five credit hours and returned in subsequent years for postgraduate courses in surgery and gynecology.[45]

"Zeb . . . Stay out of These White Women's Faces"

The University of Texas Dental Branch desegregated in 1952 as a result of a process carried out as quietly as that of the postgraduate division of the Medical Center. Officials of the dental school, wanting to head off any lawsuit, literally grew and hand-picked the blacks that would desegregate the school. The men they selected, Moritz Virano Craven and Zeb Ferdinand Poindexter, unlike the Beals, came from urbane, relatively privileged black middle-class families. Craven's father was Dr. Essex S. Craven, a prominent physician in black Houston. Poindexter's father, although he had only an eighth grade education, got a job as a dining car waiter, one of the best jobs available for black men during the 1920s. His mother taught school in Fort Worth after having studied for two years at Wilberforce University in Ohio, but she later earned her four-year degree from Wiley College. Widowed in 1941, Poindexter's mother did what she could to provide for her four children. Although financially she could only do so much to help them, she encouraged them to pursue higher education, and they each one did achieve an advanced or professional degree. A cousin of the Poindexter's, Vassar Tolbert, had become a medical doctor and taught anatomy at Meharry Medical College. Citing his example, Poindexter's mother pointed her son in the direction of the medical profession early in his life. After finishing at Terrell High School, he earned a bachelor's degree from Wiley College and then took a job as a dining car porter. Like Sweatt, who finished his degree at Wiley and felt lucky when he returned to Houston to find a job as a porter at Sakowitz Department Store, Poindexter felt no shame in working for the railroad at such a menial job. Years later, he explained how he faced the indignities and constraints of a white-dominated world and then became the first to desegregate the UT Dental Branch:

> Most people don't realize what segregation was. You didn't think about bucking the law, you went ahead and accepted what was status quo . . . what was the law at that time. Now it took a lots to rebel against the establishment and when you do usually one single individual gets punished. This is what happened to Heman Sweatt. Heman Sweatt had a nervous breakdown. It took a lots of stamina to really get through and fight the status quo.
>
> However, in my favor I had been working for Dr. Telfort for two years and he was the Dean of Admissions at the University of Texas Dental Branch . . . [and] they selected the [black] students that they wanted [to have desegre-

gate the school] so I was asked: "Zeb, we are thinking about admitting a colored student to the University here and everybody knows you, would you like to go?"[46]

Telfort hired him as a laboratory assistant in 1950 upon the recommendation of TSUN president Ralph O'Hara Lanier and science professor Robert Terry. His excellent work in TSUN's master's program and good record as a laboratory aide at the dental school convinced the school officials that if desegregation had to occur, then Poindexter would make a promising candidate. When they asked Poindexter to attend the white school, it did not take him long to respond with a "yes." A man of great personal magnetism, the future dentist had a way of looking deep into the place where a person's humors reside and with the snap of his fingers turn almost anyone into a friend. He called it his knack for selling. It served him well; sometimes too well. Shortly after UT admitted him, his charm landed him a conference with the dean of the dental school, Frederick C. Elliott. He recalled the reason Elliott, who in 1952 went on to become the executive director of the Texas Medical Center, called him in: "The girls used to come and bring me coffee and donuts when I was down there [in the laboratory] taking care of the animals—the white girls; wasn't no black women working there, the white girls. Dr. Elliott called me in his office. He say, 'Zeb,' he say, 'you in a new environment now.' I say, 'Yes sir.' I'm expecting him to ask me do I need a tutor or do I think I can't keep up with the subjects and everything. He say, 'I want you to stay out of these white women's faces.' I said, 'Yes sir.' "[47] Poindexter's personality and his being in the urban metropolis of Houston did not leave him despairing of loneliness during his four years at UT Dental School. He pursued his dental education and negotiated the daily manifestations of white supremacy, privilege, and power with a mask that always presented a smile as it concealed his innermost feelings of anger and humiliation. In 1956, he completed his course of study and became the first black man to graduate from the dental school. About a decade and a half later, the school asked him to join its faculty and he became its first black instructor. Craven also graduated, but a year after Poindexter.

A Breach in Brownsville?

Collegiate desegregation in Texas moved beyond Galveston, Austin, and Houston in 1951. In the context of the *Sweatt* decision and the sudden responses of local authorities to the lack of or unequal postsecondary educational opportunities available to African Americans, black students, often with direct ties to NAACP activists, began applying like never before to the state's institutions of higher learning that denied their admission on racial grounds. In some cities, white authorities created black junior colleges or expanded existing ones, generally in the black high school. Typically, the local white junior or senior college organized the black junior colleges as branches that would satisfy black demands for college, vocational, or adult training programs. An article in the December 1951 issue of *Texas Outlook*, the official organ of the all-white Texas State Teachers Association, reported that a "growing feeling" existed that black junior college branches "do not provide equal facilities." It noted that at least one junior college had begun admitting blacks and that suits for admission had been filed against other schools. The white teachers' group did not go so far as to advocate desegregation, but the article did suggest that it was an emerging trend, which, along with other developments, indicated that the state's junior colleges were on their way to becoming "community colleges" in the truest sense of the term.[48]

Three junior colleges took the unprecedented action of voluntarily desegregating in 1951. A close analysis of the places that admitted blacks reveal some interesting patterns. Texas Southmost College at Brownsville and Howard County Junior College at Big Spring became the first undergraduate public schools in Texas to admit black students. The details on Texas Southmost College's desegregation remain sketchy. Carter Wesley published a small article in the 8 September 1951 edition of the *Houston Informer* that reported that Howard County Junior College had followed the Brownsville school in announcing that it would admit blacks. The available historical records tend to endorse the common view that the problem of racial segregation of blacks had never been a major issue in the Rio Grande Valley, at least not for the Anglos and Mexican Americans who dominated many of the counties of the region.[49]

Established as Brownsville Junior College in 1926 with the encouragement of the University of Texas, the school very well may have had persons with some African ancestry attending the school from its earliest years. A student's mother could have been a full-blooded African, but if she had a Spanish surname, admission officers asked no questions. Despite this limited flexibility, racial segregation did constitute a significant social problem for South Texas African and Mexican Americans alike. In 1950, Cameron County, with Brownsville as its seat, led the way as the most highly industrialized county in Texas. The state's third largest cotton-producing county, Cameron hosted a wide range of industrial, international trade, tourist, and petroleum processing business activity. Its population of 125,170 inhabitants consisted of 65.8 percent Latin Americans, 33.6 percent Anglo-Americans, and a mere 0.6 percent, or 751, Negroes. Based upon the pattern of landownership and landowner-worker relations, Cameron grew up an "Anglo county," notwithstanding the fact that Anglos represented a minority group. The minutes of the junior college's board of trustees' meetings between 1950 and 1959 do not mention a policy change regarding the admission of blacks. Nor does the *Brownsville Herald* report a formal policy change. In the aftermath of the *Brown v. Board of Education* decision in 1954, John F. Barron, superintendent of Brownsville's school district and former president of Texas Southmost, stated that he saw no problem with desegregation since the town only had thirteen pupils attending its sole black elementary school. By arrangement, the city of Harlingen allowed Brownsville to transport a distance of thirty miles two black students for instruction at its high school for blacks. In relation to the *Brown* decision, Barron stated, "We'll see what the state sends down on this and do whatever they say."[50]

Cameron County Anglos accepted but did not welcome desegregation. An editorial in the *Brownsville Herald* groaned about Court's ruling in *Brown*: "We cannot rejoice with the Negroes, if they consider this a victory." Calling the Supreme Court a "College of Cardinals," perhaps revealing a trace of anti-Catholicism, the editor cautioned that "you can't legislate a social change overnight." Asserting that the ruling reflected the rule of men instead of law, the editor chastised that blacks "have accomplished nothing to increase their opportunities for real education" and predicted that "some enterpriser is sure to come up with some variation of the old Grandfather Clause." Moreover, the allure of "the fancy palaces of the white folks across the tracks" would cause blacks to lose the sense of "sacrifice and devotion" that compelled them to send their children to the small, Jim Crow school. In 1954, desegregation gradually took place in Cameron County, despite the disapproval of the Anglo masses.[51]

The Mexican American majority, on the other hand, embraced the meaning of *Brown* and took the opportunity to intensify its struggle against so-called "Mexican" schools, which were supposedly segregated on the basis of language rather than race or ancestry. This heightened struggle did not, however, take the form of additional litigation in the manner of the landmark 1948 *Delgado* case in Bastrop. Historian Guadalupe San Miguel observes that from the middle of the 1950s to the late 1960s, organizations of people of Mexican descent, like the League of United Latin American Citizens (LULAC) and the American G.I. Forum, faced an "era of subterfuge" that effectively rendered "futile" the use of lawsuits to compel desegregation. Educational equalization activism, however, took other forms. Increased direct political solidarity between African Americans and Mexican Americans emerged as one of them.[52]

In the absence of detailed information on the blacks that desegregated Texas Southmost between 1950 and 1955, the earliest black student at the junior college who can be identified is Albert A. Hunter of Brownsville. His picture appears in the school yearbook, *Scorpio*, as a freshman in the 1955–

56 academic year. Emanuel Bowser appears next in 1957–58. In the 1956–57 regular term, Texas Southmost had 1,150 students and sixty-nine faculty members, up from 763 students and twenty-seven teachers in 1952–53. Thus, desegregation did not have an adverse effect on enrollment at the junior college. Photographs of school organizations and campus life in *Scorpio* do not reveal black students entering the mainstream until 1968. Three blacks appear in the annual's class pictures, and Robert Hosey had the honor of being elected most popular sophomore and best all-around student. Students also voted Philip Turner the most popular freshman. The college, which later became the University of Texas at Brownsville, did not recruit its first black faculty until John Anderson came to the English department to teach speech in 1985.[53]

Big Spring

The desegregation of Howard County Junior College, like Texas Southmost's, took place a year after the *Sweatt* decision in an area with a small African American population. Howard County, with its ranching, farming, oil, and gas businesses, had only about 800 black inhabitants. With an overall population of 26,722, Howard was 82.8 percent Anglo, 13.9 percent Latin, and 3.3 percent African American. Big Spring had been the home of an army air force bombardier school, and in 1946, after a public vote, the hospital area of the defunct base was converted to be used as a junior college. Big Spring blacks, especially black soldiers and veterans at the nearby Webb Air Force Base, were dismayed when they found out that they would be barred from any use of the new school and would have no equal facilities created for them. When college officials announced plans to move the school to a new 100-acre campus in the southeastern part of the city effective September of 1951, the local NAACP stirred itself into action to pose a challenge based on the *Sweatt* victory. Presented with black applicants, trustees could either desegregate or hurriedly take the economically infeasible route of establishing a black junior college. In September of that year, college officials announced that qualified blacks had applied to the school and that it would admit them. On 17 September, Gwendell White and Robert L. Brown enrolled for premedical studies and Frances Louise Stewart entered as a prenursing student. The next day, Jessie Mae Davis entered with an interest in education, and a few days later Ervin D. Butler Jr. enrolled in courses in business administration. All occurred with no major opposition, and the NAACP branch and civil libertarians at Big Spring claimed a major victory.[54]

The desegregation of Howard County Junior College helped prepare Big Spring to take steps toward complying with the Courts ruling in *Brown*, but it also spurred social conservatives into action. In 1955, when school trustees gathered to discuss ending segregation, one member, R. E. Mc-Kinney, adamantly opposed any move in that direction. He bolted from the board and soon became a plaintiff in a suit to stop school district officials from ending segregation in the city's elementary schools. McKinney and fellow plaintiff Roy Bruce, another Big Spring resident, identified themselves as local representatives of the Texas Citizens' Council, a new group organized in the summer of 1955. Ted O. Groebl and John W. Currie, who professed no membership in the new council, joined McKinney and Bruce in suing for a declaratory judgment and injunction to halt allocation of foundation school funds to the schools of Big Spring unless they maintained the separate education of black and white children as stated in the state constitution and various statutes. A Dallas law firm, Carlton and Street, represented the men in what they agreed would be a test case that would determine whether the Texas state constitution requiring racial separation or the U.S. Supreme Court's interpretation of the federal constitution forbidding the same would be the valid law of the state. On 26 August, a district judge in Big Spring, Charlie N. Sullivan, denied the injunction and gave his opinion that the laws and constitution of a state must yield if they conflict with the antisegregation decision of the high court. His ruling in effect cleared the way for local school boards to begin racial desegregation of the schools. Segregationists appealed their case to the Texas Supreme Court, where justices Few Brewster, Meade Griffin, and Ruel Walker upheld Sullivan's decision and voided the "separate but equal" doctrine in the Lone Star State. That fall, seven out of the twenty-one Big Spring black children who were certified as eligible to transfer to a white elementary school entered a new social reality, putting the town on the path toward abolishing precollegiate school segregation. The other fourteen remained at the black school. The city's eighty-nine black junior and senior high school students attended school that year in a new, $210,000 building erected to provide them the separate equality that had long been denied.[55]

Amarillo

The conflict between democracy and white supremacy challenged Potter County's Amarillo College much as it had Howard County Junior College. In the 1940s, black students and servicemen at Amarillo Air Force Base, complained that they were barred access to education or training beyond the high school level while whites could attend the local junior college. In 1950, Potter County, with Amarillo as its seat, had a population of 73,366. Known in the Texas panhandle as a leader in oil and gas production, cattle raising, and wheat cultivation, the county was 92.2 percent white, 4.8 percent black, and 3.0 percent Latin American. Growing steadily since its creation in 1929, Amarillo college had about 1,000 students and fifty faculty members in the early 1950s. Soon after the Court's decision in *Sweatt*, Reverend R. H. Hines, leader of the Amarillo chapter of the NAACP, approached the city school board, which administered the college, to discuss allowing blacks to enroll. Recognizing that the lawsuit under way to open Texarkana Junior College would, in A. Maceo Smith's words, "definitely affect Amarillo and 34 other Junior Colleges in Texas which exclude Negro students," and on the strength of the *Sweatt* decision, the board voluntarily dropped the color line.[56]

On 1 October 1951, when the Amarillo School Board voted to admit black students, Hines and the NAACP claimed a major victory. However, the board approved the admission of only qualified blacks who could prove residency inside the boundaries of the independent school district. Lane McAfee, president of the school board, explained that the board adopted the residency restriction "to prevent Negro students from all over the state from entering the school." Physically and politically, the school could not sustain what it believed might be a large influx of blacks to the junior college. On 3 October, just three black women enrolled as regular day students: Celia Ann Bennett, in premedical studies; Johnnie Mae Cartez, in prenursing studies; and Dorothy Reese, in home economics. Dr. A. M. Meyer remarked that Amarillo College had experienced "no unpleasant incidents whatsoever. We have found that the students, both white and Negro, get along extremely well."[57]

The board made explicit that the decision to desegregate arose from practical interests and not out of any desire to practice social or racial reform. The good Reverend Hines and the NAACP, on the other hand, relished their roles as reformers and pushed to extend desegregation into the city's primary and secondary schools. Dr. J. O. Wyatt, a prominent black physician in Amarillo, added another dimension to the fight for equal rights and justice when he announced his candidacy for the school board in the spring elections. He did not win, but for his effort, he did get eight white boys to leave a burning cross in his driveway. He responded to the gesture: "I do not consider this an expression of public sentiment and it will not alter my plans at all. I have felt during my years of residence here that the people are not like that." Undeterred, black advocates of integration secured from the board a plan for desegregation of the local schools to begin in the fall of 1955, but when the Citizens' Council members filed their lawsuit at Big Spring, they abruptly abandoned the plan. Thus, Amarillo College and Howard County Junior College, as the first public undergraduate institutions of higher learning in Texas to admit blacks and depart from the traditions of social separatism, set examples of how to make a smooth transition to integration, but their success did not lead their respective communities toward immediate change at the precollegiate level. If anything, they made their towns become lightning rods attracting concerted, albeit futile, resistance from extreme social conservatives.[58]

Corpus Christi

Del Mar Junior College, the one other two-year institution of higher education in Texas to desegregate before the *Brown* decision, perhaps enjoyed the most successful and far-reaching transformation of caste arrangements experienced anywhere in the state prior to May of 1954. At midcentury, Nueces County, which had the coastal jewel Corpus Christi as its seat, had a population of 165,471. With a naval air station and a strong local economy driven by a diverse mix of agricultural and industrial production, commerce, tourism, and the oil and gas business, Nueces was home to an Anglo majority (57.1 percent of its population) that thoroughly dominated county life. Nueces had 7,943 blacks, who made up 4.8 percent of the population; Latin Americans made up 38.1 percent. Black Corpus Christians for decades watched as their white neighbors took advantage of Nueces being one of the richest and fastest growing Texas counties. They also observed their Mexican American neighbors rouse from their slumbers in the late 1920s and openly attack school segregation based on language. The League of United Latin American Citizens and the American G.I. Forum, founded in 1929 and 1948, respectively, were two of the major Mexican American protest groups that developed in the twentieth century. Their growth can be attributed to the work of Corpus Christi leaders like businessman Ben Garza and medical doctor Hector P. García. The latter leader, moreover, would become a key ally of the black movement for civil and human rights.[59]

When the Corpus Christi Independent School District (CCISD) established Del Mar in 1935 in the city's white senior high school, Mexican Americans could enroll, but the school barred blacks altogether. The district furnished education to blacks in three facilities: the Booker T. Washington Elementary School, the George Washington Carver School, and the Solomon M. Coles High School. In the late 1940s, Harry Coleman, president of the local NAACP branch, began an exchange of letters with the CCISD regarding the woeful conditions of the black schools. In a move contrary to NAACP national policy, Coleman requested that "our Negro schools be made equal in all respects to the other schools of the city." Ray West, president of the CCISD board of trustees, answered the NAACP equalization demand with promises that a renovation program involving all of the schools would be completed by the start of the 1950 spring semester.

He also noted that "years before it was required by law, this system [CCISD] adopted a single salary schedule for all teachers. . . . We have been trying to do the best possible for all students." The board, which administered the junior college until 1950, when it separated from the district and formed its own board of regents composed exclusively of Anglo men, also approved adult education and night school classes in English at the black high school. In 1946, when the junior college added the adult and vocational department to meet the educational demands of returning veterans, Del Mar also organized "Negro classes" at what officials dubbed the Solomon Coles Junior College for Negroes. By 1948, E. L. Williams, director of the department, boasted that twenty students would graduate from this program.[60]

In June of 1952, however, campus administrators rejected black applications to classes at Del Mar on the basis that the law of segregation prevented them from doing otherwise. With that decree, prominent black dentist and longtime NAACP member H. Boyd Hall sprung into action. Appearing before the Del Mar board of regents he apprised them that the *Sweatt* decision and other rulings of the Supreme Court nullified the state's segregation laws where it could be proven that equal education had not been provided to blacks. An investigations committee confirmed the inequality between the black and the white schools in regard to academic program, library, physical plant, courses, and schedules. Moreover, it concluded that "it would take a minimum of $300,000 to bring Coles Junior College up to Del Mar." Dr. Hall had already served notice that he would file a lawsuit for the educational rights of black Corpus Christians, so when the board of regents concluded they did not have the funds necessary to create separate equality, they determined that their only alternative was to desegregate. Thus, with no show of reluctance or negative statements, the board voted unanimously to admit blacks who lived in the Corpus Christi Junior College district area beginning 1 September. Del Mar president E. L. Harvin, formerly a history professor, expressed optimism about the decision and noted that students had registered no objections to the admission of blacks and that he anticipated no trouble.[61]

Del Mar experienced no trouble at all over its desegregation in 1952 when perhaps a dozen black students entered the student body of 3,876. Indeed, if pictures in the 1953 and 1954 annuals, the *Cruiser*, tell the story, it is one of remarkable, affirmative acceptance. Alice Fay James and Lavernis Royal, two outstanding students who desegregated the campus, became leaders looked up to by black, brown, and white students alike. James received the support of the African American, Anglo, and Mexican American student members of the LaMar Club to become its president. In women's intramural basketball, she also helped lead the club to victory and played on the All-Stars team. Royal took the art department by storm and as a student of Mary Johnson he designed and produced the thespian plaques that adorned each side of the stage in the school's Thimble Theater. He also acted on that stage as a member of the Red Masque Players. In a class photograph of an art appreciation class with five young women, Royal is pictured seated in the back row with the two white male students. In his first and sophomore years, members of his class elected him their representative to the Student Council and that body elected him council historian. In later years, the college bestowed its highest honor on Royal by inducting him into its Hall of Fame. Black students also entered vocational training classes such as auto mechanics. Apparently, even older, working-class whites accepted the presence of blacks. Corpus Christi's readiness to desegregate relative to the larger society's is indicative of many years of strong interracial solidarity-building in the city. Although the CCISD undertook desegregation in 1955, with black students enrolling in previously all-white schools, segregation of African American and Mexican American students and faculty remained a contentious issue in Corpus Christi throughout the next two decades.[62]

Roadblocks in the Deep East

NAACP southwestern regional counsel Ulysses S. Tate wrote in a letter to all branch officers on 1 August 1952 that the opening of Howard County Junior College, Amarillo College, and Del Mar Junior College in the early 1950s was "good news." He also asked local leaders not to doubt that such change could occur and reminded them that "a right GAINED and not USED is NO right at all." He told them to encourage young people to apply to their nearest junior college for admission, especially if they lived near Big Spring, Amarillo, or Corpus Christi, and to watch the battles under way to open the East Texas junior colleges in Wichita Falls, Texarkana, and Kilgore. Tate emphasized that branches should discuss their plans with the regional office before moving "into a fight" because his office had "the KNOW HOW to help you. Do not go off before you are ready. But do not stand still." He pledged that "[w]e can help you get ready" and "we will help you do the job right." Rebuking the naysayer, Tate volleyed, "Some will say that you cannot do it, but the facts prove that we can. We have done it and the white community has shown a readiness to advance with us."[63]

Despite Tate's appeal, only one other public two-year institution desegregated before the *Brown* decision: San Angelo College in West Texas. NAACP activists and others launched antisegregation efforts in several places, but their work came to no avail. In East Texas, at Hardin Junior College/Midwestern University, Texarkana Junior College, and Kilgore Junior College, resistance to desegregation proved stiff, and legal battles ensued, not ending until the fall of 1954 or later. After September of 1954, when seven junior colleges joined the five already open, the NAACP's southwestern regional office reported, "[T]he back of racial segregation in junior colleges in Texas has been broken. There is little doubt that exception [*sic*] for those in deep east Texas, the remainder of our junior colleges [will be] open to Negro applicants as soon as they present themselves and make a demand." Tate did not exaggerate the importance of the victories at the junior college level, but even with a broken back, segregation in East Texas junior colleges would prove a formidable adversary in the years ahead.[64]

Defrocking Jim Crow

An additional area of collegiate desegregation in the early 1950s involved denominational schools and religious seminaries. In September of 1950, the Austin Presbyterian Theological Seminary became the first postsecondary school in Texas to voluntarily admit blacks. The all-male seminary under the leadership of David L. Stitt opened its doors to Daniel Clark. Not much is known about his experience except that he studied on the campus of a little more than 100 students and about a dozen faculty members. The seminary was organized in 1902 and became affiliated with the largest of the four Presbyterian sects in Texas, the Presbyterian Church in the United States. It trained the vast majority of the state's educated Presbyterian ministers, and, with Clark's admission, black men, especially those from any of the twenty-one Colored Cumberland Presbyterian churches, were allowed to enroll. A year before the Austin school desegregated, the board of trustees at Trinity University in San Antonio, another Presbyterian institution, approved the admission of black servicemen to its evening division at its downtown satellite campus. In so doing, it helped the armed forces fulfill its obligation to provide equal educational opportunities to all soldiers regardless of race. Texas Presbyterians, though they have never sought nor received the credit, took the lead in dropping the color line in its institutions of higher education. The Austin seminary, moreover, became the second Presbyterian institution in the South to admit blacks after Columbia Theological Seminary in Decatur, Georgia, admitted E. E. Newberry in September of 1948. Louisville Presbyterian Theological Seminary in Kentucky opened its doors in May of 1950, but its first student did not arrive until September. The Reverend Snowden I. McKinnon, assistant pastor of Mount Corinth Baptist Church in Houston, traveled to Louisville to become the only black in the seminary's Centennial Class of 1953. The Texan attended Emmett Scott High School in Tyler, studied a year at TSUN, and received a B.A. degree with honors from Fisk University in 1950. He exemplifies how black Texans took the lead in desegregating higher education in the early 1950s, both inside and outside the state.[65]

Southern Methodist University (SMU) was the second private school to inch toward desegregation. SMU officially decreed in 1950 that it would admit blacks to its Perkins School of Theology in January of 1951. Previously, blacks had been allowed to audit classes in the theological school, but they did not receive credit nor could they obtain a degree for their work. Dean Eugene B. Hawk of the seminary explained the SMU board's motive for allowing a graduates of Huston College and Jarvis Christian College to become students at the state's fifth largest university and the premier institution of higher learning in the Dallas–Fort Worth area. We are trying, he explained, "to do something Christian for Negro students. The school can and should provide a service to a great group of people, that will go far toward saving them to the church and from the inroads of communism and other false and subtle philosophies."[66]

SMU officials refused to do anything "Christian" for black undergraduates until many years later, but opening its graduate school of theology, along with the desegregation of Austin Presbyterian Theological Seminary, encouraged other denominational schools to question its adherence to segregation. Southwestern Baptist Theological Seminary in Fort Worth and Wayland Baptist College in Plainview desegregated in the summer of 1951, and Saint Mary's University in San Antonio and Texas Christian University's Brite College of the Bible in Fort Worth entered the fold in 1952. The desegregation of these schools provides evidence that the leadership in major Christian religions — Baptists, Catholics, and Disciples of Christ — grappled with the injustice and hypocrisy of racial segregation.

Southwestern Baptist Theological Seminary (SWBTS) received its charter from the state of Texas on 14 March 1908. Originally located in Waco, it moved to Fort Worth in 1910. The school grew out of Baylor University's Theological Seminary, from which it separated in 1907. The Baptist General Convention of Texas, which ran both institutions, ceded control of the Fort Worth school to the Southern Baptist Convention in 1925. Fully accredited, the SWBTS offered bachelor's, master's, and doctor's degrees and at one time was the largest evangelical seminary in the world. Its board of trustees was also responsible for setting policy for the Southern Baptist Seminary in Louisville, the Baptist Seminary in New Orleans, and the Golden Gate Seminary in San Francisco. The latter school never "barred students of any race," but the Texas, Louisiana, and Kentucky seminaries did strictly adhere to segregation. In 1951, all three institutions ended their ban on blacks. The Fort Worth school emerged as a leader among the schools in promoting the change.[67]

Thomas Buford Maston, the social activist and theological conservative who cautiously championed a re-envisioning of the Baptist Church's views on race, was behind the victory of desegregation of the Texas seminary after almost three decades of quietly advocating such reform from within. He defined his approach: "[S]tart where the people are and keep the pressure in the right place, pointed in the right direction. This eventually would yield desirable and lasting results." Where he started was among a thoroughly reactionary, white supremacist, and socially conservative bunch of Texas Baptists. He practiced patience, kindness, balance, empathy, and restraint with his white brethren, but he also could be exhortatory, declarative, urgent, and assertive.[68]

In April of 1946, just when Heman Sweatt and the Texas University Movement had begun their nearly five-year-long battle against segregation in Texas higher education, the Fort Worth branch of the NAACP held a monthly forum at Morning Chapel CME Church and invited Maston to be its principal speaker. Forthrightly, the seminarian addressed himself to the theme of the meeting, asserting that "the church must take the lead" in the fight to "get equal educational opportunities for Negroes," for the problem of segregation "is primarily moral and spiritual." He prophesied that black and white students would eventually attend the same schools and held that such a development "ought to start on the high level — among the professionals — and there first among the church schools." The native Tennessean of impoverished, working-class origins declared that the right to equal educational opportunities was a moral right, and he explained that "right is based on the character and will of God and in his SIGHT all people are alike." Admonishing blacks to keep up the fight for their rights, he observed that "one of the biggest problems of the Negro race is to get more of 'your own people' behind such moves as this." Blacks kept fighting, and five years later Maston's seminary found itself "bringing up the rear."

For all Maston's influence among Texas Baptists, the SWBTS did not admit blacks to its regular day classes until 25 May 1951. With over 600 students in its summer session and over 1,700 in the regular academic year, the SWBTS represented the largest school to fully desegregate. In an interview years later, the ethicist claimed that the faculty of Southwestern would have admitted blacks earlier, but the trustees and Southern Baptists at the mass level effectively resisted change. When it did desegregate, however, the seminary laid no restrictions as to the field or the level of study opened to blacks. UT and SMU were larger, but they adhered to a restricted desegregation policy. The black men who first entered SWBTS and helped elevate the moral condition of the white men there were Chester Brookings, S. M. Lockeridge, and Getral Wright. When Maston spoke at the NAACP forum and said "whites cannot lift themselves by keeping the Negro down," he presented a basic moral principle that echoed ideas of Booker T. Washington and other thinkers on the race problem in the world. Of course, he

131

had earned some stripes for his public remarks, especially those in his book *Of One*, a frank study of race from a scriptural standpoint, which, when published in 1946, established him as the leading spokesman for racial justice among white Texas Baptists and embroiled him in no small amount of controversy. However, after admitting Brookings, Lockeridge, Wright, and other blacks in course, he, other faculty members, and President Lee Rutland acquired a more personal and visceral appreciation for the meaning of social equality. They had to defend their decision before the censure of prominent Baptists such as Dallas cleric W. A. Criswell, and, more important, they had to close the intellectual gap between themselves and rank-and-file members of the church for whom white supremacy remained as abiding an article of faith as the belief that Jesus Christ is the only begotten son of God who died on the cross to bring the possibility of salvation to all people. As Maston pointed out, to defend desegregation by pleading "thus saith the law" was to abdicate moral leadership to state action. What ultimately won over many church leaders, such as Criswell, was the contradiction in sending missionaries to Africa to spread the good news while practicing Jim Crow and sharing the bad news of racial discrimination at home. As for the white masses, the opening of swbts amounted to no more than a small step in challenging their racial attitudes. Indeed, it could be seen as merely the fulfilling of a duty of the superior race, another part of the white man's burden, to let the most gifted and talented black savages who desired to forsake their heathen ways come and study theology and the Christian life with the best and brightest of the great white race. Maston and many of his colleagues in 1951 may have gotten beyond such retrograde and paternalist attitudes, but their fold had not. The shepherds' work against racial hatred and hierarchy had just begun.[69]

Wayland Baptist

Immediately on the heels of the desegregation of swbts, Wayland Baptist College accepted four blacks to the 1951 summer term. The action, however, had no relation to the seminary changing its admission standards. For some time, blacks, especially school teachers needing "leveling out" courses that would enable them to renew their contracts and become eligible for promotions, had inquired whether the college might allow them to take extension courses or segregated courses, if it would not forthrightly admit them to the school. Since it was a private school, the state constitution's provision against educating blacks and whites together had no binding force. The binding force of white supremacy and separatism, however, precluded any racial intermingling up until the spring of 1951, when Annie Taylor put her story to Wayland's president, J. W. "Bill" Williams. Taylor, a teacher in Floydada, the seat of Floyd County, twenty-eight miles from the college in Plainview, the seat of neighboring Hale County, had to acquire graduate course work that summer or she could not return to her job that fall. Without her, moreover, the black children of Floydada would go without instruction. As she found leaving to attend classes at Prairie View or Houston too inconvenient, it was Wayland or bust. Williams prayed on the matter and received an inspiration. During the week of final examinations, President Williams called the student body and the thirty-and-some-odd faculty members to a general convocation to discuss "Miss Annie" Taylor's application. In a ballot on whether the college should admit her and other Negroes, only 9 out of 274 objected to the idea; no faculty members opposed her admission. Marshall took news of the vote to the meeting of Wayland's board of trustees the next night and asked them to "do right," for "if we do right, God will see we come out right." Although two trustees voted against admitting blacks, thirteen other members of the board ultimately elected to open "the academic facilities of Wayland College . . . to students of all races and nationalities."[70]

Three other local teachers followed Taylor into Wayland: Bessie Williams and Ernest and Vera Dykes. Together they made Wayland the first, private, nonseminary four-year institution to eliminate its whites-only admissions policy. President Marshall did not shy away from the opportunity to use the media attention showered on the small college to trumpet the idealism that lay behind his motivation: "We felt like it was the Christian thing to do, the thing to do in harmony with democratic principles." Dean Preston James answered reporters' queries about why the college did not set up segregated classes to accommodate Taylor and other blacks by saying such arrangements would have been impossible at Wayland. A month after the news got out that Wayland had enrolled four black students, Marshall reported that of the fifty letters the college received regarding its desegregation only five voiced regret over the board's decision. Marshall felt good about the ratio of supportive to negative correspondence, "since objectors generally voice their opinion quicker than people for a program."[71]

Although the articles about Wayland's desegregation noted that at close to fifty years of age Taylor was a mother of five with two children enrolled as students at Prairie View College, few bothered to quote Taylor regarding how she felt about integrating Wayland. Carter Wesley editorialized that Wayland's desegregation represented part of some significant "cracks in the dam the oligarchy of the South has been at pains to build to keep the Negro from equal opportunity" in that it involved religious leaders taking up the "moral question" of segregation in education. "To a very large extent," Wesley asserted, the religious leadership set "the moral tone of the community." Identifying the private colleges of the South as "leading the way" against racial discrimination, the editor noted that segregation,

Annie Taylor, a forty-eight-year-old teacher from Floydada, upon entering Wayland Baptist University in June of 1951 to take classes necessary to keep her teacher certification, made the school the first four-year, liberal arts college in the former Confederate South to voluntarily end segregation. She was joined by Bessie Williams and Ernest and Vera Dykes (Wayland Baptist University).

like chattel slavery, "has had church sanction since its inception." "If and when this sanction is removed," he continued, "all politicians in the South will not be able to keep it going." Throughout the 1950s and 1960s, Texas Baptist leadership openly debated the issue of racial injustice and changing the "moral tone" of the largest denomination in the state. Transformation of racial attitudes occurred slowly, if at all, but a crucial source of change among Baptists came from the early Christian march toward desegregation of the faith's institutions of higher learning.[72]

With 1,332,187 members in 1953, the Roman Catholic Church in Texas had a particularly strong presence in San Antonio, where it operated five institutions of higher learning. Meyer Weinberg in his *Chance to Learn: A History of Race and Education in the United States* identified Catholic colleges such as the ones in San Antonio as having been "notoriously exclusionary." The first Catholic school to desegregate in Texas and the River City, Saint Mary's University held the distinction of being the state's oldest college in continuous operation. In 1852, Bishop John Mary Odin secured the help of brothers from the Society of Mary to found the school for white boys. It became a senior college in 1926, adding a law school in 1934 and a graduate division in 1937. As the university grew, various departments went coeducational, but it did not admit women to all programs until 1963. Saint Mary's quiet move toward racial desegregation occurred a few years after Archbishops Joseph Ritter in St. Louis and Patrick O'Boyle in Washington, D.C., put Catholic schools on the road to ending racial segregation in 1947. In the early 1950s, San Antonio's Archbishop Robert E. Lucey began to lead his diocese in the direction of racial inclusiveness and would help make the city a model for the state in its peaceful transition away from the Anglocentric, separatist tradition that governed its schools and institutions. In 1952, Hattie Elam Briscoe, a licensed cosmetology instructor with a master's degree from Prairie View A&M, began taking night classes at St. Mary's School of Law. She graduated first in her class in 1956. During her initial semester at the university, someone told her she "had no business being there." She responded, "I am a woman, I am in law school and I am going to become a lawyer." At forty years old she did just that and in the process garnered a number of "first" distinctions: the first black woman to graduate from St. Mary's, the first black woman to receive a law degree from a Texas university, and one of the first black women attorneys in the Lone Star State. From her office in the Preachers Professional Building, she practiced law for more than four decades.

Texas Christian University's (TCU) Brite College of the Bible first open its doors to a black graduate seminarian in September of 1952. The divinity school had been a part of the university since 1914 and constituted the premier theological seminary of the Christian Church (Disciples of Christ) in the Southwest. The student, James Lee Clairborne, of Green-

135

wood, Mississippi, had earned his baccalaureate degree from Jarvis Christian College and become pastor of Mount Olive Christian Church in the Northeast Texas town of Henderson. His connection to the Christian Church through Jarvis proved felicitous. J. J. and Ida Jarvis of Fort Worth not only donated the 456 acres that became the campus of the black denominational college named in their honor but also had a lengthy history of donating to TCU. The two schools had significant connections through private philanthropists and members of religious organizations like the Christian Women's Board of Missions of the Disciples of Christ, which may have influenced the board to initiate desegregation.[73]

Although Jarvis and TCU lacked any formal arrangements for inter-collegiate cooperation, the white institution's board of trustees looked sympathetically at an application coming from an alumnus of its black counterpart. The board announced that it would "admit Negro students who have completed their A.B. work at a standard college and who meet all scholastic and character requirements, to Brite College of the Bible to work for a graduate degree or degrees in preparation for full time church service." The board stated that "it is understood that such Negro students must meet the same standards and requirements for this graduate work which have to be met by all other students." The rest of TCU refused to admit blacks for almost a decade more.[74]

The Road to *Brown*

On the basis of Heman Sweatt's travail, the Texas University Movement produced fourteen victories in the years before the Supreme Court ruled in 1954 that segregated education violated the Fourteenth Amendment of the U.S. Constitution. From Amarillo to Brownsville, from Houston to Big Spring, the students who entered classrooms created by people who never envisioned that a day would come when whites and blacks might sit as equals and study morality, law, art, human anatomy, and anything else their minds cared to explore had started something. What they started is minimally explained by the degrees they attained and hardly at all by the word "desegregation."

The "all-out war" of those for and against segregation in the pre-*Brown* period has been rewritten in popular memory as a prelude rather than as a period of struggle in its own right. It would become easy to diminish the accomplishments of the years between 1949 and 1954. In *A Chance to Learn*, Meyer Weinberg wrote disparagingly that "much of what was represented as the opening of southern graduate schools turned out to be an increase in graduate departments of education. Black students in graduate departments of natural sciences, social sciences, or humanities were exceedingly rare."[75]

For Texas, however, given the UT-TSUN "contract" policy, black students continued to be barred from graduate departments of education at white universities because such degree programs already existed at Prairie View or TSUN. Thus, by the time the Court ruled in *Brown*, in Galveston, Austin, and Houston, black Texans had started earning doctoral and professional degrees in the natural and social sciences, in the humanities, and in those fields where previously they had to leave the South or travel long distances to find institutions that did not ban them because of their African ancestry.

From 1949 to 1954, for the first time in history, black Texans took their struggle for human rights to the grassroots level. The campaign for the vote and the attempts of black workers to appeal to the Fair Employment Practices Commission involved important, elite-level, preparatory steps; but a more mass-based movement for racial justice fully emerged in the fight for equal education. A black consensus formed: social equality would remain elusive until the race won its right to equal educational opportunity and entered white institutions of higher learning. Whites also began to perceive that blacks had begun a process of achieving social equality, and many began to react negatively and violently. After 1954, moreover, angry white men and women began organizing to halt or at least retard blacks' march toward an integrated equality. Their organized response, among other important ramifications, polarized state politics and drew the state government into an active role as an agent of political repression.

CHAPTER FIVE

Democracy Is on the March in Texas
Black Equality versus White Power, 1955–1957

Mrs. Davis wanted to know if the Attorney General's office was investigating the White Citizen's Councils. I told her that I did not know; that I knew I wasn't investigating them. . . . The Davis's followed us out to our car, and Mr. Davis stated that "Democracy is on the march in Texas," and that this investigation would blow over as soon as it had served John Ben Shepperd's political purposes. I asked him if he was expecting me to comment on that statement. He laughed, and said, "No," and we drove off.

— Riley Fletcher, NAACP investigator, September 1956

Solicit applicants who are going to college, urging Negroes to attend desegregated colleges, and the whites to attend Negro colleges. You have very little time for this last item. Another effort should be made before the January, 1956, session begins. This work must be done. "The future belongs only to those who prepare for it."

— Texas NAACP Memorandum to Youth Councils, 8 August 1955

Through *Brown*, the civil rights movement gave the United States a new and radical interpretation of its Constitution — so much for that. Almost two years after the ruling, Thurgood Marshall, the attorney who presented the school desegregation cases before the Supreme Court, had to go about addressing critics who called themselves friends of racial justice but who chastised the NAACP for "moving too fast" in its fight against racial segregation. At the annual Conference on Human Relations at Central State College in Wilberforce, Ohio, on 14 April 1956, Marshall gave his answer to "so-called liberals" and others who felt that the NAACP was "pushing too hard" and that the war against segregation could not be won: "Saying it [desegregation] can't be done is like telling the Federal Government it can't make you pay your income tax. They can't make you pay it, but if you don't you'll be cracking rocks."[1]

Cracking rocks indeed. Who would arrest, indict, prosecute, convict, sentence, much less put on the chain gang to bust rocks: white supremacists maintaining school segregation? The "Bull" Connors of the South? Judges, legislators, and governors in the southern states? The U.S. Supreme Court that mandated no timetable for local school boards to develop or implement desegregation plans but merely exhorted them to move "with all deliberate speed" in that direction? Would the federal executive under the leadership of Dwight D. Eisenhower enforce the law? No. Marshall's analogy amounted to amusing hyperbole and nothing more. No white man would send another white man to prison to crack rocks for refusing to mix the races in the country's schools. As clear as the broad nose on the Sphinx's face, placing white girls next to black boys in the same classrooms filled many otherwise respectable white men with a fear and loathing that cut deep into their psyches. No less a respectable white man than Eisenhower himself argued the case against interracial commingling and the sexual activity to which it must, of course, lead. At a White House white men's only "stag" dinner just after oral arguments in the *Brown* case, a few months before the Court's ruling, the president explained to Chief Justice Earl Warren, Attorney General Herbert Brownell, United Nations ambassador Henry Cabot Lodge Jr., Harvard Law School dean Erwin Griswold, prosegregation attorney John W. Davis, and Princeton professor Edward S. Corwin that white men had every right to object to their daughters having to be around black boys with their overgrown sex organs and lascivious psyches. In his memoirs, Warren recalled Eisenhower remarking that whites who objected to desegregation "are not bad people. All they are concerned about is to see that their sweet little girls are not required to sit in school along side some big overgrown Negroes." Moreover, the president said, decent white men would strenuously object to the federal government intruding into southern race relations to enforce integration. This conversation among some of the most powerful men in the world's most powerful and technologically advanced country is suggestive of the dismal mental condition of certain white male elites on the eve of the *Brown* decision.[2]

Of course, other elite white men were not content to plug their nostrils and reluctantly accept the dismantling of the country's dual system of education. Rising to the defense of his state and the South on 18 May 1954, the day after the Court announced its decision in the school segregation cases, U.S. senator Price Daniel, former Texas attorney general, proceeded "to place in the Record the facts as to the past and as to the good faith of the people of 17 States in maintaining our separate school systems." His "study of the issue" of segregation compelled him "to disagree with the latest opinions of the Court," but he emphasized that his disagreement with the "new law" did not spring from an inborn "prejudice or a desire to discriminate against either white or the colored race, or because of hatred, or a feeling of superiority." He claimed he never lived among people who held to their heart such a malignant feeling for blacks: "The only defense and justification for the doctrine [of separate and equal schools] have been that in certain localities it has been impossible to maintain peace, order, and harmony among the people, and to have support for the public-school system by the taxpayers, when people are forced to mingle together against the will of the majority of each race."[3] Thus, a revisionist view of Reconstruction again reared its ugly head some four-score years later in the Texas lawyer's speech before the U.S. Congress. The myth, which could have been lifted directly from Thomas Dixon's *Clansman*, claimed that northerners foisted on the vanquished white people of the South close association with blacks, their former chattel slaves, with dire results: violence, chaos, and rupture. If a second reconstruction had to occur that would avoid the tragedies of the first one, Daniel argued, a mutually "tolerant" view would be necessary, as well as an appreciation of the "good faith shown by the people of the South and other States in attempting to provide equal school facilities through separate schools." He predicted that "if those who are disappointed in the decision are tolerant, and if those who hail the decision are tolerant, I believe these problems can be worked out in the future."[4]

Carter Wesley hailed the *Brown* decision but also urged blacks "to refuse to be inveigled, enticed or challenged into any kind of debate or discussion with whites." Calling for a slow-going, humble posture, he noted that "the Negro gained the victory with the decision, and there is nothing to be gained from arguing or discussing, or even just talking about it with whites." If blacks would shut up and let white racists vent their spleens, he forecasted, they would cool off and eventually become "harmless." He also charged that the "race issue" did not belong in the 1954 Democratic runoff race for governor between Allan Shivers, the social conservative, and Ralph Yarborough, the economic liberal. Shivers race-baited a desperate Yarborough on school desegregation to the point that Yarborough was "stupid enough to make a definitive statement on his position," Wesley wrote. Yarborough announced his support for separate schools, despite his having received the overwhelming support of black voters in the first primary election. Wesley felt that Yarborough simply should have pledged to obey the law and not have taken sides on *Brown*; nevertheless, Wesley encouraged blacks to vote against Shivers to censure him for injecting race into the campaign and to register their approval of *Brown*. The black vote in the runoff primary again went to Yarborough.[5]

The race-baiting in the gubernatorial contest of 1954 came as the sound before the fury. The aim of the rising hue and cry for massive resistance to desegregation inside Texas and throughout the South was to secure government cooperation to control school officials and to intimidate blacks from the struggle for racial justice along integrationist lines. In the short run, recalcitrant white supremacists in Texas won. Shivers and the Shiverscrats, a Texas version of Strom Thurmond's Dixiecrats, won election on a platform strongly opposed to the civil rights and liberties of blacks, Mexicans, and organized labor. Although more colleges and many school districts did begin admitting blacks after *Brown*, white power continued to deny blacks equality and kept desegregation at a token level into the 1960s. Finally, the forces of white power also came close to silencing organized integration activists and did effectively prevent the Texas civil rights movement from galvanizing a strong, mass base, especially among grassroots working people. With no enabling legislation, the attorney general's office launched a full-scale investigation into the activities of NAACP branches, which culminated in legal action that effectively killed the association in 1957. By 1954, the "season of hope" that opened with the enlargement of black political participation with the 1944 *Smith* v. *Allwright* decision had yielded to a "time of turbulence and despair."[6]

In higher education, the court's desegregation decree on 17 May 1954 had an uneven effect on the pace and course of events. That summer, North Texas State College desegregated its graduate school and Midwestern University (MU) accepted blacks under court order. In the fall of 1954, six junior colleges opened their doors to black students. Before 1958, seven public senior colleges desegregated as a result of lawsuits or threatened litigation that state officials knew they would lose. In legal precedent, litigants had all they needed in *Sweatt* to force desegregation on Texas colleges and universities. The case of Willie Faye Battle and her fellow applicants to Midwestern University proved that blacks could defeat segregation without a comprehensive ruling on *Plessy*. For civil libertarians, however, *Brown* came as manna from above. At last, it put the great charter of American citizenship, the U.S. Constitution, in their arsenal. However, for black people who took the decision seriously, *Brown* soon caused more pain and frustration than it brought joy and hope. As never before, desegregation advocates received negative sanctions from the state.[7]

Brown unfolded in two parts. The 1954 decision held that school segregation was an unconstitutional denial of equal protection of the law. A year later, the Court decreed that states must abandon the "separate but equal" principle set forth in *Plessy* and create a unitary system of public education. Contrary to the wishes of the NAACP and other civil libertarians, the Court established a flexible schedule for desegregation expressed in the ambiguous phrase "with all deliberate speed." Focusing on the fight for desegre-

141

gation of colleges, rather than the public schools, brings the meaning of *Brown* into sharper relief. Moreover, between 1954 and 1957, Texas higher education remained the most significant battleground of the civil rights struggle. The NAACP exhorted Texas branch leaders to widen the field of struggle to grade schools, public accommodations, and other fronts, but the fight to open the state colleges continued as the key arena of litigation and mobilization.

Between 1946, the year Sweatt launched his case, and 1956, one year after the second *Brown* decision, the NAACP coordinated legal battles against college segregation in seven locations, all but one involving East Texas institutions. Before the *Brown* ruling, brave plaintiffs filed three lawsuits: *Battle et al.* v. *Wichita Falls Junior College District et al.* in 1951 and *Allan* v. *Masters* (Kilgore) and *Bruce* v. *Stilwell* (Texarkana) in 1952. After *Brown*, equally courageous applicants filed four suits: *Atkins* v. *Matthews* (Denton), *Whitmore* v. *Stilwell* (Texarkana), and *White* v. *Smith* (El Paso) in 1955 and *Jackson* v. *McDonald* (Beaumont) in 1956. Significant and related movement work also occurred in Sulphur Springs, Austin, Wharton, and Kingsville. An intensive study of the clash of the forces of white power and black equality in these ten cities presents a different interpretation of what revisionist historians have called the *Brown* backlash thesis. The difference has less to do with any reputed Texas exceptionalism than with the dynamic force of ideological hegemony and its relationship to social change.[8]

Massive Resistance and Texas Higher Education

In immediate response to *Brown*, Texas commissioner of education J. W. Edgar instructed the public schools of the state to make no attempt at changing their policies of racial separatism and hierarchy. Although all districts except for the schools of Friona (which remained the West Texas town's best-kept secret until 1955) followed his edict, it did not slow the momentum toward collegiate desegregation. In the summer of 1954, North Texas State College voluntarily began admitting black students at the graduate level only. Six public junior colleges announced their desegregation, and under court order, Midwestern University opened its doors to blacks, making it the first public four-year college in Texas to fully desegregate. Although grade schools remained segregated in 1954, to hard-core white supremacists, collegiate desegregation represented the writing on the wall. The Associated Citizens' Council of Texas (ACCT), the key group in the state that organized massive resistance, grew from the leadership of men and women who had opposed the desegregation of higher education.[9]

Although a majority of Texans still favored maintaining segregation of the races at the state's colleges and universities, in 1954, the *Texas Poll* revealed a softening of attitudes from 1948 to 1954 (see Table 4). The *Texas Poll*, which surveyed all racial groups, found that the Texans most resistant to desegregation in the schools had two key characteristics: they were Anglo-American and of low socioeconomic status. Initially, so-called poor white trash relied on their better educated and wealthier kinfolk for leadership, but two groups espousing differing tactics quickly emerged: racialists who called for fighting fire with fire power and massive resistance leaders who advocated fighting fire with fire, that is to say, blocking compliance with *Brown* at the courthouse and the statehouse. The first group, representing a more primordial instinct and primitive passion, resorted to terror and coercion. The second group promoted orderly resistance to desegregation.[10]

Only two months after the court's decision in the school segregation cases, white terrorists attacked the chair of the NAACP branch in Sulphur Springs, a small town of 9,000 in rural Hopkins County (88.8 percent white and 11.2 percent black), about seventy miles east of Dallas. NAACP branch leaders Hardy W. Ridge and his wife, Eleanor, held meetings in the grocery store they owned, and from 1952 had organized parents to picket the town's lone black school demanding its equalization with the white schools. Heartened by the Court's declaration that school segregation violated the Constitution, on 12 June 1954, Ridge and other members of an antidiscrimination committee petitioned the local school board to eradicate segregated schooling in Sulphur Springs. After the group threatened to file suit, district officials responded that they would follow the order of the Supreme Court and the Texas legislature. Two days after the school board meeting, two men approached Ridge about buying his business, the Quality Drugs and Cosmetics Store. Mindful of the southern protocol of never answering white men too directly, he equivocated and withheld giving them an answer. Threats against the Ridges started and finally, before the couple left one afternoon for church, a group of men created a disturbance outside their house, yelling to the neighbors who came outside in response to the commotion "what would happen to those uppity n——s." Later that night while the Ridges attended church services, terrorists shot up their home with shotguns and pistols. Police chief Lon Bleaton, who investigated, played down the matter, saying that some of the "niggers" who lived next to the Ridges' home were unreasonably fearful that a white race riot was about to "break loose" in their neighborhood but that most of the "niggers" did not feel terrorized. When Ridge appealed to the mayor and other city officials, one official told him, "If you don't like the way we are runni[n]g things here, why don't you try living in another part of the country?" A few days after the attack on his home, someone told Ridge point-blank: "You are a marked man." Immediately, he and his wife fled

Table 4. Results of *Texas Poll* Reports, 1948–1954

Question: "As you may know, the United States Supreme Court is now considering whether or not Negroes should be allowed to go to the same university as whites. Are you for or against Negroes and whites going to the same universities?"

	1948	1950	1953	1954
Against	76%	76%	59%	57%
For	20	20	31	36
Undecided	4	4	10	7

Source: Scott, "Twenty-Five Years of Opinion on Integration in Texas," 159.

"the state in fear of their lives." They moved to Cleveland, Ohio, never to return.[11]

The Sulphur Springs episode was not an isolated instance of white supremacists violently opposing black equality. Kilgore, in the East Texas county of Gregg, the birthplace of the Citizens' Council movement, provides an even bloodier example of terrorism in the state. Known as the "Oil City of the World" and "City of the Magic Skyline" because it sat in the center of the East Texas Oil Field and had over 1,000 producing derricks within its city limits, Kilgore had a population of nearly 9,700 in 1950. Gregg County was approximately three-fourths white and one-fourth black. Desegregation of the town's municipal junior college, with a student body of about 700, would very likely bring into close association a significant number of young blacks and whites. Thus, when opponents of segregation challenged the status quo in Kilgore, they tested white supremacy in the Lone Star State at its cultural heart. Their action drew out of the sewer of race hatred an unremitting enemy of black equal rights and the leading mouthpiece of reaction.[12]

When Norma Joyce Allen and ten other blacks applied to Kilgore Junior College in 1952, they were denied entry. With the help of NAACP southwestern regional counsel U. Simpson Tate, they filed suit against President Basil Earl Masters and other officials of the college in the U.S. District Court for the Eastern District of Texas at Tyler. Judge Joe Sheehy refused to hear the case until after the Supreme Court made its ruling in the school segregation cases. After the Court's 1954 ruling, the two-year delay ended. Tate appeared before the judge on 11 October prepared only to argue some pretrial motions. When Sheehy quickly dispensed with the defendants' motions, Tate had to ask for a recess to allow him to search for the witnesses he needed to try his case. I. S. "Ike" White of nearby Longview, the "community representative" whom Tate relied on to bring the student petitioners, reported to the courthouse without them. Unable to find any witnesses during a two-and-one-half hour recess, Tate returned and faced the "shamefulness" of his position. Sheehy granted a postponement, and the case was rescheduled for early in 1955. Tate avoided censure, but he exposed a critical vulnerability. The failure of his clients to appear at a hearing on *their* case suggested that Tate and the NAACP, rather than the students, were suing to open Kilgore Junior College. At the next court date, Tate had his witnesses and presented a credible case. Sheehy, who delayed his ruling until the Court made its implementation decree on 31 May 1955 in *Brown II*, instructed Kilgore Junior College (KJC) to admit qualified black applicants. On 15 July, school officials offered to accept the applications of four of the original eleven who had sued for admission, but none of these ultimately attended the institution. Edwin Washington Jr., NAACP assistant field secretary, reported in his 1 October annual report that "a special field trip was made to Longview and Kilgore to ascertain the number of students who would apply to the Kilgore Junior College, just opened. . . . Many promised to do so, but they have not done so, thus far." Indeed, by 15 October 1961, no one had applied.[13]

Gregg County, one of East Texas's most racist regions, gave birth to a wave of repression in the 1950s that matched the savage days following the emancipation of blacks from slavery. White terrorist activity discouraged Allen and other blacks from attempting to enroll in KJC. "A series of wanton shootings on Negro schools and dwellings" occurred in the county but barely received any mention in wire services, such as the Associated Press, or local newspapers. The *Texas Observer* helped expose the rash of violent attacks, and Tom Sutherland, director of the Texas Commission on Race Relations (TCRR), called upon East Texas pastors and newspaper editors to promote peaceful race relations, but the attacks continued unabated. Then, while the rest of the country registered shock and outrage over the cold-blooded lynching of Emmett Till in Money, Mississippi, on 28 August 1955, the murder in Gregg County of a sixteen-year-old black boy named John Earl Reese passed almost unnoticed. On a pleasant Saturday evening, 22 October, Reese sat in a café near the community of Mayflower with Joyce Nelson, thirteen, and her sister, Johnnie, fifteen. They had no idea that their young lives were in danger. Two beer-drinking white men, Joe Simpson, twenty-one, and Dean Ross, twenty-two, decided they had had enough with uppity blacks and that it was time to "make a raid." Simpson got behind the wheel of an automobile and Ross rode shotgun as they searched for their quarry. When they eyed the three teenagers, Simpson sped past the café and Ross aimed a 22-caliber rifle out the window and fired several rounds, wounding the Nelsons and killing Reese. The killers later tied the murder weapon to a log and tossed it into the Sabine River. Months went by before Captain Bob Crowder of the Texas Rangers cracked the case, arrested the gunmen, and wrung confessions from them. District

Attorney Ralph Prince of Longview gave greater attention to a newspaper editor who found evidence police officers overlooked than to the murder investigation itself. He downplayed the shooting as "a case of two irresponsible boys attempting to have some fun by scaring Negroes." The Reese murder and the indifferent attitude of local authorities led to a cruel irony: the first junior college in Texas that the federal court ordered to desegregate became one of the last to actually do so. The Kilgore Junior College case parallels the more famous episode at the University of Alabama, where Pollie Anne Myers and Artherine Lucy had attempted as early as 1952 to register. They won court-ordered admission in 1956, only to have violent racists and irresponsible officials make it impossible for African Americans to enroll there until the early 1960s.[14]

Massive resistance in Texas perhaps had its deepest roots in Gregg County. Days after Judge Sheehy's ruling in *Allen* v. *Masters*, which ended de jure segregation at KJC, Basil Earl Masters organized the state's first Citizens' Council. A deacon in the Baptist Church, former dean of Paris Junior College, first president of Amarillo College, and president emeritus of Kilgore Junior College, Masters had upper-class credibility. On the strength of his name, the Kilgore Council signed up 300 members at a single mass meeting and boasted that it had a membership of 1,500 by the end of the month; if this number was correct, this meant that about half of the white men of the town were dues-paying members of the council. Masters played a leading role in organizing other councils in several towns and cities in the more heavily black populated eastern section of the state. He also helped organize the Associated Citizens' Council of Texas in November 1955 at an assembly in Dallas of 250 white councillors from ten eastern counties. The ACCT elected as executive committee chair Ross Carlton, a Dallas lawyer who had gained notoriety for representing Big Spring councillors in *Blankenship* v. *McKinney*. After the meeting, Carlton blustered that Texas councils had 20,000 members, predicted that the numbers would continue to grow exponentially, and pledged that the ACCT would wage a full-scale battle against the NAACP. "Wittingly or unwittingly," the NAACP had "become the tool of the Communist Party," Carlton claimed. The ACCT adopted a motion to call upon Attorney General John Ben Shepperd to root out communism and the NAACP from Texas. Shepperd responded a few months later with an overt "war" against the NAACP. Initially, his cautious, consensus-building approach upset staunch segregationists and their opponents alike. When he polled the legislature as to whether he should submit an amicus curiae brief to the second phase of the *Brown* case, Texas senator Jimmy Phillips of Angleton, who favored continued segregation, indignantly replied that Shepperd was "the first attorney general I ever saw who needed the legislature's permission to file a brief." Although never a stranger to criticism, Shepperd remained a tried and true friend of white supremacy, demonstrating his support for massive resistance in the numerous meetings and consultations he held with leaders of the ACCT and in his assistance of the group's efforts to be certified as an educational rather than political organization.[15]

When Shepperd left public office in 1956, Carlton stepped down from the top leadership position of the ACCT to run for attorney general. Masters continued as the fire-breathing prophet of massive resistance. Tom Sutherland, a descendant of an early Anglo-Texan filibuster and Confederate general, described Masters's techniques and the influence he could wield to great effect. Dubbing him the "guiding spirit" of the Texas Citizens' Councils, the TCRR director observed that Masters's message mixed Christianity and a semimythical version of world history with paranoiac fears of black sexual potency and genetic dominance into an emotionally charged argument for maintaining white supremacy by any means necessary. To Masters, the greatest danger confronting the white race, whom he identified as the chosen people of God, was the horror of "mongrelization," or the loss of racial purity. The football-loving educator with degrees from Yale, Baylor, and the University of Texas, would shout with all the energy in his gaunt body *his* stories of race and power: "India — once a great race . . . tall, blond people. But they mixed with Negroes and look at them today. A thousand American soldiers could whip them. Spain — once a great nation. But they were invaded by the Moors, a sort of Negro people. Not much account today." Sutherland noted that Masters repeatedly employed "the most powerful sex phobias" to whip his audience's emotions into a "high pitch." They would leave prepared to do anything to block desegregation.[16]

The ACCT, which to Sutherland was a "new style" of the old Ku Klux Klan, openly prescribed economic pressure as the primary weapon of struggle. Blacks who applied to Kilgore Junior College or who signed desegregation petitions "were threatened with the loss of their jobs." Sutherland recounted that Citizens' Council economic tactics in LaGrange, where blacks had battled for equal educational opportunity in the 1940s long before *Brown,* caused some blacks to be fired. He also pointed out that despite council members eschewing the rope and faggot methods of yesterday, "the dreadful threat of violence lurks always in the background." He speculated that many of the rank-and-file members of the council movement were "people dispossessed from a rural culture trying to find something to which they can belong" who hungered for excitement to break the monotony of a "flat life." Finally, he predicted that the councils would be defeated by the "two great forces, press and pulpit." Sutherland may have been entirely too sanguine, however, about the prospects of interracial conciliation among his fellow white Texans.[17]

Desegregation spread across the state not because racial liberalism seized the hearts and minds of the white majority but because most federal judges followed the rule of law, most college trustees ultimately behaved pragmatically, and, above all, courageous black men and women persisted in demanding change in their local communities. Wichita Falls, in the northeasternmost part of Texas, and Wharton, in the southeast, reveal the difficult situation local people faced in desegregating the municipal colleges in these towns. In both cases, without Masters or the influence of the ACCT, white supremacists took a stand, but eventually the majority of whites relented and adjusted. Wichita Falls's journey toward fair access to higher education went into high speed on 15 August 1951, when Willie Faye Battle, Helen Davis, Carl McBride, and Marilyn Menefee, all eighteen-year-olds, Wilma Jean Norris, a twenty-year-old, and Golden Era White, a twenty-two-year-old, went to the campus of Midwestern University to apply for admission. They were accompanied by Rev. L. W. Jenkins, president of the Wichita Falls branch of the NAACP, Dr. M. K. Curry Jr., a leader in the African American community, and Professor A. E. Holland, principal of the city's black high school. The next day, registrar J. H. Jamison wrote the six that their applications had been rejected. MU's board had voted unanimously the week before to maintain segregation after meeting with representatives of the Negro Council on Civic and Political Affairs, the respectable group through which Jenkins, Curry, Holland, and others organized desegregation efforts. With the help of U. Simpson Tate and W. J. Durham, the applicants filed a lawsuit against the school on 4 September in the U.S. District Court.[18]

Judge William Atwell accepted the factual record that showed MU officials conceding that the six met all the financial and academic qualifications for admission but that it had refused them "solely on the account of the[ir] race and color" and that the students would find it "much less expensive, in both time and money" to attend college in Wichita Falls rather than travel 367 miles to Prairie View or 411 miles to Texas Southern University (TSU) in Houston. Since there were no facilities in the district substantially equal to those at MU for the higher education of blacks, Atwell held that the economic hardship that denial of access to the college placed on blacks was "a discrimination which the law does not allow." His concluding remarks in his written decision on 27 November 1951 left no doubt as to where he stood:

> The Negro did not come to the United States. He was brought here. He has grown in learning and in capacity and in the performance of the duties of citizenship. He pays taxes, he puts on the uniform of the Armed Forces. That is because he has had the benefit of his association with his white brethren. He walks the same streets; he engages in the same business; he reads the same newspapers; he sings the same songs in his churches and his churches

148

are of the same denominations. It is, in truth, an united citizenship for an United States of America. Decree must go for the plaintiffs requiring their admission to the defendant college.[19]

Atwell's "united citizenship" argument did not move the college's board of trustees, the campus administration led by President James Boren, nor Attorney General Price Daniel. They appealed the ruling, but the U.S. Court of Appeals affirmed the decision of the trial court. Undeterred, they filed an application for a writ of certiorari before the U.S. Supreme Court. On 24 May 1954, the court denied the writ and the color line on admissions at Midwestern University fell.[20]

In June 1954, five black students enrolled, and that September, more than forty black students followed, making Midwestern the first publicly supported senior college to admit black undergraduates in the state. The first five included four black men who had been top students at the city's Booker T. Washington High School and were members of some of the most prominent families in the black community. The sons of NAACP branch leader Rev. Leland W. Jenkins Sr., Wynell D. Jenkins and Leland Jenkins Jr., were eighteen and twenty-one years old, respectively. Leland Jr. was married and recently had completed fourteen months as an airman second class with the Fifth Air Force in Korea. Wynell finished as the salutatorian of Washington High's class of 1954. The valedictorian, Charles Bosley, the son of a section worker for the Fort Worth and Denver Railroad, was another of MU's first black students, along with Edwin Fuller, son of Dr. C. B. Fuller. Mrs. Milton Easley, a graduate of a high school in Topeka, Kansas, and the wife of a civilian instructor at Sheppard Air Force Base, became the fifth black student to enter MU. The transition to desegregation on the campus occasioned no aggressive acts of opposition. MU's first black students had maturity and solid academic preparation going for them. The *Wichita Falls Record News* reported that white students "accepted readily without any reservations" the five.[21]

The annual for the 1954–55 school year, the *Wai-Kun*, reveals that black students were involved in many aspects of MU's curricular and extracurricular life. The Reserved Officers Training Corps' "A" and "F" Company rosters had one black each, "B" company had three blacks, and "E" company had two blacks. Students Helen E. Burnett, Ollie M. Jeffrey, Charlsie Margaret Jenkins, and Donnie M. Wilson were enrolled in the graduate school, Doris Ann McBride was a nursing student, Dorothy Battle, Ruth Faye W. Hoyt, Marilyn Menefee, and Dorothy Tarrance were in the sophomore class, and Herbert Coleman was in the freshman class, where he was elected as a representative to the student council and inducted into Alpha Phi Omega, a campus service organization. The college yearbook's inclusion of pictures of blacks perhaps represented how the presence of a large, newly desegregated military base in Wichita Falls helped to erase the color line on the MU campus.[22]

The NAACP hailed its victories at Wichita Falls and in a related case against segregation at Southwestern Louisiana Institute in Lafayette as giving "strong support for the suggestion that our Texas State Colleges at Denton, Commerce, Lubbock, Huntsville, El Paso and elsewhere are ours for the asking — if not for the asking — most certainly for the taking." Durham and Tate proudly beat their chests, for they and A. P. Tureaud had forced the South's first state-supported colleges to desegregate their undergraduate student bodies. The NAACP lawyers eagerly, perhaps too eagerly, as later events proved, sought to achieve the same goal at every public college in Texas.[23]

Wharton County Junior College (WCJC), which shared the same name as the town and county wherein it resided, gave civil libertarians another important victory in 1954. Despite the widespread disapproval of whites and without any pressure from a federal court, it eliminated the ban against blacks. What could explain this development? In almost every respect, Wharton, a city southwest of Houston, looked like a typical East Texas, southern locale: an economy heavily dependent on cotton production, a substantial black population, a cultural past rooted in chattel slavery, and a historical pattern of underdevelopment and inequality in the public school resources designated for black people. The most nontraditional aspect of Wharton from a Dixieland perspective was its large Mexican American population. In 1950, the county's 36,077 inhabitants were 60 percent Anglo, 22 percent African American, and 18 percent Latin American.[24]

Could an answer to why Wharton's junior college dropped the color line be found in the extent of Wharton County blacks' political consciousness and mobilization? Probably not. The Wharton's desegregation did not result from the work of an assertive NAACP chapter. Pioneer black professionals like physician Ennis Alexander Martin, who opened a medical practice in Wharton in 1917, never formed a chapter of the NAACP. In fact, E. O. Smith, a leader in the Houston branch, gave testimony at the Thirteenth Annual NAACP Conference as to how white supremacy in Wharton operated to stifle overt activism. In 1921, Smith recounted, two of the town's police officers went to the farm of a black family and sought to arrest a man on the charge that he had been cruel to an animal when he allegedly tied a tin can on a dog's tail. When the man objected to being taken into custody and losing a day of work on such a frivolous matter, the officers jumped him and began pistol-whipping him. The man's dog lunged at the white men, and in the melee the man's wife rushed to the scene and said, "For God sake, men, don't kill my husband." A young boy then appeared with a rifle and shot to death one of the white men holding a six-shooter. The man and the boy tried to flee the county, but they were caught and lynched. As a result of the fiasco, the man's mother lost her mind; his wife was convicted of interfering with an arrest and sent to the state penitentiary for twenty-five years; and their two little children were hunted like wild animals. Smith stated: "Every effort has been made to run down these children that they might be killed. But the [Houston] Branch [of the NAACP], acting simply as friends and relatives, has seen to it that these children have not yet been captured. We have changed their names and they are safe." For many years this event and others like it helped to suppress an overt NAACP presence from developing in Wharton.[25]

Although Wharton had no NAACP in 1954, it did have an outspoken educator, Principal Thomas Lane Pink, who would press for desegregation of the junior college. Pink, born near the all-black communities of Kendleton and Powell Point, had traveled across the United States and to Mexico and Canada as a professional baseball player in the Negro leagues before returning to his home county to teach in the "colored" schools of Hungerford and Glen Flora. During the Second World War, the Glen Flora School District constructed a new school building and named it after Pink in recognition of his popularity and service to his people and the county. In 1952, he embarked on a nonbelligerent campaign to enroll blacks at Wharton County Junior College. Reportedly, Pink and Dr. G. M. Wilkins, president of the Victoria chapter of the NAACP in nearby Limestone County, who organized a "Negro citizen's committee" that successfully petitioned for the admission of blacks to Victoria (Junior) College also in 1954, told the press that "the NAACP played no active part in the admission of Negroes to the two schools." Wilkins stated, however, that the Victoria branch "sponsored" one student's application and had been "anxious to get the girl admitted with as little controversy as possible," but had she been refused, the branch might have filed a lawsuit "to make a test case of it."[26]

Wharton County school officials dismissed Pink's petitions for fair access from 1952 until 1954. Only a few days after the *Brown* decision, school superintendent C. Graves Sivells Jr. assured parents that the Court's ruling would not affect the county's schools in any way. Noting that school attendance was not zoned in Wharton, Sivells held that "it is unlikely that colored children would prefer to attend the white school or that the white children would attend the Wharton Training School by choice, at any rate in the immediate future years." Less than a month before *Brown*, the school district announced it had purchased twenty-three acres of land adjacent to the all-black Wharton Training School and the Colorado River and would build a new school facility and a playground. The board of trustees had authorized a "negro branch" of WCJC at the Training School, but only a limited number of courses were taught. The board made no promises of expanding the branch. Pink, his determination renewed by *Brown*, again petitioned the WCJC board to drop segregation, and he set off

151

a panic in the city. This time it seemed as if black people meant to have equality even if they had to resort to the courts to get it. Pink's initiative exposed the thinness of whatever paternalistic tradition existed among Wharton County residents. In her 1964 chronicle of Wharton County's history, Annie Lee Williams, longtime public relations director for the junior college, tried to describe the paternalistic spirit that she contended exercised great influence over race relations in the region:

> The old and the new blend in Wharton County. In many ways it is still "Old South." Negroes who have long worked for the same white families are referred to, affectionately, as "my Negroes" by the white people. Men of Southern heritage give the respectful title of "Miss" to any woman when addressing her by her first name, even though she may be married and the mother of many children. There is a certain bearing and indefinable manner about the long-time residents that sets them apart from the newcomers. They have long been a part of the county, and their descendants will carry on when they are gone.[27]

Wharton physician F. J. L. Blasingame, chair of WCJC's board of trustees, first learned that blacks in the county were preparing to take the board to court over the segregation issue through the old-time paternal bond that whites cultivated through the long night of slavery and maintained during the era of segregation. "I had a really prominent black man which had been a patient of mine for some time," Blasingame recalled in an interview almost forty years later, "and he was in to see me in a routine office call and in the course of conversation [he] mentioned to me in a constructive, helpful sense, that he had heard rumors that the black people were thinking about filing a suit against the Board of Trustees" to force desegregation on WCJC. The well-known and successful young doctor immediately brought up what he had heard to J. M. Hodges, president of the college, who confirmed that his sources also had warned him that a suit was in the making. They then agreed to place the issue on the agenda of the board's next meeting, whereupon the board reached the decision to admit black students in the fall of 1954.[28]

The new policy sparked a storm of controversy. The semester commenced on 13 September with sixteen black students joining about four hundred white students at WCJC. A public outcry compelled Wharton mayor J. R. Martin to call a town meeting to discuss the desegregation of WCJC. All seven members of the board of trustees attended and sat behind a table on the college's gymnasium floor. They faced a crowd of two or three hundred Wharton County residents. Blasingame outlined the board's decision to desegregate and the reasons for it: "I made the plea that they understand" that the board members approved the admission of blacks "because we felt it was better for us to do it voluntarily than to be involved in lawsuit and be forced to do it under those circumstances." In a very tense atmosphere, he and the other trustees listened for hours while, row by row, each person in attendance received the opportunity to air his or her views. Newspaper accounts of the meeting stated that the majority of the fifty-three speakers who addressed the forum opposed the board's decision to open the main branch of the college to blacks. They demanded that blacks continue to be restricted to the college's "negro branch" and argued that the board's action was premature. "Some of the presentations," Blasingame recalled, "were very tense, loud, argumentative." However, "the majority of the people felt the decision was timely and wise." The incongruity between his recollection of the meeting and journalists' contemporary accounts may best be explained as the result of the trustees having to take a course of action at once the most undesirable and yet the wisest policy available. *Brown*, even before the Court's "with all deliberate speed" pronouncement a year later, had a decisive effect. It said that if blacks take a segregating college to court, their petition would be upheld. Thus, voluntary compliance with desegregation could in no way be considered premature. What Blasingame and other white officials saw was the need to manage the desegregation process rather than have that process manage them.[29]

There is no evidence that Pink or any other blacks attended or were allowed to attend the "public meeting." A few citizens did, however, endorse the board's action. Gus Gonzales and Barney Bernstein came straight out and supported desegregation as a matter of fairness. Gonzales reminded his fellow citizens about the Four Freedoms, the cherished values of freedom of speech and worship and freedom from want and fear for which Franklin Roosevelt said democracies always fought. He said these values were much talked about in the United States but "the place to start practicing them is right here." His remarks hit at the fact that black people from Wharton County were not free of fear, did not have equal educational opportunity, and lacked the freedom to speak out at a "public meeting" that concerned their immediate interests. Bernstein, one of WCJC's first graduates and its first president of the alumni association, also took up a theme from the Second World War. He noted that black soldiers had fought and died for the arsenal of democracy just as other Americans had. "If this is a free country," Bernstein said of the United States, then blacks "should be free." Other supporters of desegregation, such as Frank Shannon, publisher of the *Wharton Spectator*, and state representative–elect Buckshot Lane, an area attorney and high school history teacher, favored the decision on other grounds less sympathetic to their black neighbors. Some regarded the costs of providing blacks with equal facilities simply too high. Others did not like the idea of "putting off" dealing with the school segre-

gation problem. Shannon stated he had no criticism of separate equality
except that "frankly, I'm a nickel and dime boy and don't believe in that
kind of outlay." An attorney presented the group with a scenario in which
the district would spend $5,000 or $10,000 to educate a single black desir-
ing a class already available at WCJC. Area representatives from Lutheran,
Presbyterian, Catholic, and Episcopalian churches also spoke against segregation at WCJC.[30]

The majority of those who addressed the gathering cared little if at all
about the cost effectiveness of desegregation or the rights of blacks. Tom
Abell, Wharton Independent School District's school board president, expressed virulently anti–African American attitudes. He asked the people
of Wharton if white people would permit the eradication of their civilization "to appease those who come from the jungles of Africa." He vowed
that his three children would never attend a nonsegregated college. Other
whites with similar views included state representative Jack Fisk, a former
mayor of the town, a bank executive, a printer, and a medical doctor, as
well as the fathers of some students who had permitted their children to
enroll not having known that the board had opened the college to blacks.
Blasingame assured them that students could withdraw and have their
tuition fees returned to them. Fisk argued that the board had acted pre-
maturely in response to the Supreme Court's ban on segregation. He
pointed out that the Texas Democratic Party and the Texas Baptist Association remained on record in favor of the continuation of segregation. He
described the board's action as giving the NAACP "the small wedge" they
had been looking for to move into Wharton County and mount a broad
attack against segregation.[31]

After all the speeches, the board retired to a closed session and reaffirmed its earlier action. It decided not to expel the sixteen blacks who
were attending classes at the main campus but did not approve the elimination of WCJC's black branch or of its policy of not allowing blacks to take
courses at the main branch that the branch exclusively for blacks offered.
Eventually this segregationist holdover would be dropped as the junior
college enjoyed a peaceful transition to desegregation. Blasingame and
the other board members allowed President Hodges to orchestrate the
college's transition to desegregation. After the initial uproar and national
attention the college received, the officials did their best to treat the decision to admit blacks as a practical, business matter. They took no pride and
felt no shame over their position. In reflecting on the moment many years
later, Blasingame gave the desegregation of WCJC no special sentiment. He
discussed the issue in the same tone, if not with less enthusiasm, than he
did other difficult questions he faced in the 1950s, the problem of deciding which town in Wharton County the junior college should be placed,
for example. Segregation's demise at WCJC resulted from a direct chal-

lenge by blacks for equality in higher educational opportunity that compelled white officials to choose, in a charged atmosphere, to open the
college to blacks.

Once the school was opened, WCJC's first black students moved rapidly
to become fully and significantly a part of campus life. Hodges, WCJC
president, and J. D. Moore, president of Victoria College, both told a
correspondent for the *Houston Post* a year after desegregation that no dis-
courteous incidents had occurred between black and white students and
that blacks "stayed to themselves and neither they nor white students made
any attempt to fraternize." Hodges commented, however, that black students "played games with white students in the college student union
building" and "took part in the intramural sports program." Student Don
Malone joined the college's new Art Club sponsored by art instructor Elsie
Smothers, and he appeared in the group's picture in the yearbook, the
only black among the mostly female membership. In 1957, John Frankie,
physical education teacher and head coach of WCJC's Pioneer Cagers,
integrated the team with Doris "Hank" Allen as a forward.[32]

In the summer of 1954, as a federal court opened Midwestern University and colleges elsewhere also dropped segregation, UT officials finally
began to face the inevitability of comprehensive desegregation. Logan
Wilson, who replaced Theophilus Painter as president of UT, recognized
the color bar had to go the day the Supreme Court handed down its ruling
in *Brown*. The *Dallas Morning News* reported him as saying that the decision
"certainly is going to pose some critical, practical problems in primary,
secondary and higher education." He predicted that if black undergraduates deluged the university with applications, there would be a serious
crisis. "We have got to remain calm and sensible," he said, until responsible leaders could intelligently work out the how and when of the end of
segregation. At other state colleges, officials stood by the state constitution's segregation mandate and gave no hint of recognizing any impending demise of Jim Crow as a result of the Court's decree. President E. N.
Jones of Texas Technological College at Lubbock emphasized that the
state established his university "for white students" only and that he had
"no authority to make any adjustments without legislative action."[33]

James Gee, president of East Texas State College at Commerce, also dug
in his heels. "We will be governed by the policy set down by the board of
regents of the Texas State Teachers Colleges. We have no other alternative,"
he declared. Across the state, public administrators and officials alike,
including Governor Shivers, regarded the ruling as incomplete and without effect until the Court prescribed the procedure and deadline for compliance. Thus, the official view regarded *Brown I* as merely a statement of
principle. Officials hoped that the court would permit them to move toward
it, perhaps, over the course of twenty or, better still, a hundred years.[34]

155

Several black students, however, wanted UT to move toward comprehensive desegregation on a time line of a few months rather than years or decades. Houston's John Winfred Walker, an honor student at Jack Yates High School, and Marion George Ford Jr., a straight-A honor graduate from Phyllis Wheatley High School, along with Austin's John Willis Hargis, valedictorian of the class of 1953 at Anderson High School, Norcell D. Haywood, Robert Norwood, John A. Searcy, and Herman Clifton Smith, became the first blacks accepted at UT as undergraduates. Two of the men applied to the chemical engineering program, and one each hoped to attain aeronautical, electrical, and petroleum engineering degrees. The other two students had applied for course work leading to a degree in architecture. Without making any public record of a policy change, UT officials adopted the posture that these fields, even at a baccalaureate level, did not constitute regular academic undergraduate degrees but professional degrees. Therefore, under the policy established after *Sweatt*, blacks could enroll.[35]

With the admission of John Saunders Chase into the School of Architecture and the requirement that he take undergraduate classes before he could begin his graduate work (see Chapter 4), the university had anticipated accepting blacks in undergraduate courses in professional fields. UT president Wilson and the regents had enlarged upon that opening but did not announce it as a formal change. Initially, Ford had been refused admission in late June, and then in July the university reversed itself after the scholar-athlete's rejection garnered headlines across the state and nation. After admitting Ford, UT went on to accept the other six students. Ford, who once described himself as a "dark, large, looming and gruff looking Black man," had been a newsboy at age seven and a shoeshine boy at nine and had developed himself physically to a point that at twelve he worked for a packing company. While in high school making honor-roll grades, he became a lifeguard, taught swimming classes, and distinguished himself on the football field. When he received notice that he could attend UT, he stated to a reporter, either in a fit of arrogance or naïveté, that he longed to try out for the Longhorn swimming and football teams. As soon as the word had gotten out that a young black man might suit up in the burnt-orange and white, or swim in the same water with white youth, Ford and the other six blacks received letters revoking their admission to UT. Registrar Henry Y. McCown explained that a rule in the UT admissions policy required that the the engineering students first complete a year's work at Prairie View and the architecture students, at Texas Southern before they would be allowed to enroll at UT and "begin the professional courses of your program," as opposed to basic, academic course work. Ford made an appeal to the regents but then dropped the matter and accepted the cancellation of his acceptance notice. He enrolled at Wiley University and

later went to the University of Illinois on a football scholarship. He ultimately did earn a UT degree at the dental branch in Houston.[36]

A few of the other black applicants did not accept UT's double cross
as passively as Ford. Smith, Norwood (through his father), and Hargis
(through his grandmother) asked the Austin branch of the NAACP to help
them get into the university. Walker, eschewing NAACP legal counsel, filed a
motion for a temporary restraining order against UT registrar McCown,
President Wilson, and UT's board of regents in federal district court in San
Antonio before Judge Ben H. Rice Jr. The Houston firm of Dent, Ford,
King, and Wickliff represented him in his request that UT be prohibited
"from forcing Walker and others to pursue undergraduate studies at a
Negro school when other students are permitted to do all their work at the
University." He based his case on the proposition that Prairie View and TSU
were inferior schools in comparison to UT and therefore UT's action violated his constitutional right to equal protection of the law. Burnell Waldrep and Bill Lee of the attorney general's office, along with Judge Scott
Gaines, university legal adviser, countered that the court should deny the
motion until the Supreme Court wrote its decree in *Brown II*. Rice accepted the defendant's logic and refused the temporary injunction and
maintained his position in a subsequent preliminary injunction hearing.
Walker's lawyers never followed up with a motion for a permanent injunction. Tate and the staff of the NAACP regional office accepted the results of
his suit and never challenged UT's nullification of the acceptance notices
of Smith, Norwood, and Hargis.[37]

Hargis, Smith, and Norwood exiled themselves for a full academic year
to Prairie View, where some members of the administration and faculty
warmly welcomed the three political musketeers as celebrities. They got
the courses they registered for, even upper-division classes. They got their
own rooms in the campus dormitory, and they even received an invitation
to eat in the faculty cafeteria. When they applied to transfer to UT, Prairie
View officials came at the students first with sugar cubes, then with a stick.
Hargis, who had completed a year at Morehouse in Atlanta, knew from the
start that he would not stay at Prairie View. In October, not having been
among the proud and mighty Panthers a good month, he asked UT to
admit him in the spring semester of 1955, but McCown refused his request. In the spring, he made it known that he had again applied to UT and
that the school had taken his application for summer enrollment under
review pending the outcome of *Brown II*. Hargis, according to a historian
who interviewed him a year before he died, rejected offers from Prairie
View's top brass of "substantial compensation — including an automobile
and monthly payments — if he would remain there." It seems highly improbable that such a bribe occurred or that, if it was made, it was genuine.
Who would have provided the funds to make it happen? Did President

Wilson, UT alumni, or state government officials have a secret kitty they could tap to induce Hargis to stay put? Did a perennially underfinanced Prairie View have money at hand to uphold undergraduate segregation? Whatever the full story behind the promises made to Hargis or the abuse he endured when he insisted on transferring, there is no denying that UT did not want to admit him. Wanting a lawsuit even less, however, UT very quietly admitted Hargis and two other Prairie View students, Smith and David Wallace, in June 1955. Official statements to the contrary notwithstanding, these three men became the first black undergraduates at the University of Texas.[38]

The board of regents of the University of Texas System announced that it would make a formal policy statement on university segregation at its meeting in early July 1955. A five-person committee of the nine-member board had developed several recommendations for the approval of the full body. Several challenges demanded action. First, UT officials had used *Brown II* as grounds for delaying any changes, but, as of 31 May, the Court had decreed schools should make a "prompt and reasonable start" toward compliance with the principle of nonsegregation. Second, in April an NAACP-sponsored lawsuit attacked segregation at Texas Western College (TWC), a branch of UT in El Paso. The regents feared that the federal district court would open the campus to blacks and possibly strike down segregation throughout the UT system. Finally, although the regents had managed to keep the admission of undergraduates Hargis, Smith, and Wallace one of the best-kept secrets in the state, they did not relish being in such a predicament. They wanted time. No lawsuits, no exposure and censure in the press, just time to implement a plan that would settle the race problem. In the new regent policy resolution made public on 9 July, UT agreed to open Texas Western College to blacks beginning in the fall semester, to admit qualified students "without reference to racial origin" to all graduate programs at UT irrespective of whether the state-supported black institutions offered the programs, and to maintain segregation at the Austin campus until the fall semester of 1956. The board reasoned that it needed the additional time so that it could "formulate a policy of selective admissions, based on merit and applied equally to all regardless of racial origin." The centerpiece of its new selective admissions policy, having been studied for almost a year, would be the adoption of standardized entrance examinations. The examinations, biased in favor of the white cultural majority and administered in segregated arrangements, worked according to plan: from February to September 1956, about 80 percent of blacks who took the test were rejected, compared to 55 percent of whites.[39]

As for the black students at UT, conditions remained anything but pleasant. Before the end of the summer, Smith and Wallace left Hargis the lone black undergraduate. Haywood and Norwood joined him on the campus in the fall, but within a year, Norwood suffered a nervous breakdown and withdrew from the Forty Acres. Hargis and Haywood alone persevered, and in the tumultuous fall of 1956, they finally found themselves less isolated when over 100 black transfer and first-year students joined them. Meanwhile, black graduate students, with access to all of the university's programs, continued to earn advanced degrees. Galveston's Central High School principal, Leon Morgan, who permitted Herman Barnett to live in his house while he was a medical student and intern at UTMB, applied, attended, and in 1956 became one of the first blacks to earn the doctorate degree in curriculum, administration, and philosophy at UT. The desegregation process became an irreversible trend in the late 1950s, despite the tight control administrators exercised over it. Its cost weighed most heavily on the black people who initiated and endured the change.[40]

White resistance mustered two pathetic attempts to halt UT's comprehensive desegregation in 1956. Both lawsuits originated in Houston, and both efforts failed to do much more than garner a few headlines and register the displeasure of bigots, albeit organized and influential ones. The first case involved a group of sixteen Harris County men calling themselves the Citizens League for School Home Rule, counting several ex-UT students among its number. Among the primarily middle- to upper-income petitioners were five attorneys, two ranchers, two real estate agents, an insurance agent, a tax consultant, a printer, a "broker," a magazine editor, an oil operator, and a retired oil company executive named W. J. Barnes. Edgar E. Townes, a ringleader of the conservative wing of Texas Democrats who in the summer of 1955 led efforts on behalf of an antidesegregation resolution, and Fred W. Moore represented plaintiffs in the motion filed in the Texas Supreme Court on 14 October 1956. The petitioners held that the state constitution created UT for whites only and only by a constitutional amendment could it be changed to a school for blacks and whites. Neither the regents, the U.S. Supreme Court, nor the Texas legislature had the right to open UT to blacks, and thus the petitioners sought a writ of mandamus against state comptroller Robert S. Calvert to prevent him from funding the university as long as it admitted black students. In effect, the league presented a rerun of the Big Spring case in which the Citizens' Council had tried the year before to stop the desegregation of a public school district. The Texas Supreme Court dispensed with *Barnes et al.* v. *Calvert* one day after receiving the league's petition. In a brief, unpublished ruling it told the Home Rule group to go home and give up on preserving the rule of segregation at UT. The Citizens' Council of Greater Houston sponsored the other lawsuit, *Barnett* v. *Calvert*, which the Texas Supreme Court also denied.[41]

Whereas the comprehensive desegregation of UT generated noteworthy but altogether futile resistance efforts, El Paso's Texas Western College encountered little opposition to its admission of blacks in the fall of 1955. The one significant battle took place in the black community, which had put forward the challenge in the first place. A few years before UT created a mining school in El Paso in 1914, members of the city's small but growing black professional-managerial class formed one of the state's first branches of the NAACP. In the 1920s, the branch, through the activism of physician Lawrence A. Nixon, joined Houston and San Antonio blacks in the fight against the white Democratic primary. By 1949, however, the year the original mining school had grown into a senior college branch of UT with its own graduate programs, the city's NAACP branch had declined and had very few members. Dr. M. C. Donnell, the president of the branch, in 1951 called on A. Maceo Smith to help him revitalize the civil rights group. Smith made a trip there and into New Mexico and advised Donnell to rebuild branch membership and to create a "regular program." As a tactic to create enthusiasm for the association, he suggested a limited, demonstrative attack on Jim Crow at TWC. "Professor Fred Strait said that he had an interest in taking a course or courses at Texas Western University," Donnell explained. "I think that he should be urged to make immediate application, if it is not too late. If he is denied admission, we can provoke quite a lot of sentiment around it without going so far as to get into a law suit. At least we will not go that far until the branch and the community are ready for it."[42]

Early in 1954, El Pasoans readied themselves to directly assault race-based admissions practices at TWC. At an executive committee meeting on 7 March the subject arose that the branch "should be prepared to aid some student in breaking segregation at Texas Western College." The branch leadership created a committee to select a student to apply to TWC. Six months later, the selection committee reported that it had chosen Thelma White. The committee reported that it had tremendous confidence in White, who was the seventeen-year-old daughter of an employee of an El Paso garage and the valedictorian of the class of 1954 at the city's all-black, all-grades Douglass School. The executive committee discussed contributing ten dollars per month toward her expenses, as well as helping her with the steps she would need to take to file her application and bring suit upon being refused permission to enroll. She had applied through the mail, and the registrar's office had returned an unopened envelope containing her high school transcripts. For the purpose of legal action, however, White had to have a record that the university had rejected her application on the grounds of race. Branch officials, therefore, authorized a check for $22 to be paid to selection committee member Mrs. E. M. Williams to accompany White to register at TWC; and two prominent citizens would join them as witnesses. White got her formal rejection and went on that fall to attend New Mexico A&M College in nearby Las Cruces, leaving the details of her lawsuit to the NAACP's local branch and southwestern regional counsel. In March 1955, Tate filed the case styled *Thelma White, a minor, by her Father and Next Friend* v. *Alvin Arlton Smith, as President, etc., of Texas Western College of the University of Texas et al.*, in federal district court before El Paso's Judge R. Ewing Thomason.[43]

At that point, White's lawsuit intersected with the administrative maneuvers of the UT board of regents and the political-legal posture of the attorney general's office. On 18 July 1955, when the case came up for a hearing on the merits, UT presented Judge Thomason with a motion to dismiss White's suit as moot given the regent's decree earlier that month that it would graciously allow blacks to attend TWC, citing as a rationale the fact that the El Paso school board had opted in favor of ending segregation. Tate opposed the motion, arguing that *Brown* made the regent's statement of a new policy on segregation moot. By offering to allow TWC to desegregate based upon the school district's decision to comply with *Brown*, the regents tried to skirt the reality that *they* had to comply with *Brown*. Tate called on Thomason to overrule and deny the motion to dismiss, to hear the evidence, and to make his ruling. The judge agreed, and at the end of the trial he declared Article VII, Section 7, of the Texas Constitution and Article 2900 of the Revised Civil Statutes of the state contrary to the constitution and laws of the United States and therefore void. He also permanently restrained the UT regents from denying blacks the opportunity of attending Texas Western College or *any* institution in the UT system. Thomason shocked everyone, including Tate, when he extended his order to include the main branch. The regents and the state's attorneys disputed the extension of the decision beyond TWC, but for a few days they stewed in their own sweat, relieved only when Thomason sent out his written order on 25 July, which limited the force of the decree to TWC.[44]

TWC's transition to desegregation went as smoothly as its new president, Dysart E. Holcomb, and registrar J. M. Whitaker predicted. Twelve blacks, several of them servicemen from Fort Bliss and Biggs Field, joined 3,877 other students that fall, and no violent incidents on the campus resulted. Thelma White chose to continue her education at New Mexico A&M, having had a good first year there and having no wish to return to her home city as both a celebrity and a lightening rod for the enmity of staunch white supremacists. Although White chose not to enter the doors she helped to open, there appeared among the twelve apostles of a new era of racial justice at TWC a young man, Joe Atkins, who that fall semester had a lawsuit pending to open the doors of North Texas State College (NTSC) hundreds of miles away in Denton. Atkins's fight to open the doors of NTSC had its beginnings in voluntary actions the college took a year earlier.[45]

In 1954, NTSC's graduate program quietly admitted a black man. President James Carl Matthews could hardly have prayed for a better individual to help him initiate desegregation at his campus. A. Tennyson Miller, forty-one years old, had been a participant in the emerging civil rights movement in Texas from the 1940s. Born in Fort Worth the year before the First World War started, he graduated from I. M. Terrell High School, obtained a baccalaureate degree at Prairie View during the W. R. Banks era, and in 1936 went to work teaching at Fred Moore High School until 1943. He went on to taste life above the Cotton Curtain, earning his master's degree in 1952 at the University of Wisconsin. In 1946, he began a long and esteemed career first as an instructor and coach and finally as principal of Lincoln, the high school for black children in the Gulf Coast city of Port Arthur. Through the years of the *Sweatt* case and in the unfolding course of desegregation in Texas higher education, he played an active part in the Colored Teachers State Association of Texas. Miller, an ambitious, articulate charmer, exhibited strong leadership qualities.[46]

Shortly after the *Brown* ruling, Miller contacted NTSC regarding his entering its doctoral program in education. On 20 June, Matthews and Vice President Arthur Sampley met with him, in part because Miller presented fine academic credentials. From his past teaching work in Denton, he had also acquired a reputation among several faculty members at NTSC for being "a good student and a reliable person." Miller convinced Matthews of the ardor and "objectiveness" of his desire to study in the college's graduate school and emphasized that the white executive's "endorsement was of major importance; [as for him,] pursuing graduate work under adverse conditions would be a waste of time, money, and effort." He left the meeting hopeful that he would be admitted to the college in its second summer session, but a few days later he learned that the college had rejected his application. He traveled to Austin to inquire into admission at the University of Texas and also met with Assistant Attorney General Burnell Waldrep, who handled legal matters pertaining to the public school system. Subsequent to his visit to Austin, Miller wrote Matthews and informed him that UT had accepted him and that he would attend school there unless NTSC admitted him. With his wife living full time at their home in Denton, Miller had obvious reasons to prefer NTSC over UT. Miller also told Matthews that the attorney general's office "stated without hesitancy or reservation that my being admitted to any school offering the doctoral program was solely an administrative decision and that any state school was legally available to me." Furthermore, the expected implementation decree in *Brown* had no bearing on Miller's application "since neither 'separate' nor 'equal' were factors" of relevance to his situation. The high school principal added that if NTSC chose not to admit him, despite the fact that the legal watchdog of the Texas Constitution had no objections, he would direct his efforts toward UT. He did not hold out the threat of a lawsuit, but he did offer NTSC an appointment with destiny: "It is my conviction that my entrance now would contribute much to the successful, inevitable integration of Negroes into the school. My every effort would be toward the quality of deportment and performance that would dispel much of the apprehension that some may be harboring at this time. Knowing even in my own work the burdened seriousness of making an unusual decision, I understand any caution that may be yours. Yet, there are decisions to be made, and we cannot be without courage to make them."[47]

After consulting with the attorney general's office and confirming the substance of Miller's report on its position, Matthews informed the Phi Delta Kappa educator that he could enroll at NTSC in its second summer session. The college would take a step toward its "inevitable integration," but the president stressed to the media that NTSC's "policy on Negro undergraduates or Negro students working on master's degrees is not changed. They will not be admitted at this time." Miller completed his six-week course of study and returned to his principalship at Lincoln. Matthews may have received other applications from black students or heard rumors of a legal challenge being prepared against the college's ban against blacks except at the doctoral level. Whatever the impetus, toward the end of 1954, he and the NTSC board of regents drafted a plan of gradual desegregation for the college beginning with master's level students, then seniors in the fall of 1956, and proceeding a level a year until blacks were admitted in the entering class of 1959.[48]

The Dallas headquarters of the Texas NAACP, however, envisioned a more immediate timetable for gaining the constitutionally protected right of blacks to attend the North Texas college. Willie Atkins of Dallas and his son Joe took Matthews, Sampley, and the NTSC board before Judge Joe W. Sheehy of the U.S. District Court for the Eastern District of Texas. The younger Atkins, who had completed a year of study at Philander Smith College in Little Rock, Arkansas, sought a court ruling that would force NTSC to recognize that he had a legal right to attend the school. His petition also sought to declare the state's notorious constitutional Article VII, Section 7, and statutory Article 2900 "repugnant to the Fourteenth Amendment to the Constitution of the United States" and therefore null and void. He attempted to enroll in NTSC's first summer session in June of 1955. Admission officers found that he met the college's entrance requirements, but on 18 July, Vice President Sampley wrote Atkins that he would not be admitted because he was a Negro and the present policy of the board permitted people of his race for study for the doctorate degree only. Atkins and his father secured legal counsel from the NAACP. U. Simpson Tate assumed the role of lead attorney, but after a near disaster in Wichita Falls, Robert L. Carter and Thurgood Marshall of the national office signed on as co-counsel.[49]

They filed a petition on 11 August, requesting a temporary restraining order against NTSC so that Atkins could attend the school in the fall semester. Judge Sheehy granted a hearing on the motion for temporary injunction to take place in Tyler on 2 September. Despite Tate's careful work on the case, he lost the preliminary decision on a technicality: a federal marshal had failed to serve a subpoena to one of the regents. Without the temporary restraining order, NTSC would begin its fall 1955 semester with its undergraduate division and its master's degree programs continuing on a segregated basis. Atkins, however, still went on to attend a white state-supported college that fall, becoming one of the first blacks to attend Texas Western College at El Paso. Nonetheless, permanent injunction trial proceedings against NTSC occurred on 14 November. Billye Lee and Horace Wimberly, from the attorney general's office, presented Matthews as NTSC's sole witness. Matthews testified that the college, in large part, refused to admit Atkins because of overcrowdedness, operating at "102 per cent capacity at this time." Matthews also stated that subsequent to Atkins filing his suit, the board had adopted a schedule, to commence in the fall of 1956, for admitting black undergraduates one classification level per year, beginning with the senior class, in descending order. The defendants' lawyers argued that in *Brown II* the Court, in recognition of the considerable complexity involved in the process, left to local school authorities the task of deciding when, how, and at what pace to desegregate. They asserted that Judge Sheehy should rule in favor of NTSC's gradual, phased desegregation plan as evidence of its willingness to obey and respect the new law of the land "with all deliberate speed."[50]

After the brief hearing, shortly before the noon hour, Sheehy returned with his ruling. He expressed sympathy for the difficult problems NTSC officials faced and for their class-per-year proposal, but the law left him no alternative but to rule that the college had to admit blacks without delay. The problem of size could not be used as a reason to single out blacks as a group and refuse them admission, nor would any race-based gradual admission plans be allowed. Sheehy drew a distinction between public grade schools, the context for the Court's decision in *Brown II* granting districts time to end segregation, and a college like NTSC. "Public schools below college level, both for students of the white race and students of the Negro race," he stated, "are provided for and conducted on a local district basis and to a substantial extent attendance of a child, regardless of race or color . . . is compulsory. Whereas a college such as the Defendant College is conducted on a state wide basis [with] attendance being purely on a voluntary basis." If an individual white person could not stomach the possibility of sitting next to a black person in a classroom at NTSC, then the person had the choice to go elsewhere or not go to college at all. No law or state power demanded or compelled the mixing of blacks and whites at the collegiate level. Sheehy, joining the ranks of other federal judges in Texas who had ruled against postsecondary school segregation, decreed that NTSC had to judge black applicants "on the same basis as if they were members of the white race" and that officials of the college were "forever restrained and enjoined from refusing admission to the minor Plaintiff or any other Negro student of the same class as the Plaintiff to the College solely because of their race or color." The state attorneys, despite their own and Judge Sheehy's opinion that it would be "futile," held out the possibility that they would appeal the case. The attorney general's office extended to NTSC an offer to appeal the decision to the Supreme Court, but the board and Matthews declined and opted to make the best of things as a desegregated institution in the spring of 1956.[51]

A forty-one-year-old Fort Worth piano teacher, bookkeeper, and housewife named Irma Etta Loud Sephas became the first black undergraduate student to meet NTSC's entrance requirements. The daughter of J. Q. Loud, a retired Methodist minister, she took care of her disabled father who lived in her home along with her husband and three-year-old daughter, Vicki. Classified as a sophomore because NTSC accepted work she had completed at Huston College in Austin over two decades before, she enrolled for fifteen hours. The business major and music minor told curious reporters on her first day at the campus that she would not seek student housing but would commute between Fort Worth and Denton. Her plans included bringing her daughter to Denton and leaving her at a nursery for NTSC students' children. When Sephas began attending classes without incident, she and the Denton community gave a deep sigh of relief. The editor of the *Denton Record-Chronicle* commended the students of NTSC "for their patience and understanding," noting how "the college's civilized, Christian treatment" of the desegregation problem was "a direct contrast to the mob violence being displayed at the University of Alabama," where Artherine Lucy, admitted to the school by a federal court order, faced stones, rotten eggs, curses, and threats from Tuscaloosa whites. Mob violence kept Lucy out despite international exposure of her case. The editor expressed regret not that an American-born woman had been denied her constitutional rights but that the incident would provide "fodder for Communist propaganda" that "long accused" the United States of "racial hatred, intolerance and gangsterism." The "large majority" of the students of NTSC, however, believed in the Golden Rule and gave evidence of a more compassionate white America, thereby winning the admiration of the newspaper.[52]

While white Texans patted themselves on the back for not being as bad toward *their* Negroes as white Alabamians, black Texans confronted a difficult and at times treacherous situation at NTSC. In June, when about six black undergraduates and between fifty and seventy black graduate students, most of whom were teachers, enrolled at the college, the need for housing on campus for black students became acute. Two black women graduate students, Gwendolyn McDonald Jackson of Wichita Falls and Rosa Lee Thomas of Dallas, secured permission to move into Terrill Hall, a female dormitory.

Jackson, the wife of C. Emerson "Prof" Jackson, had played a behind-the-scenes role in the desegregation of Midwestern University. They both worked at Wichita Falls's colored school, her husband as its principal and she as the band director and organizer of its choral groups, and put there jobs in jeopardy to help recruit the students that filed suit for admission to Midwestern. With that experience and with news of Sephas breaking the color line that spring semester, they went to NTSC to speak with Matthews about her enrolling in the doctoral program in education as their good friend Tennyson Miller had done two years earlier. Jackson, however, could not commute from Wichita Falls to Denton every day of class as Sephas had done. Her husband explained to Matthews, "My wife just lost her mother and wants to change things, not stir up trouble." Jackson did not want to sue for the right to live on campus; she simply wanted her rights. Matthews took the matter to the NTSC board, and upon its approval, he arranged for Jackson and Thomas to live in a dormitory where young, lower-division girls lived. He reasoned that problems were less likely to result from the two older women living among younger girls than if they lived with other graduate students closer in age. The former country school principal had wisely assessed the situation. The white girls accommodated Jackson and Thomas, and NTSC became the first school in Texas to desegregate university-owned housing without incident. By the end of the summer, however, some Klansters had to demonstrate that not everyone in the area acquiesced to what they viewed as black equality steamrolling over white supremacy. At about nine o'clock on a Wednesday night in late August, students discovered a six-foot-tall, gasoline-soaked cross burning a few yards from the NTSC library. A college night watchman prevented a staff photographer with the *Denton Record-Chronicle* from taking pictures. No one, he said, would be allowed to photograph the occurrence "unless authorized by Dr. Sampley." Campus officials strictly enforced a gag rule on any media coverage of racial matters, whether positive or negative. Police Chief Glen Lanford helped Matthews play down the cross-burning, saying, "I don't think it's serious" and by identifying it as the work of "teenage pranksters."

Despite the occasional hostile act and the isolation they faced on the campus, as well as their being completely unwelcome or segregated in the stores, restaurants, theaters, and public accommodations off campus, black Texans flocked to NTSC and quickly made it the most desegregated public institution of higher education in the state. In the fall of 1956, the college had two blacks on the football team, Abner Haynes and Leon King, a fact that did much to contribute to NTSC's image as an "Island of Integration," as a journalist once described the college. Black enrollment seemed to support the moniker: in September 1957, an unofficial count (the college did not keep statistics on the ethnic breakdown of the campus population) put the number of black students at 181, more than at any other desegregated college in the state.[53]

As North Texas grappled with the problem of desegregation, four-year colleges in South Texas also encountered black challenges to racial discrimination. In August 1954, emboldened by *Brown*, Russell Hayes, a twenty-three-year-old veteran and lifelong resident of Kingsville, met with Texas College of Arts and Industries (A&I) president Ernest H. Poteet about enrolling at the school. Hayes had graduated from the town's Frederick Douglass High School in 1948 and had just received an honorable military discharge in July. As a veteran he had funds from the GI Bill to begin his college education, and Hayes asked Poteet to let him begin his studies right in his hometown. Poteet responded that he could not admit him since the college's governing board had previously discussed admitting blacks and concluded that the enabling act that created A&I clearly stated that the college had been established exclusively "for the white youth of the state." Hayes protested the board's decision and pointed out, "I laid my life on the line for my country." Between 1948 and 1954, he had served in Okinawa, Japan, and in Korea. "I don't want any exceptions," he explained, "I just want my rights." He disavowed any connection to the NAACP and said he regarded his case as a matter of veterans' rights. If he was not admitted, he would appeal to the Veteran's Administration (VA) to take away the college's status as approved for GI Bill disbursements. He also rejected the idea of his attending Prairie View or TSU, observing that the VA did not pay transportation costs. As a taxicab driver, he could not afford to travel to Houston or Waller County for the same education he could get at home.[54]

Poteet agreed to pass on Hayes's request to the board, and, instantly, the young applicant became a local celebrity. As part of the price of notoriety, Hayes received a threatening letter in the mail a day after his conversation with Poteet. He handed it over to post office authorities, who, in turn, referred the matter to the Federal Bureau of Investigation. No one was ever prosecuted, but the news caused quite a stir in Kleberg County. Known for cattle ranching, oil production, agriculture, and the Naval Auxiliary Air Station, the county, with its seat in Kingsville, had a population in 1950 of 21,991, half of which was Anglo, 46 percent Latin American, and 3.6 percent black. For generations past, blacks had never openly contested the disparities in white and black education, economic standing, and political participation. Then suddenly, it seemed to the whites of Kleberg, blacks were raising their voices on an issue that had to be reckoned with.[55]

167

Meanwhile, A&I's board of directors concurred with Poteet's initial response to Hayes's application. Hayes persisted, maintaining to the board that he did not come as a black man seeking to enter the college but as "a veteran with approval of the Veterans Administration." Board president John F. Lynch of Corpus Christi, formerly a regent at Del Mar Junior College when it underwent desegregation, stated that the board had voted to refuse to admit blacks "until either a court decision or the legislature expressly opens the college to such applicants." The board, saying it was uncertain what it had a legal right to do under the restrictive language in the college's charter, opted to "stay within the law" and ignore the U.S. Supreme Court's ruling in *Brown* as well as *Battle*, which three months before had opened Midwestern. Rather than filing a lawsuit, Hayes pleaded with the Veteran's Administration to intervene in his behalf. Early in October, however, a VA official in Washington, D.C., informed Hayes that "retention or admission of students or trainees are matters entirely within the discretion of the particular education institution or training establishment in which enrollment is sought."[56]

Hayes's highly visible challenge, however, aroused H. Boyd Hall, a Corpus Christi dentist and "old fire horse" activist within the NAACP, to give the board the lawsuit it asked for before it would break the color line. He notified college officials that another veteran of the Korean War, "a sample applicant" who A&I had rejected in March of 1956, intended to use legal proceedings to obtain his right to enter the college. He hoped, however, that the South Texas institution would follow "the pattern of Del Mar College in Corpus Christi, Pan American in Edinburg, and Victoria Junior College. All desegregated on their own accord. None was sued." In May, A&I's board finally reversed itself and ordered that "no young man or woman, a citizen of the State of Texas, shall be denied admission to this college by reason of race or color." In June, two local teachers with degrees from TSU, Ellen King Lambert and Irma Rebecca Summers, entered A&I. More black students enrolled in the fall, and desegregation continued without incident. Kingsville resident Nancy M. Nelson recalled years later that none of the black students "had a hard time. . . . They didn't have no, you know, big to-do, over" the killing of Jim Crow at A&I.[57]

The Turning Point at Lamar Tech

The "big to-do" over desegregation lurked in the Piney Woods of East Texas. Kilgore Junior College pointed to the difficulty the black equal rights movement faced in that part of the state. The most violent and massive episodes of white resistance to black equality occurred at Lamar State College of Technology in Beaumont and Texarkana Junior College

168

in Texarkana. The clash at Lamar climaxed a protracted antidiscrimination campaign that developed after the Second World War, escalated in 1949 when the college grew from a locally supported junior college to a state-supported senior college, and became a legal dispute in March of 1956. College administrators responded to the demand for integration, both inside and outside the courtroom, with a pragmatic philosophy, but privately the men who governed the college endorsed white supremacy. A plantation mentality reigned over Lamar from its creation in 1923 as South Park Junior College, the second junior college established in the state. In a speech before the Kiwanis club in June 1923, its first president, Louis R. Pietzch, who was "closely associated" with the Beaumont Ku Klux Klan of the 1920s, counted the development of both the new college and the local branch of the Klan among the city's most outstanding achievements. "Beaumont has gained fame from its Spindletop oil field, from its open shop association, from its Ku Klux Klan," and, he said, the city "is about to gain more fame because of its new junior college at South Park." Although by the end of the 1920s the Klan's fame turned to shame, under Pietzch's leadership, South Park Junior College became a key regional college. With the help of Governor Allan Shivers, a native of the area, it became a state-supported senior college in 1951.[58]

Although the rapid industrialization of Southeast Texas and the GI Bill helped to spark a tremendous increase in Lamar's enrollment figures, black veterans of World War II who returned home found extremely limited opportunities for postsecondary education or vocational training. The only institution beyond high school open for blacks, a business school, had a poor reputation and district officials were seeking to close it. A group of black leaders calling itself the Negro Goodwill Council had protested to Governor Beauford Jester about the educational inequality in the city and the exclusion of blacks from Lamar State College. In 1947, when a bill was put before the legislature to change Lamar into a state-supported senior college, the council attempted to block its passage. John Gray, Lamar's president, reacted immediately to the group's protest, promising separate facilities for blacks. A year later, a black branch of Lamar, Jefferson Junior College, opened with evening classes held at Charlton-Pollard High School. Dr. Harvey Johnson, principal of the black high school, welcomed the creation of a black junior college.[59]

Black civil libertarians, however, gave no support to the power holders' belated attempt to move toward separate-but-equal facilities, and soon after the *Sweatt* decision, they made plans to desegregate Lamar State College. They fired their first salvo at the college's race-based admissions criterion in 1952. In January, James Briscoe, a native Beaumonter and graduate of Charlton-Pollard High School, applied to Lamar. Briscoe's parents were laborers with little formal education and members of the

Beaumont chapter of the NAACP. They courageously supported their son's effort to attend the school and avoid the inconvenience of studying long distances from home. Briscoe, a student at Morehouse College in Atlanta since 1950, at the urging of his parents and the Beaumont NAACP, agreed to participate in the test case.[60]

Initially, Lamar accepted Briscoe. Apparently, the admissions office did not realize that he was a student at a black college in Atlanta. The school notified him that on the basis of his transcript from Morehouse, he was qualified to enroll for the spring term of 1951. On 29 January, Briscoe went to Lamar with his acceptance letter in hand to register for classes. Aaron Jefferson, a grocer, charter member of the Beaumont NAACP, and a distributor and local writer for the *Informer*, accompanied Briscoe to witness the historic moment. Lamar's acting president, G. A. Wimberly, met with Briscoe and explained that a mistake had been made and suggested he apply to TSUN. State law, he said, created Lamar for whites only.[61]

Briscoe prodded the NAACP for action on his case. Archie Price Sr., the principal of Beaumont's Hebert High School and the pastor of West Tabernacle Baptist Church, to which the Briscoes belonged, opposed desegregation of the college. He warned the Briscoes that they would lose their jobs if they persisted and with six children to support, they would be ruined. The prediction of the prominent preacher-teacher came true when Briscoe's father was fired. Many of the Briscoes' neighbors also put pressure on the family, warning that their attack on segregation would cause white rioting similar to what took place in the city in 1943. Some even ended all association with the family. Local NAACP leaders supported the Briscoes' decision to relent and not file a lawsuit. They reasoned that they had gotten the attention of influential members of the white community and should try to let biracial negotiations produce the final victory.[62]

The Beaumont Chamber of Commerce organized the sixty-member United Racial Council (URC), with a white chairman and an executive committee composed of three whites and three blacks. The URC shifted focus away from the desegregation of the college to ending segregation in city parks and recreational facilities. Dr. Ed Sprott, leader of the local NAACP, characterized the biracial group's work as ineffective but a learning experience: "For their first act, they picked two parks without swimming pools for desegregation, got the council's approval and also that of the city authorities. Two days after issuance of the Mayor's proclamation, the authorities reversed their stand. Considerable protest had arisen, including threats like 'Blood will flow down the valley.' Negro leaders, recognizing that if the top echelons of both groups could not work together, their only recourse had to be in the courts. Legal action was taken, and . . . the URC never met again."[63]

The legal action to which Sprott referred was a 1954 NAACP lawsuit,

Fayson v. *Beard*, to open the city's golf course and other park facilities to blacks. The case came before Judge Lamar Cecil, who ruled in September 1955 that Booker T. Fayson and all members of his race had to be granted "the free and unrestricted use and enjoyment of Central and Tyrrell Parks in the City of Beaumont." With a victory in that case in 1955, as well as in court-ordered actions in higher education at UT in 1950 and Midwestern, TWC, and NTSC after 1954, Sprott, Octave Hebert, and other branch leaders returned to the NAACP's method of direct attack and successfully recruited seven black students to seek admission to Lamar. In the summer of 1955, two 1948 Beaumont graduates, Martin High's Versie Jackson, who went on to attend Texas Southern for a year, and Charlton-Pollard's Henry Cooper Jr., who had studied three years at TSU, led the group. The other five were 1955 graduates of high schools in Beaumont or Port Arthur. With the students' participation secured, the NAACP branch's education committee wrote Lamar president Floren Lee McDonald encouraging him to correct the "ser[i]ous injustice" of restricting attendance on the basis of "race." The committee presented four reasons that segregation should be ended at the college. First, the inaccessibility of Lamar put a heavy economic hardship on families and made it almost impossible for lower income blacks to send their children to college. Second, as taxpayers, blacks had a right to "nondiscriminatory access" to all public colleges. Third, segregation constituted a "repudiation of our professed belief in the equality of all." And, fourth, Lamar's policy helped maintain the economic backwardness of the South by causing "the loss of the talents and capabilities of an arbitrarily selected group." In reply, the Lamar board of regents granted the committee a hearing at its meeting on 23 August 1955.[64]

News that the regents had plans to take up "the problem" of admitting black students quickly set in motion white organized resistance. On 19 August, a group of forty-seven whites, mainly workers at Magnolia Petroleum Company and residents of South Park, a heavily working class neighborhood with a reputation for hostility toward black residents in the area, signed a letter opposing any attempt to desegregate Lamar. Addressed to the regents, it stated: "We, many of whom are students at Lamar Tech, and all citizens of Jefferson County Texas, do hereby appeal to you to rule against any integration of the white and colored races at Lamar State College of Technology. We believe in equal but separate educational facilities and we think that the NAACP is trying to usurp the power of the state of Texas." Their appeal mixed the idea of racial hierarchy and separation with the old state's rights argument.[65]

A few days later, at 1:30 on the morning of the regents' meeting on the "Lamar Negro Issue," a night watchman discovered a blazing fifteen-by-eight-foot cross laid out on the ground south of the main entrance to the campus. When the regents arrived, the police reported that juvenile pranksters, probably from the South Park area, had set the fire. Proceeding with the business at hand, the officials voted to deny admission to the seven black students. Taking the same position as the A&I board a year earlier, the regents declared that the state legislature created the school in 1949 for "whites only," and for whites only it would remain. They added, just as NTSC had, that "an unprecedented growth in student population" prevented Lamar from accommodating any additional students. The regents pledged to reconsider the matter after it had time to look into plans to accommodate the additional student load that black admissions might create. The board's delaying tactics left the NAACP no other option but to resort to legal action.[66]

When *Jackson* v. *McDonald*, as the suit to open the college was styled, came before Judge Lamar Cecil, the students and their lawyers had good reason to expect he would rule in their favor. The Beaumont native graduated from Rice Institute and the University of Texas School of Law and made ties to prominent Texas Republicans like former U.S. representative Ben Guill and multimillionaire oilman H. L. Hunt. The relatively isolated minority party to which he belonged shaped the views he held, and it was to the party he owed his political debts. In 1954, he was appointed by President Dwight D. Eisenhower to a newly created judgeship for the Eastern District, an appointment for which he owed nothing to the socially conservative Democrats he lived among. In addition, Cecil had never held a state or local judgeship or political office prior to his appointment.[67]

Cecil did not hide his opinion on the desegregation issue from either side of the Lamar lawsuit. He wanted the regents and the students to reach an agreement and release him from having to issue a court order. On 14 March 1956, local attorneys Elmo Willard and Theodore Johns, as well as NAACP southwestern regional counsel U. Simpson Tate, filed a complaint on behalf of the students and a trial brief that made specific reference to *Brown*, Texas higher education desegregation cases *Atkins* and *White*, and the Louisiana higher education desegregation case *Constantine* v. *Southwestern Louisiana Institute*. The Attorney General Shepperd's office filed its answer to the plaintiff's charges on 5 April and offered no new defense whatsoever. Shepperd himself argued that Lamar's statutory language established it for whites only. Also, the college was overcrowded and had made no plans for a sudden influx of Negroes. If the school was forced to admit blacks, he asked that it be allowed to do so gradually by accepting upper-division transfer students in the 1957–58 school year and first-year students in 1958–59. Shepperd, in a new tact, urged Cecil to approve a "pepper and salt," or tripartite, system of higher education in which the state would provide choices of racially mixed, all-black, and all-white colleges, with Lamar remaining an all-white institution. As Price Daniel had six years before in the *Sweatt* case, Shepperd warned of gloom and doom if the judge forced Lamar to admit blacks: "It is not well for turmoil and discontent to be aroused in a community nor between the races residing there by a too hasty forcing of a claimed right of two puppets dangled before this court by the operators of a national racial organization." Taking a dig at Thurgood Marshall and the NAACP leadership, Shepperd added, "A liberty of choice in this regard should not be abolished just to appease the inordinate desires of those officers in certain negro organizations to chalk up a record of 'victories.' "[68] Judge Cecil was openly "critical" of the state's answer. In May, the NAACP offered to drop its suit and to have the students waive enrollment in the summer session if the college would voluntarily desegregate in September. Lamar's board knew it had lost but refused this settlement. Instead, it asked the attorney general's office to get Cecil to render his decision as early as possible.[69]

On 30 July 1956, Lamar's Jim Crow admissions policy received its death blow. After brief testimony from Versie Jackson and Lamar's president, Cecil took only a few minutes before announcing his decision that qualified blacks had a right to become students at Lamar. He stated that the "separate but equal" doctrine was no longer in effect "whether we like it or not" and that he would "follow the Supreme Court" as long as he sat on the federal bench. Lamar officials, however, refused to accept the unconstitutionality of its white youth–only provision. They sought a stay of execution of Cecil's order, citing the need for time to solve local implementation problems. Although blacks had already enrolled, on 25 September, Shepperd's office filed both a notice of appeal and a motion for Cecil's judgment to be suspended pending Fifth Circuit appellate court action.[70]

The regents' deep-seated and publicly stated belief in segregation, their legal efforts, and their delaying tactics may have encouraged white extremist violence. At 9 A.M. on 1 August, six "hooded figures" set ablaze a twelve-foot-tall, gasoline-soaked wooden cross. Police Chief Jim Mulligan suspected that Lamar students erected the flaming cross. On 11 August, police found two more crosses burning in the vicinity of Lamar, one near the Baptist Student Center, and blamed them on "youthful pranksters." At the same time, less youthful white militants unleashed a campaign of terrorism against local black activists. Attorneys Theodore Johns and Elmo Willard, for example, received death threats and their offices were vandalized. Other NAACP members, and Hebert and Sprott in particular, also were harassed and even terrorized with bombings. The comments of Frances Lightfoot, who ran for mayor of Beaumont in 1956, got the most votes in the first election, and then lost the runoff by a narrow margin, summarized the mood in Southeast Texas. "We don't like . . . the mulatto NAACP leader in town [Ed Sprott]," she told Warren Breed, an undercover agent of the Anti-Defamation League of B'nai B'rith. "He's got a mansion on the outskirts of niggertown," she added; "somebody has tossed rocks at his windows. He may be leaving town." Lamar's desegregation in 1956 represented a watershed event for East Texas, but it occurred at no small cost.[71]

On 18 September, a "committee" endorsing the "continued segregation of the races" met with McDonald and submitted a statement urging officials to "not permit Negroes to enroll in Lamar Tech for the September, 1956 term." Led by Charles Howell, future president of the Beaumont Citizens' Council, the group asked the board to deny black admission pending the resolution of the appeal of Judge Cecil's decision and to maintain segregation even in defiance of the federal court order. As evidence that such a policy would be in step with the desires of most Texans, the committee referred to the "overwhelming vote" in July's Democratic primary for a referendum opposing the "mixing of the races in any tax-supported school." McDonald replied that the college was doing everything it could to uphold segregation. After his meeting with the group, he wrote regent W. R. Smith informing him of "a little effort on the part of out-siders [*sic*] to interfere, but up to now I have everything under good control."[72]

Massive white resistance to desegregation lacked organization and leadership with a clear-minded strategy. Politically unsophisticated, the race militants engaged half-heartedly in relatively passive activities such as visiting college officials and opinion-makers, gathering signatures on petitions, and writing letters. Their impulse tended toward violent resistance. They wished to drive terror into the hearts of blacks and thereby elicit the cooperation of white power holders. Walking the border between violent tactics and massive resistance and doing neither fully, the opponents of desegregation were not very effective. A few days after Howell's group met with McDonald, another group emerged to protest the "integration of the races" at Lamar with a petition of 160 signatures, mostly of people from the small, all-white town of Vidor, about ten miles east of the campus. On 25 September, the second day of classes, Vidorian Eleanor Parker gave the petition to McDonald. It ended with an ominous warning: "Please remember what happened in our city back in 1943." The petition of the Vidor citizens, who apparently had no problem claiming Beaumont as "our city," contained a none too subtle threat that an attempt to end segregation at the college would ignite a bloody riot.[73]

Lamar's governing board did not support violent resistance to desegregation, but it also did nothing to discourage massive resistance. W. R. Smith explained in a letter to another board member: "I am not sure whether we should or not consider the possibility of violence such as occurred at the University of Alabama. I am aware of the bloody riots between the two races. While I am absolutely opposed to violence in any form, I would hate to be a party to anything that might bring it about." Smith rationalized, "If we proceed with too much speed we may do just this. The possibility of such trouble may require us to be a little more deliberate than otherwise." His reading of the Alabama episode, however, may not have been accurate or truthful.[74]

Once the board understood the federal courts would demand an immediate end to segregation at the college, it still refused to prepare whites for the inevitable. It chose instead to continue to present itself as fighting what more than a dozen senior and junior colleges in Texas had already done. If it had spent more time trying to prepare the region for desegregation, Lamar officials might have stemmed some of the turbulence that marred the college's transition to desegregation.[75]

On the first day of the fall semester at Lamar, five blacks enrolled. By the third day, there were eleven. Official figures released on 1 October, in the second week of school, revealed that a total of twenty-six blacks had been accepted in various departments of the college as part of a record enrollment of 5,455 students. Lamar's first black students included Harriot Anderson, Freddie Mae Bell, Betty Jean Booker, Alfred Briscoe III, Mattie Lee Cobb, Lonnie Flanagan, Winona Frank, Edward Frank Jr., Versie Jackson, Alice Jefferson, Theodore Johns Jr., Herbert Joseph, Lillie Mae Joseph, Lexsee Nixon Jr., Alvin Randolph, Lillian M. Rhodes, Jimmie Rice, Elnora Riggs, Robert Sampia, Clarence Sams, Hazel Thibodeaux, Vara Vincent, and Adam Wade. Most of them had attended college before, and a few who had official connections to the NAACP (like Johns) entered the college merely to make certain that the legal victory had not been in vain.[76] As black students entered Lamar, the massive resistance movement desperately tried to create a lawless, riotous atmosphere. McDonald requested the help of the sheriff and the chief of police in averting "any un-necessary [*sic*] incidents." He also met with student leaders and won their support for peaceful desegregation of the college. The president's organization of a united front of faculty, staff, and students helped keep white extremism from gaining a foothold on the campus once the semester began.[77]

On the first day of class, pickets appeared in front of most of the eleven entrances to the campus. Picketers also forced black students from classrooms, and the police had to remove others as a precautionary measure. Unable to attract enough support to close the campus or bar black students, the picketers became openly hostile, insulting and jeering whites who entered the campus. History professor Ralph Wooster recalled how they referred to him and his colleagues as "scabs" and threw things at one staff member who escorted a black student onto the campus. The picketers, he remembered, "seemed by their appearance to be lower white middle class, because they were not very well clad; in fact . . . one of the ladies didn't even have shoes on. These were real hillbilly types."[78]

175

Into the second week of the semester the Beaumont hillbillies, as Mc-
Donald put it, "got pretty rough." Picketers soon tried to stop everyone
who entered the campus parking lots or driveways. In response, the president had signs posted at all entrances prohibiting "loafing," but police
officers and the two Texas Rangers he "quietly arranged" to come to
Lamar refused to enforce the law banning loiterers from campus property.
Consequently, a number of serious incidents took place. The picketers,
McDonald reported in a newsletter his office circulated during the crisis,
"beat up one negro while a police officer stood idly by. This happened on
one of my parking lots. They broke a taxi cab's window as it delivered a
negro student and later the negro driver was found to have a pistol in his
car." Noting the biased and unprofessional policing of the campus, Mc-
Donald observed, "By Thursday it was obvious that the law enforcement
agencies were not going to discontinue the insulting of any teachers and
students, and I decided that public opinion was sufficiently crystalized in
my behalf to go on the offensive. The Editors of the Beaumont papers
agreed to help me and I blasted away at the lack of law and order in
Beaumont in front page headlines." The negative publicity, he averred,
"brought the Mayor over to my side and he called in the Police Chief and
told him to clear the pickets from the area. At 1:00 P.M. on Thursday the
police drove about 50 picketers from our eleven entrances to the campus,
arresting one. At 6:00 the pickets were back and the police again drove
them from the campus, arresting three including Mrs. A. W. Lightfoot,
one of the ring leaders."[79]

On Friday, 5 October, the day after the arrests, Lamar operated without
pickets for the first time since classes had started. That night, however,
crosses were burned on both the Lamar campus and in front of city hall.
Mayor Cokinos received numerous death threats and had to have twenty-
four-hour police protection after bombs exploded at the church he attended and, in an apparent mistake, at the house directly behind his.
Attorneys Johns and Willard, Ed Sprott, Octave Herbert, and other NAACP
leaders were also victims of terrorism.[80] The picketing at Lamar resumed
on Monday and continued peacefully for a week. On 15 October, however,
Mrs. H. T. Mercer of Vidor informed the media that her group had chosen
to end the picketing permanently in order to concentrate on organizing a
rally in Beaumont's Sportatorium, which ACCT president Basil Masters
would keynote. Mercer revealed the strategy behind the picket movement
in a statement to the *Beaumont Journal*: "Our one and only purpose in
picketing Lamar Tech . . . was to show public disapproval and aversion
to having negroes forced into our all-white schools, which is against the
laws of Texas, the laws of God, and the laws of personal morality and personal freedom. When we dared voice our protest to Dr. McDonald, and
our picketing of the college, we had faint hopes that the people of Beau-

mont, or a portion of its white population, would become conscious of their white blood and the danger threatening their children (and mine), and awaken to what was happening." Mercer's statement also indicates that a mood of resignation had come over whites in their defense of white supremacy.[81]

The council rally drew a crowd of over 600, many of whom paid one dollar to become a member of the new Beaumont Citizens' Council. Not one of the women who led the picket movement at Lamar won election to any of the group's twenty leadership positions. Only men, many of them the husbands of these women, took office.[82]

The demise of segregation at Lamar involved not only a racial conflict but also a "class cleavage." In 1956, "the falling common whites" in Beaumont's factories, refineries, and shipyards reacted to what they saw as an attack on their economic status and the erosion of the social contract that guaranteed for all classes of whites their incontrovertible superiority over blacks. Bourgeois whites, like the Lamar regents, also loathed the assault on "Southern customs" that *Jackson* v. *McDonald* posed, but for their class, the imperative goal of law and order forced them to permit a revision of the region's unwritten social policy. Both bourgeois and working-class whites, however, feared that racially mixed education would lead to miscegenation. Frances Lightfoot explained the attitude of many Southeast Texas whites when she said, "We like niggers here. We like a nice sweet collie dog, but we don't like 'em in bed with us. We'll help 'em out whenever we can, as white folks have always done in the South. But just don't let 'em get uppity on us." When she parroted Masters and warned that "if the white race doesn't rise up, we'll have a nation of mongrels in two generations," she spoke not only for many white "working folks" but likely for bankers like John Gray, lawyers like W. R. Smith and J. B. Morris, and businessmen like Otho Plummer. In her view, "cafe society" whites, the "froth" of the city, deeply opposed desegregation but were spineless. The regents fought it in the courtroom and the boardroom, but for Lightfoot, when they and the majority of Beaumont's affluent whites refused to help foment a crisis in which Governor Shivers would be forced to authorize Texas Rangers to remove black students from Lamar as a public safety measure, their reluctance to take part in massive resistance amounted to a betrayal and a refusal to "take a stand." She explained to Warren Breed: "You take the upper crust—bankers, lawyers, and businessmen. I know them and I have yet to see one of them come out and take a stand. But I'll be downtown and some of them will come up to me and say, 'Mrs. [Lightfoot], here's $10 or $1, take it and use it, but don't quote me. I can't afford to be in this publicly. We're not fighting the niggers, we just want to keep our customs.'" Lightfoot deeply resented upper-class whites' reluctance to openly oppose the African American freedom struggle.[83]

177

Amid such animosity on campus and across the city, Lamar's black students tried to attend classes. Lonnie Flanagan's determination to enter the college met a severe test. At about 9:00 A.M. on 4 October, Flanagan crouched down out of sight in the back seat of his stepfather's taxicab, while Clarence Mason, the forty-two-year-old driver for Flanagan Taxi Company, drove in a circle near Lamar's rear entrance. Mason would stop the car when a propitious moment arose for Flanagan to run from the car through Lamar's rear gates to his class. Flanagan had successfully used this method the day before, but on this day he encountered sentries on the back gates. When the cab passed an entrance, Tom W. Sanford, a thirty-eight-year-old Beaumont fence salesman, ran out in front of the cab and motioned to Mason to stop the car. Mason slowed down and then tried to speed away when Sanford yelled to other picketers, "He's got a nigger in the back!" Sanford dropped his placard, leaned into the car, and made a grab for the steering wheel in an attempt to stop the car. As Mason dragged Sanford the distance of a "city block," he drew his pistol and pointed it at the white man's head. Sanford still refused to let go of the car. He later said, "I told him to go ahead and shoot, but he didn't. He started beating my hands with the gun." Mason finally stopped the car when a police vehicle with two of the fifty officers that patrolled the campus pulled in front of his car. With the help of Ranger captain Johnnie Klevenhagen, the officers quickly took Mason, Flanagan, and Sanford away from the scene to police headquarters for questioning. The police released Flanagan from jail after he gave them a statement. Flanagan later learned that his brother, Mansfield Flanagan, a twenty-one-year-old cab driver, had his rear window smashed after dropping off a black student minutes before the incident with Sanford. Police did not charge any of the white picketers for destroying Flanagan's window, and the picketers did not press charges against him for allegedly "nearly hitting" two of their ranks.[84]

Lonnie Flanagan's later experiences at Lamar improved markedly after the incident. In an interview with Lamar professor Kirkland Jones, Flanagan said "his classmates were unusually kind and that both students and professors transported him to and from school when his stepfather could not drive him. Some of his professors even tutored him in areas where he needed special help." Alvin Randolph had similar memories. He most vividly recalled a white female student who offered to share her notes with him for the three weeks of classes he missed during the picketing crisis. But Randolph also remembered driving along Port Arthur Road in front of Lamar's main entrance and seeing several white female picketers chasing Lillie Mae Joseph into the road. She avoided a stoning, beating, or worse only because Randolph stopped his car for her and drove her to safety.[85]

Although the behavior of students contrasted sharply with that of the picketers, intense isolation remained the dominant characteristic of the black experience at Lamar. After the picketing ended, the college ceased to be the scene of open racial strife but remained far from being hospitable to blacks. President McDonald's "policy of gradual integration" prevented black students from moving into the mainstream of campus life until well into the early 1960s.[86] McDonald, in a letter to the chairman of the board of advisers of the Beaumont Citizens' Council, came out as 100 percent prosegregation but passed the buck for his actions onto the desk of higher authorities: "As I have repeatedly stated, I am not in sympathy with the Supreme Court's ruling regarding the mixing of the races in educational institutions. I was opposed openly to the admission of negroes to Lamar. However, you and members of your organization should clearly keep in mind that I am merely an employee of the Board of Regents, and as such, I do not make the decisions on such important matters of policy. I am only carrying out the orders which have been given to me by the Federal Court and my Board of Regents." He went on to assure the council members that the Lamar board of regents had only acted "in accordance with the Attorney General's interpretation of the law" in its policies affecting the operation of the college.[87]

In another letter, McDonald tried to allay the fears of a Galveston father who was concerned about his daughters who attended Lamar:

> I am sure you know I am very definitely apposed [sic] to integration as is the Board of Regents. We have done everything in our power to keep from having negroes. As a parent you will be interested to know that there are only about ten negroes in the day classes where your daughters are concerned. No two are in any one classroom and no white student need sit by or in any way be in contact with one. If you are at all concerned, I will be glad for you to telephone me; however, I think that everything will work out and we are having a very wonderful fall session. Our enrollment has jumped from 4680 to 5600 and no class work has been interrupted at all. The students have been a real inspiration to me as I try to make the wisest decisions over these great troublesome problems.[88]

Segregated seating arrangements, the college's disinclination to accept younger blacks with no prior collegiate experience, and the policy of restricting the number of blacks to one or two per class are but a few examples of the latitude that McDonald gave himself in handling the "great troublesome" problem of desegregation.

Warren Breed, in his study of how students and the "campus community" adjusted to desegregation, conducted an informal poll of thirty-one white students. He found the group divided about evenly, with sixteen supporting equality for blacks and the remaining fifteen being indifferent or nonsupportive. His sample revealed no enthusiastic "integrators" but did include five students who felt bitter, two of whom "seemed vindictive and emotionally angered" by the admission of blacks at Lamar. With regard to desegregation, "girls were markedly more favorable than boys." Breed learned of only two white students who left Lamar in protest: "One was in an English course. At the first lecture, a white student remained seated, visibly angered. The instructor went over, and the student said he could not stand Negroes in his classroom. The instructor said, 'That's just fine.' The student never returned. The second student was in a shop course, and about 50 years old. He told his instructor he was 'just too old to start going to school with niggers.' "[89]

Black students had a different adjustment experience. White students had to make a transition from a traditionally white campus to accommodating twenty-six blacks. Black students had to make a transition from exclusion from the Lamar campus to reluctant acceptance in a tense setting. After the ugly period of picketing, blacks continued to experience the pain of discrimination and prejudice. Winona Frank recalled that "once classes began, I felt myself surrounded by whites staring at me, gawking, and talking behind my back in their little groups that I was never asked to join." She had no hostile encounters with picketers and never missed a day of class during the disturbances. In addition, because Frank was a light-skinned Creole and a product of Catholic schools, where she learned English primarily from Irish nuns and priests, she looked, spoke, and appeared white. Her husband, Edward, who was attending Lamar on the GI Bill, was more racially identifiable as a Negro. When they walked hand-in-hand to their classes they sometimes created a sensation. One instructor, unaware of Frank's race, requested that she come to his office one day. Referring to her husband, he asked her, "What is that man to you?" When she told him they were married, the instructor became visibly upset and began treating her with less respect than before.[90]

Frank and five other black students persevered against many injustices before they received their degrees from the college in May 1958. Bell, Flanagan, Frank, Rice, and Vincent, all education majors, and Randolph, a business major, became Lamar's first black graduates. Surviving the long, cold winter of discrimination earned them a little adulation in the black community, a sort of consolation prize.[91]

Trouble in Texarkana and the State Repression of the NAACP

As white power battled black equality in Beaumont, another front in the struggle raged in Texarkana. Although the fight to open Texarkana Junior College (TJC) was the first continuously active campaign to desegregate a public institution of higher education in the state after Heman Sweatt filed his suit against the University of Texas, ultimately it was the NAACP's most difficult and disastrous battle. Through the influence of two native sons of Texarkana, the Texas State Conference of NAACP Branches' executive secretary, A. Maceo Smith, and its president, John J. Jones, blacks began discussing applying to the junior college as early as 1948. Dr. and Mrs. A. H. A. Jones and their son George volunteered for the campaign. A few months later, John L. Montgomery and his daughter, Betty Jo Taylor, a senior at Dunbar High School, agreed to be a part of a "total effort," including legal action. Smith praised him for offering his family to be involved in "opening up this whole question of educational inequalities provided Negro students." A lawsuit, however, did not make its way to trial until June 1952. After such a long road to the promised land of justice, *Bruce* v. *Stilwell*, named for Geraldine I. Bruce, one of the black petitioners, and TJC president H. W. Stilwell, ended up being dismissed because the plaintiffs had not appealed to the State Board of Education, which, it turned out, claimed no authority over the admission policy of the school. By the time the Fifth Circuit Court of Appeals reversed the lower court's judgment in April 1953, another challenge to segregation at the junior college already had begun.[92]

John J. Jones, a prominent black mortician in Texarkana since 1914, eagerly desired to gain bragging rights among state and national NAACP leaders by winning a victory against segregation at the junior college. With the *Bruce* case pending before the court, Jones, Montgomery, and other local NAACP leaders encouraged blacks to continue applying to the school. During the opening week of the 1952 summer session at TJC, nine of Dunbar's newest graduates went to the campus seeking admission. The first black applicants arrived as a group. Bobbie Jean Whittaker, Wilma Jean Whitmore, and Bettie Lee Edwards, along with the adults who accompanied them, met with the college's dean and the registrar. They were referred to Hale Parker, president of the school board of the junior college district, and Parker, in turn, told them that the trustees would take up their request for admission at their 9 June meeting. The six women and three men in the group, along with several family members and friends, appeared that night for what became a lengthy discussion. The board approved the creation of a biracial negotiating committee, consisting of trustees and the black students and their adult supporters, and stipulated that the group "meet in an effort to work the matter out in a manner satisfactory to all." The simple-sounding task, however, proved to be utterly impossible.[93]

Tate, in his annual report, noted that TJC district officials had "commanded every divisive machination that their collective genius could conjure to frustrate the purpose of the petitioners." The committee trustees came up with some unique proposals. One plan they suggested, which was very similar to proposals put forth in various cities when blacks sued for access to city parks and recreational facilities, entailed white students attending the junior college in the morning and black students in the afternoon, or vice versa. They held that such a policy would maintain racial separation and, since both races would be "using the same facilities and having the same curriculum and the same teachers," no inequality would exist. Black committee members flatly rejected the scheme. Next, the trustees proposed construction of a new building staffed and equipped like the existing junior college, with the same courses. Blacks would then be permitted to choose TJC's building or the new building for their very own junior college. The black students also refused to sanction this separate school plan. The board, however, went ahead with creating a black branch of TJC.[94]

The board authorized the addition of three classrooms to Dunbar High School and hired three instructors, giving one of them, the holder of a Ph.D., the title of president. In September, when the school opened its doors to the black community, not a single student enrolled. District officials closed the branch school, found its teachers jobs in the high school, and faced another suit to open TJC to blacks. Tate gave the credit to the "high quality" of John Jones's leadership for the "cohesiveness of the community" behind the desegregation of TJC. "He has," the regional counsel wrote, "simply refused to let Jim Crow sprout new roots" in Texarkana. Judge Joe Sheehy, who in November 1954 heard and decided the new suit, *Whitmore* v. *Stilwell*, dismissed the suit on technical grounds. TJC administrators, unlike those at most other white colleges, never stipulated that the black applicants possessed all qualifications for admission other than race and color. District secretary Thomas A. Bain wrote that because of Article 7, Section 7, and Article 2900, the students were "not qualified to attend the Texarkana Junior College." Sheehy also suggested that Dunbar, from which they had graduated, might not have been an accredited high school at the time of their graduation. He also loaded his opinion with other technical matters, such as the failure of the plaintiffs to properly name all seven members of TJC's board as a party to the suit; the students' failure to reapply that fall semester "in the light of the ruling laid down in the *Brown* case"; and, contrary to the previous point, the pendency of the court's final implementation decrees in *Brown*. Tate and his co-counsel, W. J. Durham, appealed Sheehy's ruling to the Fifth Circuit Court, which a year later saw past the smokescreens and overturned the case. Despite Bain's eleventh-hour attempt to inject other irrelevant matters, the circuit court observed that the TJC's use of race as an admissions criteria remained the only issue in the case, and it declared the practice of such a policy unlawful.[95]

NAACP leaders in Texarkana recruited several students from Dunbar's class of 1956 to apply to TJC in for fall semester. President Stilwell and the board searched for every means to evade complying with the law. Stilwell and board member Bill Williams even went so far as to encourage the growing forces of massive resistance in the area. In Bowie County, whites outnumbered blacks three to one. Texarkana, half of which was in Texas and half in Arkansas, erupted the first week in September on both sides. When eighteen-year-old Jessalyn Gray, seventeen-year-old Steve James Poston, and a few other black students presented themselves for registration, officials asked them to reconsider but let them take their entrance exams, pay fees, and buy books. When the news spread that blacks were about to enter TJC, violence and massive protests took over the city. Death threats against blacks rang throughout the black community. Violent outbreaks included a shotgun blast fired into a service station owned by an NAACP leader and a cross and a Negro burned in effigy on the campus. On 6 September, just hours after black students enrolled at TJC, a Citizens' Council meeting convened. Keynote speaker Stilwell exhorted the crowd: "It is not only your right but your duty to resist" being mixed with blacks. To admit blacks to TJC would lower the school's educational standards, he asserted, and would lead to the desegregation of the grade schools, even to the "babies who can't help themselves."[96]

Roused by such rhetoric, an estimated 500 whites mobbed the entrance of TJC on 10 September, the first day of classes. Most of the jeering, placard-carrying group were men, the older ones dressed in overalls and working boots, the young ones wearing rolled up denim trousers and penny loafers. They chose to lose a day of work to come and stand guard against Gray and Poston. The eight-year-long legal battle had come to this: two black teenagers waiting, books in hand, facing angry white men who yelled and held signs reading "No Mixed Classes" and "Go Home Niggers!" Waiting in the hot sun for what? TJC board member Williams stood in the crowd hooting right along with the rest. Four Texas Rangers and Bowie County police officers observed the standoff at a distance. When Gray asked a Ranger for help, he told her that Governor Allan Shivers had not sent them to be an escort service for black students but to keep the peace and maintain order. When the two students tried to walk through the mob, some men threw rocks at them, separating them briefly, and one kicked Poston. At that point, some blacks who were watching at a distance sent in a taxicab to get Gray and Poston out of harm's way. According to a newspaper report, "After 15 minutes packed with tension the Negroes climbed into a taxi and rolled away." During the days of turbulence in the city, authorities arrested seven black teenagers for throwing rocks at a carload of white youths who taunted them. Justice may have been blind, but, in Texarkana in the fall of 1956, it was not color-blind.[97]

The Citizens' Council's "peaceful riot," as one of its leaders dubbed the event, convinced blacks to back off their campaign to desegregate TJC. By telephone, John Jones and Tate responded by filing a motion citing Stil-

In September 1956, Steve Poston and Jessalyn Gray were greeted by a racist mob that prevented them from attending their first day of classes at Texarkana Junior College. State law enforcement officials did not intervene, and the college remained segregated for another decade (photo by Joseph Scherschel, Getty Images, Inc.).

well and Williams with contempt of the federal court order that required them to admit blacks to the school. Tate entered the suit against the TJC officials in Judge Sheehy's court without ever having met or spoken with his clients. On 26 September, the day before Judge Sheehy's pretrial hearing on the matter, Assistant Attorney General L. W. Gray went to Texarkana. He hauled Jessalyn Yvonne Gray and her father, Clarence, along with Steve James Poston and his mother, Rosa, before a court of inquiry presided over by a Bowie County justice of the peace. Frightened by the presence of armed police officers, the Grays and the Postons told the court that they had known nothing about the lawsuit against the TJC officials until they read about it in the newspapers. They did not know, had never met, nor had even spoken with a Ulysses Simpson Tate, much less retained him. Clarence Gray testified that he had not discussed or given his permission to Jones, Tate, or anyone else to file a lawsuit for his daughter to go to TJC. He said he thought Tate was the city attorney. Likewise, Steve Poston denied knowing Tate or agreeing to be a party to any lawsuit. He added that he did not know Jones was an NAACP leader nor had he ever attended a meeting of the NAACP. Rosa Poston also professed no knowledge of a lawsuit, but when asked what she thought about Steve's going to TJC, she replied, "My idea is he could go there and be at home. It would be more cheaper and lighter on him." Getting into TJC, however, had proven anything but light.[98]

After Gray and Poston disclosed that they had not hired Tate to file a lawsuit, Clarence Gray knew the case before Sheehy the next day easily could be demolished. At the hearing, Sheehy permitted TJC's lawyer, John Raffaelli, to put witnesses on the stand to show that the petitioners, Jessalyn Gray and Steve Poston, did not wish to intervene and sue Stilwell and Williams for obstructing the execution of the court order arising from *Whitmore* v. *Stilwell.* Tate testified that before that day, he had never seen the clients he claimed to represent and that Jones was his sole contact with Gray and Poston. Next Raffaelli put A. H. Jones and John Montgomery on the witness stand. Through their cogent testimony, his argument began to crumble, and he grew more impatient. When he finished with one witness, he would call the next one immediately, forcing Sheehy to intervene so that Tate could cross-examine his witnesses. His trump card, however, was Gray and Poston. Gray initially testified that she had not asked anyone to file a suit on her behalf. But as Raffaelli continued to question her, she started to crack. Her problem, she explained, arose from the fact that she did not know the exact "nature of the situation." She said she told Jones to use her name and that he promised her that the NAACP was going to "do something" about her being denied entrance to TJC. Raffaelli reminded her of her testimony the day before and then began to hammer the soft-spoken youth with direct, yes or no questions. With Sheehy barking to her to "speak out louder," she started to give the lawyer what he wanted to hear. She affirmed that Montgomery contacted her and asked to use her name, but she denied he ever told her he would be hiring a lawyer for her. Under cross-examination Tate put her at ease, but her testimony became confused and contradictory. She answered that she still desired to attend TJC but then added, "What I really wanted to do is just to go to college." Tate elicited answers that helped put the NAACP's actions in a better light. He ended by asking her if she wanted a lawsuit if that was what it would take to get her into TJC. She answered meekly, "I suppose so." "I'm not asking what you suppose," Tate retorted, "I am asking you, do you want a law suit [*sic*] now?" When she replied that "expenses and things like that" associated with the suit left her uncertain, Tate asked the court's permission "to dismiss this petition as to Miss Gray." Sheehy granted the motion.[99]

Poston gave Raffaelli no trouble at all, clearly stating that he knew nothing of a lawsuit until reading about it in the news and that he had not authorized anyone to file a lawsuit for him. He mustered the courage to say that he had been willing to let his name "be used in trying to get admission for my right," but he said he never knew that his name would be used for legal action. Not bothering to cross-examine Poston, Tate made another motion for dismissal and ended the hearing. Sheehy took the opportunity to rebuke Tate and to demand that in the future he be sure he was properly employed by the party he purported to represent before setting foot in his courtroom. "I want the Court to know," Tate responded, "I appreciate very much the situation." In an instant, eight years of litigation to open TJC ended. With the town perilously close to a full-blown race riot, the NAACP had moved teenagers like chess pieces in a gambit where their lives and means of survival could be taken away. Neither Jones's wealth and prestige, brilliant NAACP lawyers, nor constitutional principles would protect them from the immediate threat they perceived. The state attorney with armed officers had the power to take them from their homes and terrorists could bomb them out permanently. The Grays and Postons folded, but not out of an irrational fear. They assessed the risks, the strength of the enemy, and made a costly strategic retreat. From the Ku Klux Klan to the suit-and-tie-wearing Citizens' Council, from local Texarkana folks to agents of the state government, the forces of white supremacy in 1956 kept TJC off-limits to black folks for another eight years. The junior college did not admit its first black students until 1963.[100]

The defeat in Judge Sheehy's Tyler courtroom marked only the first act in a farce of monumental proportions. The next day, a temporary injunction hearing in the case *The State of Texas* v. *The National Association for the Advancement of Colored People, a corporation, et al.*, began. At issue was the continued existence of the NAACP in Texas and the right of citizens in a democracy to protest and change the status quo. The case followed similar prosecutions that year in Alabama, Louisiana, and other southern states. In June, an Alabama judge granted a temporary restraining order against the NAACP on the grounds that the organization had been operating as a business in the state without registering. The next month, the judge ordered the NAACP to turn over various records, including its membership lists for all branches in the state. When the NAACP refused to give up the lists, the judge cited it for contempt of court, imposed stiff fines, and maintained the injunction barring it from collecting dues or accepting contributions. Legal action between the state and the NAACP continued for the next eight years, during which period the NAACP ceased to function in Alabama. Louisiana also faced a major assault on civil liberties beginning in 1956. Using an old anti-Klan law, state officials banned the NAACP until its leaders turned in branch membership lists. Of this wave of repressive action, Numan V. Bartley wrote nearly three decades ago in *The Rise of Massive Resistance*: "The war on the NAACP represented the gravest overt threat to basic civil liberties during the 1950's." Thurgood Marshall called the Tyler trial the "greatest crisis" in the organization's history.[101]

The scheme to repress the NAACP sprung from the white supremacist's elemental belief that blacks accepted inequality in educational opportunity and other public goods and services because they were smart enough to know that whites were a superior race and deserved what they had and that blacks, being an inferior race, knew they did not deserve to have absolute equality. If blacks began to seek equality through desegregation, then there had to be some outside force that had disturbed their normally contented minds. Texas attorney general Shepperd, Governor Shivers, and other segregationists genuinely believed that Communists, through the NAACP, had stirred up blacks, aiming ultimately to pollute the social and biological essence of the master race. Naturally, they had to stop it.[102]

Prior to appearing before Judge Otis Dunagan, Shepperd engaged a team of lawyers and a former FBI agent to investigate the NAACP. Sterling Fulmore Jr., assigned by the attorney general to the probe, submitted on 11 September 1956 an interoffice memorandum titled "N.A.A.C.P. Communist Front Affiliation." In it he provided details tying key NAACP activists to Communists and subversive groups. He cited U. Simpson Tate, Juanita Craft, Lulu B. White, Kenneth Lamkin, and Arthur DeWitty for involvement with the Harlem-based Civil Rights Congress (CRC). In the late 1940s, Attorney General Tom Clark and the Congressional Committee on Un-American Activities found the CRC "to be controlled by individuals who were either members of the Communist Party or openly loyal to it." Hard hit by the U.S. government's Subversive Activities Control Board, the CRC dissolved in 1956. Fulmore's memorandum drew from the study "Individuals from Texas Reported as Having Been Affiliated with Communist-Front Organizations — As Compiled from Official Government Reports," which identified over 200 Texans from various ethnic, educational, and occupational backgrounds. The document, written by a Houston woman, named prominent figures at the University of Texas such as Clarence Ayres, J. Frank Dobie, Homer Rainey, George I. Sanchez, and Carlos Castaneda; college executives such as the UT Medical Branch's Chauncey Leake, Thomas W. Currie of the Austin Presbyterian Theological Seminary, and Texas Christian University's Colby D. Hall; religious leaders like Rabbi Hyman Judah Schachtel of Houston and Archbishop Robert Lucey of San Antonio; and labor leaders, outright Communist party members, and almost all of the NAACP's leadership. For most of the blacks, including Huston-Tillotson College president Mary E. Branch, A. Maceo Smith, John Jones, Rev. M. K. Curry of Wichita Falls, and TSU president Ralph O'Hara Lanier, membership in the CRC, the Southern Conference for Human Welfare, the National Negro Congress (the parent body of the CRC), or the National Federation for Constitutional Liberties got them placed on the list. These individuals were cited in light of the official findings of two leading anti-Communist Texans in Washington, D.C., Martin Dies, chair of the House Un-American Activities Committee, and Attorney General Tom Clark. Shepperd had also considered linking his assault on the NAACP to the Cold War by adding to the list of charges violations of the Communist Control Act of 1954. On the advice of his assistants, however, he decided it would be impractical to take such an approach.[103]

The case Shepperd did undertake alleged that the NAACP had "exceeded the bounds of propriety and law." He asked for an injunction against the operation of the civil rights organization and its legal arm, the Legal Defense and Education Fund, Inc., known as the LDF, on the grounds that they had violated barratry laws against soliciting litigation; that the two groups were corporations organized under the laws of New York and were operating illegally in the state of Texas; and that, since they were "foreign" profit-making entities, they had evaded paying state franchise taxes. Judge Dunagan approved an order restraining the NAACP for seven days until he could hear its answer to the charges. A temporary injunction hearing was held on 1 October 1956 to decide whether the ban on association activities should be extended several more months until a permanent injunction hearing would be held. In collaboration with Marshall and the LDF, Tate, Durham, Johns, Willard, and other Texas attorneys had pioneered a new kind of public-interest law practice in the state, and now a state court would scrutinize their practice from top to bottom. Tate, in his eagerness to win victories against Jim Crow and show his colleagues the way forward, sometimes failed to heed special counsel Marshall's advice to exercise caution in his work against white supremacist laws. Tate had to rely heavily on local NAACP leaders (and lawyers in the rare case of Beaumont and the Lamar suit) because of the sheer size of Texas, as well as financial and organizational considerations. He briefed them by mail and by phone on the steps to take toward the college in each area, but he could not afford the time to go to each locale, and local plaintiffs and NAACP branches seldom could afford the expense to bring him to Kilgore, Wichita Falls, Kingsville, El Paso, Austin, Denton, Texarkana, and all the other places at every stage of preparing a suit to go to trial. At the same time, the desire of plaintiffs, like Jessalyn Gray, to get on with their education, made it very difficult for local communities to get volunteers who were willing to tie up their lives in litigation for a year or more. Moreover, the rising tide of white resistance to social change, the violence, the threatening letters and phone calls, the economic pressure, and the police and state repression put the NAACP and the LDF between a rock and a hard place: do nothing or go to court and run the risk of being charged with stirring up lawsuits.[104]

To civil rights advocates, the Tyler trial was the most important court battle in the history of the state, except, perhaps, for the *Sweatt* trial. The case named as defendants all 112 branches of the NAACP in Texas, the Texas State Conference of Branches, and the NAACP southwestern regional office. Before the hearing, agents of the attorney general's office visited citizens who had challenged segregation at Texas colleges or grade schools, current and former plaintiffs in school desegregation cases, and the officers of more than a dozen NAACP chapters. Tate, in a deliberate overreaction, denounced the use of state troopers who accompanied assistant attorney generals during their investigations: "We consider some of the methods now being used by the Attorney General as highly improper and unlawful. It now appears that this is ceasing to be a lawful investigation. It is becoming a campaign of coercion and suppression designed to deprive Negro citizens of Texas of their civil rights and to threaten them with danger and harm to their person." Tate had a case against the state's intimidation tactics, but he was speaking to the media and to the record, not to the court in which the case was being tried.[105]

The activities in September 1956 of Riley Eugene Fletcher, an assistant attorney general, are illustrative of the typical "raid" on an NAACP branch, as well as of how this wave of state repression directly tied local civil rights activists to the Tyler trial. Fletcher, accompanied by a Texas Highway Patrol captain and two patrolmen, began making unannounced visits to NAACP members in the Beaumont area. Their first stop was Sprott Clinic to see Ed Sprott Jr., president of the Beaumont NAACP branch. After waiting thirty minutes to see the physician, Fletcher asked him to produce all "papers, books, minutes [and] official correspondence" of the branch. Sprott replied that he kept nothing pertaining to the organization at his office but then vacillated when the state attorney told him to bring out whatever he had. After haranguing Fletcher on the merits of the NAACP, Sprott produced a few leaflets and referred his interrogator to the NAACP secretary Pauline Brackeen and the NAACP vice president Marion Lewis. Fletcher went to the Brackeen residence, but a neighbor, Leah Saint Julian, told him no one was at home and that they were out of state on vacation. He then went to the law offices of Johns and Willard and showed the local attorneys who handled the Lamar State College case his "official visitation letter" and his identification card. They opened their files to him, and he took four documents from the Lamar College case file and went to the office of County Clerk Fred Hill, who had the documents photocopied at no charge. After treating his armed escorts to lunch, Fletcher worked until close to midnight, visiting two more residences in Beaumont and two locations in Port Arthur. Mrs. Charles Graham, a Beaumont branch NAACP Youth Council adviser, after looking at the visitation letter and identification card, let the men into her living room. She denied that she held any post in the branch, then stated that she had been elected an adviser at a meeting she had not attended and had never served in that capacity. Upon request, she retrieved some NAACP papers she had but then became "perturbed" when Fletcher began copying down information from one of the letters. She asked what he was doing, and he responded that she should call the branch attorneys, Johns and Willard, and follow their counsel.

After phoning Johns she told Fletcher to go ahead and finish what he had begun. At his visit with Marion Lewis, Fletcher collected nine documents to photocopy. After patrolman J. S. Moses replaced one of his escorts, Fletcher went to visit NAACP officers in Port Arthur. Branch vice president Damon Davis, a Caucasian chemical engineer at the Gulf Oil refinery, and his wife, who was active in the membership committee, gave the men a chilly reception. Moses told Fletcher that the Davis family held biracial committee meetings at their home, a fact that caused some of their neighbors to no longer speak to them. "Quite agitated" by the surprise visit of the state official, Damon Davis asked whether he had to answer any of Fletcher's questions. The attorney replied that he did not but that failure to cooperate could "jeopardize the corporation's [NAACP's] right to do business in Texas." Davis also objected to bringing out any organizational papers, saying that they were private. At that point, as Fletcher related in his summary report to Attorney General Shepperd, "his wife spoke up, and said, 'Get him all the papers, we have nothing to hide. There are no Communists under that sofa.' Davis said to his wife, 'I thought you were just going to come in here and listen.' Davis went to another room, and got a large brown, Manila envelope, from which he removed a stack of papers, and started thumbing through them. I told him, 'Just remove all purely private and personal matters. I just want to see the official papers.' Mrs. Davis spoke to her husband in a sharp tone, and said, 'Give him the whole stack! We've got nothing to hide!' "[106] Davis handed over the entire stack of NAACP documents. Fletcher went through it, removed what he wanted, and returned the rest. Davis and his wife stated that they felt that the investigation was an act of pure "political persecution" on Shepperd's part to serve his own purposes. They asked whether his office also was investigating the White Citizens' Council and whether Shepperd would probe other groups to which they belonged such as the Parent-Teachers Association. Before Fletcher left, Davis talked at length about the black honor graduates who sought admission to Lamar, how they were "fine people" and "would have been a credit to the college" but instead had to attend school at TSU or Prairie View. Fletcher politely dismissed these comments and left to visit Jessie Gardner, a black housewife and the secretary of the Port Arthur branch. She brought out her records, and he began manually copying names from the membership rolls until he found his "eyes were failing." He returned to his motel room just before midnight.

Fletcher had no time to waste. Shepperd needed all the information he could get before the Tyler trial started, and news of Fletcher's visits had spread quickly among NAACP members, some of whom managed to avoid meeting with him or simply did not cooperate. He had to seize the time in order to maintain the element of surprise. The next day, after sending Shepperd a message via teletypewriter, he returned to Port Arthur. When the state attorney arrived at the house of Leroy Horton, the black refinery worker and president of the local NAACP branch met him in his yard and greeted him by name, saying he had been waiting for him to come all morning but had to leave for work. Taken by surprise, Fletcher said he would see him another day and then drove off, but then he decided to double-back and demand to see whatever NAACP papers Horton possessed. Horton replied as state and national leaders had instructed branch leaders to respond, that he had only one, the official charter for the branch. Fletcher looked at the charter, returned it, and left.

Fletcher then traveled to Orange, the third city in what locals call the Golden Triangle, where he visited the president, vice president, and secretary of the NAACP branch. At the home of the vice president, Dr. M. F. Harris, and his wife, the couple demanded to know what the investigation was about and whether the Citizens' Councils had also been targeted. Harris, a black physician, was indignant but conceded that it was beyond the branch's power to prevent Fletcher from seeing its records. Fletcher coyly suggested that Harris could prevent the inquiry by refusing to produce the papers. Harris, however, was aware that a couple of months earlier, an Alabama judge held the association in contempt of court for refusing to provide the state with membership rolls and correspondence and fined it $100,000. Harris told Fletcher that he would authorize branch secretary Louise Pritchard to provide him with the minute book and membership roll. Fletcher went there and copied names from the membership roll, noting that it was a partial list. Finally, he visited branch president J. L. Arnold Jr., a black refinery worker, and went through a stack of papers and letters Arnold produced. After taking a few documents for photocopying, he asked Arnold about the number of branch members and other matters before leaving for supper.

That evening, Fletcher made copies of the documents he had netted during the day. He then made his second trip to the Gardner home. "It became apparent very shortly," he noted, "that her attitude had changed since we were there the preceding night." She began arguing with the men about bringing out the books until Fletcher told her sharply, "Let's get them out, the clock's running, and we are wasting time." She brought the books out but protested about having to stay up while they did their work. After saying she was going to bed she came into her kitchen, where the men were working, and, as Fletcher recorded it, "turned on a portable radio about two feet from my ear; played it quite loud, listening to a Negro high school foot ball game, and hollering in a loud voice to her boy in another room. Then she got the insect spray gun, and went over the kitchen, filling it full of spray." Her exerting control over her living space made a clear impression on the attorney.[107]

Later that night, Fletcher learned that newspaper reporters had discovered he was in town conducting anti-NAACP raids. The secrecy of his mission had been blown. The next morning, Fletcher called Assistant Attorney General John Davenport to report on his work. Davenport relieved him of carrying out his scheduled visits in the nearby town of Liberty and told him he "could come on home." That Friday, 21 September 1956, Davenport obtained from Judge Otis Dunagan in Tyler a temporary court order to shut down the operations of the NAACP. In the days ahead, Shepperd and his battery of lawyers put together the material Fletcher collected in Beaumont, Port Arthur, and Orange, with records that other assistant attorneys obtained in raids at the national New York offices of the NAACP and the LDF, at the large chapters at Houston and Dallas, along with material gathered from other local Texas branches such as Austin, El Paso, Texarkana, Mansfield, Fort Worth, Abilene, Monahans, Pecos, Odessa, Brownwood, San Angelo, Midland, Wharton, and Gainesville.

During the near month-long hearing, the state produced over five hundred exhibits and more than a million words of testimony that came primarily from its raids and three courts of inquiry. Jessalyn Gray and Steve Poston testified, as they had at the Texarkana inquisition, that they had not authorized a suit to be filed against TJC. Gray added that "she was so scared by the white officers wearing guns who summoned her to the court of inquiry that she would now be afraid to file a lawsuit to enter the college." A contract dating back a decade in which Tate agreed to pay Heman Sweatt an $11,500 stipend to support him and pay for his education once his lawsuit opened the University of Texas Law School was another major piece of damaging evidence against the NAACP. After Marshall, Durham, and C. B. Bunkley put on the NAACP's defense and both sides made masterful closing arguments, Judge Dunagan rendered his decision restraining the NAACP and LDF from operating in the state of Texas until a final hearing could be held. On 8 May 1957, Judge Dunagan signed and entered a permanent injunction and ended the *Texas* v. NAACP affair. The NAACP, after some internal wrangling, chose not to appeal the ruling.[108]

Shepperd's raids, the Tyler trial, and Dunagan's ban were not the only troubles the association faced, nor were they the only assaults on the movement for the desegregation of public education. In 1956, snuff-dipping Jerry Sadler, an attorney and a 1946 gubernatorial candidate representing the tiny East Texas backwater of Percilla, announced plans to introduce two bills aimed at restricting the NAACP and nine bills directed at preserving school segregation. The latter bills would put into effect the proposals the Shivers-appointed state Advisory Committee on Segregation in Public Schools adopted in September 1956 by a thirteen to five vote. The odious anti-NAACP measures, which followed examples set by other states, "would make it unlawful for any state or municipal government agency or any school to employ a member of the NAACP and would require all persons and organizations to register with the Secretary of State if their principal function is either to promote or to oppose racial integration." In the wake of Dunagan's temporary injunction and prosegregation Price Daniel's win over the liberal Ralph Yarborough in the gubernatorial election, it must have seemed at the end of 1956 that Houston NAACP leader Christia Adair's prophecy that Texas would fall under the rule of the Citizens' Council was coming true.[109]

A 20 December 1956 summit meeting of twenty of the 181 Texas legislators (31 senators and 100 members of the House) at Marshall, a major East Texas city in which blacks comprised more than half its population, consolidated a core group around Sadler's bills in advance of the opening of the legislative session in January. With its equal opportunity provision against those promoting *or* opposing racial integration, the notorious "thought permit" bill did not fare well. It was passed by the House, but when it went before a senate committee the members referred it to the new attorney general, Will Wilson, who declared it unconstitutional. As for the other anti-NAACP bill requiring all state and city employees to sign sworn statements that they were not members of the NAACP, in March 1957, Reagan R. Huffman, Marshall attorney and summit host, got it onto the floor for argument. "We can take care of our Negro citizens," Huffman told his House colleagues; "they don't want the trouble caused by the NAACP." When George Thurmond, the South Texas lawyer from Del Rio, asked if the NAACP had ever been found guilty in a court of law of being a subversive organization, Huffman answered, "No, sir. But I'm going to answer with this: We have evidence that [the] NAACP is infiltrated with members of the Communist Party." Although several lawmakers doubted the legality of the bill, HB 32 passed in the House seventy-five to forty-nine.[110]

A group of South and West Texas senators, who came to be known as the "filibusteros," opposed the bill. Its leaders, Henry Gonzalez of San Antonio and Abraham Kazen Jr. of Laredo, both the sons of immigrant Catholics, took turns speaking continuously for thirty-six and one-half hours as part of a marathon filibuster that killed the anti-NAACP measure and led to the defeat of all but two prosegregation bills. Although the Senate floor was conspicuously empty during periods of the "talkathon," a crowd of blacks and whites largely supportive of the senators filled the galleries cheering them on — until the presiding officer who had warned the group against demonstrations ordered them cleared. Gonzalez, a former city councilman who made the motion to desegregate all San Antonio's public facilities, had eschewed advice in his first term in the state legislature that as a junior senator he not take so bold a stand on a controversial matter. Outmaneuvering veteran senators like Wardlow Lane of Center, Gonzalez shrewdly observed to the press that "time worked in our favor. We did serve the purpose of focusing public opinion on this type of legislation." Letters and telegrams flooded the legislature during the highly publicized filibuster, but for perhaps the first time, a significant amount of the mail opposed the extreme attempts to uphold segregation, putting the white supremacists on the defensive.[111]

With the NAACP humbled, the church stepped up to lead the opposition to racial extremism. Organized labor also ended its virtual silence on the abuse of civil rights and liberties by the state and its citizens. Shortly after Dunagan's temporary injunction, Rev. A. A. Lucas, president of the Missionary Baptist General Convention of Texas and former president of the Texas State Conference of NAACP Branches in the 1940s, gave a passionate and moving speech to about 100 black ministers and lay leaders in Dallas. He implored them to be alert to "what's happening to our people" and to not create "a substitute for the NAACP" but to carry on its work. "If anyone should want to enjoin the church, let them do it," he said. "If the church goes to jail, it will pray itself out." In Fort Worth, the Texas State Council of Methodist Women approved a resolution against efforts to thwart the implementation of *Brown*. Endorsing a report from its committee on human rights, the Texas State Congress of Industrial Organizations Council added its opposition to "the program of the 'hate' organizations" and called on its members to work to abolish racial discrimination in public agencies and schools. Texas Council of Churches leader Harold Kirkpatrick got church leaders to barrage the legislature with telegrams opposing passage of the prosegregation bills. Thus, within two years of *Brown*, racial moderation in Texas had not died; it had just begun to thrive.[112]

Citizen Council aggression and state repression disrupted the NAACP's momentum and neutralized much of its local base, but the NAACP by no means disappeared. In January 1958, NAACP leader Roy Wilkins wrote NAACP activist H. Boyd Hall, saying he knew "that the situation within the state conference and among the branches is not an easy one." He nonetheless expressed his "hope that our Texas members and branches are going to snap out of it in 1958. Apparently they were a little dazed and confused by the 1957 situation, but by now they ought to be ready to go ahead."[113]

Slowly the NAACP and the movement for civil rights in Texas did stumble to their feet. Of all the movement's experiences — the legal battles, the great speeches, the sanctions levied against it by fanatical white supremacists in the streets and in state government — what most helped the association to resume its role in the political and legal arena was the bravery shown by blacks, especially the youth, in demanding their rights. An editorialist in the *New York Post*, far removed from the heat of the struggle, made the point most poignantly:

Do the Jim Crow legions believe such victories [as Dunagan's order] can halt the drive for equality? We suggest they look at the photographs of the quiet, resolute Negro children defying jeers and violence and sadism. The NAACP may be hounded and driven underground; but who will smother the valiant kids, and who will say they can be permanently detoured by stones or injunctions? Some day they will be able to tell their own children of how they endured this ordeal. There will be few comparable moments of glory for the adult delinquents leading this desperate last stand of white supremacy.

With the images of courageous youth like Marilyn Menefee, Joe Atkins, Jessalyn Gray, and Lonnie Flanagan facing down virulent and age-old hatreds to stoke the cause, the struggle to advance democracy continued.[114]

CHAPTER SIX

Plowing around Africans on Aryan Plantations
Access without Equity at Texas Universities, 1958–1965

Negro students have been desegregated but not integrated. . . . We are cut off
from the general stream of university life.
—Anthony Henry, a black sophomore at UT, December 1957

In the aftermath of the state's assault on civil liberties, Texas white supremacists began to realize that sanctions against the democratic movement for racial integration could only slow the pace of change; it could not
reverse its direction. By disrupting the work of the NAACP, the attorney
general's office had curtailed the momentum of the civil rights revolution.
The ideas of equal protection of the laws and equal educational opportunity and access and the discrediting and abandoning of the philosophy
of racial superiority, however, continued to challenge segregation at state
universities and colleges. In 1958, Richard Morehead of the *Dallas Morning
News* reported the findings of the first survey on desegregation of Texas
colleges. Morehead had mailed questionnaires to the presidents of over
100 public and private institutions of higher learning in Texas and disclosed that thirty-six schools had desegregated and nine others had open
policies (see Table 5).[1]

At the hold-out schools, administrative boards clung to the concept of
Texas supporting all-black colleges, several mixed universities, and a number of all-white colleges. The idea of a tripartite system of higher education
came to be known as the "salt-and-pepper plan." It was based on a simple
analogy to how people like to season their food: some like the taste of salt
but cannot stand pepper; others like pepper but cannot handle the salt;
still others prefer both salt and pepper. In the same way that a restaurant
accommodates all three preferences among its diners, so too, went the
argument, should the state provide institutions for blacks and whites who

Table 5. Desegregated Texas Senior and Junior Colleges in 1958

Institution, City	Year Desegregated	No. Black Students	No. White Students
Amarillo College, Amarillo	1951	23	1,346
Borger City Junior College, Borger[b]	1954		
Cisco Junior College, Cisco	1956	11	323
Del Mar Junior College, Corpus Christi	1952	25	2,100
Gainesville Junior College, Gainesville	1956	1	303
Howard County Junior College, Big Spring	1951	8	476
Lamar State College of Technology, Beaumont	1956	57	5,003
Laredo Junior College, Laredo	1954	4	773
Midwestern University, Wichita Falls	1954	16	1,435
North Texas State College, Denton	1956	133	5,855
Odessa Junior College, Odessa	1954	5	1,500
Pan-American College, Edinburg[b]	1954		
Paris Junior College, Paris	1956	4	382
Saint Philips College, San Antonio	1955	800	200
San Angelo College, San Angelo	1953	12	787
San Antonio College, San Antonio	1955	70	4,950
Southwestern Medical College, Dallas	1958	1	409
Temple Junior College, Temple	1957	11	368
Texarkana Junior College, Texarkana[a] opened by *Whitmore* v. *Stilwell*	1955		
Texas College of Arts and Industries, Kingsville	1956	15	2,785
Texas Southern University, Houston[a] opened by board of directors in 1956	1958		
Texas Southmost College, Brownsville	1951	2	900
Texas Western College, El Paso	1955	20	3,550
University of Texas at Austin	1950	165	15,925
University of Texas Medical Branch, Galveston	1949	22	480
University of Texas Dental School, Houston	1952	8	343
Victoria Junior College, Victoria	1954	8	947
Wharton Junior College, Wharton	1954	22	1,041
Totals		642	51,572

Sources: "Status of Texas Colleges," *SSN*, April 1958, 11, and February 1959, 2
Note: These figures are for black students enrolled at traditionally white institutions. The figures for Saint Philips College, a municipal, traditionally black institution, are not included.
[a] Desegregated by court order
[b] Open to both black and white students at inception

preferred or did not mind going to college together and exclusive facilities for those students who preferred to matriculate strictly with "their own kind." Two college systems formed the exclusive, salt-or-pepper parts of the plan: the six-member State Teachers College System and the four-member A&M College System (including Prairie View as the pepper-only campus). Killing Jim Crow at these institutions would be exceedingly difficult, especially in the absence of a strong NAACP and LDF challenging discrimination in the courts. The governing boards of these hold-out systems held fast to the "salt-and-pepper" slogan John Ben Shepperd introduced in the Versie Jackson trial in 1956 and ignored the fact that the federal judge in the case found the scheme unacceptable.[2]

Black Texans kept up the struggle to end segregation in higher education because they felt it represented a grave injustice and because they knew *Brown* made it an unlawful practice. The NAACP, moreover, had proven that the reform ideology of civil libertarianism could produce changes in the social order of the South that only prophets or lunatics dreamt possible. After the Court's ruling in *Brown*, the civil rights movement gained support from the federal judiciary and the U.S. Congress. The Civil Rights Bill of 1957, the first legislation since Reconstruction that involved the federal government in protecting the long-assailed and almost-forgotten citizenship rights of blacks was proposed as a direct result of *Brown*. As it worked its way through the House, Senate Majority Leader Lyndon Johnson played a major role in watering down and narrowing the scope of the original bill that Dwight Eisenhower's administration had drafted; and when it reached the Senate the Texas politician weakened it further. He had an interest, however, in passing some form of civil rights legislation. By convincing his southern colleagues in the Democratic Party to allow a toothless federal civil rights bill to get through Congress, Johnson knew he would prove his statesmanship and send his own presidential ambitions soaring. Johnson presented himself as maneuvering the bill past the vehement opposition of Dixiecratic stalwarts like Strom Thurmond on one side and legislative leaders like Democrat Hubert Humphrey and Republican Williams Knowland who backed a stronger version of the bill on the other. He handed Eisenhower a limited voting-rights protection measure, and on 9 September 1957, over the objections of many black and white critics, the president signed the compromise package into law. The act created two federal agencies: the U.S. Commission on Civil Rights (CRC) and the Civil Rights Division of the Justice Department.[3]

Immediately, the CRC launched into its mission as a "fact-finding body" and produced the document *Equal Protection of the Laws in Public Higher Education, 1960*. In 1959, it prepared questionnaires on enrollment by race and on admission policies and distributed them to fifty public institutions of higher learning in Texas. Out of twenty universities and four-year colleges, eighteen responded to the survey, and of its thirty junior colleges, twenty-three responded. Eleven traditionally white institutions and one traditionally black college reported that they still maintained segregation. Five schools said they excluded blacks on the grounds that their establishing acts determined that they were for white students only. In the six desegregated colleges that enumerated their enrollment by race, black students accounted for between 0.1 and 3.5 percent of the total student bodies. Of the twenty-three junior colleges that responded to the commission survey, fifteen reported that they had desegregated, five stated they had an all-white enrollment despite having a racially nondiscriminatory admissions policy, and three said they continued to deny admission to black applicants. Twelve of the desegregated junior colleges reported that in the fall of 1959, blacks made up between 0.2 percent and 4 percent of their student populations. In addition, at San Antonio's traditionally black Saint Philips Junior College, which was desegregated since 1955, whites (most of whom were persons of Mexican descent) constituted one-third of its enrollment.[4]

Compared to other states, Texas, half of whose fifty-three publicly supported institutions of higher education had dropped the color ban, was moderately desegregated. All the public universities and colleges in the Deep South states of South Carolina, Georgia, Mississippi, and Alabama remained completely segregated. In Louisiana, four state colleges had admitted black students; and in Florida, after a legal battle that spanned almost entire decade, the University of Florida had accepted its first blacks into its graduate and professional degree programs. By 1960, about half of the public and nearly one-third of the private institutions of higher learning in all seventeen southern and border states had desegregated. Relative to the region's public elementary and secondary schools, higher education had come a long way. Nonetheless, the CRC suggested in a report released in January 1961 that the government withhold funds from segregated public colleges:

The Supreme Court has held that the Federal Government is prohibited by the Constitution from maintaining racially segregated educational institutions. It is not sound policy for the Federal Government to subsidize the unconstitutional operations of others; to do indirectly what it is not permitted to do directly.

It is not sound policy for the Federal Government to disburse public funds in such a manner that it increases the adverse effects on some citizens of denials of equal protection of the laws by states and political subdivisions thereof.[5]

The Texas State Advisory Committee to the CRC, however, stood by the position it took in 1959 opposing "the exercise of force or undue pressure from any quarter." The eight-member committee pointed out that "no great unpleasantness has taken place in Texas as an outgrowth of the efforts to bring about a recognition of the rights of citizenship of those belonging to minority groups" and stated that coercive actions by the government would "only serve to engender bitterness and resentment, which inevitably will delay the realization of just and righteous aims." The committee, with white supremacist William B. Bates on one end and wealthy black businessman Mack H. Hannah on the other, concluded that securing equality for national minorities in the state had best be left to "persons of good will" coming together "in an atmosphere of spiritual understanding and trust." Their lofty-sounding conclusion had no basis in political reality. The desegregation of the remaining institutions of higher education required more than goodwill. In the end, the ultimate triumph of desegregation came from additional initiatives in the federal courts, threats of legal action, and the passage of national legislation that prohibited the practice of racial discrimination by federally funded institutions.[6]

After the repression of the NAACP in 1957, no other traditionally white four-year colleges in Texas desegregated until 1960. Between 1957 and 1960, students broke the color line at only one university, the very school set up originally to demonstrate the state's good faith in honoring the separate-but-equal doctrine. In 1958, Texas Southern University finally admitted Caucasians to a university created for Negroes. A decade before, TSU's board of directors rejected Jack Coffman, the first white student to apply to the school, after Attorney General Price Daniel issued Opinion No. V-645 on 31 July, declaring that "since substantially equal courses of study are offered for white students at The University of Texas and other State colleges, a white student may not be legally admitted to the Texas State University for Negroes." In January 1949, another white, Harold Schachtel, attempted to enter the black university as part of a joint antiracist effort of the NAACP Youth Council and the Young Progressives of Texas. The board also refused his application on the basis of Daniel's opinion.[7]

In the fall semester of 1955, whites' attempts to enter TSU again made headlines. TSU rejected six nonblacks, Warren Martin, an associate pastor of a Methodist church in Houston; Albert Kaszcyke, the seventeen-year-old son of a Polish war refugee who recently moved to Houston from Chicago; Thomas C. Brunson Jr., a Baylor graduate and navy lieutenant on duty in the Pacific; John August Solomon Jr., a resident of Dallas; William A. McAnear, a resident of Houston; and Aiko Awata, a resident of Tokyo, Japan. When their names became public, Kaszcyke, Brunson, and Solomon explained to the press that their applications had been misdirected. Kaszcyke stated he did not realize that TSU was only for blacks; Brunson said he intended to apply to UT for graduate work; and Solomon said he had intended to apply to the University of Houston (UH). Martin, a native of Kerrville who previously had worked at a black church in Waco, applied to Houston's TSU because it was the school he could best afford. The young preacher told the press that "all men are brothers" and that he supported the "elimination of segregation." Nevertheless, when the semester started he found himself studying at a segregated UH.[8]

The applications from Caucasian men and a Japanese woman prompted board members to reconsider TSU's segregated admissions policy. At their September 1955 meeting, the executive committee recommended the immediate adoption of a racially nondiscriminatory admissions policy. George Allen, a black board member from Dallas, supported the recommendation. But Dr. H. D. Bruce, a white board member, moved to table further discussion of the matter until the board convened in closed session. Allen objected and called for the matter to be discussed openly before the press, but the other members overruled him. In closed session the board voted 5–1 to postpone a decision on desegregation until its next meeting. Mack Hannah, chairman of the board, explained to the media that he and his colleagues voted to delay a final vote in order to give TSU's new president, Dr. Samuel M. Nabrit, time to settle into his position.

On 10 January 1956, the board met and approved the desegregation of TSU by a vote of 6–1. W. R. Banks, president emeritus of Prairie View, Hannah, Bruce, Price Crawley, J. O. Nobles, Dr. J. C. Chadwick, and Houston attorney Ralph Lee attended the meeting. Lee's dissenting vote excepted, the board agreed to admit "all qualified applicants without regard to race, color or creed." Lee protested that the board's action might be illegal without a specific court order but then moved that TSU desegregate its faculty and staff saying, "If [integration] were proper for the students it was proper for the faculty." His motion carried unanimously. For the next two years, despite TSU's declaration of an open policy, no whites entered the school. In the fall of 1956, several white students were admitted but they never registered. Nabrit gave them each "special counseling" by phone or in a letter, and none followed through on enrollment. What the president told the prospective students is not recorded, but his words and Houston's opposition to school desegregation apparently combined to keep whites out in 1956, and possibly in 1957 as well. TSU kept no record of the race or ethnicity of its student body as a matter of official policy.[9]

The massive resistance movement may have discouraged whites from entering TSU, but, ironically, it provided the university with one of its first publicly acknowledged white students. On Monday, 15 September 1958, E. A. Munroe, leader of the Missionary Baptist Temple and an ardent segregationist, applied to TSU. Accompanied by twenty-five members of his flock, including children who carried the church banner, the U.S. flag, and prosegregation placards with slogans like "Intergration [*sic*] Leads to Intermarriage" and "We Believe in a Government by the People Not by Nine Men," Munroe registered for classes and wrote a check for $83.50 for his tuition and fees. Wearing white high-heeled boots, a dark serge suit, "a broad-brimmed white Stetson hat and tie with fuchsia sequins and gold lame stitching," the comical figure told newspaper reporters who immediately swarmed the campus that he entered the school to "show the stupidity of integration and our defiance of the Supreme Court verdict on integration." He added, "My purpose is to serve as an object lesson to show how stupid and inconsistent it is for me to enroll in a colored university as a white man when we have so many fine white schools and universities." He indicated that he wanted a bachelor's degree in religion and registered for classes in psychology, philosophy, and a survey course on the Old Testament. But he also stated that he "had no idea tuition would be so high. . . . Looks like I'll have to sell my Fleetwood Cadillac to pay the tuition."[10]

The board split on whether to admit Munroe. The minority, Lee and Hannah, opposed his admission, saying that he applied only for "propaganda purposes" and to embarrass the university. The majority of the board, however, accepted Nabrit's advice that TSU had to enroll him regardless of his motives. After a few days of classes, Munroe dropped out and stopped payment on his check, saying that he encountered an "awful lot of prejudice and discrimination" from TSU's black students, which he claimed proved that most blacks, as well as whites, did not want integration. Another white minister enrolled after Munroe but without all the grandstanding. Clayton McMahill, pastor of St. Thomas Methodist Church, wanted to counter the Baptist preacher's views, saying he was taking a stand for "a world Christian brotherhood" in desegregating TSU. He did not report any negative reactions from blacks.[11]

Elsewhere in the state, no additional campuses were desegregated until 1960. On 11 February, ten days after four college students in Greensboro, North Carolina, launched the sit-in movement, John Matthew Shipp Jr. sued West Texas State College (WTSC) and gained for blacks the right of nondiscriminatory access to the institution. The college, located in Canyon, the seat of Randall County (where the population was 99 percent Anglo), offered four-year degree programs to students in the Panhandle area. The public junior college in nearby Amarillo had dropped segregation nine years earlier, and the city' grade schools were desegregated in 1956. Shipp, a product of Amarillo's desegregated public schools and a graduate of Amarillo College, sought to finish his undergraduate education at the institution nearest to home. Henry Braswell, an assistant attorney general that represented WTSC in *Shipp* v. *White*, brought up the old "salt-and-pepper" idea, but U.S. District Court judge Joe Dooley struck it down saying that he did not believe it would "pass muster under our present understanding of law." Dooley told the defendant board, which governed five other segregated state colleges, that "the law of the country has now been decided by the Supreme Court" and that by its rulings in school segregation cases, it "has settled for me the matter of barring admittance of students solely on grounds of color." He ordered Frank White, the other members of the board of regents of the State Teachers College System, and college president James P. Cornette to admit Shipp on "the same terms and conditions that white citizens are permitted to enroll, study, and receive instruction." For the Anglo judge in an almost all-Anglo region, the Court's decisions on school segregation may have reconciled him to the equal rights of blacks under the law, but the regents of the Teachers College System continued to stonewall in the face of challenges to segregation at its other campuses.[12]

The board of regents of Texas Woman's University (Texas State College of Women until 1957), an independent body that governed the all-female college in Denton, also vigorously opposed admitting blacks. Texas Woman's University (TWU) officials exhibited their racist convictions in 1952 when an executive committee met and reviewed its policy toward "the problem of the Negro visitor or delegate to meetings held on the College campus." By a unanimous vote of the deans, directors of various departments, and the president, the committee went on record as reaffirming "its belief in and support of the policy, rooted in Texas law, which does not permit Negro visitors to participate in meetings on the College campus."[13] Three years later, TWU's regents faced a more serious problem. In December of 1955, the executive committee met at the request of the board to consider how the college should handle the desegregation problem. The committee wrote a statement that urged that the board be guided by three principles:

(a) Strongly discourage admission of Negro students until after the present long session, but if an insistent case is encountered at the beginning of the second semester admit the Negro student concerned, provided that she is a resident of Texas and meets all entrance requirements and standards; (b) Admit fully qualified Negro applicants after the present long session but, if legally possible, resist the admission of out-of-state Negroes for an indefinite period; (c) Refuse indefinitely to house Negro students in the same dormitory or dormitories with white students.[14]

Effectively, the committee's proposal put it in the hands of John A. Guinn, TWU's president, to do all he could to prevent desegregation; but if a qualified, in-state black could not be dissuaded from pursuing her right to admission, then the college would capitulate and admit her, but not to student housing. Guinn managed to persuade blacks against applying to TWU, but in the spring of 1957 the widening stream of applications again

203

brought the issue to the surface. The executive committee cited five reasons for its belief that "any immediate step to integrate TSCW would be likely to involve the College in violent controversy." Citing the July 1956 Democratic primary vote in favor of three prosegregation referenda, the "attitudes" of the 55th Legislature, the rise in "bitterness" among segregationists Southwide, threats of violence that had been made at UT over desegregation, and the policies of other institutions that remained segregated (i.e., A&M, Texas Tech, the schools in the Teachers College System, and A&I), the committee unanimously revoked its 1955 statement on desegregation. Strangely, TWU officials chose to ignore North Texas State College's successful, ongoing experience with desegregation, even of campus housing. On 14 May 1957, a few days from the third anniversary of *Brown*, the group recommended to the board "that voluntary integration at the Texas State College of Women be indefinitely postponed . . . even under insistent pressure, until such time as the mores of the citizenry of Texas would tolerate integration in their institution of higher learning exclusively for women students, an institution set up specifically for white women students in 1901." On 3 June 1957, the board accepted the executive committee's statement on integration policy and for the next four years determined that the Texas "citizenry" remained vehemently opposed to TWU dropping the race bar.[15]

TWU changed its policy in 1961. Alsemia Ann Dowells, a graduate of a Dallas high school that year, applied for admission as a resident student. On 24 August, by a unanimous vote, the board adopted a resolution stating that since the Supreme Court had ruled TWU's "white girls only" statute "unconstitutional and inoperative" and since the school was faced with applications from other black female students, it authorized the president to admit blacks "commensurate with school policy relative to the qualifications for other students." That fall semester, Dowells became TWU's first and only student of African descent. An all-female environment in no way mitigated or lessened the stultifying white-supremacist attitudes she encountered. In the spring of 1962, she concluded she had endured enough terrifying isolation and abandoned the campus, never to return. The door she opened enabled six black women to attend TWU that fall semester: Gloria Brannon of Texarkana, Marvia Elmore of El Paso, Ruby Griffin and Betty Person of Temple, Carolyn Washington of Fort Worth, and Minnie Smith of Dallas. With the exception of Washington, these women became TWU's first black graduates (along with Arnetis Green and Liz Williams of Houston) in 1966. Almost thirty years later, in a series of interviews published in TWU's campus newspaper, *Daily Lasso*, the women described both high and low moments in their years at the college. Griffin summarized the ordeal: "Looking back, I don't think I'd want any daughter of mine to do what I did. But we didn't think about it at the time. We just did it."[16]

In 1961, with a similar "just do it" attitude, blacks entered Texas Technological College in Lubbock for the first time. The Reverend Merrell T. Reed, president of the Lubbock branch of the NAACP and pastor of Mount Vernon Methodist Church, approached the board supporting three black applicants to the college. The board rejected the students, explaining that the act that established the school restricted it to white or Caucasian students only, which was a boldface lie. Nothing in the 1923 enabling legislation made any reference to race. The major obstacle they faced on the board was J. Evetts Haley, the West Texas rancher, author-historian, and ideologue-for-hire who perfectly married anticommunism with white supremacy. He maintained a position identical to the UT regents of the 1940s that the desegregation of Texas Tech would only occur over his dead body. Reed and many other blacks may have hoped mightily that lightening might strike Haley down and remove him from the board, but where divine intervention proved unforthcoming, they patiently waited for a less dramatic event to take him out of the picture: the expiration of his term on 19 February 1961. Price Daniel refused to reappoint the crusty reactionary who ran a poor fourth against him in 1956 in the first gubernatorial primary race. When Haley finally announced his retirement, blacks in Lubbock breathed a collective sigh of relief. A reporter for the city's *Avalanche-Journal* quoted Reed as saying of Haley that he was "a good man — a good man to have off the board."[17]

With Haley out of the way and the threat of a lawsuit imminent, the board debated what it should do. For several weeks, Lubbock's mayor, David Casey, facilitated negotiations between the board and the black students who were preparing to go to court. In July, the regents implemented a new policy of admitting all qualified applicants regardless of color. While the college's president, Robert Cabaniss Goodwin, underwent back surgery in Florida, Texas Tech accepted its first black students. Board president, C. I. Wall, imposed a tight gag order on the campus, forbidding campus officials from releasing any information to the public about the opening of the college to blacks and from keeping any records of student enrollment by race. The campus dormitories, varsity athletics, and eating and recreational facilities remained segregated, with change coming ever so gradually. Undaunted by such indignities, however, the woman who threatened legal action against the college, Lucille Graves, led the way for black students when she enrolled in the summer of 1961. Ophelia Moore became the first black to earn a degree at Texas Tech. In 1967, Coach J. T. King recruited star athlete Danny Hardaway to become the Red Raiders' first black football player. His excellence on the gridiron helped "thaw" race relations at the campus, but academic difficulties in his senior year forced him to transfer to Cameron State in his hometown of Lawton, Oklahoma.[18]

The opening of Texas Tech, a member of the Southwest Conference and the second largest state-supported university after UT, represented a key victory for the civil rights movement in Texas. Its desegregation made the remaining hold-outs' stand more untenable than ever. Two colleges, UH and Arlington State College (ASC), desegregated in 1962 and signaled the true beginning of the end of Jim Crow's stranglehold on Texas higher education. UH, which immediately became the second largest university in Texas once its state-supported status went into effect, symbolized the future of higher education. The admission of blacks there meant segregation had no future. UH also became the first institution in East Texas to withdraw from the principle of racial separatism since Lamar Tech's forced desegregation in 1956. The desegregation of ASC, the sixth largest college in the state and a branch of the A&M College System, signified the ultimate unraveling of the "salt-and-pepper" construct. If blacks breached the walls of the A&M colleges, with the militaristic and patriarchal-chauvinist tradition of its main campus in College Station, then no Texas college could long keep them out.

UH's implementation of what its officials claimed was a long-planned-for desegregation strategy occurred in the summer of 1962. "On a selective basis as part of a study," the university admitted Charles P. Rhinehart Jr., a faculty member in TSU's Department of Music.[19] Vice President Patrick J. Nicholson, in charge of public relations and the keeper of UH's image as an up-and-coming urban institution of higher learning, summarized the "situation" to a journalist: "The initial move this summer toward integration of the university was a part of a study began several years ago by the board. At that time it was decided that at the proper time, we would accept any Negro student into our graduate divisions who met the requirements of admission. This was effected this summer. As far as I know, there were no incidents involved. The integration was a normal development of the school's program. The situation has quietly taken care of itself."[20] Indeed, under the presidency of Clanton Ware Williams, the university initiated a "study" of desegregation in 1959. When UH launched its campaign to secure full state support, shortly after its number one benefactor, Hugh Roy Cullen, died on 4 July 1957, university officials knew they would no longer be able to forestall admitting blacks. A. R. "Babe" Schwartz, a Jewish attorney and Democratic politician from the Galveston area who served in the Texas legislature, observed that racism was a key part of the moss-backed opposition to UH becoming a state-supported institution. State senators from rural areas in East and West Texas formed a powerful bloc and frequently rallied together against measures benefiting urban areas exclusively. The coalition of rural, Anglo politicians believed that if UH became a state university it would attract to it primarily "poor [whites] and minorities." Schwartz contended that the dirty secret of the anti-UH bloc's opposition was that it regarded public funding of UH as an expansion of the welfare system. The Texas Senate, nevertheless, approved Senate Bill No. 2, and on July 1961, Governor Price Daniels signed legislation that made UH a state university beginning in the fall semester of 1963. During the transition period of 1961–63, college officials decided to desegregate and avert the negative publicity a lawsuit would generate.[21]

In November 1962, Nicholson told a reporter from the student newspaper, the *Daily Cougar*, "Integration is a large, complex problem and we are moving along without an exact time schedule, but we have had it under study for three years." UH regents took no action in the direction of integrating its living and dining facilities and maintained that they were studying the problem. UH admitted black undergraduates in the fall of 1963. In 1965, President Philip Hoffman authorized the recruitment of blacks into university athletic programs.[22]

Blacks who sought entry to Arlington State confronted the to-hell-and-be-damned-if-they-don't-understand, "Gig 'Em Aggie" tradition of the college's main branch in College Station. They also encountered a school theme and campus culture that openly celebrated white supremacy. The school, entering the A&M system in 1923, adopted the mascot Junior Aggies, but in 1949 it changed its nickname to the Blue Riders. After two years, then president E. H. Hereford charged a group of student leaders to come up with a new school theme, one that would evoke greater school pride, unity, and enthusiasm. At an assembly of the student body in the first week of the fall semester of 1951, the winner of a standing vote was the Dixie Rebel. The ASC Rebels stuck, and in time all the accouterments of the Old South hero appeared on the campus: Confederate battle flags, Daniel Decatur Emmett's "Dixie" as the school song, Johnny Reb as the mascot, Confederate decor in the main room of the University Center, and, perhaps worst of all, the annual Old South Week, with its slave auction, complete with whites (particularly the Kappa Alpha fraternity) in Confederate soldier uniforms and others in blackface wearing shackles. College administrators and faculty, whose general reaction to the evolution of the school theme during the 1950s ranged from toleration to encouragement, did not look forward to desegregation of the college.[23]

Nevertheless, they and the ASC student body and alumni had to face the end of their Dixie fantasy land in the summer of 1962 when three students petitioned Dr. Jack R. Woolf, ASC president, for admission and threatened to sue if they were rejected based on their race. Woolf thought he had a couple of months to quietly prepare the campus and area community and to secure from the local media "their support in handling the release of the information [that ASC had revised its admission policy] in a way which would not be detrimental to the College or the students." But when a luncheon meeting he arranged to have with the managing editors of newspapers and radio and television stations was reported by one of the news organizations as a press conference to announce the desegregation of ASC, his hopes of covertly accepting black students vanished. A&M system chancellor Marion Thomas Harrington wrote the regents and explained that the exposure given "the decision to admit Negroes to Arlington State College was not as President Woolf had planned." At the next meeting of the board on 29 July 1962, it formally affirmed what had become public knowledge: ASC would become the first college in the A&M system to desegregate. Campus officials did not keep records of enrollment by race or ethnicity, but about thirty blacks are estimated to have attended the school in the 1962–63 school year. An article in the school newspaper, the *Shorthorn*, reported that all college facilities operated on a nonracial basis, and the writer predicted that "Negro students will participate in all phases of college life." News reporters scoured the campus looking for trouble at the beginning of the semester but left storyless.

One story they did not look for was Phala Mae Price's. In 1961, pregnant and without a high school diploma, Price, through the help of a white friend became the first of her race ever to be hired there, as a food server in the cafeteria of ASC's University Center. "I was here when the first black students came through the lunch line," she recalled many years later. "I didn't say anything, but I was proud deep inside." Without a single word, the presence of the black students at ASC began to refute what a white supremacist world had taught her about her people, their proper "place," and the future she could envision for her newborn daughter. Despite the confederate decoration around her and the white folks' air of superiority, she knew that with "faith and patience . . . [and] the help of God" the life possibilities for an African American were not forever frozen. She and her husband, Phianous, sent all three of their children to the college where she worked for twenty-seven years.[24]

The desegregation of ASC also made a difference in the strange career of Jim Crow at the main branch of the A&M system. When system regents opened ASC to blacks, they also decided to allow Texas A&M to admit academically qualified male students "regardless to race or color." This decision did not, however, become public knowledge until after 3 June 1963, when A&M enrolled three black students. Leroy Sterling, at home in nearby Bryan for the summer, wanted to study at A&M so that when he returned to TSU in the fall he would have enough hours to be a senior and could complete his degree in languages by that next June. Two junior high school science teachers, Vernell Jackson of Bryan and George Sutton of Fort Worth, attended A&M that first summer session after receiving National Science Foundation (NSF) scholarships to do six weeks study in advanced science course work. Jackson claimed that he did not state a desire to study at A&M on his application to the NSF. If A&M had refused to accept the NSF-sponsored students, it undoubtedly would have gone against the college's future chances of securing grants from the federal agency. In the next session, six more blacks enrolled, four undergraduates and two graduate students, one of whom was a woman. Each year, A&M allowed about 200 women to take classes during the summer, but in the fall of 1963, women were accepted as regular students for the first time in the college's history. The white males of A&M had to adjust to both women and blacks as students. Between the two, the gender change apparently overshadowed the racial change.[25]

A&M's admission of women came as a result of a series of Fourteenth Amendment legal challenges patterned after the cases of black civil libertarians. Blacks had not threatened a lawsuit against A&M, but two factors readied the regents for desegregation. First, the growth of A&M's student body had not kept apace with colleges like UT, UH, or even ASC. Many believed if the school went coeducational and announced the end of racial segregation, its rate of growth would catch up with the other large state universities.

Second, the executive offices of the nation and the state had moved toward taking a public position in support of college desegregation. The Kennedy-Johnson administration and John Connally, the Texas governor since January of 1963, were closely aligned in political ambitions and party operations. The desegregation of higher education might drive a wedge between the administration and Governor Wallace in Alabama but not Connally. The national spectacle of Wallace standing in the door of the University of Alabama's Foster Auditorium drew a line dividing southern Democratic stalwarts and the rest of the party. In July, before leaving for the National Governors Conference at Miami, Connally appeared on television in a statewide broadcast to make his position known. He presented what amounted to a report card on the progress of civil rights in the state. He boasted of how Texas had taken "tremendous strides" in the realm of desegregation, especially in public education. He noted that sixteen out of twenty-one senior colleges and universities and twenty-six out of thirty-three junior colleges had dropped segregation. Connally, in tones that paralleled those in Kennedy's nationwide television speech just a few hours after black students Vivian Malone and James Hood desegregated the University of Alabama, praised the end of segregation in Texas. He also noted that the hold-out schools were preparing to get on the bandwagon. His comments, combined with efforts at the national level to pass a new and tougher civil rights bill, were the first breaking rays on the political horizon of a new day. The dark clouds of a silent and inept Eisenhower administration and of the racist demagoguery and repressive actions of Shivers, Daniel, Shepperd, and company had finally passed.[26]

The dawn of a new day does not, however, necessarily bring good weather. In the same month as Connally's national declaration and the tempest in Tuscaloosa, one state-supported senior college in Texas jumped on the civil rights train and another tried to get in front of it. Sul Ross State, an all-white West Texas college in the State Teachers College System, admitted its first black students without litigation. Southwest Texas State Teachers College, on the other hand, became the last institution of higher learning in Texas legal history that required a federal court order before it would end segregation. Ironically, Southwest was Lyndon Johnson's alma mater.

The story of desegregation at Sul Ross centers on a young, gifted black girl named Christine Young. Her early education in Alpine occurred at the all-black Morgan School. While she was in the seventh grade, the year of the *Brown* decision, she transferred to the Centennial School, an all-Latino junior high school in the barrio. She excelled there, became bilingual, and graduated as valedictorian of her class. Thereafter, she attended the formerly all-white Alpine High School, where she graduated with honors in 1960. She applied to Sul Ross, but on 29 March 1960, registrar Robert Decker explained in a letter that her enrollment was "not legally possible." The college's enabling act, he stated, limited who could attend Sul Ross to "White Students Only." Decker suggested three ways the restriction could be overturned whereby the college could then admit her: (1) an act of the Texas Legislature, (2) a court order or, (3) an act of the board of regents of the State Teachers Colleges, "subject to legal question." Extremely disappointed by the news, Young looked to get on with her life. Her family did not have the wherewithal to send her away to college, so she joined the Women's Army Corps and left Alpine until 1963. Young could have attended Sul Ross merely by claiming she was Hispanic. Someone suggested she "pass" for a Mexican or a Native American, as a cousin of hers had done in 1955. Young refused this route, possibly because of the risks it might have entailed but also because, as one writer who interviewed her discovered, she wanted to be "true to herself . . . to be accepted as she was." She simply could not "betray her heritage" and pretend to belong to a culture that was not her own.[27]

Young's application was not without support from the black, Mexican, and white communities of Alpine. Three years later, when she returned from her tour of duty and confronted the same racist barrier, an influential group of educators and local political leaders rallied to support her admission to Sul Ross. Pete Gallego Jr., a businessman, a Sul Ross graduate, and member of the board of trustees for the Alpine Independent School District; Charles Wade, one of Young's teachers at Alpine Centennial School; Dr. W. E. Lockhart, Alpine's mayor and a prominent physician; Dr. Delbert Dyke, Sul Ross's dean of academic studies; Gene Hendryx, a businessman and a former state representative; and others began meeting to discuss the problem of segregation at the college. Blacks made up less than

1 percent of the population of Brewster County and the town of Alpine. Anglos and Mexicans each comprised about fifty percent of the population. The public schools had already desegregated. To the business, professional, and especially the educational leaders of the community to forbid the admission of Young and other blacks who could pass the entrance requirements to Sul Ross was anachronistic and unjust. Hendryx emerged from the meetings and called Texas attorney general Waggoner Carr, who, in turn, contacted Newton Gresham of Houston, the chairman of the board of regents for the State Teachers Colleges. The Alpine community indicated it wanted Sul Ross to drop its ban against blacks and that it did not want to go through a lawsuit, which would very likely be filed if the racial barrier did not come down. After meeting on the matter, the board gave Sul Ross's president, Dr. Bryan Wildenthal, permission to open the college to all students regardless of race or color. On 3 June 1963, Young entered Sul Ross after a three-year delay. She went both summer sessions and accumulated twelve hours before the start of the fall semester, when eight black athletic scholarship recipients joined her at the college.[28]

Simultaneous with the events leading up to Young's admission to Sul Ross, the regents of the State Teachers College System grappled with another showdown on the segregation issue at Southwest Texas State College (SWT) in San Marcos. In 1962, upon graduating from Austin's Anderson High School, Dana Jean Smith had the school send a copy of her transcript to SWT, which she followed with a letter indicating that she would take the American College Test on 23 June 1962 and have her scores reported to the college. On 22 June, SWT president John Garland Flowers wrote the teenaged girl that although her high school grades convinced him that she met SWT's "academic qualifications for admission admirably," the law that created the college did not allow him to admit someone of her "racial background." Smith, however, did not give up after receiving Flowers's rejection letter. On 13 September, she and her attorney, J. Phillip Crawford, went to the office of SWT's registrar, Clem Jones, to ask that the college honor her right to attend the state-supported institution. Jones replied that unless a court ordered him to admit her, he would not do so then or at any future date. Shortly thereafter, she filed suit in the Austin division of the U.S. District Court before Judge Ben H. Rice Jr., who set the case to be heard on 4 February 1963. Three days before the trial, the system regents met at the Driskill Hotel in Austin, the same hotel where twenty-five years before state officials decided to reject a black man who tried to attend a class at the University of Texas, and there they officially requested the state attorney general to represent them at trial in the case *Smith v. Flowers*. With various points of fact having been stipulated by both sides, the only issue before Judge Rice concerned whether or not the law permitted swт to deny Smith and other blacks admission to the college solely based on their race. He ruled that the law did not allow it to do so and ordered Smith admitted "forthwith." That fall semester of 1963 when she enrolled, Flowers, who had been president of swт since 1942, personally assisted Smith and allowed a photograph to be taken recording the event. The school annual published the photograph and reported that Flowers was pleased with the "maturity of the students" who enabled swт to accomplish desegregation "so smoothly." Other blacks attending the college with Smith included three San Marcos women, first-year student Carolyn Burleson and sophomores Gloria Odums and Georgia Hoodye; and a freshman from Waco, Oswald Cockrell. The *Smith* decision, however, did not compel the system regents to formally announce a change of policy regarding the other colleges under their governance.[29]

The regents of the A&M system, meanwhile, approved the elimination of race as an admissions criterion at Prairie View and Tarleton State in 1963 when they opened Texas A&M. But they kept the action secret and left it up to the presidents of the two colleges to make the change when and how they saw fit. These institutions had come under no threat of a lawsuit; indeed, no whites applied to Prairie View and no blacks to Tarleton. But they did begin to inform newspaper reporters that they had dropped segregation. Prairie View stepped out first to disclose that it had abandoned its "Negroes-only policy" in the fall of 1963. The first qualified white applicants did not seek admission to the college until 1966, however. These students. who mostly came from Waller or other nearby counties and towns, often were teachers who found the college to be the most convenient and affordable place to do graduate work. Tarleton also may have accepted its first black students in 1966. Regardless of when those campuses actually ended segregation, the struggle for civil and human rights won a great victory in early 1964 with the announcement that all the colleges in the A&M system had desegregated.

That left the State Teachers College System's three East Texas campuses as the last hold-outs.[30] Blacks had attempted at least since 1954 to enter Sam Houston State Teachers College at Huntsville, Stephen F. Austin State College (sfa) at Nacogdoches, and East Texas State College at Commerce. The large black populations in these areas, which ranged from 15 to 37 percent, had long imbued many local whites with an absolute dread of blacks becoming fully free and empowered and of any new increase in interracial contact, particularly on a socially equal level. How much importance college and state government officials should accord to the prejudices of these whites and for how long should they trample the constitutional rights of blacks to appease white supremacists remained the critical questions. On 12 August 1955, the regents of the state teachers colleges answered by directing the six institutions under its governance to "advise

Dana Jean Smith, shown here with Southwest Texas State president John Garland Flowers, in 1964 became the last African American student in Texas to require a federal court order before she could be admitted (Southwest Texas State University 1964 *Pedagog* Year Book).

each [N]egro applicant who has or may apply for admission to such college, that such admission is denied because (1) neither the charter nor the existing facilities at the college in question . . . permit such admission; (2) the citizenry of the respective communities has not yet been conditioned to the point of acceptance of the abolishment of segregation."[31]

The East Texas colleges played up the Anglo community's unpreparedness for desegregation, but in the early 1960s advocates of civil rights shifted the momentum. A case that originated at Sam Houston but sent shock waves throughout the state and nation involved what C. Vann Woodward described in a *Harper's Magazine* article as the regents' "high-handed firing" of Rupert Koeninger. At the end of the 1962 school year, Koeninger, head of Sam Houston's sociology department for fifteen years, suddenly found himself dismissed from his job with no explanation. President Harmon Lowman related to the fifty-five-year-old diminutive scholar of criminology that his speeches encouraging school desegregation had been

213

at the heart of the board's decision to drop him from the faculty. One speech that the regents especially complained about occurred in 1955. In May of that year, Koeninger read a paper in which he reviewed the first year of changes in the schools since *Brown*. As one of the keynote speakers at the Southwestern Regional Conference on Integration, he explained that "you cannot expect integration to come about just by edict of the Supreme Court." More troubling than what he said, which he had discussed beforehand with Lowman, was where he delivered his speech. Held in Houston and drawing an evenly divided biracial crowd of about 150 persons, the meeting had been sponsored by the Southern Conference Educational Fund, an offshoot of the Southern Conference for Human Welfare. Extreme conservatives and anticommunists, like members of the John Birch Society, which was active in Huntsville in 1962, believed the fund was actually a front organization of the Communist Party, USA. The Texas Association of College Teachers conducted an investigation of the firing and reported that Birchers and regent chairman C. S. Ramsey pressured the board to discharge the professor. Koeninger did not stay long without a job. That fall semester he started teaching at Texas Southern University. Meanwhile, fifteen teachers left Sam Houston in protest of the incident, and the American Association of University Professors placed the college on its censured list for violating Koeninger's right of academic freedom. It did not remove Sam Houston's name from the list until 1970, when a settlement occurred involving the payment of $10,000 to the professor.[32]

The straw that broke the regents' resolve to avoid desegregation emerged out of the struggle of Maxine Haywood, a Texarkana schoolteacher, and Carolyn Jean Kirkwood, a May 1964 graduate of a Huntsville high school. The two women applied to the college during the spring and received letters of rejection based on their race from Reed Lindsey, the acting dean of admissions. They retained the services of attorney Weldon H. Berry, an active member of the Houston NAACP branch. On 5 June 1964, he filed a lawsuit before Ben Connally, a federal district judge in Houston. On the same day, system regents met in Austin and discussed the segregation question. They agreed that none of the campuses under their governance would continue to refuse students "solely on the basis of race." News of the decision rang out across the state on 8 June, and a day later, John Connally broadcast throughout the nation that Texas had completed the desegregation of its public, four-year colleges. He made the Texas-sized brag at a panel discussion on civil rights and at the National Governors Conference held that year in Cleveland, Ohio. The boast supposedly verified his argument that the problem of civil rights in education, employment, and other areas was "essentially local and the most effective solutions could be reached by local groups" acting voluntarily and without pressure from the federal government. With an eye toward the Civil Rights Bill, which President Johnson would sign into law in less than a month, Connally was attempting to deny the need for such a sweeping measure and to project his political leadership in a favorable light. Still, following his widely publicized comments, blacks had to fight to compel officials at the hold-out schools to get into the new era — to enter, at last, the twentieth century.[33]

John Patrick, valedictorian of the class of 1964 at Huntsville's Sam Houston High School, helped to bring Sam Houston out of the racist darkness of the nineteenth century. On 8 June, he enrolled, and the next day he began attending classes in history and mathematics. "No one even glanced in his direction," observed one reporter who went to the campus to record the historic event. Acting president Elliott Bowers gave the reporter the attitude of officialdom: "He's just another student as far as we're concerned." How quickly the official attitude had changed. In January 1968, Patrick graduated with a bachelor of science degree in mathematics and chemistry. The process of change by then seemed irreversible.[34]

The black equal rights struggle did not generate a lawsuit to open Stephen F. Austin State College, but the filing of *Kirkwood* v. *Sam Houston State Teachers College* hastened desegregation throughout the State Teachers College System. The rights revolution came slowly to "NaKKKogdoches," as young blacks dubbed the town. A true East Texas city, it had a reputation for "hard core" racial attitudes. The county, sharing the same name as its leading town and seat of government, split into whites and blacks at about a two-to-one ratio. Ralph Steen moved to the area in 1958, leaving his long-held position as professor of history at Texas A&M to become president of SFA. At his inaugural ceremony, his mentor, Walter Prescott Webb, gave the keynote speech. He offered those attending the occasion a parable: A farmer took a plow and went out onto his field to earn his daily bread but then discovered that "one of those big pine trees had fallen down. The tree was too big to move and too green to burn, and so [the farmer] just plowed around it." The wise farmer found it best to "go on and plow around one great obstacle in order to get on with [his] crop." Webb, renowned as one of the most brilliant white supremacists in Texas history, spoke through this story to the destiny of "Aryan civilization" as it faced the long-dreaded dark hour of social equality with the African. The meaning of the tale was simple and direct: an inferior black person entering the schools and colleges of whites was an enormous problem, but not one that should absorb too much of the energies and emotions of the civilization-builders who taught and helped to mold white youth. Men like Steen should simply accept the presence of blacks on their campus and get on with their crop, the cultivation of the Aryan race. In time, like the fallen tree, blacks would lose their greenness, the momentary political vigor they were exhibiting, and could be cut into pieces, moved, or burned away. The moral of his story did not escape Steen.[35]

215

Through the years of massive resistance, SFA's president dutifully spurned black applicants to the college and assured whites who worried about the coming of blacks that when change occurred they would not be put upon in the least. By 1963, Steen predicted that the ban against blacks would end within a year's time. In October, he offered SFA as the host campus for the annual meeting of the American Studies Association scheduled for December of 1964. Since the association opposed meeting on segregated campuses, he assured members of the American Studies community that the college would be integrated before then. When the system regents publicly announced that all the colleges they governed were free to admit blacks, Steen first opened SFA's graduate programs. He found the perfect kind of black student SFA could tolerate the best. As one eyewitness explained, "Steen stacked the deck in integrating the school. The first black to enroll was an old black preacher. With hat in hand, he was not the type of person to offend anybody." And, indeed, no violent incidents took place. If the preacher was a character like Kingfish in Amos 'n' Andy, then he undoubtedly amused most whites. But whether or not he was like the Kingfish, Uncle Tom, or any other white stereotype, he paved the way for more blacks to enroll, including undergraduates. Approximately twenty blacks attended SFA in the fall, but none lived on campus. The university's dormitories were not desegregated until 1965. Steen's administration had begun to "plow around" the blacks on his campus.[36]

At East Texas State College, the last of the state teachers colleges to desegregate, an estimated six blacks enrolled for summer courses in 1964. At least ten years before they crossed the color line, blacks had made attempts to enter the college but President James Gee routinely turned down their applications. Described as an ardent segregationist, the native of South Carolina had served as a staff officer under General George Patton in the Second World War. He could take orders whether he liked them or not. He knew by the early 1960s that blacks would enter the school before long. In 1962, he appointed various members of the faculty and his administration to a secret, ad hoc committee charged with studying collegiate desegregation and recommending the best policies and procedures to take whenever the college had to face the elimination of its racial rules. The group studied Lamar, Arlington, and North Texas and recommended two major moves: First, Gee should bring together all the personnel of the college, from executive vice presidents to the yard men, inform them that blacks would be admitted, and secure their cooperation — a procedure McDonald used at Lamar to satisfactory ends. Second, the college news director should contact the media to garner their support in bringing about a "dignified integration." When Velma Waters became the first black to enter East Texas State, Gee acted according to the committee's recommendations. The speech he gave to prepare the college staff two weeks before the summer term began seemed to announce the end of the world. Local papers printed the text of the speech, the theme of which centered on the need to be civil:

> Our attitudes, our personal conduct, and the manner in which we exercise the utmost of practical and active good citizenship and self-control will be forever recorded in the annals of this institution, this county and the State of Texas as being irreparably bad or infinitely good. . . . Let us each here pledge to ourselves and to each other that our individual and joint efforts will always be motivated by the best interest of this college. . . . It is my devout wish and fervent prayer that the integration of this college will come about in an orderly manner.[37]

With President Gee having rejected Waters's original application in 1960, the young Commerce native showed tremendous persistence in finally entering the school four years later. The challenges that lay ahead deeply tested her stamina, but again she prevailed. When she took her seat in a classroom full of whites a ring of empty chairs would appear between her and her classmates. She had to take classes with professors who did not want to talk to her outside of class nor would ever call on her during class. Others graded her work unfairly and even tried to flunk her out of the school. Nonetheless, she had some good experiences such as the help of anonymous donors when she lacked the funds to remain in school. In 1968, Waters became one of the first blacks to get a degree at East Texas. That same year, at 325, blacks comprised nearly 6 percent of the college's student body. The desegregation of SFA, Sam Houston, and East Texas State symbolized a start in the softening of the hardest core of racist recalcitrance in the state. Texas's accomplishments in social justice and race relations, however, like those of its native son in the White House, became overshadowed by a war in Southeast Asia, fading into that blur that Michael Eric Dyson has called the United States of Amnesia.[38]

Coda

I have great respect for that unsung army of black men and women who trudged down back lanes and entered back doors, saying "Yes, sir" and "No, Ma'am" in order to acquire a new roof for the schoolhouse, new books, a new chemistry lab, more beds for the dormitories, more dormitories. They did not like saying "Yes, sir" and "No, Ma'am," but the country was in no hurry to educate Negroes, these black men and women knew that the job had to be done, and they put their pride in their pockets in order to do it.
— James Baldwin, *The Fire Next Time* (1960).

By 1965, in order to secure greater access to educational opportunities for themselves and their children, Negroes had, as James Baldwin wrote in his book *The Fire Next Time,* stuffed "their pride in their pockets" to the point that they began to burst. Even as African Americans won the enlarged access they had long sought, their individual and collective sense of self could no longer be stuffed down into pockets of pragmatic necessity. Heman Sweatt and others whose names styled desegregation lawsuits like Joe Atkins, Dana Jean Smith, Versie Jackson, John Shipp, Carolyn Jean Kirkwood, Wilma Jean Whitmore, Willie Faye Battle, and Thelma White, and many others whose names did not but who often took greater risks, had let the genie out of the bottle. Responding to William Faulkner's silly advice to the freedom fighters to "go slow" with desegregation, Baldwin answered, "Any real change implies the breakup of the world as one has always known it, the loss of all that gave one an identity, the end of safety." White Texans resisted change and refused to surrender their dreams of unending racial hierarchy. Black students after 1965, however, refused to surrender their parents' dream of a world where all races had equal rights and justice. As students, they began to question the meaning of university access without acceptance, integration with continuing inequities.[1]

At the same time, powerful voices called them to follow Dr. Martin Luther King Jr. in the building of a beloved community, to do their part to change the world. Colored rituals of integration penetrated to the core of black pride itself—the black educational tradition. Ever in the lead, even when black folks were going backward, the Colored Teachers State Association of Texas began discussing the factors that made their association separate from whites' "untenable." In 1963, CTSAT's executive committee authorized dual memberships after the formerly segregated Texas State Association of Teachers joined the CTSAT in removing racial restrictions on membership. On 30 November, about 2,900, or one-fourth, of CTSAT members joined the TSTA. After passage of the Civil Rights Act of 1964 and the federal government's Health, Education and Welfare Department and the National Education Association issued various pro-integration mandates, talks of unifying the CTSAT and the TSTA accelerated. At a call meeting of the association in August of 1966, the membership voted without dissent to merge with the TSTA. The members voted to begin a new history, building on the sure foundation of decades of struggle for a united nation. Optimism was palpable.[2]

In carefully listening to southern crusaders for justice, African American author Alice Walker has found that the term "civil rights" does not work well to describe what the democracy-seekers sweated and shed blood for. Perhaps in a solipsistic act of owning the words that defined their deepest longings, perhaps because of their deep southern accents, Walker heard from black mouths: "silver rights—I want my silver rights." The democratization of higher education in the United States, like the civil rights movement before warriors like Fannie Lou Hamer, Mae Bertha Carter, and Bernice Johnson Reagon started lifting hearts, was without poets and singers. Lawyers, politicians, and bureaucrats created the language of the struggle for access and equity in higher education. When Dr. King moved on from dreamy images of black and white girls and boys atop hills singing old Negro spirituals to the pressing reality of the Vietnam War and the contradiction it posed to a nonviolent world where war was waged against poverty and not people, the language of social transformation became more militant and strident. At the same time, as black southerners attended college with whites and discovered that the "ordeal" of integration did not produce a transformed mainstream, words laced with fire captured their imaginations. In a world so long and difficult in its arrival but still so distant from what they sought, black folk had to have songs that sang out their agony and their hope.[3]

As James Brown, the Godfather of Soul, announced in 1966 that "Papa's Got a Brand New Bag," young warriors of the African American freedom movement made Black Power their battle cry, Maulana Karenga established Kwanzaa, the Black Panther Party for Self-Defense formed, and the interracial crew on Star Trek beamed into millions of homes. On 16 August 1966, at Arthur Smith Studios, in Charlotte, North Carolina, the Godfather recorded "Don't Be a Dropout" to make it clear that "without an education you might as well be dead." The next year, African American coeds and their peers who wanted change launched serious struggles for academic departments of Black Studies, an increase in the number of black professors at historically white collegiate institutions, and a transformation of the liberal arts general education curriculum. Aretha Franklin, the twenty-five-year-old Queen of Soul who put in song the rising mood, became Billboard's top vocalist of 1967. In 1968, she became the first black woman to appear on *Time* magazine's cover. Her hit "R-E-S-P-E-C-T" had as much to say about the New African generation's challenge to a white American culture that continued to belittle its black sisters and brothers as it did about a person demanding respect from an indifferent lover. In return "for a little respect" the wronged woman in her song promises a healthy relationship full of honesty and honey-sweet kisses. But if the cheating and disrespect persisted, then the offending mister "might walk in" and "find out I'm gone."

If the Queen left room for any ambiguity about how African Americans felt, then the Godfather, Soul Brother No. 1, banished all doubt in 1968 with his "Say It Loud, I'm Black and I'm Proud." James Brown recorded the song four months after Dr. King's assassination amid political eruptions all over the United States, on college and high school campuses, in offices and boardrooms, and in the streets. Brown once explained the intense yearning for American democracy to live up to its potential and to work for black people this way:

> There are a lot of people who think they're in the system, but they're really not in the system. Any time an Afro-American kid, 9 or 10 years old, can get up and say, 'Mama, I think I'm gonna study hard because I want to be president,' and have a shot at being president, then we've got America. When you can go on any side of town and not be frantic, or curious, about what might happen to you, and be at home at any place in America, we won't have to worry about 'Say It Loud (I'm Black and I'm Proud).' Other than that, we've got a name and we're trying to find out what it means.

The African American quest for meaning of words like "America" and "democracy" can be heard in soul music, but the search has found its greatest expression in the struggle for access and equity in higher education.

By the end of the 1960s, the higher education struggle in Texas and across the United States had reached a watershed. The African American freedom movement, first led by intelligent, brave, and eloquent leaders in Texas, rendered unjust, undemocratic, and unspeakable the idea that whites had the moral authority and the constitutional legitimacy to claim public spaces — college campuses, seats on a bus, jobs, parks, water fountains, ballot boxes, political offices — for their own exclusive use and benefit. Their victory did not prevent whites from continuing to maintain the supremacy of their race; and, here and there, down to our own time, the struggles continue. New tactics and strategies, policies and practices, lawsuits and court rulings would rise and fall, hopeful yearnings and dreams would be deferred, and promises would be made and broken. That story, too, the history of the African American freedom movement in the second century after chattel enslavement, must also be written. When that story is told, let future historians look upon the men and women in the years from 1865 to 1965 with humble and respectful eyes knowing something of the sense of pain and conviction they felt as they put their pride aside to do a job that had to be done.

As we study history, I and many of my generation have learned humility and have discovered a higher level of respect for our parents, for who they are and all they had to put up with. No longer do the tears flood as we say to ourselves, "If only they had not let us forget the price of the ticket." I entered the University of Texas in 1977 not knowing any of the names in this book except for my kinfolk; and, even in their case, I knew nothing about their deeds recounted here. I knew nothing about the price of the ticket that made it possible for me to be a student at UT. Dick Gregory, who gave a talk on the campus in my junior year, helped further break my consciousness from, as Ayi Kwei Armah put it in *Two Thousand Seasons*, "the pull of old habits of destruction's empire." Gregory's humor, like Richard Pryor's, pushed me into a remembering and a project of recuperating my history. The comedian stood before the large room filled with a few more whites than blacks and said something to this effect: "Integration is a beautiful thing. It's a beautiful thing especially for my black folks. Under segregation we thought y'all were everything. But thanks to integration, baby, we learned y'all ain't about nothing." I laughed so hard I fell out of my seat. He uttered a secret truth that shook my reality like an earthquake. He revealed publicly what four years of a "white" high school and two years at a "white" university made self-evident but unutterable: a morally bankrupt whiteness rules the empire. Still, a naked emperor is still the emperor and still capable of the destruction of bodies, the death of souls.[4]

One of the emperor's senators, a man of stone named Trent Lott, publicly fantasized about a world in which Strom Thurmond had become the emperor in 1948. If Thurmond had been emperor, Lott averred, all would be right in the world. One must suppose that if Lott's fantasy were reality, Herman Barnett would never have gone to UT's medical school, nor would John Saunders Chase, Heman Sweatt, or George Washington Jr. have studied architecture or law at UT. Nor indeed would I have attended the school. African Americans would have remained in their proper place, and the United States would not be beset by crime and a lack of morals, bulging prisons, bloated federal spending on welfare and other dependency-producing programs, foreign terrorists, and so-called affirmative action that lowered standards to allow less qualified blacks to take places in the finest colleges and universities in the country that would otherwise go to all those infinitely more deserving white women and men. Lott's hooey, which some claim most whites (certainly most white southerners) believe to be true, stripped him of his leadership post in the Senate. The new emperor, a Texan named George W. Bush, berated Lott and hastened his demise. Was he a victim of simple ignorance or evil intention? The question is beyond the scope of this coda, but it does highlight the importance of remembering and learning, of really knowing the price of the ticket that started us all moving in the direction of becoming one people, one democracy, with one destiny. Advancing democracy will not occur by intensifying the oppression of black folk. That much was clear in 1948 to most European Americans and African Americans alike. It took two decades of African Americans taking tremendous risks and engaging in courageous actions to demonstrate that the reduction of racial oppression in the United States need not ruin the country. That there have been missteps, misspoken words, misdeeds, and misbegotten policies in the name of affirmatively acting to reduce racial oppression remains the subject of another chapter and another book. They have occurred just as the log of democratic principles and practice has been plowed around on numerous campuses and fields of public life. For now, though, we must, as Armah writes of another terror-soaked age, "end this remembrance, the sound of it. It is the substance that continues."[5]

Notes

Abbreviations

DMN	*Dallas Morning News*
FLMP	President Floren Lee McDonald Papers, John and Mary Gray Library, Lamar University, Beaumont, Texas
HC	*Houston Chronicle*
HD	*Houston Defender*
HI	*Houston Informer*
HP	*Houston Post*
Integration File	Integration File, Special Collections, Texas Woman's University Library, Denton, Texas
JCMP	James Carl Matthews Papers, Willis Library, University of North Texas, Denton, Texas
NAACP Papers	Papers of the National Association for the Advancement of Colored People, Library of Congress, Washington, D.C. (The designations preceding the abbreviation are the group number, the series letter, and the box number, e.g., II-A-29.)
NYT	*New York Times*
PD Papers	Governor Price Daniel Papers, Sam Houston Regional Library and Research Center, Liberty, Texas
SSN	*Southern School News*
Texas v. *NAACP* Papers	*State of Texas* v. *NAACP*, Attorney General's Papers, Center for American History, University of Texas, Austin, Texas
UTAL	University of Texas at Arlington Libraries Special Collections Division
UTPOR	University of Texas President's Office Records, Center for American History, University of Texas, Austin

Introduction

1. Mortimer J. Adler helped inform my sense of what were the great books of the world. His *Great Ideas from the Great Books* (New York: Washington Square Press, 1963), came into my hands by way of the library of my high school philosophy teacher, John Conway. As for UT ranking at the top of my list of universities, it rated so highly because I knew that my uncle, Grant Saint Julian Jr., was one of the first Negroes to attend the school as a microbiology graduate student. He became a scientist, and from as young as I can remember he represented for me the finest living example of an educated person. I should note here that throughout this book I deploy the wide variety of names used to denote people of African descent in the United States of America: niggers, n/Negroes, coloreds, blacks, Afro-Americans, African Americans, and New Africans both in direct quotations and in my own text. My approach is sometimes synchronic and at other times idiosyncratic. If the reader is flexible and good humored, no confusion at all should occur.

2. E. Culpepper Clark, *The Schoolhouse Door: Segregation's Last Stand at the University of Alabama* (New York: Oxford University Press, 1993).

3. Mark Tushnet, *The NAACP's Legal Strategy against Segregated Education, 1925–1950* (Chapel Hill: University of North Carolina Press, 1987); Mark Tushnet, *Making Civil Rights Law: Thurgood Marshall and the Supreme Court, 1936–1961* (New York: Oxford University Press, 1994).

4. Adam Fairclough, *Race & Democracy: The Civil Rights Struggle in Louisiana, 1915–1972* (Athens: University of Georgia Press, 1995).

5. James D. Anderson, *The Education of Blacks in the South, 1860–1935* (Chapel Hill: University of North Carolina Press, 1988). *A History of Negro Education in the South from 1619 to the Present* (Cambridge: Harvard University Press, 1967), is an important classic written by the Texas-based sociologist Henry Allen Bullock. He wrote the book after becoming a faculty member at UT and following a long career at Prairie View A&M University.

6. Manning Marable, *Beyond Black and White: Transforming African-American Politics* (New York: Verso, 1995), 18.

7. The late Prairie View A&M historian George Ruble Woolfolk described a Kulturkampf, or cultural struggle, between the Anglo-Protestant and Latino-Catholic regimes, with Africans caught in the middle. See Woolfolk, *The Free Negro in Texas, 1800–1860: A Study in Cultural Compromise* (Ann Arbor: University Microform, 1966), 12–35.

8. *Gratz* v. *Bollinger*, 122 F. Supp. 2d 811 (E.D. Mich. 2000); *Grutter* v. *Bollinger*, No. 97-CV-75928-DT, 2001 U.S. Dist. LEXIS 3256 (E.D. Mich. Mar. 27, 2001); *Hopwood* v. *Texas*, 78 F.3d 932 (5th Cir.), *cert. denied*, 518 U.S. 1033 (1996); *Johnson* v. *Bd. of Regents*, 263 F.3d 1234 (11th Cir. 2001); *Smith* v. *University of Washington Law School*, 233 F.3d 1188 (9th Cir. 2000), *cert. denied*, 69 U.S.L.W. 3593 (U.S. May 29, 2001) (No. 00-1341). Justice Lewis F. Powell's opinion in *Regents of the University of California* v. *Bakke*, 438 U.S. 265 (1978), represents the controlling law that all the above cases seek to overturn. In *Bakke*, the U.S. Supreme Court upheld the use of race as a "plus factor" in higher education admissions, holding that "the interest of diversity is compelling in the context of a university's admissions program," because it contributes to "the robust exchange of ideas" (ibid., at 314–15). Justice

Powell relied on the U.S. Supreme Court's ruling in *Sweatt* v. *Painter* in his finding that "our tradition and experience lend support to the view that the contribution of diversity is substantial," particularly in the area of legal education. Heman Sweatt certainly felt that diversity was a substantive value; had he not, he would never have sued to enter the UT School of Law.

Chapter One

1. Juneteenth is the name black Texans gave to their 19 June emancipation day celebration that marks the day in 1865 when a military officer at Galveston announced the news of the end of chattel enslavement.

2. Frederick Eby, *The Development of Education in Texas* (New York: Macmillan, 1925), 266.

3. On the forty acres issue, see Amilcar Shabazz, "Land, Reparations and the Freedpeople: Some Lessons of History," in *The Forty Acres Documents* (Baton Rouge: House of Songhay, 1994). For the Texas state constitution, see C. R. Granberry and Helen Avery, *Texas Legislative Manual: 45th Legislature* (Austin: Von Boeckmann-Jones, 1937), 66. For his hypothesis as to why Texas legislators wrote Article 7, see Alton Hornsby Jr., "The 'Colored Branch University' Issue in Texas—Prelude to *Sweatt* vs. *Painter*," *Journal of Negro History* 76 (April 1973): 51. Although his opinion of the effect of the South Carolina higher educational experience is plausible, Hornsby offers no citations to support it. The University of South Carolina had two blacks on its board of regents from as early as 1869 and accepted black people as students and as faculty members from 1873 to 1877. See Joel Williamson, *After Slavery: The Negro in South Carolina during Reconstruction, 1861–1877* (Chapel Hill: University of North Carolina Press, 1965), 232–33, and George Brown Tindall, *South Carolina Negroes, 1877–1900* (1952; reprint, Baton Rouge: Louisiana State University Press, 1966), 18, 227, 291–92.

4. On Alta Vista's fitness for farming, see Henry C. Dethloff, *A Centennial History of Texas A&M University, 1876–1976*, vol. 1 (College Station: Texas A&M Press, 1975), 312. Dethloff notes that Alta Vista's land turned out to be more suitable for agriculture than that of the main A&M branch in College Station. For summaries of the legal and institutional history of higher education in Texas, see Texas Legislative Council, *Higher Education Survey*, Part I (Austin: Texas Legislative Council, 1951), 1–19; and Graham Blackstock, *Staff Monograph on Higher Education for Negroes in Texas* (Austin: Texas Legislative Council, November 1950), 1–11.

5. Dethloff, *Centennial History of Texas A&M*, 313. On Alta Vista's failing "completely" and blacks of the 1870s having "not the faintest notion of scientific farming," see Eby, *Development of Education in Texas*, 274–75.

6. Cuney's statements are quoted from Maud Cuney Hare, *Norris Wright Cuney: A Tribune of the Black People* (1913; reprint, Austin: Steck-Vaughn, 1968), 37–38.

7. Cuney's daughter also resisted the rituals of white supremacy. In 1897, as a talented pianist who had studied at Boston's New England Conservatory of Music and a pupil of Edmund Ludwig in Austin, Maud Cuney Hare refused to hold a recital at the Austin Opera House because its management insisted that colored members of the audience sit in the balcony away from whites. She and Ludwig

canceled the engagement and instead performed at the Deaf, Dumb, and Blind Institute, where the demeaning requirement of segregated seating would not be practiced. See Hare, *Norris Wright Cuney*, 32–33, 214–15. On Cuney as a "strong" but compromised black leader, see Merline Pitre, *Through Many Dangers Toils & Snares: Black Leadership in Texas, 1870–1890*, 2d rev. ed. (Austin: Eakin Press, 1997), 211, 215–16.

8. David A. Williams, "The History of Higher Education for Black Texans, 1872–1977" (Ed.D. diss., Baylor University, 1978), ch. 2, and George Ruble Woolfolk, *Prairie View: A Study in Public Conscience, 1878–1946* (New York: Pageant Press, 1962), ch. 5, discuss the struggle for the constitutional "colored" university.

9. Lawrence D. Rice, *The Negro in Texas: 1874–1900* (Baton Rouge: Louisiana State University Press, 1971), 209, 239.

10. In surveying the relevant literature, no works adequately address the development of public education in Texas. Rice, *Negro in Texas*; Eby, *Development of Education in Texas*; and C. E. Evans, *The Story of Texas Schools* (Austin: Steck, 1955), particularly fail to show how black Texans contributed to the growth of public education; James M. Smallwood, *Time of Hope, Time of Despair: Black Texans during Reconstruction* (Port Washington, N.Y.: Kennikat Press, 1981), 68–95, does, however, give it some attention.

11. See Barry A. Crouch, *The Freedmen's Bureau and Black Texans* (Austin: University of Texas Press, 1992), ch. 2, and William Lee Richter, "The Army in Texas during Reconstruction, 1865–1870" (Ph.D. diss., University of Texas, 1971), 192. Additionally, Kiddoo founded a school at Galveston that educated African American troops in the area and produced several teachers who stayed in Texas after their muster-out.

12. Richter, "Army in Texas during Reconstruction," 193.

13. Smallwood, *Time of Hope*, 94. Diane Neal and Thomas Kremm, " 'What Shall We Do with the Negro?': The Freedmen's Bureau in Texas," *East Texas Historical Journal* 27 (Fall 1989): 30, found that total black enrollment was 6,449.

14. From "An Act of the United States Congress," 30 March 1870, quoted in Graham Blackstock, *Staff Monograph on Higher Education for Negroes in Texas* (Austin: Texas Legislative Council, 1951), 2–3.

15. Charles W. Ramsdell, *Reconstruction in Texas* (Gloucester: Peter Smith, 1910), 300.

16. From "An Act of the Texas Legislature," 6 February 1884, quoted in Blackstock, *Higher Education for Negroes* (1951), 5. Barry A. Crouch and L. J. Schultz, "Crisis in Color: Racial Separation in Texas during Reconstruction," in *African Americans and the Emergence of Segregation, 1865–1900* (New York: Garland, 1994), 49, write that racial hierarchy and separation in Texas "did not wait until the decade of *Plessy vs. Ferguson* to solidify. Rather, it was a basic fact of life during the years 1865 to 1877." The "basic fact" emerged because of specific actions of certain whites that certain blacks did there best to contest.

17. My analysis differs sharply at points from Lawrence Rice's conclusions in his *Negro in Texas*, 276–80. Until 1896, whites correctly interpreted black demands for equal rights as a desire for social integration and racial equality, despite the frequent denials of leaders like Cuney. There is no evidence to prove that black Texans "accepted" an inferior caste status in the social structure of the state and

nation. Thus, the Supreme Court's "separate but equal" doctrine was "out of harmony" with the "racial mores of the South" to the extent that black southerners were recognized as a part of the South. The construction of blacks as slaves, as a class, and as a caste subordinate to whites has always been contested and was never accepted on an ontological level. The efforts of blacks to oppose white hegemony have had their high tides and low ebbs, but the challenge to historians is to discern why and how patterns of resistance succeed or fail and not to declare some cut-off score at which the conclusion is drawn that all blacks then believed in the white view of their innate, biological, intellectual, or cultural inferiority to whites.

18. Harrison Beckett's Works Progress Administration interview is in George P. Rawick, ed., *The American Slave: A Composite Autobiography*, supp. 2, ser. 2, vol. 2, Texas Narratives, pt. 1 (Westport, Conn.: Greenwood Press, 1972), 230–32.

19. Ibid., vol. 6, pt. 5, 1951.

20. The order "spread like wildfire in Texas," after Texas legislator David Abner Jr. founded the first lodge on 13 January 1879. See Charles Brooks, *The Official History and Manual of the Grand United Order of the Odd Fellows in America* (Freeport: Libraries Press, 1971), 150, and J. Mason Brewer, *Negro Legislators of Texas* (Austin: Pemberton, 1970), 42.

21. Quoted in Eugene D. Genovese, *Roll, Jordan, Roll: The World the Slaves Made* (New York: Vintage Books, 1976), 566.

22. Rawick, ed., *American Slave*, suppl. 2, ser. 2, vol. 6, Texas Narratives, pt. 5, 2344.

23. Robert Blauner, *Racial Oppression in America* (New York: Harper & Row, 1972), provides a sociological model for analyzing the historical context of blacks in Texas between 1865 and 1965. The model has been criticized on many grounds, one crucial deficiency being its failure to account for so-called upward mobility for some blacks inside the internal colony. I embrace its language here because it emphasizes the conquest and enslavement experience and a racial labor principle that put black workers at a special disadvantage in global terms.

24. Sources on the CTSAT include Vernon McDaniel, *History of the Teachers State Association of Texas* (Washington: National Education Association, 1977), 145, and Melvin J. Banks, "The Pursuit of Equality: The Movement for First Class Citizenship among Negroes in Texas" (Ph.D. diss., Syracuse University, 1962).

25. Booker T. Washington, "Atlanta Exposition Address," *Up from Slavery* (1900; reprint, New York: Bantam Books, 1963), 156. On the CTSAT, see the "Report of a Committee on Industrial Education" quoted in Eby, *Development of Education in Texas*, 271.

26. Eby, *Development of Education in Texas*, 270–73. Population figures are taken from U.S. Bureau of the Census, *Negro Population in the United States, 1790–1915* (1918; reprint, New York: Arno Press, 1968), 36.

27. A portion of the bibliography in William Riley Davis, *The Development and Present Status of Negro Education in East Texas* (1934; reprint, New York: AMS Press, 1972), 139–45, provides a reliable compendium of the reports and bulletins of federal, state, institutional, and philanthropic organizations on education, especially higher education for blacks in Texas, up to 1932.

28. Thomas Jesse Jones was the director of research for the Phelp-Stokes Fund. On his "critical attack upon black higher education," see James Anderson, *The*

Education of Blacks in the South (Chapel Hill: University of North Carolina Press, 1988), 250–51; see also his discussion of the influence of industrial philanthropy, such as the General Education Board, on black institutions of higher learning (245–78). On the founding of the Division of Negro Education, see Bruce Glasrud, "Black Texans, 1900–1930: A History" (Ph.D. diss., Texas Technological College, 1969), 243.

29. Artemisia Bowden, "Education, Negro," in Walter Prescott Webb, ed., *The Handbook of Texas*, vol. 1 (Austin: Texas State Historical Association, 1952), 544–45. C. E. Evans, *The Story of Texas Schools* (Austin: Steck, 1955), 252, notes that the legislature granted the State Board of Education no more than "advisory authority" over the board of directors of the Agricultural and Mechanical College; this limited the DNE's power to improve conditions at Prairie View in particular and the higher education of blacks in general.

30. George A. Works, *Texas Educational Survey Report*, vol. 8 (Austin: Texas Educational Survey Commission, 1925), 218.

31. Ibid., 1:247–48.

32. Anderson, *Education of Blacks*, elaborates on the board's overall view of "negro" higher education in the South. He stresses how the board favored the Hampton-Tuskegee model of industrial education and favored a drastic reduction in the number of public and private institutions trying to provide blacks with an opportunity for higher education. Many of the recommendations of the *Survey*, by way of Favrot, were consistent with Anderson's observations.

33. L. D. Coffman et al., *Texas Educational Survey Report: Higher Education*, vol. 6 (Austin: Texas Educational Survey Commission, 1925), 73.

34. Woolfolk, *Prairie View*, 228–31. See also Dethloff, *Centennial History of Texas A&M*, 321.

35. Arthur Klein, *Survey of Negro Colleges and Universities*, Bulletin, no. 7 (Washington: GPO, 1929), 3.

36. Dethloff, *Centennial History of Texas A&M*, 321; see also Woolfolk, *Prairie View*, 236–41, for more on the Klein survey and his follow-up survey of 1930 (specifically focused on land-grant colleges), and Prairie View principal Banks's use of the Conference of Presidents of Negro Land-Grant Colleges to help convince A&M officials of his sense of Prairie View's needs.

37. See Woolfolk, *Prairie View*, 244–58, on the "North-South pivot," that is to say, the purposes that Banks would seek to satisfy through spearheading a variety of conferences at his college.

38. *Proceedings of the First Annual Session of the Conference on Education for Negroes in Texas* (Prairie View: Prairie View Standard, 1930), 5.

39. *Proceedings of the Eighth Educational Conference* (Prairie View: Prairie View College State Normal and Industrial, November 1932), 5.

40. Woolfolk, *Prairie View*, 268, discusses how Bullock, among others, would receive fellowships from groups like the General Education Board. In exchange, Banks or his representative attended conferences these groups held or the college supplied the "constant request from field agents of critical professional information" and other data. A near complete list of the studies and bulletins from all of the annual conferences up to 1941 was published in *Proceedings of the Eleventh Educational Conference* (Hempstead: Prairie View College Press, November 1940), 6.

41. See *Eleventh Educational Conference*, 3.

42. *Eighth Educational Conference*, 6.

43. Ibid., 11–12.

44. Ibid., 19.

45. Ibid., 25, 69.

46. Eby, *Development of Education in Texas*; he was also noted for his *Education in Texas Source Materials* (Austin: University of Texas, 1918).

47. Frederick H. Eby, "History of the Development and Expansion of Public Education in Texas," in *Eighth Educational Conference*, 16–17.

48. I. Q. Hurdle, "The Program of the State Association for Colored Teachers and Its Effectiveness in Increasing the Availability of Education for Negroes in Texas," in *Eighth Educational Conference*, 86. On the CTSAT's complete slogan, see McDaniel, *Teachers State Association*, 145.

49. Hurdle, "Program of the State Association for Colored Teachers," 86. Hurdle's admonition that members of the teaching profession "be sure to cultivate the habit of love for people" is indicative of a contrasting function of black education to white and of a black-white difference in mentality. The teacher as a source of affection and empathy was central to the existence of "Negro Education as a Way of Life," as Henry Allen Bullock puts it in *History of Negro Education*, 147–66. Bullock's discussion, despite its many limitations, is one of the most suggestive interpretations available of the segregated black school's role in shaping an antisegregation, antiracist social movement. He termed the school-based process of counter-hegemonic production, that is to say, of creating "uppity" Negroes, "a school system in unconscious rebellion" (157, 160–66). The analysis presented here departs in a substantial way from Bullock's interpretation. He exaggerates the overdetermination of the economic structure to a point that it becomes difficult to see how black schools contributed, as he argues they did, to the production of anticaste social revolutionaries. He is inspiring, however, in his attempt to contextualize the dissident function of black higher education.

50. Hurdle, "Program of the State Association for Colored Teachers," 86.

51. On the influence of the "classical sociological view of social movements" on the contextualization of the "black freedom struggle" in historical literature, see Clayborne Carson, "Civil Rights Reform and the Black Freedom Struggle," in Charles W. Eagles, ed., *The Civil Rights Movement in America* (Jackson: University Press of Mississippi, 1986), 19–32. Carson usefully suggests that historians view civil rights in a larger historical context.

52. Darlene Clark Hine, *Black Victory: The Rise and Fall of the White Primary in Texas* (Millwood: KTO Press, 1979), ix.

53. Ibid., 235.

54. It is likely that many schoolteachers supported the movement. McDaniel, *Teachers State Association*, 33–34, 145–53, indicates that the legal campaign against the white primary was of great concern to the CTSAT.

55. U.S. Bureau of the Census, *Special Reports: Occupations at the Twelfth Census* (Washington: GPO, 1904), 392, 396; U.S. Bureau of the Census, *Thirteenth Census of the U.S. Taken in the Year 1910*, Occupation Statistics (Washington: GPO, 1914), 520–22; U.S. Bureau of the Census, *Fourteenth Census of the U.S. Taken in the Year 1920* 4, Occupations (Washington: GPO, 1923), 1022–25; U.S. Bureau of the

Census, *Fifteenth Census of the U.S.: 1930* 4, Occupations, by States (Washington: GPO, 1933), 1582–84; U.S. Bureau of the Census, *Sixteenth Census of the U.S.: 1940* 3, The Labor Force, pt. 5 (Washington: GPO, 1943), 488, 492.

56. Hamilton may have learned of the unsuccessful *Hocutt* case, in which a black student sought admission to the law school at the University of North Carolina in 1933, but there is no evidence that he was inspired by the incident. He may just as well have read about West Virginia's enactment of a measure in 1933 that provided assistance to blacks who had to leave the state for graduate and professional education.

57. J. Mason Brewer, *Heralding Dawn* (Dallas: Mathis Publishing, 1936), 17.

58. On the DNCC, see Marvin Dulaney, "What Happened to the Civil Rights Movement in Dallas, Texas?," in John Dittmer, George C. Wright, and W. Marvin Dulaney, *Essays on the American Civil Rights Movement*, ed. W. Marvin Dulaney and Kathleen Underwood (College Station: Texas A&M Press, 1993), 70. While the Klan had declined considerably by 1926, it still exerted influence in Dallas and elsewhere in Texas into the 1930s. See Kenneth T. Jackson, *The Ku Klux Klan in the City, 1915–1930* (New York: Oxford University Press, 1967), ch. 6. "In March 1931," wrote Jackson, "fourteen armed Knights abducted and flogged two Communist organizers in Dallas for making speeches against Jim Crow (segregation) laws and the lynching of Negroes" (80).

59. Smith has not yet received the full-length biographical treatment he deserves, but one source on this important leader is a sketch in Effie Kaye Adams, *Tall Black Texans: Men of Courage* (Dubuque, Iowa: Kendall-Hunt, 1972), 22–27; the Antonio Maceo Smith Papers are in the possession of his widow, Ms. Fannie Smith of Dallas. See Dulaney, "What Happened," 92 n. 12, on the DNCC's hiring of Smith.

60. Adams, *Tall Black Texans*, 23.

61. Michael L. Gillette, "The Rise of the NAACP in Texas," *Southwestern Historical Quarterly* 81 (April 1978): 393–94.

62. See Jacquelyn Dowd Hall, *Revolt against Chivalry* (New York: Columbia University Press, 1979), 59, 62, and 294–95 n. 13, for information on TCIC activities that Ames led; namely, state support for a home or "training school" for delinquent black girls, the erection of a tuberculosis hospital, the securing of greater services for blacks from the state Department of Health, and a drive for adoption of textbooks on black history. On the rise of the CIC in response to the cutting off of communication between the races, considered an "insidious" product of the Progressive era's perfecting of segregation, see Jack Temple Kirby, *Darkness at the Dawning* (Philadelphia: Lippincott, 1972), 179.

63. R. T. Hamilton, "Resolution Presented Inter-racial Commission at Prairie View," UTPOR, group VF 18/C.

64. All letters and documents in UTPOR. All of the letters are dated 11 March 1936, except for the one to Virginia, dated 29 June 1936.

65. "Proposed Bill," UTPOR, avoided any mention of race by referring to "such persons" unable to pursue certain courses of studies offered at the University of Texas or some other state-supported institution "because of provisions of Section 7 of Article VII of the Constitution of Texas." The draft bill authorized the appropriation of $15,000 each year from 1937 to 1939 for out-of-state tuition assistance.

66. Banks, "Pursuit of Equality," 400, states that the new graduate division was established "to forestall a suit." There is, however, no evidence that such a suit was seriously impending in 1937 or that state legislators acted in reaction to such a concern.

67. Banks, "Pursuit of Equality," 359 n. 144. The quotation is from Neil Gary Sapper, "A Survey of the History of the Black People of Texas, 1930–1954" (Ph.D. diss., Texas Tech University, 1972), 358 n. 143. Sapper states that Hamilton and other school-aid-campaign supporters did not trust the lobbyist who drafted the bill and guaranteed its passage for an additional $3,000.

68. "Negro Education," *Dallas Dispatch*, 1 March 1937.

69. "Dallas Negroes Ask State Aid for Education," *Dallas Express*, 26 February 1937. Evidence has not been found to substantiate the claim that Hamilton and the editor of the *Dallas Dispatch* made that most of the faculty members of the black colleges of Texas had come from the North. Hamilton's estimate of 97 percent, however, might not have been too badly exaggerated, if he had said that most black faculty members had received some part of their education in a northern school. See Michael R. Heintze, *Private Black Colleges in Texas, 1865–1954* (College Station: Texas A&M University Press, 1985), 120–26.

70. "An Appropriation that Should Be Voted," *Dallas Times Herald*, 27 February 1937.

71. *HI*, 5 June 1937, 1–2. Spurred by the U.S. Supreme Court's decision in the *Gaines* case (see Chapter 2), in early 1939, Governor James Allred called for the legislature to pass the student assistance bill. See Sapper, "Survey," 360–61.

72. Larry D. Hill and Robert A. Calvert, "The University of Texas Extension Services and Progressivism," *Southwestern Historical Quarterly* 86 (October 1982): 253. The authors point out an element of hypocrisy when they write that "in spite of avowed nonelitism, progressivist extension services for many years generally did not encompass black schools" (231 n. 1). To be sure, Texas segregationists left the matter in the hands of Prairie View and the other black colleges; but they must have overlooked the effect that inadequate funding had on the ability of these colleges to reach the black population.

73. Sapper, "Survey," 360.

74. Quoted in Michael L. Gillette, "Blacks Challenge the White University," *Southwestern Historical Quarterly* 86 (October 1982): 321.

75. Ibid., 321–22. See also Sapper, "Survey," 360.

76. *Gaines* v. *Canada*, 305 U.S. 337 (1938).

77. Jessie P. Guzman, *Twenty Years of Court Decisions Affecting Higher Education in the South, 1938–1958* (Tuskegee, Ala.: Tuskegee Institute, 1960), 3–4.

78. R. T. Hamilton, "Professional Training Problem of Negroes," *Dallas Times Herald*, 31 December 1938.

79. "Scholarship Funds Inadequate; Negroes May Enter A. & M. College," *Dallas Express*, 22 April 1939.

80. Murphy to President, 15 January 1939; Hayes to George E. Bethel; Goss to J. W. Calhoun; and Jackson to Registrar, 6 March 1939, all UTPOR.

81. *Dallas Express*, 9 September 1939, 1, and 16 December 1939, 3.

82. Brewer, *Heralding Dawn*, 17.

83. John Lee Brooks, "J. Mason Brewer," in ibid., 3.

84. Brewer, *Heralding Dawn*, 20–21.

85. Henry Allen Bullock, "Negro Higher and Professional Education in Texas," *Journal of Negro Education* 18 (Summer 1948): 380–81.

Chapter Two

1. Several works examine the legal struggle against segregation. Among the most important studies are Mark V. Tushnet, *Making Civil Rights Law: Thurgood Marshall and the Supreme Court, 1936–1961* (New York: Oxford University Press, 1994) and *The NAACP's Legal Strategy against Segregated Education, 1925–1950* (Chapel Hill: University of North Carolina Press, 1987). Also see Richard Kluger, *Simple Justice: The History of Brown v. Board of Education and Black America's Struggle for Equality* (New York: Vintage Books, 1977); M. M. Chambers, *The Colleges and the Courts, 1946–50* (New York: Columbia University Press, 1952); Loren Miller, *The Petitioners: The Story of the Supreme Court of the United States and the Negro* (New York: Pantheon, 1966); Ozie H. Johnson, *Price of Freedom* (n.p., 1954); and Henry Allen Bullock, *A History of Negro Education in the South from 1619 to the Present* (Cambridge: Harvard University Press, 1967).

2. Abram Harris and Sterling Spero provided this ideological quartet in their essay "The Negro Problem," in *Encyclopaedia of the Social Sciences*, vol. 11, ed. E. Sebigmann and A. Johnson (New York: Macmillan, 1933), 346. See William Darity Jr., ed., *Race, Radicalism, and Reform: Selected Papers, Abram L. Harris* (New Brunswick: Transaction Publishers, 1989), 14–21, for a succinct overview of these contending social philosophies as Harris analyzed them. Typologies are always fraught with difficulties, but I prefer Harris's framework to the three "trends" in John Cell, *The Highest Stage of White Supremacy: The Origins of Segregation in South Africa and the American South* (New York: Cambridge University Press, 1982). Cell identified accommodation, confrontation, and separation as the major responses to segregation of blacks in the United States and South Africa. Accommodation corresponds to the interracial conciliation position used here; confrontation corresponds less neatly to the civil libertarianism and class consciousness positions; and separation represents a part or a potential part of the militant race consciousness position.

3. An insightful article on the Second World War as a "watershed" in modern black history is Richard M. Dalfiume, "The 'Forgotten Years' of the Negro Revolution," *Journal of American History* 55 (June 1968): 90–106. For the concept of ideology that helps guide the present work, see Martin Seliger, *The Marxist Conception of Ideology: A Critical Essay* (Cambridge: Cambridge University Press, 1977). He defines what he termed the "inclusive conception" of *ideology* as "[The] sets of factual and moral propositions which serve to posit, explain and justify ends and means of organized social action, especially political action, irrespective of whether such action aims to preserve, amend, destroy or rebuild any given order" (1).

4. Banks was undoubtedly one of the most powerful men of color in Texas in the 1930s and 1940s. He exercised his power cautiously and constructively. Unfortunately, no biography exists of him nor is he included in a collective biography of black college presidents during his era. Much of his memory remains in legend and

folklore and, of course, the built environment at Prairie View. His style may be suitably epitomized by an anecdote of undetermined origin or veracity. It goes that Banks discovered a young faculty member sitting with his legs propped up reading an edition of *Academe*. He asked the man if he was an employee of the college, to which the scholar came to attention and answered in the affirmative. Banks, who had clearly seen what the man was reading, told him to stop wasting time and that if he had nothing better to do to go and move some boxes that were in the corridor.

As another story goes, as told to me in 1993 by a Prairie View faculty member, who has asked that her identity not be disclosed, Banks was on one of his many trips to the offices of the General Education Board. He was brought to a room that housed what might have been the country's largest collection of the catalogues of historically black colleges and universities. Upon encountering the holding, Banks commented that this must surely be the greatest collection of fiction in the world. Irony, ambiguity, and paradox are surely in no short supply in the life story of W. R. Banks.

5. George R. Woolfolk, "W. R. Banks: Public College Educator," in Alwyn Barr and Robert A. Calvert, eds., *Black Leaders: Texans for Their Times* (Austin: Texas State Historical Association, 1981), 132. Also see Woolfolk's discussion of how Banks got the principalship of Prairie View. He states that there was an attempt by a group of blacks to "smear" Banks as a radical by pointing to his "ties to Du Bois" (135). To debunk this effort to derail his candidacy for the Prairie View job, Woolfolk writes, Banks wrote a series of letters to A&M president T. O. Walton, "claiming closeness to Booker T. Washington." I have been unable to find these letters. Walton did not leave his papers at Texas A&M, and their whereabouts are unknown.

6. *HI*, July 19, 1941, 15. See also Neil Gary Sapper, "A Survey of the History of the Black People of Texas, 1930–1954" (Ph.D. diss., Texas Tech University, 1972), 403–4.

7. Woolfolk, "W. R. Banks," 147–48; quotation on page 147.

8. T. S. Montgomery, *The Senior Colleges for Negroes in Texas: A Study Made at the Direction of the Bi-Racial Conference on Education for Negroes in Texas* (n.p., April 1944), 4. The meeting took place in the Senate chamber of the Texas state capitol.

9. Montgomery, *Senior Colleges*, 12. Brown's scholarly output is interesting, but there is little biographical material on this Texas woman. In 1939, when Congress directed the U.S. Office of Education to make a study of the higher education of blacks, she was selected to join the survey staff as senior specialist in social studies. In the resulting four-volume work called the *National Survey of the Higher Education of Negroes*, Brown authored the first volume, titled *Socio-Economic Approach to Educational Problems* (Washington: GPO, 1942). The BCNET's generous use of all four volumes, especially Brown's, attests both to the work's methodological strength and to its neutrality toward segregation. Brown did, however, present a strongly analytical and critical discussion of American race relations, the content of which moved John W. Studebaker, U.S. commissioner of education, to submit a draft of the chapter to a panel of scholars for their criticisms. UT had three members on the panel: President Rainey, Robert Sutherland (director of the Hogg Foundation), and Mary Decherd (assistant professor of pure mathematics). Noted anthropologists Melville Herskovits and W. Lloyd Warner, as well as the eminent Howard Odum, director of the University of North Carolina's Institute for Research in

Social Science, were the best-known white scholars that were sent drafts of Brown's second chapter. Black scholars invited to critique her work were Charles Thompson, dean of Howard University's College of Liberal Arts and editor of the *Journal of Negro Education* (arguably one of the most important scholarly periodicals produced by blacks in that period); Charles S. Johnson, director of Fisk University's Department of Social Science; and John W. Davis, president of West Virginia State College. Will W. Alexander, Jackson Davis, Frances C. McLester, and John Pomfret were the other invited critics. Brown explained that two roads lay before America: integration of the Negro or the perfection of a racially balkanized, antidemocratic nation-state such as what loomed on the South African horizon. She endorsed the preservation of democracy in America by the elimination of the "nonrational" barriers to social mobility the white majority imposed on blacks. Negro integration into American life, Brown insisted, would "not come about as a result of fiat or force" and could not "be achieved either rapidly or by arbitrary methods, and any great progress toward such a goal must, perhaps, be counted by generations rather than by years." See Brown, *Socio-Economic Approach to Educational Problems*, 20.

10. Montgomery, *Senior Colleges*, 12–13. It is ironic but customary that Montgomery chose to cite the white managing editor of the Louisville *Courier-Journal*, Mark Ethridge, for a summation of black aspirations and desires and for black folks' ideological position on race, national identity, miscegenation, and the political economic order. The citation also appears to have been gratuitous, since this passage closely resembles Brown, *Socio-Economic Approach*, 19–20.

11. Montgomery, *Senior Colleges*, 83–84.

12. Orville Bullington to John A. Lomax, 7 January 1944, "The Homer Rainey Controversy" file, John A. Lomax Papers, Center for American History, University of Texas, Austin. That an educated man like Bullington would send out a letter with "Negro" consistently spelled in lowercase form can only be taken as additional evidence of the contempt in which he held people of African descent. On antidiscrimination provisions in government contracts, especially concerning the U.S. Navy, see Dennis D. Nelson, *The Integration of the Negro into the U.S. Navy* (New York: Farrar, Straus and Young, 1951); John W. Davis, "The Negro in the United States Navy, Marine Corps and Coast Guard," *Journal of Negro Education* 12 (Summer 1943): 348; and Bernard C. Nalty, *Strength for the Fight: A History of Blacks in the Military* (New York: Free Press, 1986).

13. The black press became self-consciously militant during the years of the Second World War, more than at any other time in the first half of the twentieth century. The reference to white supremacists as "American Hitlers" was quite common. Such a reference appears in *HI*, 5 November 1938. The black conservative and iconoclastic columnist George Schuyler stated flatly: "Our war is not against Hitler in Europe, but against Hitlers in America" (quoted in Dalfiume, " 'Forgotten Years,' " 94). See also Lee Finkle, "The Conservative Aims of Militant Rhetoric: Black Protest during World War II," *Journal of American History* 60 (December 1973): 692–713, and Harvard Sitkoff, "Racial Militancy and Interracial Violence in the Second World War," *Journal of American History* 58 (December 1971): 661–81. Sitkoff notes that the NAACP repeatedly compared "Hitlerism with American racism" (665) and encouraged blacks to protest Jim Crowism at every chance. Dorie Miller was killed in action on the *Liscome Bay* aircraft carrier

when a Japanese torpedo tore into its aft on 24 November 1943. See Effie Kaye Adams, *Tall Black Texans: Men of Courage* (Dubuque, Iowa: Kendall-Hunt, 1972), 113–15.

14. Montgomery, *Senior Colleges*, 84.

15. Ibid. For a discussion of the regional education program, see Jessie Parkhurst Guzman, ed., *The Negro Year Book, 1952: A Review of Events Affecting Negro Life* (New York: Wise & Co., 1952), 231–35.

16. Montgomery, *Senior Colleges*, 85.

17. Ibid., 87.

18. Woolfolk, "W. R. Banks," 149.

19. Woolfolk notes that Rhoads was a contender for the principalship of Prairie View but the A&M board of directors passed over him in favor of Banks (ibid., 134). On the two men's educational background, see Woolfolk on Banks in ibid., 132; see also Vernon McDaniel, *History of the Teachers State Association of Texas* (Washington: National Education Association, 1977), 127. Apparently, Michael R. Heintze, in *Private Black Colleges in Texas, 1865–1954* (College Station: Texas A&M University Press, 1985), erred or meant an honorary degree where he credits Banks as earning an master's degree from Paul Quinn College in 1922. Quinn was "striving" to get the Texas State college examiner to recognize its four-year programs and had no graduate degree offerings whatsoever. On Paul Quinn College, see Arthur J. Klein's study for the U.S. Department of Interior, Bureau of Education, *Survey of Negro Colleges and Universities*, Bulletin no. 7 (Washington: GPO, 1929), 856–65. Klein chided the college for granting "a very excessive number of honorary degrees" (862). In 1924–25 the college conferred twelve honorary doctor of divinity degrees but granted fewer than that in academic degrees. Banks may have gotten such a degree in like manner.

20. On Hamilton, see Tempie Virginia Strange, "The Dallas Negro Chamber of Commerce: A Study of a Negro Institution" (M.A. thesis, Southern Methodist University, 1945), 10, 12–13, 58, 174, 243–44.

21. See McDaniel, *Teachers State Association*, 49–51, and Melvin J. Banks, "The Pursuit of Equality: The Movement for First Class Citizenship among Negroes in Texas, 1920–1950" (D.S.S. diss., Syracuse University, 1962), 347–401.

22. Sources on the Texas CODE include McDaniel, *Teachers State Association*, 41–42, and Banks, "Pursuit of Equality," 354–64, which notes that CODE "planned the strategy" while the NAACP supplied "legal advice and defense" and that TCNO acted as the "spearhead and shock absorber" of the University Movement and the fight to equalize the salaries of black and white public school teachers (363).

23. For information on Wesley, see Nancy Ruth Eckols Bessent, "The Publisher: A Biography of Carter Wesley" (M.A. thesis, University of Texas, 1981), 125–68. In 1940, moreover, Wesley added the influential *Dallas Express* to his chain of papers.

24. Charles Hamilton Houston, "Statement on the University Cases," II-A-29, NAACP Papers.

25. Walter White, "Keynote Address," 1941 Annual Conference, II-A-30, NAACP Papers.

26. Tushnet, *Making Civil Rights Law*, 122.

27. NAACP Youth Section Resolution, 1941 Conference, II-A-30, NAACP Papers.

28. A. Maceo Smith to Marshall, 9 April 1945, II-A-147, NAACP Papers.

29. The Texas Primary Case refers to *Smith* v. *Allwright* (the lawsuit of a black dentist in Houston, Lonnie Smith—of no relation to A. Maceo Smith), which ended in the 1944 U.S. Supreme Court ruling that blacks could not be barred from voting in the Democratic Party primary. See Darlene Clark Hine, *Black Victory: The Rise and Fall of the White Primary in Texas* (Millwood: KTO Press, 1979), 222–25.

30. *HI*, 6 January 1945; *HP*, 31 May 1945. On the Permanent University Fund, see Berte R. Haigh, *Land, Oil, and Education* (El Paso: Texas Western Press, 1986), especially 296, where it is noted that UT and Texas A&M split the proceeds from the fund on a two-thirds and one-third basis, respectively; David F. Prindle, "Oil and the Permanent University Fund: The Early Years," *Southwestern Historical Quarterly* 86 (October 1982): 277–98, is useful on some of the machinations of the UT regents in relation to the fund and how Texas A&M got into the honey pot, but it is silent on the legislature's refusal to permit Prairie View to obtain some revenues.

31. Merline Pitre, *In Struggle against Jim Crow: Lula B. White and the NAACP, 1900–1957* (College Station: Texas A&M Press, 1999), ch. 5; "Black Houstonians and the 'Separate but Equal' Doctrine: Carter W. Wesley versus Lulu B. White," *Houston Review* 12 (1990): 23–36.

32. Tushnet, *NAACP's Legal Strategy*, 107–9. Kluger, *Simple Justice*, 523, presents Thurgood Marshall as vacillating on the timing of a direct-assault strategy against segregated education as late as 1951.

33. Founded in 1919, the CIC was the South's premier interracial organization for nearly two decades. It successfully attracted support from a small constituency of white southerners in locales where the NAACP garnered little or none. In November 1943, however, it was voted out of existence. Remnant branches of the organization in Texas cities like Houston continued functioning into the 1950s, although they were more of a *function* in a meeting sense than actual organizing or work projects, even after they went on record opposing segregation. See "Elimination of Segregation Stressed during Party of Interracial Commission," *HI*, 29 January 1949, for a description of the 1949 annual meeting of the Texas CIC. See also Raymond Gavins, *The Perils and Prospects of Southern Black Leadership: Gordon Blaine Hancock, 1884–1970* (Durham: Duke University Press, 1977), 146, and David R. Goldfield, *Black, White, and Southern: Race Relations and Southern Culture, 1940 to the Present* (Baton Rouge: Louisiana State University Press, 1990), 40–43.

34. Wesley to Marshall, 11 August 1943, Wesley File, II-B-218, NAACP Papers.

35. Southern Regional Council, *The Southern Regional Council: Its Origin and Purposes* (Atlanta: SRC, 1944), 4. See also George B. Tindall, *The Emergence of the New South, 1913–1945* (Baton Rouge: Louisiana State University Press, 1967), 719, where he states that credit for the idea of a black summit should go to a white woman, Jessie Daniel Ames, who "prodded" Hancock to call for the Durham conference. Gavins, *Perils and Prospects*, 117–19, and Hall, *Revolt against Chivalry*, suggest that Hancock was already thinking along the lines of a conference independent of Ames.

36. Wesley to Marshall, 11 August and 25 October 1943, II-B-218, NAACP Papers.

37. Wesley to Attorneys A. P. Tureaud et al., 1 May 1945, II-B-218, NAACP Papers.

38. Wesley to Marshall, 12 July 1945, II-B-218, NAACP Papers.

39. Marshall to Wesley, 16 July 1945, II-B-218, NAACP Papers.

40. Marshall to Wesley, 17 December 1943 and 28 January 1944, II-B-218, NAACP Papers.

41. Wesley to Marshall, 28 January 1944 and 3 September 1945, II-B-218, NAACP Papers.

42. Marshall to Wesley, 21 August 1945, II-B-218, NAACP Papers. In the same file, see also Wesley to Marshall, 3 September 1945; Wesley notes that Marshall's summary "substantially states the agreement we made." He goes on to chide Marshall for being a "turn-coat" sending out "a damn fool directive . . . calculated to set up two organizations" when "a straightforward letter" to Wesley would have drawn the SNC-EEO's "pre-acknowledgement" that it would not "curtail the field of operation of the NAACP" (Marshall to Wesley, 26 September 1945, ibid.). The special counsel replied in a testy manner to Wesley: "I told you that I was wrong in sending out the memorandum without personally acquainting you with the fact. I told you personally I was wrong, and you continue to remind me that I was wrong. What do you want, an affidavit?" He also noted that there was no "good plaintiff for the law school," and he suggested starting a case at the primary or secondary school level.

43. Marshall to Byrd, 15 April 1946, II-B-218, NAACP Papers. Marshall wrote Byrd two days after the conference, apparently believing that the meeting was scheduled for 20 April. In Byrd to Marshall, 18 April 1946, ibid., Byrd replied that he "didn't think much of" the conference. "The committee sppears [*sic*] to be weak and poorly organized and uncertain as to what steps to take next," wrote Byrd. He continued, "I feel that if Carter Wesley steps down as President, and he insists upon stepping down, this will be the end of the Committee." He also observed that the SNC-EEO went on record commending the NAACP for taking action in Texas with the Sweatt case and in a school case in Texarkana, as well as in Kentucky "and other communities spear heading the attack for equal educational facilities."

44. Open letter from Smith and Wesley to Friend, 3 September 1946, II-B-218, NAACP Papers.

45. Lulu White to Walter White, handwritten note on Smith and Wesley's open letter, stamped 14 September 1946, II-B-218, NAACP Papers. White stated, "I know full well [the TNCEE] is Maceo's idea. He has attempted before for a compromise." Among other factors, what infuriated Lulu White was Smith and Wesley using a mailing list she regarded as the private property of the NAACP. Given Smith's role as an executive officer and spearhead in both the TCNO and Texas State Conference of NAACP Branches, White's perception may have been blurred by her fury. Whether her charge of their unauthorized use of NAACP property was merely a low blow or a valid complaint, Wesley and Smith saw no impropriety in their conduct.

46. Walter White to Marshall, 12 September 1946, II-B-218, NAACP Papers.

47. Marshall to Wesley, 18 October 1946, II-B-218, NAACP Papers.

48. White to Marshall, 11 December 1946, II-C-193, NAACP Papers.

49. "The Colossal Fraud," *HI*, 7 December 1946. The sociologist Henry Allen Bullock was a columnist for Wesley's papers. He wrote strident articles challenging

Prairie View officials to not involve the school in makeshift arrangements that would make it "a Benedict Arnold of Negro education." See *HI*, 30 March 1946.

50. "Quit Kidding," *HI*, 14 December 1946 and 28 December 1946; Pitre, "Black Houstonians," 31–32.

51. When Lulu White finally resigned as Houston branch executive secretary in June of 1949, she stated that the time had come to "OBEY" her husband as she had vowed at their marriage to do until death did they part. "We must recognize [Wesley] to be the enemy that he is," she bitterly wrote in letter of resignation published in full in Wesley's paper. See "NAACP Sec'y Quits," *HI*, 18 June 1949.

52. A biographical study of Julius White would make interesting and enlightening reading. Two historians use "truculent" to describe him. See Michael L. Gillette, "The Rise of the NAACP in Texas," *Southwestern Historical Quarterly* 81 (April 1978): 409, and Darlene Clark Hine, *Black Victory*, 207. The fullest account of White can be found in Pitre, *In Struggle against Jim Crow*.

53. Walter White to Marshall, 30 December 1946 and 6 January 1947, II-B-218, NAACP Papers.

54. "NAACP Sec'y Quits," *HI*, 18 June 1949.

55. Wesley to Jones, 2 January 1947, II-B-218, NAACP Papers.

56. Minutes of the Meeting of the Executive Committee, Texas NAACP, 18 December 1946, II-B-218, NAACP Papers. The defendants' claim that they would open in Houston a Negro law school by 1 February satisfied Archer that the separate-but-equal doctrine had been upheld.

57. Wesley to Marshall, 23 December 1946, II-B-218, NAACP Papers. In this letter Wesley stated that the TNCEE and TNCO were one and the same organization by "gentlemen's agreement" between him and A. Maceo Smith. To the extent that Wesley is accurate in this claim, Tushnet, *NAACP's Legal Strategy*, 107, is far off the mark in his idea that the conference "existed almost exclusively on paper." Indeed, it existed in the dollars, sweat, and tears of scores of the Lone Star State's most influential black leaders and activists. "Jester to Address Negroes of Austin," 22 March 1947, *Informer*, indicated the existence of a county branch of the TNCEE, the Travis County Association for the Equalization of Educational Opportunities. The association sponsored a mass rally and invited Governor Beauford Jester to the Dorie Miller Auditorium to speak on the Texas University for Negroes "among other vital topics."

58. Marshall to Wesley, White to Wesley, 27 December 1946, II-B-218, NAACP Papers.

59. Wesley to Marshall, Wesley to White, 30 December 1946, II-B-218, NAACP Papers.

60. White to Marshall, 6 January 1947, II-B-218, NAACP Papers.

61. Marshall to Wesley (draft), 6 January 1947; Wilkins to Marshall, 7 January 1947; Marshall to Wilkins (memo), 7 January 1947; Marshall to Wesley, 7 January 1947; all in II-B-218, NAACP Papers.

62. Wesley to Marshall, 9 January 1947, II-B-218, NAACP Papers.

63. Marshall to Wesley, 13 January 1947, II-B-218, NAACP Papers.

64. Wesley to Local Branch (Houston) NAACP, 17 January 1947; Wesley to Marshall, 18 January 1947; Marshall to Wesley, 22 January 1947; all in II-B-218, NAACP Papers.

65. Nabrit to Wesley, 30 January 1947, II-B-218, NAACP Papers.

66. Marshall to Wesley, 5 February 1947, and Wesley to Marshall, 13 February 1947, II-B-218, NAACP Papers. The NAACP did not count Wesley out altogether. When called upon to send a congratulatory note on the seventh anniversary of Wesley's New Orleans *Informer*, Walter White had a letter drafted for his signature hailing the paper as carrying out the "sacred duty" of "uncompromisingly" focusing "attention upon the discrepancies in our nation between the democratic ideal and democratic fact." See White to Harrington, 26 April 1947, and White to Wesley, 6 May 1947, II-B-218, NAACP Papers.

67. Memorandum to Gloster B. Current from Thurgood Marshall, 8 July 1947, Marshall File, NAACP Papers.

68. Alan Scott, "Twenty-Five Years of Opinion on Integration in Texas," *Southwestern Historical Quarterly* 48 (September 1967): 158. Gale L. Barchus, "The Dynamics of Black Demands and White Responses for Negro Higher Education in the State of Texas, 1945–1950" (M.A. thesis, University of Texas, 1970), 21–22, notes that the poll was published widely in Texas newspapers. He does not provide a citation for the poll data he furnishes but does state that "trained colored interviewers" were used so that black respondents would be encouraged to report their true opinions.

69. *HP*, 11 and 12 February 1947; Barchus, "Dynamics of Black Demands," 23–24.

70. "Segregation Intensifies Suspicion and Distrust, Sociologist Asserts in Sweatt Hearing at Austin," *HI*, 17 May 1947. See also Barchus, "Dynamics of Black Demands," 33–34; *Sweatt* v. *Painter, Transcript of Records*, U.S. Supreme Court (October 1948), 189–208; and *DMN*, 15 May 1947. On the emergence of an antiracist and antisegregation argument among American social scientists, see Thomas F. Gossett, *Race: The History of an American Idea* (New York: Schocken Books, 1963), 409–30, 453–57. Despite the paucity of commentary on Redfield's appearance as an expert witness in the *Sweatt* case, *The Social Uses of Social Science: The Papers of Robert Redfield*, edited by Margaret Park Redfield (Chicago: University of Chicago Press, 1963), has two articles, particularly Redfield's 1946 piece, "Race and Religion in Selective Admission," that help reveal his political and ethical concerns. He criticized quotas that limited the numbers of Jews admitted to graduate and professional schools and also gave strong support to the black struggle to democratize higher education: "It is notorious that educational facilities offered Negroes are inferior to those provided for whites," he wrote. "The Gaines decision is now eight years old, but it will not be claimed that Negroes find ready for them everywhere state institutions of higher learning and professional training equal to those open to whites. . . . Decisions of the Supreme Court have given legal recognition to local practices of segregation, but they have not made racial or religious discrimination lawful. It is the duty of every citizen to work to overcome such discrimination" (174).

71. "NAACP Sets Stage to Enter Hearne Suit," *HI*, 27 September 1947.

72. R. M. Blocker, Arthur Mack, General Washington, C. G. Jennings, Luell Mack, and J. Wesley Simms, "Petition of the Negro Citizens Committee of Hearne, Texas," II-B-147, NAACP Papers.

73. A. Maceo Smith to Lulu White, 14 August 1947, II-B-147, NAACP Papers.

74. Ray Osborne, "Negro Pupils Quit Classes: White School Denies Hearne Girl Entry," *DMN*, 18 September 1947.

75. The communication between Sanchez and Marshall is suggestive of a heretofore unexamined connection between the Mexican American legal work against segregated education and the NAACP's work, which reached a watershed with the *Brown* ruling in 1954. Sanchez held that the testimony of experts so effectively used in the *Mendez* case might be useful to the NAACP legal effort. "Our segregation suit," he boasted, "was won before we went to Court!" If there had been a trial, he explained, "we had certain procedures in mind that would have gone a long way toward proving our case. All these may have some value to you in your field." Al Wirin initiated the correspondence between Sanchez and Marshall. The NAACP special counsel stated he would contact Sanchez on his next trip to Texas. See Sanchez to Marshall, 6 July 1948, and Marshall to Sanchez, 14 July 1948, II-A-147, NAACP Papers.

76. A. Maceo Smith to Carrie Mack, 19 October 1948 and 5 May 1949, II-B-147, NAACP Papers. Smith to Marshall, 22 October 1948, II-B-147, NAACP Papers, reveals some of the problems and plans, at least in Smith's mind, for carrying forward the Hearne suit and preparing the way for the launching of suits in "other centers." The Hearne schools did not begin to desegregate until twenty-five years later.

77. Tushnet, *NAACP's Legal Strategy*, 152.

78. Sitkoff, "Racial Militancy," 671. It has been twenty years since any historian has looked over and dug into the Beaumont Race Riot of 1943, but the need and opportunity for research on the event and the larger issue of domestic terrorism is pressing. See James A. Burran, "Violence in an 'Arsenal of Democracy': The Beaumont Race Riot, 1943," *East Texas Historical Journal* 14 (Spring 1976): 43, and James Olson and Sharon Phair, "The Anatomy of a Race Riot, 1943," *Texana* 11 (Spring 1973): 64–72.

79. On the Negro Goodwill Council of Beaumont, see Nancy Dailey, "History of the Beaumont, Texas, Chapter of the National Association for the Advancement of Colored People, 1918–1970" (M.A. thesis, Lamar University, 1971), 45–46. See also Amilcar Shabazz, "The Desegregation of Lamar State College of Technology: An Analysis of Race and Education in Southeast Texas" (M.A. thesis, Lamar University, 1990), 76–81, on the black branch of Lamar; and Amilcar Shabazz, "The African-American Educational Legacy in Beaumont, Texas: A Preliminary Analysis," *Texas Gulf Coast Historical and Biographical Record* 27 (1991): 73–74, on the education of blacks in Beaumont after 1948.

80. David Levering Lewis, *W. E. B. Du Bois* (New York: Henry Holt, 2000), 313, 497–99, 511, and 512, offers a picture of Marshall as chivied by Du Bois and his anticolonial and socialist agenda draining precious pennies from NAACP funds.

81. "Strutting Across the Stage," *HI*, 12 July 1947; "We Query the NAACP," *HI*, 5 September 1947.

82. Marshall, "Preliminary Statement," 5 September 1947, II-B-218, NAACP Papers.

83. Marshall to Martin, 3 October 1947, II-B-218, NAACP Papers.

84. Marshall to Wesley, 3 October 1947, II-B-218, NAACP Papers.

85. Marshall to Wesley, 16 October 1947, II-B-218, NAACP Papers.

86. Wesley to Marshall, 27 October 1947, II-B-218, NAACP Papers.

87. See Clayborne Carson, "Civil Rights Reform and the Black Freedom Struggle," in *The Civil Rights Movement in America*, ed. Charles W. Eagles (Jackson: University Press of Mississippi, 1986), 19–32.

88. Marshall to Wesley, 6 December 1947, II-B-218, NAACP Papers.

89. See Lewis, *W. E. B. Du Bois*, 335, 345, on Du Bois's 1934 flack with the NAACP, and 534, for the 1948 falling out. Wesley published Du Bois's "My Relations with the NAACP" in the *Houston Informer* in two parts beginning in the 27 October 1948 weekly issue. The quote is from the 30 October 1948 issue. See Howard Jones, *The Red Diary: A Chronological History of Black Americans in Houston and Some Neighboring Harris County Communities* (Austin: Nortex Press, 1991), 160, on Du Bois's lecture in Houston. Greater research is needed on his appearance at TSUN and his relationship with Wesley.

90. Barchus, "Dynamics of Black Demands," 53–54, is the only source for this debate and is a problematic one. Barchus cites as his source an article in the 26 February 1948 issue of the *Houston Informer*. In that year, however, *HI*, which always came out on Tuesdays and Saturdays, was published on 28 February 1948. I studied this issue carefully using microfilmed editions of the paper at both the University of Houston and Houston Metropolitan Research Center. I found no article discussing such a debate. An issue of *HI* did appear on 26 February 1949, but the microfilmed edition at both libraries was incomplete for that date. Barchus's citation error does not suggest that the debate never occurred. It seems likely, however, that it occurred in 1949; Barchus's account must be relied on until a copy of the article is located. An added problem arises from Barchus furnishing only the last name, Shaw, as the co-debater with Wesley. An educated guess would identify Charles Shaw as the person he meant. Shaw is profiled in Andrew Webster Jackson, *A Sure Foundation* (Houston: A. W. Jackson, 1940), 25–27.

Chapter Three

1. Michael L. Gillette, "The NAACP in Texas, 1937–1957" (Ph.D. diss., University of Texas, 1984), 25–27.

2. See Michael L. Gillette, "Heman Marion Sweatt: Civil Rights Plaintiff," in *Black Leaders: Texans for their Times*, ed. Alwyn Barr and Robert A. Calvert (Austin: Texas State Historical Association, 1981), 175–77, and Mark V. Tushnet, *Making Civil Rights Law: Thurgood Marshall and the Supreme Court, 1936–1961* (New York: Oxford University Press, 1994), 126–36.

3. On Sweatt's becoming the "test case," see Gillette, "Heman Marion Sweatt," 158–61, and "Heman Sweatt Twenty-Five Years Later: The Price and the Product of Black Efforts to Integrate White Institutions," 13 August 1973, from the private papers of Albert H. Miller, in possession of the author. Professor Miller shared these papers with me when I was a student in his course "The History and Philosophy of Education" at the University of Houston.

4. "Texas Prexy Asked to Admit Negro Student," *HD*, 9 March 1946.

5. Ibid.

6. Ibid.; see also Gillette, "Heman Marion Sweatt," 167–68.

7. "Sweatt Denied Entry to University of Texas: Sellers, Stevenson Say Negroes Must Have Law Training," *HI*, 23 March 1946.

8. The Texas A&M makeshift was located in Houston at 409½ Milam Street in the McDonald, or U.B.F., Building. The lawyers involved with W. R. Banks in this scheme were Henry Stuart Davis and W. M. C. Dickson, who had practiced law from his office on Milam for almost forty years after completing studies at Boston University in 1907. See *HI*, 7 December 1946; *HP*, 28 November 1946; and Gale L. Barchus, "The Dynamics of Black Demands and White Responses for Negro Higher Education in the State of Texas, 1945–1950" (M.A. thesis, University of Texas, 1970), 15–16. For information on Dickson and Davis, see Carter Wesley, "Archer Welches, Marshall Argues, Sweatt Appeals," *HI*, 21 December 1946.

9. Newspaper article clipping, "Class of '50' Starts Work: Only One Chair Needed as Law School Opens," II-A-147, NAACP Papers.

10. *HD*, 9 March 1946.

11. Tom Allen, "Lone Negro Law Student Resigned to Segregation," *Daily Texan*, 25 September 1947; Sweatt to Marshall, 21 September 1947, and Marshall to Carl Murphy, 30 September 1947, NAACP Papers. Carl Murphy was editor of the *Afro-American* newspaper from 1922 to 1967. He and Marshall were frequent correspondents.

12. See Howard Jones, *The Red Diary: A Chronological History of Black Americans in Houston and Some Neighboring Harris County Communities* (Austin: Nortex Press, 1991), 182–83; Michael L. Gillette, "Blacks Challenge the White University," *Southwestern Historical Quarterly* 86 (October 1982): 344; and William Henry Kellar, *Make Haste Slowly: Moderates, Conservatives, and School Desegregation in Houston* (College Station: Texas A&M University Press, 2000), 89–92, for Doyle's involvement in Houston's major integration cases. Also, Marshall to Murphy, 30 September 1947, NAACP Papers, shows the special counsel's indignant attitude toward Doyle: "He should have added [to his analogy about accepting segregation] that while the white people will be eating the breast, the thigh and the other good portions of the chicken in the house, he is not only eating in the backyard, but his eating is limited to the neck and the feet." Marshall probably discloses here more about his view of segregated legal education than what Doyle actually experienced. In 1970, Gale Barchus, a graduate student at UT, interviewed Doyle for his master's thesis. Doyle reported to him that he felt he got a "good education," perhaps even a better one than the white students on the Forty Acres. As proof for his contention, he cited the individualized attention and the ability to recite and have in-depth discussions on points of law with his professors (among the best at the law school). In his first year at the makeshift law and graduate center at Austin, Fornie Brown and Heaulin Lott were his classmates. They did not join him when the classes were relocated to the Houston campus, whereupon he became the first black man to get a law degree inside the state of Texas. Lott, however, was co-counsel on the Houston city schools desegregation suit. On Doyle's involvement in the cafeteria desegregation case, see Barchus, "Dynamics of Black Demands," 45–47.

13. Painter to Davis, 16 May 1947, and Davis to Painter, 24 March 1947, UTPOR, VF 18/C.

14. Morton is profiled in Effie Kaye Adams, *Tall Black Texans: Men of Courage* (Dubuque, Iowa: Kendall-Hunt, 1972), 91–93.

15. Craft to Wilkins, 27 April 1946; Morton to Smith, 3 December 1946; Marion C. Ladwig to Walter White, 4 April 1947; all in II-B-193, NAACP Papers.

16. Thurgood Marshall wrote to Carter Wesley that "the position taken by the students of the University of Texas to my mind is one of the most important vantages we have yet run across" (Marshall to Wesley, 20 December 1946, II-B-218, NAACP Papers). In Wesley to Marshall, 23 December 1946, ibid., the publisher, wishing to downplay the importance of the UT student supporters as evidence of the need for the NAACP to have exclusive control of the movement, commented that he did not "care what the students of the University of Texas said, did, promised, or may do." He felt the UT students "were fighting for a principle, not for the NAACP or for Sweatt individually." Marshall in a letter to Donald Jones, 29 October 1947, ibid., revealed a more race-conscious position: "I have been told about the white students of the University of Texas forming a chapter of the NAACP, as if that had some mysterious power in it. Brother, the NAACP still depends on the masses of Negroes, and it will get that support in proportion as it serves them, and as it cooperates with the leaders throughout the state." See also "UT Student Joins Youth Council in Protest against Two-Room Law School Here," *HI*, 14 December 1946, which focuses on student leader John W. Stanford. Marion Ladwig fingered Stanford as a member of the communist club or "cell" at UT. He contended that there were three cells in Austin: a weak and unorganized one at Samuel Huston College, which may have involved J. H. Morton Jr., son of the NAACP Austin branch president; a small one at UT composed of "some of the most active, sincere, capable leaders" from various UT student groups, and a strong one in downtown Austin (Ladwig, "Misguided Talents," Speech to the Wesley Foundation, University Methodist Church, 13 April 1947, Austin File, II-B-193, NAACP Papers). For the reaction of Austin branch leaders to the UT campus chapter's political developments, see DeWitty to Walter White, 1 April 1947, Ladwig to Walter White, 4 April 1947, and Ladwig to Gloster Current, 12 April 1947, ibid. Apparently, the controversy between Ladwig, the UT college chapter, and the Austin branch led Gloster Current, director of branches, to draft a new policy governing the relationship between college chapters and local branches, giving the former complete autonomy from the latter; see Memorandum from Current to Walter White et al., 12 April 1947, ibid.

17. Smith to Morton, 12 December 1947, II-B-193, NAACP Papers.

18. Durham to Smith, 9 December 1948, II-B-193, NAACP Papers.

19. In Austin, beside the aforementioned application of Ben Davis, a school teacher named Veola Hicks Young applied to UT for graduate work in counseling psychology; see Painter to R. O'Hara Lanier, 26 November 1948, UTPOR, VF 18/C. Although the lawsuit of black dentists Everett H. Givens and James H. Carlock (who intervened and made it a class-action suit) demanded the establishment of a black dental school over desegregation of the school for whites in Houston, it nevertheless added to the charged atmosphere in Austin; see *Givens* v. *Woodward* 207 S.W. 2nd 234. From Marshall, Texas College education professor J. Nathaniel Nelum applied for work through UT's Extension Division. Painter informed him that UT had arranged to offer classes to "qualified Negroes" on a contract basis with TSUN; see Nelum to Painter, 2 March 1948, VF 18/C, UTPOR, and Painter to Nelum, 10 March 1948, ibid. A white challenge to segregation at

TSUN came in the form of an application from Jack Coffman, "a white citizen of Houston, who represents that he is a social science major from Penn College, Oscaloosa, Iowa, desires to be admitted to the Texas State University for Negroes for the purpose of taking courses in social science"; see Attorney General Price Daniel to TSUN Board of Directors, Opinion No. V-645, 31 July 1948, II-B-205, NAACP Papers. Another white, Harold Schachter, applied to TSUN later that year, and the TSUN Board denied him admission on the grounds of the V-645 opinion. The names Coffman and Schachter suggest that both these whites were Jews. In the latter case, the student may have been a member of the Houston Youth Council of the NAACP; see "NAACP Youth Council Protests Exclusion of Whites from Texas State University," *HI*, 22 January 1949. Black-Jewish relations, especially the development of Afro-Jewish cooperation regarding the problem of segregation and civil rights, are virtually an uninvestigated area in Texas history. The involvement of Coffman and Schachter in the antisegregation struggle is likely evidence for the need and opportunity for research in the area.

20. "What the Regions Are Doing," Southwest, *Crisis* (April 1949): 119.

21. Morton quoted in "37 Negroes May Seek to Enter UT," *Daily Texan*, 27 April 1949; see also *Crisis* (June 1949): 183–85, and the photograph on page 220 in *Crisis* (July 1949).

22. Virginia Forbes, "UT Refuses Admission to 33 Negro Students: College Seniors Seek Graduate School Entry," *Austin Statesman*, 27 April 1949.

23. Kirk quoted in "35 Placard-Carrying Negroes Are Refused Admission to UT," *Daily Texan*, 28 April 1949 (from "Integration Scrapbook," Center for American Studies, University of Texas); Forbes, "UT Refuses."

24. See George Norris Green, *The Establishment in Texas Politics: The Primitive Years, 1938–1957* (Norman: University of Oklahoma Press, 1979), 101–20. Green noted that while Jester would make speeches about "racial purity," he was unlike other governors during what he calls "the primitive years" of Texas politics: "Jester would sit down and talk with black political activists" (120). He would sit, but he never deigned to offer a chair to his black visitors. Neil Gary Sapper ("A Survey of the History of the Black People of Texas, 1930–1954" [Ph.D. diss., Texas Tech University, 1972], 155–56) argued that Jester's meeting with five members of the TCNO "elicited hope among black Texans" (156). On another black delegation that Jester received, the Negro Goodwill Council of Beaumont, see Nancy Dailey, "History of the Beaumont, Texas, Chapter of the National Association for the Advancement of Colored People, 1918–1970" (M.A. thesis, Lamar University, 1971), 46. On the Fifty-first Legislature, see Rupert N. Richardson, Ernest Wallace, and Adrian Anderson, *Texas: The Lone Star State*, 5th ed. (Englewood Cliffs: Prentice Hall, 1981), 422–25.

25. Arthur DeWitty, "State Medical School to Enroll Herman Barnett," *HI*, 27 August 1949. See also Painter to Barnett, 18 August 1949, UTPOR.

26. Craig F. Cullinan to Painter, 11 February 1948, UTPOR; attached to this cover letter is a duplicate of the original contract dated 24 January 1948. Copies of contracts that extend this agreement are in the same file; see also letters of request from TSUN president R. O'Hara Lanier to Painter, 15 September 1948, 30 April 1949, ibid.

27. On the opening of the Houston Negro Hospital, see Howard Jones, *Red*

Diary, 88–89. John O. King, *Joseph Stephen Cullinan: A Study of Leadership in the Texas Petroleum Industry, 1897–1937* (Nashville: Vanderbilt University Press, 1970), 214, observed that the Pennsylvania oilman made the $80,000 endowment as a memorial to his eldest son, John Halm Cullinan, who died in 1920 of a pulmonary ailment. In 1937, Cullinan, the child of Irish immigrants, died and left as the largest charitable bequest in his will $524,000 to the Houston Negro Hospital.

28. Leake to Painter, 26 August 1946, UTPOR. At the time Leake wrote this letter he was fifty years old, had a stellar reputation in the field of pharmacology and in the history of medicine, and was a well-respected and well-connected medical educator and administrator. He accommodated white southerners' peculiar oppression of blacks but probably had misgivings over barring the admission of qualified black students from UTMB. See "Conversations with Chauncey Leake, Sr. Founder and Chairman of the Department of Pharmacology, University of California, San Francisco," University of California, San Francisco Campus History Project, in Chauncey Leake Papers, Moody Medical Library, Blocker History of Medicine Collection, UTMB, Galveston, Texas. Of particular interest is M. Rita Carroll's interviews with Leake conducted between November 1976 and April 1977 in which he recollects his involvement in the desegregation of UTMB (107–9, 113).

29. Cullinan to Painter, 13 July 1949, UTPOR.

30. Green dubbed the political elite that dominated state governance since 1939 the "Establishment" in his *Establishment in Texas Politics*, 3–10. By this moniker, Green attempts to finesse the liberal-conservative ideological dichotomy that V. O. Key Jr. (*Southern Politics* [New York: Vintage, 1949], 255) contended had "real meaning" in the one-party Democratic politics of Texas. His description of a provincial, paternalistic, reactionary, individualistic, anticommunist, pro–Ku Klux Klan, moralistic, anti–New Deal Anglo-Texan ruling class oversimplifies but remains useful as a starting point for analyzing mid-twentieth-century politics in the Lone Star State.

31. Cullinan to Painter, 13 July 1949, and the reply letter from Painter to Cullinan, 15 July 1949, UTPOR.

32. In the 1930s and early 1940s, Barnett could have been inspired by the examples of aviators of other ethnic groups but few from his own. Bessie Coleman, a native Texan who obtained her pilot's license in France in 1921 but died in 1926 at thirty-four years of age, may have captured young Barnett's imagination. See Ruthe Winegarten, *Black Texas Women: 150 Years of Trial and Triumph* (Austin: University of Texas Press, 1994), 155–57. Also, the close proximity of San Antonio, where Barnett went for his high school education, very likely brought him in contact with airmen and the idea of flying since the city was home to a large military air base.

33. Wylma White Barnett, interview by author, 16 July 1995. On Tuskegee airmen see Charles Dryden, *A-Train: Memoirs of a Tuskegee Airman* (Tuscaloosa: University of Alabama Press, 1997); Robert J. Jakeman, *The Divided Skies* (Tuscaloosa: University of Alabama Press, 1992); and William Wolf, "USAAF Pilot Training in World War II," *Historical Aviation Album* 16 (1980).

34. Barnett interview.

35. "Says Time Ripe for Negroes to Enter Texas Med School," *Informer*, 12 March 1949.

36. "NAACP Hails First Break in U. of Texas Jim Crow," Press Release, 26 August 1949, NAACP Papers.

37. DeWitty, "State Medical School."

38. Barnett interview; R. O'Hara Lanier to D. Bailey Calvin, 10 September 1949, UTPOR; R. O'Hara Lanier to C. D. Leake, 21 October 1949, UTPOR. Barnett's widow noted that her husband's erstwhile lab partner apparently took the experience with Barnett to heart such that many decades later, when he died, his survivors had the act recorded in his obituary as one of the most important moments in his life. She also recalled that a white woman of some wealth in Galveston wrote out a blank check in Barnett's name for him to use when he needed something for his education and did not have the money for it. Barnett appreciated the gesture but never used the check ("Conversation with Chauncey Leake," 107).

39. Barnett interview.

40. Barnett to Morton, 19 November 1949, NAACP Papers.

41. Quoted in "Along the N.A.A.C.P. Battlefront: Southwest Region, Barnett Regular Student," *Crisis* (December 1950): 727–28. Carter Wesley's *Informer* broke the story of the VA tuition imbroglio in "TSU Pays for Barnett! Segregation Costs up $6000 for State," *Informer*, 14 October 1950. The VA's nonpayment of Barnett's tuition (and another black veteran's tuition in the 1950–51 school year) resulted from a "legal technicality." The VA paid tuition to a university only for courses listed in its official catalog. TSUN had no medical courses in its catalog because it had no medical school. The VA could not pay UTMB directly the tuition because it did not recognize the enrollment of Barnett nor any other black student. TSUN chairman of the board W. R. Banks had no quarrel with TSUN paying the $3,000 per-year sum per black student attending UTMB on a contract basis. "Why we'll simply have to pay it," Banks stated, "We don't see why we should expect the federal government to take care of a state obligation."

42. "Along the N.A.A.C.P. Battlefront," 727–28.

43. Barnett interview. In "Conversations with Chauncey Leake," 107, Leake remembered the standing ovation for Barnett, whom he referred to as an "excellent man. He did well."

44. "Conversations with Chauncey Leake," 108; Barnett interview; "Will the Brutal Beating of Dr. Barnett Be Whitewashed?" *Informer*, 18 July 1953.

45. "TSU Pays for Barnett!"; "Houstonian to Enter U. of Texas Medical School," *Informer*, 10 July 1954. McMillan did not complete her studies at UT. She went on and finished at Meharry in 1959.

46. Lanier to Painter, 9 January 1950, UTPOR.

47. Painter's assurance that he would maintain segregation was reported in "Negro Student Due to Begin Study at U. of T. in Austin," *HC*, 9 January 1950. Luciel Decker to Theophilus Painter, 9 January 1950, UTPOR.

48. Painter to Decker, 3 February 1950, UTPOR.

49. Brogan to Painter, 24 January 1950, UTPOR.

50. Omega Psi Phi fraternity to Painter, 21 January 1950, UTPOR. There is no evidence that Painter ever replied to the fraternity's letter.

51. Kirk to Dolley, 3 February 1950; Simmons to Smith, 4 February 1950; Dolley to Professor H. A. Calkins et al., 15 February 1950, all in UTPOR. The other faculty members were W. E. Gettys, H. E. Moore, E. S. Redford, C. A. Timm, and O. D. Weeks.

52. "Negro Enters, Quits Texas U.," *NYT*, 7 February 1950. Kirk to Dolley, 7 February 1950, and McCown to Kirk, 9 February 1950, UTPOR.

53. Kirk to McCown, 15 February 1950, UTPOR.

54. French F. Stone to Kirk, 2 March 1950, UTPOR; on Kirk's ultimate graduation from UT, see Alwyn Barr, *Black Texans* (Austin: Jenkins, 1973), 215; for an example of an antisegregation fight Kirk led to victory, see "Austin City Council Opens Library Facilities to Negroes," *HI*, 5 January 1952; and on the imbroglio created after the Associated Press reported that Kirk had approved of the resolution of the Kansas Board of Education that upheld noncompliance with the Supreme Court's finding in *Brown*, see "State School Board Hedges on Stopping Jim Crow in Schools," *HD*, 17 July 1954, and "Texas," *SSN*, September 1954, 11.

55. "Let's Not," *Time*, 27 March 1950.

Chapter Four

1. Ronnie Dugger, *Our Invaded Universities* (New York: Norton, 1973); George Fuermann, *Reluctant Empire* (New York: Doubleday, 1957); and George Norris Green, *The Establishment in Texas Politics: The Primitive Years, 1938–1957* (Norman: University of Oklahoma Press, 1979), discuss Texas in the fifties and sixties and briefly treat themes such as white supremacy and racial politics. However, "the period since 1954 is particularly in need of historical treatment," writes Alwyn Barr, "Black Texans," in *A Guide to the History of Texas*, ed. Light Townsend Cummins and Alvin R. Bailey Jr. (New York: Greenwood Press, 1988), 121; also on this point, see Alwyn Barr, "African Americans in Texas: From Stereotypes to Diverse Roles," in *Texas through Time: Evolving Interpretations*, ed. Walter L. Buenger and Robert A. Calvert (College Station: Texas A&M University Press, 1991), 78; and Buenger and Calvert, "Introduction: The Shelf Life of Truth in Texas," ibid., ix–xxxv, which makes an impassioned plea to historians not only to address issues of race, ethnicity, community, gender, and class (which they argue Texas historians have "ignored because they conflict with the pristine image of the past") but also to overturn the "Anglo Texas myth" that straitjacketed previous histories (xxxii–xxxv). Two recent students of Barr's also have contributed related works; see Martin Kuhlman, "The Civil Rights Movement in Texas: Desegregation of Public Accommodations, 1950–1964" (Ph.D. diss., Texas Tech University, 1994), and Virginia Lee Spurlin, "The Conners of Waco: Black Professionals in Twentieth-Century Texas" (Ph.D. diss., Texas Tech University, 1991).

2. "Let's Not," *Time*, 27 March 1950.

3. Attorney General Price Daniel, open letter to Attorney Generals, undated, PD Papers. Daniel's closing words wishing a happy Christmas season indicates that he sent this letter out in December 1949.

4. Connor to Hare, 10 January 1950, and Connor to Daniel, 10 January 1950, PD Papers, Box 58. On Albert Carmichael see V. O. Key Jr., *Southern Politics* (New York: Vintage, 1949), 332–33. On Folsom, whose first gubernatorial administration went from 1947 to 1951, see Key, *Southern Politics*, 42–44, 57; Robert J. Norrell, *Reaping the Whirlwind: The Civil Rights Movement in Tuskegee* (New York: Knopf,

1985), 64–65, 91; William D. Barnard, *Dixiecrats and Democrats: Alabama Politics, 1942–1950* (Tuscaloosa: University of Alabama Press, 1974); and two biographies, Carl Grafton and Anne Permaloff, *Big Mules and Branchheads: James E. Folsom and Political Power in Alabama* (Athens: University of Georgia Press, 1985), and George E. Sims, *The Little Man's Big Friend: James E. Folsom in Alabama Politics, 1946–1958* (Tuscaloosa: University of Alabama Press, 1985).

5. "Southern States Support Texas in Sweatt Case," 23 March 1950, II-B-147, NAACP Papers; Brief of the States of Arkansas, Florida, Georgia, Kentucky, Louisiana, Mississippi, North Carolina, Oklahoma, South Carolina, Tennessee, and Virginia, Amici Curiae in Support of Respondents at 20–25, No. 44 [*Sweatt v. Painter*] (Oct. Term 1949) (USSCL). Those states not joining Texas included Alabama, Delaware, District of Columbia, Maryland, Missouri, and West Virginia.

6. W. R. Hughes to Daniel, 4 April 1950, PD Papers, Box 58.

7. "High Court Will Rule in Segregation Cases," *NYT*, 5 April 1950, p. 39, c. 6.

8. "Southern States Support Texas in Sweatt Case," 23 March 1950, II-B-147, NAACP Papers.

9. Edna B. Kerin, "Separate Is Not Equal," *Crisis* (May 1950): 292. Kerin also cites the Japanese-American Citizens' League as among those filing briefs in support of the NAACP position in the *Sweatt* and *McLaurin* cases. Amici curiae briefs specifically filed in behalf of Sweatt include (by date) the Motion and Brief of the Committee of Law Teachers Against Segregation in Legal Education in Support of Petition for Certiorari (9 May 1949); Brief for Congress of Industrial Organizations in Support of Petition for Certiorari (13 May 1949); National Citizens' Council on Civil Rights (25 May 1949); and the American Veterans Committee (26 May 1949). On Solicitor General Perlman's brief, see "Separate Not Equal," *Crisis* (April 1950): 244; and on the Texas Council of Negro Organizations hiring a Dallas-based law firm to prepare an amicus curiae brief see "Sweatt Case," *Crisis* (March 1950): 181. Interestingly, no Mexican American organizations, which for four decades had been fighting in the courts for educational equality in Texas, submitted an amicus curiae brief, or if they did, the NAACP or the Supreme Court did not accept it. George I. Sánchez, a leading figure in the Mexican American educational rights struggle as president of the League of United Latin American Citizens (LULAC) and chair of several educational committees, knew of Marshall and the NAACP's legal campaign; but his absence and the absence of LULAC at the fateful hour of the *Sweatt* case remains a mystery. The New York City headquartering of the NAACP legal staff and black leaders in Texas having built, at best, weak political ties with their Mexican American neighbors must offer a partial explanation for the lack of a strong alliance between African and Mexican Americans in regard to the abolition of discrimination in education. The two groups did not experience identical problems in this area, but their source, white Anglo supremacist control, did represent a potentially unifying common denominator. On the Mexican American fight for educational equalization, see Guadalupe San Miguel Jr., *"Let All of Them Take Heed": Mexican Americans and the Campaign for Educational Equality in Texas, 1910–1981* (Austin: University of Texas Press, 1987).

10. Thomas I. Emerson, John P. Frank, Alexander H. Frey, Erwin N. Griswold, Robert Hale, Harold Havighurst, and Edward Levi, "Segregation and the Equal Protection Clause: Brief for the Committee of Law Teachers Against Segregation in

Legal Education," *Minnesota Law Review* 34 (March 1950): 327–28. See also, "Law Teachers Hit Texas Segregation," *NYT*, 20 January 1950. For the reaction of Price Daniel and Dean Ozie Johnson of the TSUN School of Law, see " 'Irrelevant Factors' Are Charged by Dean in Texas University Segregation Complaint," ibid. Daniel suggested the law educators did not know the factual record of the case, and he turned the idea of racial inferiority back on the opponents of segregation, stating that the professors "think less of the ability of Negroes to build and operate their own schools than the people of Texas." Dean Johnson, the head Negro in charge of building the black law school, answered that his school had received the approval of the American Bar Association and that all the fuss about equality stopped there.

11. "18 Back Negro's Suit to Enter U. of Texas," *NYT*, 16 January 1950. See also SCEF Press Release, NAACP Papers, and "Eighteen Back Negro's to Enter U. of Texas," *NYT*, 16 January 1950. NAACP officials mistrusted the SCEF, an attitude that was carried over from its dealings with SCEF's parent organization, the Southern Conference for Human Welfare. See Linda Reed, *Simple Decency and Common Sense: The Southern Conference Movement, 1938–1963* (Bloomington: Indiana University Press, 1991), 114–16. The NAACP's organ, the *Crisis*, did, however, publish the findings of a SCEF poll of 15,000 (3,375 replied) staff and faculty members at 181 accredited colleges and universities in fourteen southern states regarding desegregation. On the poll, see "Southern College Teachers Repudiate Jim-crow Education," *Crisis* (January 1950): 25–26; for the complete report, see "Attitudes of Southern University Professors toward the Elimination of Segregation in Graduate and Professional Schools in the South," *Journal of Negro Education* 19 (Winter 1950); and *Southern Patriot* 10 (November 1949). The key event SCEF organized against higher educational segregation, which took place on 8 April 1950, four days after oral arguments in the *Sweatt* case (and on the day the Supreme Court justices secretly conferred on the matter), was its First Southwide Conference on Discrimination in Higher Education at Atlanta University. The conference was also the last event of its kind that SCEF pulled off. Howard University president James M. Nabrit Jr., who addressed the conference, discussed "the Legal Approach," but he did not mention Marshall or the legal work of the NAACP by name. In fact, according to the proceedings of the conference published in *Discrimination in Higher Education* (New Orleans: Southern Conference Education Fund, n.d.), only one speaker referred to the NAACP; he mentioned a booklet that the NAACP and the American Jewish Congress co-published.

12. Kerin, "Separate Is Not Equal," 292. Although no wave of violence came in the wake of the Court's decision prohibiting the exclusion of blacks from the primary elections of the Democratic Party in the state, subterfuges such as the formation of the Jaybird Democratic Association, as well as the poll tax and other economic pressures, especially in rural East Texas, confirm that blacks had hardly become "part and parcel" of the electoral process. See Darlene Clarke Hine, "The Elusive Ballot: The Black Struggle against the Texas Democratic White Primary, 1932–1945,." *Southwestern Historical Quarterly* 81 (April 1978): 224–29, and Robert Calvert, "The Civil Rights Movement in Texas," in *The Texas Heritage*, ed. Ben Procter and Archie P. McDonald (Arlington Heights, Ill.: Forum Press, 1980), 150–51. For a detailed treatment of the showdown in the Supreme Court on

segregated universities, see Mark Tushnet, *Making Civil Rights Law: Thurgood Marshall and the Supreme Court, 1936–1961* (New York: Oxford University Press, 1994), 137–49.

13. Clark quoted in Dennis J. Hutchinson, "Unanimity and Desegregation: Decisionmaking in the Supreme Court, 1948–1958," *Georgetown Law Journal* 68 (1979): 89–90. For Clark's background, see Jan Palmer, *The Vinson Court Era* (New York: AMS Press, 1990), 12–13; Mary Beeman, "New Deal Justice: Tom Clark and the Warren Court, 1953–1967" (Ph.D. diss., University of Texas at Austin, 1993); A. Timothy Warnock, "Associate Justice Tom C. Clark: Advocate of Judicial Reform" (Ph.D. diss., University of Georgia, 1972); and Michael Philip Fricke, "Justice Tom Clark and Civil Rights," Report, Austin: Public Affairs, 1992.

14. Hutchinson, "Unanimity and Desegregation," 20–21.

15. Painter to Banks, 1 May 1950, UTPOR.

16. *Sweatt* v. *Painter*, 339 U.S. 637. The *Pittsburgh Courier*, 17 June 1950, reprinted the full text of the decision.

17. Joseph J. Rhoads, *Advancing the Cause of Democracy in Education* (Marshall: Texas Commission on Democracy in Education, 1951).

18. Ibid.

19. "TCNO Slates Dallas Meeting," *HI*, 1 July 1950; "Texas Council of Negro Organizations Vows 'To Fight Segregation Until It Disappears' at Dallas July 4th Meeting," *Shreveport Sun*, 15 July 1950; Tushnet, *Making Civil Rights Law*, 147. For a listing of antisegregation suits in Texas up to the early summer of 1950, see Price Daniel to Judge A. O. Newman, 19 June 1950, PD Papers, Box 58.

20. "Klan Launches Member Drive in Texarkana," *Dallas Express*, 8 July 1950. On Allan Shivers's rejection of the NAACP's plea that he get the Texas Rangers more involved in helping the Dallas Police Department with its investigations, see "Governor Refuses to Intervene in Bombing of Negro Houses in Dallas," *HI*, 15 July 1950. For an interesting study of white supremacy in Dallas in the middle of the twentieth century that is framed around the South Dallas bombings of 1950, see Jim Schutze, *The Accommodation: The Politics of Race in an American City* (Secaucus, N.J.: Citadel Press, 1986). Schutze notes that the July bombings were part of a wave of terror that started in February of 1950 and lasted into 1951. The *Sweatt* decision is not identified in his undocumented work as a catalytic agent for the June and July bombings, but the possibility that the decision sparked the bombings is not inconsistent with his picture of a rising level of reaction among working- and middle-class whites to the crumbling of segregation, especially in their residential areas.

21. "Talmadge Defiant; Others Hail Court," *NYT*, 6 June 1950; "Problems for the South Seen," *NYT*, 7 June 1950; Talmadge and Guill quoted in "Anti-Bias Rulings Denounced," *NYT*, 7 June 1950.

22. "Rehearing is Sought in Texas Bias Ruling," *NYT*, 21 June 1950.

23. Carter Wesley, "Ram's Horn," *HI*, 14 October 1950.

24. Robert B. Kelley to Daniel, 18 May 1947, and S. C. Hobbs to Daniel, 19 May 1947, PD Papers, Box 56; George W. Hawkes to Daniel, 16 February 1948, PD Papers, Box 57.

25. A. R. Kavanaugh to Daniel, 6 June 1950; Edith Robeson to Daniel, 7 June 1950; E. M. Brady to Daniel, 10 June 1950; and Herbert B. Harlow to Daniel, 12 June 1950, all in PD Papers, Box 58.

26. Charles A. Howell to Daniel, 14 June 1950, PD Papers, Box 58.

27. Sam Kinch and Stuart Long, *Allan Shivers: The Pied Piper of Texas Politics* (Austin: Shoal Creek, 1973), 81–89; O. Douglas Weeks, *Texas Presidential Politics in 1952* (Austin: Institute of Public Affairs, University of Texas, 1953), ch. 8. See also Clint Pace, "Daniel Advises Rights Battle," *DMN*, 10 May 1950; Jay Walz, "Court Gives U.S. Top Rights to Submerged Coast Oil Land," *NYT*, 6 June 1950; and "Daniel Says Court Erred on Tidelands," *HC*, 21 June 1950.

28. "Negro Situation," undated handwritten letter, UTPOR.

29. Painter to Lanier, 9 May 1950; Robert R. Douglass to Frances Grimes, 11 May 1950; Brogan to Painter, 29 May 1950; and Painter to Lanier, 30 May 1950, all in UTPOR.

30. Lanier to Painter, 20 April 1950; Lanier to Painter, 11 May 1950; McCown to Chase, 4 May 1950; McMath to Dana Young, 8 May 1950; and W. R. Woolrich to McMath, 18 May 1950, all in UTPOR. See also "First Negroes Enter U. of Texas: Students from Austin and Waco Seek Degrees," *HC*, 7 June 1950, and "Texas University Enrolls 2 Negroes," *NYT*, 8 June 1950.

31. "Texas University Enrolls 2 Negroes"; "First Negro Enters University of Texas," *NYT*, 9 June 1950; Jessie Parkhurst Guzman, ed., *The Negro Year Book, 1952: A Review of Events Affecting Negro Life* (New York: Wise & Co., 1952), 240.

32. "First Negro Enters University of Texas." Chase went on to become the first black to earn a degree from UT's School of Architecture. In 1993, he received the UT Ex-Student Association's Distinguished Alumnus Award and won a $4.7 million contract to build a five-story parking facility at the campus. See Robert C. Newberry, "John Chase Integrated UT, Now He's Designing It," *HP*, 18 January 1994, A-17, and Nia Dorian Becnel, "John S. Chase," *Texas Architect* (November/December 1989): 47.

33. Pence to McMath, 10 June 1950, from papers in the possession of John Chase Sr. Also in these papers is a favorable letter Masood Ali Warren, a sculptor in Los Angeles, sent to McMath on 11 June commending him for his "democratic gesture in welcoming student John Chase into the Department of Architecture and into the University of Texas."

34. Anonymous note to McMath, undated, copy in Chase's personal papers; the original is in the archives of the School of Architecture; John Chase, interview by author, 1 March 1996.

35. The quote about Chase's marital status is from "UT Approves 3 Negroes for Immediate Entrance," unidentified clipping, in Chase papers.

36. See Tracy Shuford, "Sipping Tea with John Chase," *Texas Alcalde*, March/April 1996, 20–25; and Chase interview.

37. Painter to Lanier, 7 July 1951, and Lanier to Painter, 17 July 1951, UTPOR.

38. Wright, Warren, and Hartshorn to Lanier, 19 September 1951; Lanier to Painter, 20 September 1951; Painter to Lanier, 24 September 1951; and Hartshorn, E. S. Richards, and Warren to Lanier, 19 September 1951; all in UTPOR.

39. Washington is quoted in "When the Barriers Fall," *Time*, 31 August 1953, 40. Sweatt to Marshall, 28 October 1950, NAACP Papers; Michael L. Gillette, "Heman Marion Sweatt: Civil Rights Plaintiff," in *Black Leaders: Texans for their Times*, ed. Alwyn Barr and Robert A. Calvert (Austin: Texas State Historical Association, 1981), 181–82. See also "Heman Sweatt's Victory," *Life*, October 1950, for pic-

tures of him in class seated next to white students in the back row and walking with
a white student in front of the UT tower.

40. See Gillette, "Heman Marion Sweatt," 157–84. I am also indebted to Albert
H. Miller for sharing "Heman Sweatt Twenty-Five Years Later: The Price and the
Product of Black Efforts to Integrate White Institutions" (proposal and paper
delivered at the 1974 Annual Meeting of the American Educational Research
Association); Helen C. Moore, "The Lonely Struggle of Heman Sweatt" (paper
presented to Dr. Albert Miller, University of Houston, Houston, Texas, 9 May
1973); and other insights and documents in his possession related to Sweatt's life
and times. Moore's paper contains many lengthy quotes from seventeen hours of
tape-recorded interviews between Sweatt and Michael Gillette. She received access
to the tapes from James L. Sweatt, the brother of the late Heman Sweatt.

41. "When the Barriers Fall," 40.

42. Grant Saint Julian, interview by author, 25 February 1996.

43. *The Handbook of Texas*, s.v. "Anderson, Monroe Dunaway," and "Texas Medical Center" (W. J. Battle); Dr. Anthony Wayne Beal, interview by author, 18 August
1995. My gratitude goes out to Dr. Dashiel Geyen and Dr. Janis Beal Geyen for their
helping me obtain this most enlightening and delightful interview.

44. Beal interview.

45. Beal interview; certificates dated 1950–51 and 1952 and signed by Kelsey
and the school's dean (illegible) that were hanging on the wall in Beal's office.

46. Zeb Poindexter Sr., interview by author, 8 March 1996; "2 Negroes to Attend
Texas U. Dental Unit," *NYT*, 11 September 1952; "2 Negroes Will Enter Dental
Unit," *HC*, 10 September 1952.

47. Poindexter interview. Dr. John V. Olson replaced Elliott as dean. See Walter
C. Stout, *The First Hundred Years: A History of Dentistry in Texas* (Dallas: Egan, 1969),
233–34.

48. "Texas Junior Colleges Are Community Colleges," *Texas Outlook*, December
1951, 10.

49. "Howard County Junior College Accepts Negroes," *HI*, 8 September 1951.
Neil Gary Sapper, "A Survey of the History of the Black People of Texas, 1930–
1954" (Ph.D. diss., Texas Tech University, 1972), 451, cites the same source and
dates Texas Southmost's desegregation in 1951. However, Guzman's *Negro Year
Book*, (240), an otherwise accurate and complete source on southern colleges'
early moves toward desegregation, does not include Texas Southmost. This may be
because the school either did not receive or did not return his questionnaires. It is
most unlikely the school would have sent out a press release on its admitting blacks.
Adding to the mystery is the U.S. Commission on Civil Rights' *Equal Protection of the
Laws in Public Higher Education, 1960* (Washington: GPO, 1961), 67, assertion that
Texas Southmost College did not issue a declaration of an open policy until the
1958–59 academic year. This statement is most likely an error, however, since the
junior college definitely had blacks enrolled by 1954. For an interesting take on
the black experience in Brownsville, see Matt Thomas, *Hopping on the Border: The
Life Story of a Bellboy* (San Antonio: Naylor, 1951). Milo Kearney's studies of Brownsville's general and educational history did not prove to be useful on the subject of
black education or the demise of Jim Crow.

50. "Problem Not Important in the Valley," *Brownsville Herald*, 17 May 1954. On

the history of Texas Southmost see Donald W. Whisenhunt, *The Encyclopedia of Texas Colleges and Universities: An Historical Profile* (Austin: Eakin Press, 1986), 153; June Rayfield Welch, *The Colleges of Texas* (Dallas: GLA Press, 1981), 202; and Dallas Morning News, *Texas Almanac, 1954–55* (Dallas: A. H. Belo, 1954–87), 420. On Cameron County see ibid., 527–28. On Cameron County as an "Anglo county," see David Montejano, *Anglos and Mexicanos in the Making of Texas, 1836–1986* (Austin: University of Texas Press, 1987), 244–52. Minutes of the college's board of trustees are housed at the Rio Grande Valley Historical Collection of the main library of the University of Texas at Brownsville. I must thank the collection's archivist, Yolanda Gonzales, for her generous assistance in going through the haystacks.

51. "Court Strikes Down South's Traditional Segregation," *Brownsville Herald*, 18 May 1954, 4. See *Statistical Summary of School Segregation-Desegregation in Southern and Border States* (Nashville: Southern Education Reporting Service, November 1961), 39–40, where it lists Brownsville, Harlingen, LaFeria, and San Benito as desegregated districts. The study cites the year of Texas Southmost's desegregation as 1955.

52. San Miguel, *"Let All of Them Take Heed,"* 134. Mexican American parents followed *Delgado et al.* v. *Bastrop Independent School District et al.* (1948) with six other lawsuits aimed at eradicating the segregation of their children into inferior schools. The last of these until the late 1960s, *Hernández* v. *Driscoll Consolidated Independent School District*, won a favorable decision in 1957 but did not result in the desired change in local school practices. Mexican Americans, like African Americans, ran into a wide variety of evasions and gradualist schemes that enabled local school districts to maintain segregated schools.

53. *Scorpio*, 1956, 1958, and 1968; Sessia Wyche, interview by author, 24 July 1995. Wyche, who became an assistant professor of mathematics in 1988, probably became the second black faculty member at UT-Brownsville and the first in the math department, followed a year later by Deloria Nanze-Davis. Also, Harlingen was the only Cameron County town to have a chapter of the NAACP in the 1940s and early 1950s. It is not clear how much of a role, if any, it may have played in the desegregation of Texas Southmost.

54. Guzman, ed., *Negro Year Book*, 240; "Howard County Junior College Accepts Negroes," *HI*, 8 September 1951; "Texas: Test Suit Filed," *SSN*, October 1954, 13. On the junior college's history, see Whisenhunt, *Encyclopedia*, 64; and on the county, see Dallas Morning News, *Texas Almanac, 1954–55*, 566.

55. *McKinney* v. *Blankenship*, 282 S.W.2d 691; "Integration Settlement Due Soon," *Austin American Statesmen*, 4 October 1955; "More Than 60 Texas Districts Opening with Mixed Classes," *SSN*, September 1955, 9; "Texas Supreme Court Knocks Out School Segregation Law," *SSN*, November 1955, 6.

56. A. Maceo Smith to Hines, 20 October 1950, *Texas* v. *NAACP* Papers; on Amarillo College see Whisenhunt, *Encyclopedia*, 5; and on the college and Potter County, see Dallas Morning News, *Texas Almanac, 1954–55*, 418, 596.

57. Quoted in "College in Texas Long Integrated," *NYT*, 10 October 1954; on the first blacks to enroll, see Guzman, ed., *Negro Year Book*, 242.

58. "More Than 60 Texas Districts Opening," 9; on Dr. Wyatt, see "Texas: Other Developments," *SSN*, April 1955, 15.

59. On Nueces County see Dallas Morning News, *Texas Almanac, 1954–55*, 591–

92; on Garza and LULAC and García and the G.I. Forum and the problem of school segregation see San Miguel, *"Let Them All Take Heed,"* 67–86, 113–34.

60. "Answers NAACP Letter: School Board Cites Program for Improving Negro Schools," *Corpus Christi Caller-Times,* 31 July 1949; "Adult and Vocational Department Trains 868 City Adults," *Foghorn,* 5 March 1948; *Cruiser,* 1947, 1948. The *Foghorn* was the student newspaper and the *Cruiser* was the yearbook of Del Mar, or Corpus Christi Junior College, as it was formerly known as. The 1947 *Cruiser* had a photograph of a classroom of black students listening to a "pronoun lecture." In the 1948 yearbook three photographs of night school English classes showed two large classes of Mexican American students and one small group of black students. In both pictures of black classes there appear to be black instructors.

61. "Regents Vote to Admit Negroes at Lamar [*sic*] Jr. College," *HI,* 26 July 1952. Although Glen E. Kost's article, "50 Years: Del Mar Recalls Its Colorful Past in This Half-Century Birthday Year," in *Voyageur,* Fall 1984, 6–7, contained several inaccuracies such as 1954 as the year of Del Mar's desegregation and that black students enrolled in night classes "at Del Mar" in 1948, it is also informative. Kost apparently interviewed Dean Grady St. Clair and retired insurance executive V. G. Woolsey, two of the three members of the board's site investigations committee who returned with the $300,000 figure. St. Clair stated that *Harper's* and *Life* sent reporters to "do a story on the integration issue but there was no conflict so they did not print it."

62. Dallas Morning News, *Texas Almanac,* 1954–55, 418; *Cruiser,* 1953, 1954; Kost, "50 Years," 6–7; "1954–1971: 17 Years Later," Corpus Christi Schools–Desegregation, 1970–71, Vertical Files, Del Mar College Library, Corpus Christi, Tex. Many thanks are extended to Noe M. Guerra, head of public services at Del Mar College, for assisting me in the college's library and in meeting Glen Kost, director of development and executive director of Del Mar College Foundation, who is working on a history of the college. On how women in Corpus Christi played an instrumental role in Del Mar's desegregation, see Ruthe Winegarten, *Black Texas Women: 150 Years of Trial and Triumph* (Austin: University of Texas Press, 1994), 252–53. She inaccurately states that the college was the first institution in the South to desegregate and did so "even before the law was changed," but she interestingly observes that interracial "lines of understanding dated back to the organization of the local YWCA in 1945 by a diverse group of black and white women working together."

63. U. S. Tate to Branch Officers, 1 August 1952, *Texas* v. *NAACP* Papers.

64. Annual Report, NAACP Southwestern Regional Office, 1 October 1954, NAACP Papers. The junior colleges that desegregated immediately after *Brown* were Frank Phillips College, in Borger City; Odessa Junior College; Pan-American College, in Edinburg; Victoria Junior College; Wharton County Junior College; San Antonio College; and Hardin Junior College/Midwestern University, in Wichita Falls.

65. On Clark's admission and on other white private educational institutions in the South admitting blacks by 1951, see Guzman, ed., *Negro Yearbook,* 241–42. On Austin Presbyterian Theological Seminary, see Whisenhunt, *Encyclopedia,* 11; on the school and on Presbyterian sects in Texas, see Dallas Morning News, *Texas Almanac,* 418, 433. On Trinity University, see Donald E. Everett, *Trinity University: A*

Record of One Hundred Years (San Antonio: Trinity University Press, 1968), 190. On McKinnon see Guzman, ed., *Negro Yearbook*, 242; and the photograph and caption in *HI*, 16 June 1951.

66. "Jarvis and Sam Houston Grads Admitted to SMU," *HI*, 20 January 1951.

67. On the Southern Baptist Convention and the racial policies of its seminaries, see "Seminary Ends Negro Ban," *NYT*, 16 March 1951; and on Southwestern Baptist Seminary see Whisenhunt, *Encyclopedia*, 129.

68. On Maston see John W. Storey, *Texas Baptist Leadership and Social Christianity, 1900–1980* (College Station: Texas A&M University Press, 1986), chs. 4 and 5.

69. Ibid., 119–21, 124–27, 132–35, 139. For a description of SWBTS extension classes in Southeast Texas, interracial Bible conferences, and Southern Baptist paternalism toward black Texans, see Storey, *Texas Baptist Leadership*, and Ronald C. Ellison, *Southern Baptists of Southeast Texas, A Centennial History, 1888–1988* (Beaumont: Golden Triangle Baptist, 1988), 135–38, 160–61. Our interpretive differences to one side, I am grateful to Storey for sharing with me his research and contacts on Texas Baptists.

70. "To Do Right," *Time*, 18 June 1951.

71. Guzman, ed., *Negro Year Book*, 242; first quote is from "First Negro Pupil Has Been Admitted to Wayland College," *HC*, 1 June 1951; second quote is from "Wayland Accepts Four for Summer, Expects Many More for Fall," *HI*, 14 July 1951.

72. "The Private Colleges," *HI*, 16 June 1951.

73. On Brite and TCU see Whisenhunt, *Encyclopedia*, 146; and on Jarvis see Michael R. Heintze, *Private Black Colleges in Texas, 1865–1954* (College Station: Texas A&M University Press, 1985), 39–40.

74. Quoted in "James L. Clairborne to Enter Brites Seminary," *HI*, 13 September 1952.

75. Meyer Weinberg, *A Chance to Learn: A History of Race and Education in the United States* (Cambridge: Cambridge University Press, 1977), 300.

Chapter Five

1. Norman Pearson, "Lashes out at Critics: Attorney Says High Court 'Has Spoken,'" *Springfield New-Sun*, 15 April 1956.

2. Quoted in Earl Warren, *The Memoirs of Earl Warren* (Garden City: Doubleday, 1977), 291. Eisenhower's attorney general, Herbert Brownell, essentially confirms Warren's recollection in his own memoirs, but he defends the chief executive against the chief justice's charge that his statement was meant to influence his decision in *Brown*: "As best as I can reconstruct the scene at the dinner, Ike had expressed his personal sympathy for the mothers of young white children in the South who had been reared in a segregated society and feared the unknown — the arrival of a time when the public schools would be desegregated." Brownell states that Eisenhower was infuriated when Warren went public with the conversation because he felt strongly that his stag dinner conversations were entirely "off the record." This explanation hardly disproves that Eisenhower's remarks were not intended to sway Warren in some way (Herbert Brownell, *Advising Ike: The Memoirs*

of Attorney General Herbert Brownell [Lawrence: University Press of Kansas, 1993], 174). See also, Robert F. Burk, *The Eisenhower Administration and Black Civil Rights* (Knoxville: University of Tennessee Press, 1984), 142.

3. Price Daniel, "Supreme Court on Separate Schools," *Congressional Record*, 18 May 1954, 2.

4. Daniel, "Supreme Court on Separate Schools," 7–8. For a representation of the South in chaos from black domination during the Reconstruction era, see the original fiction work by Thomas Dixon Jr., *The Clansman: An Historical Romance of the Ku Klux Klan* (1905; reprint, Lexington: University Press of Kentucky, 1970); and for a cogently argued secondary source, see Joel Williamson, *A Rage for Order: Black/White Relations in the American South since Emancipation* (New York: Oxford University Press, 1986), 36–43.

5. All quotations are from Carter Wesley, "Ram's Horn," *HI*, 7 August 1954; see also Sam Kinch and Stuart Long, *Allan Shivers: The Pied Piper of Texas Politics* (Austin: Shoal Creek Publishers, 1973), 159–60, where Allan Shivers himself lambastes Ralph Yarborough as the "captive candidate of the CIO and NAACP"; on Yarborough's eleventh-hour statement opposing the "forced commingling of our races in our public schools," see "Texas," *SSN*, September 1954, 11.

6. David R. Goldfield, *Black, White, and Southern: Race Relations and Southern Culture, 1940 to the Present* (Baton Rouge: Louisiana State University Press, 1990), 62.

7. Ulysses S. Tate, NAACP southwestern regional counsel, filed the case of *Battle et al.* v. *Wichita Fall Junior College District et al.* on behalf of Battle and a group of black students in the Wichita Falls Division of the U.S. District Court for the Northern District of Texas on 4 September 1951. In November of that year, the court ruled in favor of the petitioners, but the defendants appealed to the U.S. Court of Appeals at New Orleans, where the lower court's decision was affirmed. On further appeal to the U.S. Supreme Court, the university's writ for certiorari was denied on 24 May 1954, a week after the *Brown* decision. By the fall semester, more than forty black students were enrolled at Midwestern University. Through the period of the lawsuit, the school is referred to as Hardin, or Wichita Falls, Junior College, the name of the lower division unit from which the senior college evolved. See Annual Report, NAACP Southwestern Regional Office, 1 October 1954, 11, NAACP Papers.

8. My study of how *Brown* changed race relations in Texas differs in significant ways and arrives at different conclusions than Michael J. Klarman, in "How *Brown* Changed Race Relations: The Backlash Thesis," *Journal of American History* 81 (June 1994), 81–118. He made no attempt to look at Texas, but since his historiographical essay is derived purely from secondary source material, this oversight is understandable as no study exists on massive resistance and civil rights in the state. The Texas experience, however, shows that Klarman's argument that *Brown* had a minimal direct impact on school desegregation cannot be sustained. He contends that the ruling's only significance lies in an indirect effect it had, namely, the fomenting of a racist white backlash that decimated the ranks of racial moderates in the South and later brutally suppressed civil rights demonstrations. This suppression, he says, produced a national consensus that got civil rights legislation passed in the 1960s, and those new laws are what brought about genuine social change. The Texas story did not work as he suggests. Black activists did draw inspiration from *Brown*. The major repression of civil liberties in the 1950s had as

much to do with race as with McCarthyism or anticommunism, and the Court's decree ultimately did more to build racial moderation than to polarize the state into racial fanatics and radical integrationists.

9. On Edgar's edict, see "Texas," *SSN*, September 1954, 11; on collegiate desegregation in 1954, see "Texas," *SSN*, October 1954, 13, and Annual Report, NAACP Southwestern Regional Office, 1 October 1954, 12, NAACP Papers.

10. Alan Scott, "Twenty-Five Years of Opinion on Integration in Texas," *Southwestern Social Science Quarterly* 48 (September 1967), 159.

11. Chief Lon Bleaton is quoted in "NAACP Seeks Protection for Victim of Terror," *HI*, 24 July 1954, and "Texas: Only One Incident," *SSN*, September 1954; the statements of unidentified officials and individuals in Sulphur Springs are quoted in "Texas: Negro Couple Flees," *SSN*, November 1954. For Hopkins County's and Sulphur Springs' 1950 population figures, see Dallas Morning News, *Texas Almanac, 1954–1955* (Dallas: Belo, 1953), 565.

12. *The Handbook of Texas* (Austin: Texas State Historical Association, 1952), s.v. "Kilgore, Texas."

13. Annual Report, NAACP Southwestern Regional Office, 1 October 1954, 11, NAACP Papers; Annual Report, Edwin C. Washington, 1 October 1955, 3N162, *Texas* v. *NAACP* Papers; see also transcripts of testimony of NAACP branch president I. S. White and parents of various students of the Kilgore Junior College District case in 3N158, folder 6, *Texas* v. *NAACP* Papers. The *Statistical Summary of School Segregation-Desegregation in Southern and Border States* (Nashville: Southern Education Reporting Service, November 1961), 40, listed the junior colleges in Kilgore, Alvin, Blinn, Henderson County, Lee, Panola County, Ranger, San Jacinto, and Texarkana and the black and white junior colleges in Tyler as segregated in 1961.

14. Quoted in "Editor Faces Quiz in Negro's Slaying," *Austin-American Statesman*, 28 January 1956. The editorial "Good Will in East Texas Needed in Tense Times," *Daily Texan*, 9 November 1955, noted that Sutherland appealed for "a more thorough investigation of the outbreaks in East Texas, and the influence — if any — the so-called Citizens' Councils have played on them." It ended with the hope that the council encourages "neither racial violence nor ill-treatment, as they have in Mississippi."

15. Neil R. McMillen, *The Citizens' Council: Organized Resistance to the Second Reconstruction, 1954–1964* (Urbana: University of Illinois Press, 1971), 104–5. For Phillips's quote, see "Texas: Questionnaires Distributed," *SSN*, October 1954, 13.

16. Thomas S. Sutherland, as told to Hart Stilwell, "I'm Proud of Texas," *Coronet* (February 1956): 50–51. Other sources on Masters include Joe F. Taylor, *The AC Story: Journal of a College* (Canyon: Stacked Plains Press, 1979), 4–26, which describes his six years as president of Amarillo College; and McMillen, *Citizens' Council*, 104–5, 310, which provides some information on the council leader. See also Basil Earl Masters, "A History of Early Education in Northeast Texas" (M.A. thesis, University of Texas at Austin, 1929). Although sometimes referred to as "Dr.," Masters never earned a doctoral degree.

17. Sutherland, "I'm Proud of Texas," 50–51.

18. *Battle et al.* v. *Wichita Falls Junior College District et al.*, 101 F. Supplement, 82–83. Midwestern University was a four-year municipal college that only a year before used

to be Hardin Junior College (which became the name of the university's lower-division unit). The blacks who broke down segregation at Midwestern have not been properly acknowledged in previous studies. Other writers have cited Texas Western College, North Texas State College, or the University of Texas as the first public senior colleges that dropped the race bar at the undergraduate level but forget that the Wichita Falls battle led the way. Partly this has been the result of the different names of the school used in the legal record and press accounts. Nonetheless, the *Battle* lawsuit opened all of Midwestern University, not only the junior college division. Sources on the history of the university include Donald W. Whisenhunt, *The Encyclopedia of Texas Colleges and Universities: An Historical Profile* (Austin: Eakin Press, 1986), 87, and Billy Richard Gray, "The Growth and Development of Midwestern University, 1922–1957" (M.A. thesis, University of Texas at Austin, 1959).

The fight to desegregate MU (or Hardin College, as it was known then) had begun in 1948 with the applications of Emzy Downing and James O. Chandler. Their bids sparked plans for the creation of a Negro junior college. See "The Negro College Plans," *Wichita Falls Record News*, 18 April 1948. For the later events, see "Negro Delegation Will Meet with MU Board," *Wichita Falls Daily Times*, 30 July 1951; "Midwestern University Rejects Negro Students," *The Call* (Kansas City, Mo.), 16 August 1951; "MU Rejects Negro Student, Tax Hike Bid Fails," *Wichita Falls Record News*, 17 August 1951; and "Negroes May Ask Court Aid in Bid to Enter MU," *Wichita Falls Daily Times*, 17 August 1951.

I am deeply grateful to Gwendolyn Jackson, a retired educator and an eyewitness to many of the actions involving MU's desegregation (as well as that at North Texas State), for sharing her extensive research on the history of blacks and education in Wichita Falls, especially on the desegregation of MU.

19. *Battle et al.* v. *Wichita Falls Junior College District et al.*, 86. Judge William Atwell, known for his unpredictability, ruled against the desegregation of the Dallas public schools in his decision in *Albert Bell, a Minor, by His Stepfather and Next Friend, Theodore D. Dorsey, et al.* v. *Dr. Edwin L. Rippy, as President of the Board of Trustees of the Dallas Independent School District, Dallas County, Texas, et al.*, U.S.D.Ct., Northern District, Texas, 19 December 1956, 146 F. Supp. 485. The decision with commentary is reprinted in "The Dallas Case: Text of Atwell Decision Challenging High Court," *SSN*, January 1957, 10.

On the lengthy litigation process, see "Negroes May Ask Court Aid in Bid to Enter MU," *Wichita Falls Daily Times*, 17 August 1951; "Wichita Falls Junior College Petition to Enter College Filed by Parents of 6 Students," *The Call*, 4 September 1951; "Plea for Three-Judge Court in University Suit Refused," *Wichita Falls Record News*, 18 September 1951; Frank O. Hall, "Negroes Win College Suit," *Wichita Falls Daily Times*, 17 August 1951; and Jean Walsh, "Ruling Admits Negroes to MU," *Wichita Falls Record News*, 28 November 1951.

20. See "MU Board Decides to Appeal Court Decision," *Wichita Falls Daily Times*, 19 December 1951; "MU Files Appeal on Negro Issue," *Wichita Falls Record News*, 22 December 1951.

21. Quoted in "Five Negroes Enrolling at Hardin Junior College," *Wichita Falls Record News*, 8 June 1954; see also "Negro Students Admitted to Hardin Junior College," *Wichita Falls Daily Times*, 4 June 1954, and "Negro Students Admitted to Hardin Junior College," *Wichita Falls Record News*, 6 June 1954.

22. *Wai-Kun 1955*, the MU annual, n.p. The *Wai-Kun 1956* annual shows that a growing number of blacks were in the ROTC. There is also a picture of a black woman in a pottery class (p. 208) and a group picture with black student nurses Sonja Taylor, Olivia Fobbs, and Opal Sanders. The *Wai-Kun 1957* annual indicates that blacks entered new groups: Clara Hale joined Eta Epsilon (p. 141); a picture of the Baptist Student Union shows blacks seated throughout the group (p. 6); and Patricia Ann Thomas of Cooper, Texas; Gertrude Pope from Calvert, Texas; and Joyce Munden of Munden, Virginia, were Roustabouts (pp. 101–2, 105). The staff of Moffett Library, especially Director Melba Harvill and librarian Billye W. Jeter, at Midwestern State University, greatly assisted me in finding several sources. I am especially grateful that they helped direct me to Gwendolyn Jackson.

23. Annual Report, NAACP Southwestern Regional Office, 1 October 1954, 11–12, NAACP Papers. Michael G. Wade, in "From Reform to Massive Resistance: The Desegregation of the Louisiana State Colleges, 1954–1964" (Paper delivered at the Annual Meeting of the Southern History Association, New Orleans, La., October 1995; copy in author's possession), 1, 3–4, correctly observes that Louisiana lead the way in undergraduate state-supported college desegregation in Lafayette in 1954, but he might have mentioned that the older Wichita Falls case also helped blaze the trail.

24. Seventy percent of the people of the area lived in rural areas, and nearly a third lived in an urban environment with some industrial activity in sulphur, oil, and natural gas production, and a few other manufacturing enterprises.

25. For the presentation given by Smith, who was the only delegate present from Texas at the conference, see Report of Branches, Thirteenth Annual NAACP Conference, June 1922, NAACP Papers, 12–15; on Ennis Martin, see Wharton County Historical Commission, *Wharton County Pictorial History, 1846–1946*, vol. 1 (Austin: Eakin Press, 1993), 208. On other prominent Wharton blacks in the early 1900s, see Annie Lee Williams, *A History of Wharton County, 1846–1961* (Austin: Von Boeckmann–Jones Press, 1964), 115–16. On the idea of blacks in Fort Bend, a neighboring county of Wharton, along with state and national NAACP leaders, deeming it unwise to organize a branch of the association in the area, see Pauline Yelderman, *The Jay Birds of Fort Bend County: A White Man's Union* (Waco: Texian Press, 1979), 201–2.

In the 1930s, Yelderman was active in the Jay Bird Democratic Association of Fort Bend County, a white supremacist organization that controlled the politics of the region from Reconstruction for nearly eight decades. She later wrote a master's thesis on the Jay Birds at the University of Texas and became an associate professor of political science at the University of Houston. Her book, which indicates that she underwent no small ideological reconstruction, drew upon interviews with a number of blacks in the area, including T. L. Pink, who, together with Willie Melton, president of the Fort Bend County Civic Club, organized the desegregation of Wharton County Junior College.

26. Jim Mousner, "In Classrooms There's No Friction: Wharton, Victoria Junior Colleges Face Second Year of Desegregation," *HP*, 7 August 1955, 9, 15; for biographical material on Thomas Lane Pink, see Wharton County Historical Commission, *Wharton County Pictorial History*, 141, 209 (photo of the Black Elks, a team for which Pink played).

27. Annie Lee Williams, *History of Wharton County*, 290.

28. Sources on the desegregation of WCJC include James O. Holley, "Wharton College Sticks to Desegregation Stand," *HP*, 19 September 1954; "Negro Admissions at Junior College Discussed Publicly," *Wharton Spectator*, 24 September 1954; Mousner, "Wharton, Victoria Junior Colleges," 9, 15; and F. J. L. Blasingame interviewed by Joe Tom Davis, 15 June 1993, produced by ITVM Department, Wharton County Junior College. I am grateful to Patsy Norton, director of WCJC's J. M. Hodges Library, for her assistance, especially in my obtaining a copy of Joe Tom Davis's oral history interview with Dr. Blasingame. Also, I am indebted to E. Kelly Rogers, a native of Wharton, for significant research support.

29. Blasingame interview; Holley, "Wharton College Sticks"; "Negro Admissions."

30. Holley, "Wharton College Sticks," *HP*. None of the newspaper articles reports any women speaking on desegregation. Mary Lee Shannon Brown, editor of the *Wharton Spectator* and daughter of its publisher, gave some hints of her opinion on the matter in her editorial column, "Sincerely Mary." On Friday, 17 September, the day before the public meeting, she opined: "We have all 'held up our hands in horror' about the problems that will confront us when the Supreme Court decision is integrated into our school system. If we all just go along as calmly as we can and not get excited and fly off the handle half-cocked, the problems may just sort of solve themselves as each detail of the matter is met and dealt with." Her statement brings to mind the saying "The devil is in the detail." That is to say, white supremacy can be most effectively reestablished not in an overt, ultimately futile fight against the court's edict but in organizing white power to get what it wants in the details of policy formation and implementation. Experienced "school people," free from the "interference" of "us bystanders" and "well meaning, no doubt, but blundering citizens trying to tell them what to do," she felt, could best safeguard the interests of whites. Brown saw the coming of a single school system to educate both white and black children as inevitable and sought "a basis of reconstruction that will do the least harm to our colored and white children and to their parents."

31. Holley, "Wharton College Sticks," *HP*.

32. Mousner, "Wharton, Victoria Junior Colleges." Malone was pictured as a member of the WCJC Art Club in the 1955 *Pioneer Log*, the student annual. Hank Allen is not in the basketball team's group photo, but he is cited as a letterman from Glen Flora in the 1958 *Pioneer Log*, and he also appears in photos of the team in different issues of the *Trailblazer*, the student newspaper.

33. Quoted in Dawson Duncan, "Step Poses Problems for Texas," *DMN*, 18 May 1954.

34. Quoted in ibid. On views regarding the state's compliance with *Brown*, see also Richard Morehead, "No Rush Seen in Texas Shift," *DMN*, 19 May 1954, and Richard Morehead, "Presidents of Negro Schools See Continued Need for Them," *DMN*, 25 June 1954.

35. Henry Y. McCown to Marion G. Ford Jr., 23 July 1954, UTPOR; W. Byron Shipp to Logan Wilson, 25 August 1954, UTPOR. For UT's modified policy on admission for graduate and professional work not offered at the state-supported black universities, see an excerpt of a letter from McCown to Ford reprinted in "Texas," *SSN*, October 1954, p. 13. On the undergraduate desegregation of UT, see also Richard B. McCaslin, "Steadfast in His Intent: John W. Hargis and the

Integration of the University of Texas at Austin," *Southwestern Historical Quarterly* 95 (July 1991): 20–41. McCaslin's article draws upon a 1985 interview he conducted with Hargis (archived at UT's Center for American History), as well as conversations with friends of the chemical engineer who graduated from UT in 1959. Hargis died in 1986, so McCaslin's interview and article are valuable sources on his experience with UT. The article has several errors, including the statement that UT was "the first institution of higher education in the South to admit blacks to its graduate and professional degree programs" (p. 22) and that blacks did not successfully enter Lamar State College of Technology in 1956 and it "remained segregated through the end of the decade" (p. 32). In fact, several private and public southern institutions admitted black students years before UT opened its Galveston and Austin campuses. As discussed below, Lamar admitted blacks and conferred degrees on black students as early as 1958.

36. McCown quoted in *SSN*, October 1954, 13. On Ford's life see Burt Levine, "Defying the Odds: Dr. Marion Ford Dances His Way Past Adversity," *Houston NewsPages*, 4–10 May 1995, 10.

37. Quoted from "Negro Student Seeks Injunction," *Daily Texan*, 24 September 1954; see also "NAACP Will Not Sue for Negro Admission," *Daily Texan*, 6 December 1955, and "Test Suit Filed," *SSN*, October 1954, p. 13. On the Austin NAACP branch and the case, see Rev. M. L. Cooper Jr. to U. Simpson Tate, 17 September 1954, 3N162, *Texas* v. *NAACP* Papers.

38. Quotation from McCaslin, "Steadfast in His Intent," 26–31.

39. Quotation from *Brown II*, 349 U.S. 294 (1955), reprinted in the appendixes of Daniel M. Berman, *It Is So Ordered: The Supreme Court Rules on School Segregation* (New York: Norton, 1966), 148. On the UT regents' action, see "Segregation Decision Due," *Summer Texan*, 8 July 1955; J. C. Goulden, "Committee's Agreement Is 'Substantial'" and "Thought, Not Haste Was Regents' Criteria," *Daily Texan*, 12 July 1955; McCaslin, "Steadfast in His Intent," 29–30, 32–33; and "Maintain Policy," *SSN*, August 1955, 2–3.

40. Rev. Emanuel Eugene Rice, "Request from Citizens Concerning Naming of New Elementary School," 13 July 1977, Leon A. Morgan Papers, Rosenberg Library Archives Department, Galveston, Texas.

41. E. L. Wall, "Suit to Halt Integration at U.T. Filed," *HC*, 15 September 1956; "Court Bars Suit U.T. Integration," *HC*, 18 September 1956; "Fund Halt Denied," *SSN*, October 1956, 14; and on Judge Edgar E. Townes, see photo caption in *DMN*, 14 July 1955.

42. A. Maceo Smith to M. C. Donnell, 20 September 1951, *Texas* v. *NAACP* Papers. On Nixon and the early history of the NAACP El Paso branch, see Darlene Clark Hine, *Black Victory: The Rise and Fall of the White Primary in Texas* (Millwood: KTO Press, 1979), 72–75. On the history of TWC, see Whisenhunt, *Encyclopedia*, 172–73, and Charles H. Martin and Rebecca M. Craver, eds., *Diamond Days: An Oral History of the University of Texas at El Paso* (El Paso: Texas Western Press, 1991). I am grateful to Charles Martin for sharing his paper presented to the annual meeting of the Texas State Historical Association on 4 March 1994, "Integrating Undergraduate Studies in Texas: The Case of Texas Western College" (copy in author's possession).

43. Minutes of the Executive Committee of the NAACP El Paso Branch, 7 March and 5 September 1954, in *Texas* v. *NAACP* Papers; "TWC Admittance Asked by

Negro," *Daily Texan*, 31 March 1955; for Thomason's order in *White* v. *Smith*, United States District Court, Western District, Civ. No. 1616, 25 July 1955, see *Race Relations Law Reporter* (1956), 324–25.

44. "Legal Action," *SSN*, August 1955, 2; "Order," *White* v. *Smith* in *Race Relations Law Reporter* (1956), 324–25.

45. "University Ban Going Down," *SSN*, February 1956, 9.

46. Biographical information on A. Tennyson Miller may be found in Vernon McDaniel, *History of the Teachers State Association of Texas* (Washington: National Education Association, 1977), 133. On page 153, McDaniel erroneously cited Miller's entrance into NTSC as occurring in 1955.

47. A. Tennyson Miller to J. C. Matthews, June 1954 (no day indicated), JCMP. The primary source material on Miller's enrollment and the general desegregation of NTSC is plentiful and easily accessible thanks to the excellent efforts of the library staff of the Willis Library at the University of North Texas, especially Richard Himmel, who was personally very helpful to my research work. Despite the good archival material, including several oral histories, secondary work on UNT and blacks is very limited. Ronald E. Marcello, "The Integration of Intercollegiate Athletics in Texas: North Texas State College as a Test Case, 1956," *Journal of Sport History* 14 (Winter 1987): 286–316, is a worthy piece on one aspect of the college's desegregation. Marcello was responsible for collecting the aforementioned oral interviews. Richard Himmel and Robert S. La Forte, *Down the Corridor of Years: A Centennial History of the University of Texas in Photographs, 1890–1990* (Denton: University of North Texas Press, 1990), 166–67, however, was not very serviceable. James L. Rogers, *The Story of North Texas: From Texas Normal College, 1890, to North Texas State University, 1965* (Denton: North Texas State University Press, 1965), had nothing on the college's desegregation. Rogers taught journalism at NTSU for many years.

48. "1st Negro Student Admitted at NTSC," *Denton Record-Chronicle*, 20 July 1954; "North Texas State Admits First Negro Student in History," *Dallas Times Herald*, 20 July 1954; "North Texas State Admits First Negro," *Dallas Times Herald*, 21 July 1954. On Miller's reputation with NTSC faculty members, see Matthews to Reverend Grady W. Metcalf, 17 September 1963, JCMP. The gradual desegregation plan is outlined in Matthews to Board of Regents, 2 December 1954, JCMP. Marcello, "Integration of Intercollegiate Athletics," 289, cites the development of the plan as evidence that Matthews, far from being a "crude" racist, sought a deliberate, controlled path to desegregation. While a plausible interpretation, Marcello's comments that civil rights activism had not achieved a high level of organizational strength and had placed no "direct pressure" on Matthews and the board to do anything is not accurate. Miller's application represented the high state of consciousness and the high level of activism in the Denton area. Also, the city's proximity to Dallas, which was a major political center of the Texas civil rights movement at that time, cannot be dismissed. NTSC officials recognized and acted in response to the reigning reality in Texas higher educational policy: college administrators were on their own in how they would handle black challenges to segregation at their campuses. The attorney general's office and the state legislature had abdicated to local administrators the duty of upholding the segregationist constitutional articles and statutes.

49. "Order Denying Plaintiff's Motion for a Preliminary Injunction," *Joe L. Atkins, A Minor, by His Father and Next Friend, Willie Atkins, v. James Carl Matthews, President, North Texas State College, et al.*, U.S. District Court, Eastern District, Texas, Civ. No. 1104, 19 September 1955; "Negro Files Suit against NTSC after Denied Entry," *Denton Record-Chronicle*, 11 August 1955; "NTSC Named in Suit Filed to Gain Entry," *DMN*, 11 August 1955; "North Texas Faces Lawsuit: Dallas Negro Seeks Order for Admission," *Campus Chat*, 12 August 1955.

50. "Memorandum Opinion," *Joe L. Atkins, A Minor, by His Father and Next Friend, Willie Atkins, v. James Carl Matthews, President, North Texas State College, et al.*, U.S. District Court, Eastern District, Texas, Civ. No. 1104 (59th Dist.), 8 December 1955; "Segregation at NT Abolished by Court: Atkins Case Ruled on in Sherman," *Denton Record-Chronicle*, 2 December 1955. The *Denton Record-Chronicle* article, a front-page but brief piece with a large headline, had no post-trial comments from Matthews or any of the regents. "Bulletin," *Campus Chat*, 2 December 1955, gave the issue even less consideration. Matthews attempted to minimize public attention given to NTSC's desegregation and emphasized overcrowded conditions as the only reason Atkins had been refused admission in June; see "Integration Becomes Spring Possibility Following Injunction by District Court," *Campus Chat*, 7 December 1955. On Matthews's policy of "deliberately discouraging media coverage," see Marcello, "Integration of Intercollegiate Athletics," 288–90, and the oral history (OH) collections on James Rogers, former director of the NTSC News and Information Service, at the University of North Texas, "Oral Interview with James Rogers," OH 519:3–5; and Matthews, OH 633:22.

51. On the court decision, see "Memorandum Opinion," *Atkins v. Matthews et al.*, 5–6; and "Segregation at NT Abolished by Court." On Sheehy's sympathetic disposition and the attorney general office's opinion that an appeal would be futile, see Matthews to Board of Regents, 2 December 1955, JCMP. Regent B. E. Godfrey, an attorney in Fort Worth, felt that NTSC "would not be in good graces to appeal the Joe Atkins decision" (Godfrey to Matthews, 7 December 1955, JCMP). Other members felt the college should continue the fight against desegregation, irrespective of how futile it might be, but, in the end, the majority of the board went along with Matthews's leadership on the issue.

52. "Negro Woman Set to Enroll at N. Texas," *Denton Record-Chronicle*, 2 February 1956; "Fort Worth Negro Qualifies to Enter as Undergraduate," *Campus Chat*, 3 February 1956; "Fort Worth Negro Woman Set to Enroll Today at NTSC," *Fort Worth Star-Telegram*, 3 February 1956; "Mrs. Sephas Enrolls at North Texas," *Denton Record-Chronicle*, 5 February 1956; quotations from "NTSC Attitude Is Direct Contrast to Alabama Case," *Denton Record-Chronicle*, 7 February 1956. On the Lucy episode, see E. Culpepper Clark, *The Schoolhouse Door: Segregation's Last Stand at the University of Alabama* (New York: Oxford University Press, 1993), esp. chs. 3 and 4.

53. On the uneventful placement of Jackson and Thomas in a campus dormitory, see "Texas: In the Colleges," *SSN*, July 1956, 6, and "NTSC Is Fully Integrated as Enrollment Nears 3,000," *Denton Record-Chronicle*, 7 June 1956. Quotation is from Gwendolyn Jackson, telephone conversation with author, 2 May 1996; Jackson also discussed other aspects of her desegregation experience at NTSC during the interview. On the cross-burning, see "Cross Burned on NT Campus," *Denton Record-Chronicle*, 8 August 1956. On Abner Haynes and Leon King and the influ-

ence of desegregated sports on the process of racial adjustment at NTSC, see Marcello, "Integration of Intercollegiate Athletics," 291–98. For other sources on the desegregation of NTSC, see Matthews to Rev. Grady W. Metcalf, 17 September 1963, JCMP; Sue Connally, "Spotlight on N.T.S.C.: Integration without Tumult," *DMN*, 20 April 1958; and Lewis Harris, "Nowhere for Negroes to Go: NTSU — 'Island of Integration,' " *DMN*, 19 May 1963.

54. "Negro Veteran Seeks Admission: Law Says A&I Created for Whites," *Kingsville Record*, 25 August 1954. I am deeply grateful to Dan Eggleston, who indexed and compiled the relevant articles from the *Kingsville Record*, and to Cecilia Hunter with the South Texas Oral History Collection of the John E. Conner Museum at Texas A&M University at Kingsville for pointing out this resource.

55. "Negro Seeking Admission to A&I Says Threat Letter May Be Prank," *Kingsville Record*, 1 September 1954; "Negro Would Plead Case before Texas A&I College Board," *Kingsville Record*, 8 September 1954; Dallas Morning News, *Texas Almanac, 1954–55*, 575–76.

56. "Negro Would Plead Case before Texas A&I College Board"; see also, in a small bulletin item in *Kingsville Record*, 15 September 1954, a quote from Hayes's letter to the VA, in which he said if the VA could not help him that he would take his case to Congress. On Lynch and the board's decision, see "A&I Directors Reject Negro's Application," *Kingsville Record*, 29 September 1954. On the VA's answer to Hayes, see "V.A. Rejects Negro Veteran's A&I Entry Plea," *Kingsville Record*, 6 October 1954. This article also notes that a Houston publisher (perhaps Carter Wesley of the *Informer*) had notified Hayes to suspend his efforts to establish a paper in Kingsville and to relocate to Houston for a job on its staff. Hayes expressed great disappointment over his inability to launch a newspaper in his hometown and the VA's inability to respond to his exclusion from A&I.

57. H. Boyd Hall quoted in "A&I College Remove Barriers to Negro Enrollment," *Kingsville Record*, 23 May 1956; Ellen King Lambert and Irma Rebecca Summers are identified as the first black students at A&I in an item in *Kingsville Record*, 6 June 1956. On Hall's opening of A&I, see "Report of U. Simpson Tate, Regional Counsel, NAACP Legal Defense & Educational Fund, Inc., Southwest Region," May 1956, NAACP Papers. Hall described himself as an "old fire horse" with his own "method of desegregating schools" in Hall to Roy Wilkins, 25 August 1959, III-C-148, NAACP Papers. See also Nancy M. Nelson interview by Gene Brooks, undated transcript, Black Community Project, South Texas Oral History & Folklore Collection, South Texas Archives, Texas A&M University at Kingsville, Texas. Pan American College at Edinburg in the Rio Grande Valley, desegregated in the fall of 1954, was the second publicly supported senior college in Texas to admit blacks after Midwestern.

58. On the development of Lamar, see Ray Asbury, *The South Park Story* (Fort Worth: Evans Press, 1972), 41–42, and C. Robert Kemble, "Lamar in Perspective," *Texas Gulf Historical and Biographical Record* 19 (November 1983): 24, 32. On the connection between Lamar and white supremacy, see Thomas E. Kroutter, "The Ku Klux Klan in Jefferson County, Texas, 1921–1924" (M.A. thesis, Lamar University, 1972), 160. For the Louis R. Pietzch quotation, see "Kiwanis Hears about College," *Beaumont Journal*, 23 June 1923.

59. See Nancy Dailey, "History of the Beaumont, Texas, Chapter of the National

Association for the Advancement of Colored People, 1918–1970" (M.A. thesis, Lamar University, 1971), 46; Robert B. Lee, "Black Schools Here Date Back More Than 100 Years," *Beaumont Enterprise*, 9 November 1980; and "Efforts Pushed to Continue Operation of Negro College Now Part of Lamar Setup," *Beaumont Enterprise*, 10 August 1951.

60. Kirkland C. Jones, "Writer Enumerates LU's Black History," *University Press*, Lamar University Sixtieth Anniversary Supplement, 16 September 1983, 29. Charlton-Pollard's principal, Harvey Johnson, wrote a confidential letter to John Gray in support of Briscoe's application to Lamar (see Lola Johnson, telephone interview by author, 29 November 1990). See also Edna Briscoe, interview by author, 3 August 1989.

61. "Negro Refused Admittance to Lamar College," *Beaumont Enterprise*, 30 January 1951; Michael L. Gillette, "The NAACP in Texas, 1937–1957," (Ph.D. diss., University of Texas, 1984), 237.

62. Charles E. Sherman to Thurgood Marshall, 26 March 1952, and Mrs. T. C. Brackeen to James R. Briscoe, 1 March 1952, both in *Texas v. NAACP* Papers. See also Briscoe interview.

63. Edward Sprott quoted in Warren Breed, *Beaumont, Texas: College Desegregation without Popular Support*, no. 2, Field Reports on Desegregation in the South (New York: B'nai B'rith, 1957[?]), 5.

64. Juanita Jackson and Jean Wallace, *A Directory of Black Businesses, Churches, Clubs, and Organizations in Beaumont, Texas* (Beaumont Public Library, 1981), n.p., in author's possession; Theodore Johns, interview by author, 16 June 1989; "Seven Negroes Apply for Admission to Lamar Tech," *Beaumont Journal*, 28 July, 1955. See also "Lamar Negro Issue Is Left up to Regents," *Beaumont Journal*, 1 August, 1955. By the time Tate actually filed the suit, only two students, Versie Jackson and James Anthony Cormier, actually became plaintiffs.

65. Letter from L. F. Chester et al. to Lamar Board of Regents, 19 August 1955, FLMP. Magnolia Refinery welders, clerks, office managers, and other workers comprise the majority of the list of names attached to this letter. The first signer L. F. Chester, however, was an attorney for First Federal Savings and Loan.

66. "Lamar Tech Hasn't Room for Negroes, Regents Announce," *Baytown Sun*, 24 August 1955; "Desegregation Foes Suspected: Cross Discovered Blazing on Campus at Lamar Tech," *Beaumont Journal*, 23 August 1955. A week after the cross-burning at Lamar, Klansters fired up a cross at North Texas State College. One wonders whether the two incidents were related in any way. Quotations are from Board of Regents, *Resolution*, Lamar State College of Technology, 23 August 1955. For the enabling legislation that created Lamar as "a co-educational institution of higher learning for the white youth of this State," see "Lamar State College of Technology: Chapter 403: H.B. No. 52," in *General and Special Laws of the State of Texas* (Acts 1949, 51st Legislature), 751–54. The "white youth" clause was not repealed until 1971.

67. Mary Cecil, telephone interview by author, 14 July 1989. See also, Major T. Bell, "Lamar Cecil—The Days That Were His," *Texas Gulf Historical and Biographical Record*, 12 (November 1976): 24. For a study that describes the characteristics of federal judges based on a quantitative study of the judicial behavior of twenty-eight districts in eleven states of the traditional South from May 1954 to October 1962,

see Kenneth N. Vines, "Federal District Judges and Race Relations Cases in the South," *Journal of Politics* 26 (1964): 337–57. The pioneer work along this line is Jack W. Peltason, *Fifty-Eight Lonely Men: Southern Federal Court Judges and School Desegregation* (New York: Harcourt, Brace and World, 1961).

68. From "Defendants' Reply to Complaint," *Jackson* v. *McDonald*, quoted in Dailey, "History of the Beaumont, Texas Chapter of the NAACP," 61. On John Ben Shepperd's "pepper and salt" idea, see "Legal Action," *SSN*, May 1956, 12.

69. Jim Krupnick, "Negro Admission to Lamar is Upheld," *Beaumont Journal*, 30 July 1956; "Lamar Tech Appeal on Negroes Dismissed," *Beaumont Journal*, 21 May 1957; letter from J. B. Morris to Horace Wimberly, FLMP. In "Report of U. Simpson Tate, Regional Counsel," May 1956, NAACP Papers, the lawyer expressed his surprise that at a pretrial hearing before Cecil on 4 May, "some two-hundred-odd high school and college students with teachers and . . . the entire Board of Regents of the college" were present. He reported that "as a public demonstration for the benefit of the audience," the judge had Theodore Johns, Elmo Willard, and himself argue the merits of his case. However, in rebuttal, the state-paid lawyers for the defendants "completely avoided the fact issues and went off on a wild goose chase in the field of irrelevance and pure viciousness."

70. Quotations from Krupnick, "Negro Admission." For a summary of Cecil's ruling, see "Report of U. Simpson Tate, Regional Counsel," June and July 1956, NAACP Papers; on the state's appeal, see "State Will File Lamar Tech Appeal on Negroes," *Beaumont Enterprise*, 26 September 1956. On a legal level, their case and subsequent appeals had no merit at all, did not delay the desegregation process, and had no appreciable influence on their white working-class compatriots, who had no use for symbolic gestures or statements for the record. See "Move to Suspend Integration at Lamar Denied," *Beaumont Enterprise*, 30 October 1956, on Judge Cecil's refusal of a motion to suspend execution of his order. On the Fifth Circuit Court of Appeals' 21 May 1957 affirmance of Cecil's desegregation order, see "Lamar Is a Major Force in Economy," *Beaumont Enterprise*, 11 June 1989.

71. "Blazing Cross Found Burning at Lamar Tech," *Beaumont Enterprise*, 2 August 1956; "At Lamar: Police Eye Students in Cross-Burning," *Beaumont Enterprise*, 2 August 1956; "Burning Crosses Believed Work of Pranksters," *Beaumont Enterprise*, 12 August 1956; Johns interview; Breed, *College Desegregation*, 16 (the "note" in parentheses is Breed's; Breed also used letters in place of names in the interview, but Lightfoot was undoubtedly speaking of Sprott).

72. Statement submitted by Charles A. Howell to F. L. McDonald and the Board of Regents, 18 September 1956; letter from F. L. McDonald to W. R. Smith, 18 September 1956, FLMP. McDonald may have expressed some measure of class bias in calling the members of Howell's group outsiders. Since Howell, Gertrude Carruth, and the two other women on the committee all resided in Beaumont, they must not have had children attending the college or appeared to be not very educated, urbane, or middle class. On the prosegregation referendum questions voted on in the 28 July party primary, see "Texans Approve 3 Issues," *SSN*, August 1956, 14. Early returns reported the vote as 782,693 for continued school segregation and 227,479 against. The other questions, one on approving interposition against "federal encroachment on state authority" and the other on strengthening laws against interracial marriages, also won at the polls by a near four-to-one margin. Citizens'

Council backer Longview oilman Robert Cargill's Texas Referendum Committee sponsored the proposals.

73. "State Will File Lamar Tech Appeal on Negroes," *Beaumont Enterprise*, 26 September 1956; Petition to the President and Board of Regents (undated), Lamar State College of Technology, FLMP.

74. Letter from W. R. Smith to J. B. Morris, 30 March 1956, FLMP.

75. Robert Lasch, "Along the Border," in *With All Deliberate Speed*, ed. Don Shoemaker (New York: Harper and Brothers, 1957), 61–63; Wallace Westfeldt, in "Communities in Strife," in ibid., 53, noted that advanced warning "does have an affect, but it can be taken either way."

76. "State Will File Lamar Tech Appeal"; Sim Myers, "Picketers Escort Negro Students from Lamar," *Beaumont Enterprise*, 2 October 1956; "5,455 Students Register at Lamar for All-Time High," *Beaumont Enterprise*, 2 October 1956. F. L. McDonald, "Progress Report," 6, in FLMP states that twenty-seven blacks had enrolled.

77. Letter from F. L. McDonald to Sheriff Charley Meyers, 11 September 1956, FLMP.

78. For descriptions of the picketers, see Myers, "Picketers Escort Negro Students from Lamar"; Ralph Wooster interview by author, 23 June 1989; and Breed, *College Desegregation*, 5–7.

79. F. L. McDonald, "Newsletter from the Office of the President" to the Board of Regents, 5 October 1956, FLMP.

80. "Lamar Tech Quiet as Pickets Observe Mayor Cokinos' Ban," *Beaumont Enterprise*, 6 October 1956; Patrick K. Graves, "Leaders Recall Time of Civil Rights Act," *Beaumont Enterprise*, 2 July 1989; G. P. Cokinos, Letter to the Editor, *Beaumont Enterprise*, 15 July 1990. On violence against blacks, see "Vandalism at Office of Negro Attorney Probed," *Beaumont Journal*, 9 October 1956, and Johns interview.

81. Quoted from "Statement: Mrs. Mercer Clarifies Picket Role," *Beaumont Journal*, 16 October 1956. See also "Voluntary End of Picketing Comes at Lamar," *Beaumont Enterprise*, 16 October 1956.

82. See "Citizens' Council Plans Increase in Membership," *Beaumont Enterprise*, 18 December 1956. Two weeks after the mass meeting, a Beaumont newspaper ran an article that reported that a "considerable number" of Beaumont police officers had joined the council. See "Other Texas Municipalities Forbid Such Membership: Beaumont Police Officers and Other City Employes [*sic*] Join White Citizens Council," *Beaumont Journal*, 25 October 1956.

83. Breed, *College Desegregation*, 15–16.

84. Quotations are from Sarah Marstellar, "Violence Erupts at Lamar Tech; Picket Is Beaten," *HC*, 4 October 1956. See also "Rangers Patrol at Lamar Tech; Pickets Halt 7," *HC*, 3 October 1956; "Negro Cab Driver and White Picket Held after Rift," *Beaumont Journal*, 4 October 1956; and Cynthia Pommier, "Segregation Is a Thing of the Past," *Beaumont Enterprise*, 17 February 1990.

85. Quotation from Jones, "Writer Enumerates LU's Black History," 30. See also Alvin Randolph, interview by author, 22 June 1989.

86. On Lamar's policy of "gradual integration," see F. L. McDonald, "Ten Year Progress Report [1951–61]," an unpublished report prepared for the Board of Regents of Lamar State College of Technology, 6, FLMP. U.S. Commission on Civil Rights, *Racial*

Isolation in the Public Schools (Washington: GPO, 1967), v, noted how "racial isolation" in public schools persisted even after "formal segregation" had ended.

On the occasion of her son's graduation from Lamar in 1992, Noila Woods told a reporter how in 1958 she had rocks thrown at her and was the victim of other attacks when she tried to attend the college. See "Family Rights a Wrong with Diploma," *Beaumont Enterprise*, 19 December 1992.

87. McDonald to Charles Howell, 26 December 1956, FLMP.

88. McDonald to Charles Butts, 8 October 1956, FLMP.

89. Breed, *College Desegregation*, 11-12.

90. Winona Frank, interview by author, 4 November 1990.

91. The *Cardinal*, Lamar State College of Technology annual, 1958.

92. Smith to Dr. and Mrs. A. H. A. Jones, 21 June 1948, NAACP Papers; quotation in Smith to J. L. Montgomery, 20 September 1948, NAACP Papers; *Bruce et al. v. Stilwell et al.*, 206 F.2d 554; U. S. Tate, Annual Report, NAACP Southwestern Regional Office, 1 October 1954, 11, NAACP Papers.

93. "Memorandum Opinion," *Whitmore et al. v. Stilwell et al.*, U.S.D.Ct., Eastern District, Texas, Civ. No. 366, 2 November 1954, 2.

94. Tate, 1954 Annual Report, 12 (first quotation); "Memorandum Opinion," *Whitmore v. Stilwell*, 3 (second quotation).

95. Tate, 1954 Annual Report, 12; "Memorandum Opinion," *Whitmore v. Stilwell*, 3, 5-7; *Whitmore v. Stilwell*, U.S.Ct. of Appeals, Fifth Circuit, No. 15743, 23 November 1955, 227 F.2d 187 (Judge Hutcheson's opinion is reprinted in *Race Relations Law Reporter*, February 1956, 1[1]:122); "Texas," *SSN*, December 1954, 14; "Legal Action," *SSN*, December 1955, p. 5. See also Gillette, "NAACP in Texas," 217-18.

96. Quoted from "Race Tension Brings Gun Blast in Texarkana, Mob Clash in Kentucky," *HC*, 7 September 1956. For Stilwell's and Williams's alleged role in blocking black students from entering TJC, see "Stilwell Hails Victory in Court over NAACP," *Texarkana Gazette*, 28 September 1956.

97. Quoted from "Texarkana Crowd Turns away Two," *HC*, 10 September 1956. See also "The Lonely Hostages of a South in Strife," *Life*, 24 September 1956, 46-47. On the arrest of black youth, see "Texarkana Disorders," *SSN*, October 1956, 14.

98. The description of the mob blockade at TJC is taken from "Lonely Hostages," 47. The excerpted testimonies of the Grays and Postons to the court of inquiry on 26 September 1956 is from 3N158, *Texas v. NAACP* Papers. On the police officers intimidating Gray and Poston, see "Legal Action," *SSN*, November 1956, p. 8.

99. A transcript of the federal hearing on the Motion to Intervene in Civil Action No. 366, *Whitmore v. Stilwell*, on 27 September 1956, is found in 3N158, *Texas v. NAACP* Papers. The state subpoenaed as witnesses A. Maceo Smith, Edwin C. Washington, and Tate, all from the NAACP southwestern regional office in Dallas. Tate unfortunately chose to go to Tyler on 26 September to try to persuade Sheehy to quash the subpoena against Smith because the officer who served him failed to tender to him his per diem and mileage fees as required by law. Saving Smith from having to testify under oath proved fruitless, unnecessary, and a diversion from where Tate really needed to have been, which was in Texarkana at the court of inquiry proceedings.

100. Transcript, *Texas v. NAACP* Papers; "Public Protests and Violence Accom-

pany Desegregation Moves," *SSN*, May 1964, 12. The NAACP held no malice against Gray, probably sympathizing with the state of duress the ordeal put her through. She went on to attend NTSC in the spring term of 1957 and received $100 from NAACP lawyer W. J. Durham to help her purchase her books. Dallas NAACP leader Juanita Craft helped her find housing, and, through the intercession of Thurgood Marshall, a 33rd degree Freemason, the Southern Jurisdiction's United Supreme Council of the Ancient and Accepted Scottish Rite of Freemasonry contributed $200 toward her education. She expressed her gratitude to Marshall and all her supporters, stating, "I hope when I finish my college work to make a contribution to the cause that you [Marshall], Mr. Durham, and others have given so much for" (from Gray to Marshall, 25 February 1957, Group III: Box J5, "Misc-Jessalyn Gray" file, NAACP Papers). See also Gray to Marshall, 4 June 1957; Alice B. Stovall to Richard L. Plaut, 13 November 1956; Plaut to Gray, 14 November 1956; Gray to Marshall, 7 November 1956; Marshall to Hon. Louis W. Roy Sr., 30 October 1956; Marshall to Gray, 30 October 1956; and Roy to Marshall, 25 October 1956, all NAACP Papers. On Gray's motivation for trying to enter TJC, see Gillette, "NAACP in Texas," 308.

101. Numan V. Bartley, *The Rise of Massive Resistance: Race and Politics in the South During the 1950's* (Baton Rouge: Louisiana State University Press, 1969), 213.

102. Following a violent episode at a high school in Mansfield, Texas, Shepperd and Shivers revealed how closely their views of the NAACP as "paid agitators" stirring up blacks against southern custom, especially segregated schools, coincided with the position of the Citizens' Council. The federal courts in *Jackson* v. *Rawdon* opened the town's white high school beginning in the fall of 1956 despite the district's request for an additional year to prepare the local community to accept the decree. When the school year commenced, mob rule took over and Shivers intervened by sending in the Texas Rangers to keep the black students out and by requesting the trustees to transfer out of the district students whose presence might be likely to provoke violence. When Marshall criticized the governor's action, Shivers and the attorney general countered with accusations that impugned the motives of the NAACP in its fight with Jim Crow. See "School Boards and Schoolmen," *SSN*, October 1956, 14.

103. Memorandum from Sterling Fulmore Jr. to John Ben Shepperd, 11 September 1956, *Texas* v. *NAACP* Papers; Helen Thomas, "Individuals from Texas Reported as Having Been Affiliated with Communist-Front Organizations—As Compiled from Official Government Reports," 1956, in *Texas* v. *NAACP* Papers. The CRC, created in 1946 and led by William Patterson, a member of the Communist Party, U.S.A., since 1927, played a crucial national role in cultivating what historian Harold Cruse called the "new Negro leftwing integrationist elite" (Harold Cruse, *The Crisis of the Negro Intellectual: From Its Origins to the Present* (New York: Morrow, 1967), 177). On the CRC, see Mari Jo Buhle, Paul Buhle, and Dan Georgakas, eds., *Encyclopedia of the American Left* (Urbana: University of Illinois Press, 1992), s.v. "Civil Rights Congress," and Gerald Horne, *Communist Front? The Civil Rights Congress, 1946–1956* (Rutherford: Fairleigh-Dickinson University Press, 1987). On Dies and the Communist Control Act, see Buhle, Buhle, and Georgakas, eds., *Encyclopedia of the American Left*, s.v. "House Committee on Un-American Activities, a.k.a. House Un-American Activities Committee (HUAC)."

104. The state's attack on the NAACP in Tyler is well documented in the archival collection *Texas* v. *NAACP* Papers. Michael L. Gillette's dissertation, which created this collection, is also very useful; see Gillette, "NAACP in Texas," ch. 8. Mark Tushnet, *Making Civil Rights Law: Thurgood Marshall and the Supreme Court, 1936–1961* (New York: Oxford University Press, 1994), 272–73, briefly discusses the case, tying it to the broader assault on civil rights lawyers, the NAACP, and the LDF. See also George Fuermann, *Reluctant Empire* (New York: Doubleday, 1957), 214–16; American Jewish Congress, *Assault Upon Freedom of Association: A Study of the Southern Attack on the National Association for the Advancement Colored People* (New York: American Jewish Congress, 1957), 26; and Bartley, *Massive Resistance*, 216.

105. "NAACP Charges Undue Pressure by Attorney General in Investigation," News Release, 21 September 1956, NAACP Papers. The attorney general clearly intended the presence of the troopers to intimidate and cow investigated persons into cooperating with the probe. Gillette, in "NAACP in Texas," writes that "the use of police personnel by the attorney general's office appears to have been somewhat routine, and there were no instances of heavy-handedness or overt attempts to instill fear" (289–90). He cites as his source for this evaluation the testimony of various state attorneys at the Tyler trial and subsequent interviews he held with some of the investigating attorneys some twenty-five years later. From the standpoint of the black and white communities where these investigations took place, however, he states that the troopers had an "upsetting" effect on branch officials and "cast a pall of suspicion over the NAACP." When armed troopers and state attorneys took away a local NAACP official from his or her place of work, he says, "onlookers concluded that the Association was in trouble with the law." This is an understatement: the NAACP *was* in trouble with the law, "the law" meaning the repressive authority of the state. Moreover, treating members like dangerous criminals and subversive radicals by using armed and uniformed state police and the legendary Texas Rangers as part of an inquiry into the actions — and not as part of arrests — of a corporation cannot be regarded as routine. In the popular mind the Texas Rangers were associated with Mexican "bandits" and Bonnie and Clyde–and John Dillinger–type outlaws.

106. Fletcher to Shepperd, "Investigation of Beaumont, Port Arthur, and Orange, Texas, Branches of the N.A.A.C.P.," 19–20 September 1956, 5–6, *Texas* v. *NAACP* Papers. The attorney general's staff first went into action at NAACP offices in Dallas and Houston on 13 September. For a newspaper account of the raids, see Bob Gray, "Shepperd Probing NAACP in Texas," *HP*, 14 September 1956. The NAACP's public relations office responded to the attacks with news releases that emphasized that the association was "a law-abiding organization"; see "Texans Probe NAACP Records: Membership Lists Withheld," 20 September 1956, NAACP Papers. In 1962, Fletcher went to work as a staff attorney for the Texas Municipal League, from which he retired in 1987 at the age of seventy-five. Described as "the epitome of the Southern Gentleman," he died 1 September 1998 in a "Care Center" in Granbury, Texas. See "In Memory of Riley Eugene Fletcher," *Texas Town & City*, October 1998, 10.

107. Fletcher to Shepperd, "Investigation," 10.

108. Ibid., 11. On Gray's testimony, see "Hearing at Tyler in Recess," *Texarkana Daily News*, 13 October 1956 (quotation), and "Jessalyn Gray Testifies at NAACP

Trial," *Texarkana Gazette*, 13 October 1956. On the contract between Sweatt and the NAACP, see Gillette, "NAACP in Texas," 306 (see also 336 n. 24, where Gillette states that Judge Dunagan provided him with a copy of the contract in 1981); "Barratry, Sweatt Stipend Figure in NAACP Hearing," *Texas Observer*, 3 October 1956; and "Produce Contract," *SSN*, October 1956.

109. "Texas Solon Plans to Submit Two Anti-NAACP Bills to Legislature," News Release, 28 December 1956, NAACP Papers (quotation); on Shivers's segregation committee, see "Legislative Action," *SSN*, October 1956; and on Rep. Jerry Sadler, see "Legislative Action," *SSN*, January 1957, and George Norris Green, *The Establishment in Texas Politics: The Primitive Years, 1938–1957* (Norman: University of Oklahoma Press, 1979), 90, 94, 96. Sadler was at the end of his first term representing Anderson County, which was approximately one-third black in 1956 (see Dallas Morning News, *Texas Almanac, 1958–1959*, 363–64, 523).

110. See Fuermann, *Reluctant Empire*, 216–17, for the exchange between Huffman and Thurmond (which Fuermann spells "Thurman"). On the Marshall summit, see "Legislative Action," *SSN*, January 1957, 10.

111. Gonzalez is pictured and quoted in "Legislative Action," *SSN*, June 1957, 2; see also Stuart Long, "White Supremacy and the 'Filibusteros,'" *The Reporter*, 27 June 1957, 15, and Fuermann, *Reluctant Empire*, 218.

112. For the quotation by A. A. Lucas and material on the Methodist women's group and state CIO council, see "What They Say," *SSN*, January 1957, 13; on the involvement of the Texas Council of Churches, see Long, "White Supremacy," 15.

113. Wilkins to Hall, 29 January 1958, NAACP Papers.

114. "The Law of Disorder," *New York Post*, 24 September 1956.

Chapter Six

1. Richard Morehead's coverage of Texas education was a regular feature in *SSN*. A refreshingly honest and rare instance of reporting on the desegregation experience from the perspective of the black student appeared in *SSN*, December 1957, 5. Anthony Henry, a black student at UT, observed how he and other African Americans had to endure restrictions in regard to where they could live and eat and that in some cases they would receive a Negro "welcome treatment," which they found as embarrassing as discrimination.

2. The A&M system consisted of four colleges and several other units (e.g., Forest Service and Rodent Control Service). The colleges included A&M, Prairie View A&M, Arlington State, and Tarleton State. The State Teachers College System consisted of East Texas at Commerce, Sam Houston at Huntsville, Southwest Texas at San Marcos, Stephen F. Austin at Nacogdoches, Sul Ross at Alpine, and West Texas at Canyon. See Texas Legislative Council, *Higher Education Survey*, Part I (Austin: Texas Legislative Council, 1951), 1–15, 37–48.

3. On the passage of the Civil Rights Act of 1957, see Robert Frederick Burk, *The Eisenhower Administration and Black Civil Rights* (Knoxville: University of Tennessee Press, 1984), 204–26, and Manning Marable, *Race, Reform, and Rebellion: The Second Reconstruction in Black America, 1945–1990* (Jackson: University of Mississippi, 1991), 41–42.

4. U.S. Commission on Civil Rights, *Equal Protection of the Laws in Public Higher Education, 1960* (Washington: Government Printing Office, 1961), 64–68; "In the Colleges," *SSN*, July 1955, 12; Donald W. Whisenhunt, *The Encyclopedia of Texas Colleges and Universities: An Historical Profile* (Austin: Eakin Press, 1986), 114–15.

5. Quoted in Homer Babbidge Jr. and Robert Rosenzweig, *The Federal Interest in Higher Education* (New York: McGraw-Hill, 1962), 175. Babbidge and Rosenzweig observe that the CRC split 3–3 on the question of withholding funds from private colleges, where the government has an even greater responsibility to uphold equal protection of the laws. Citizens denied their rights at a public college have recourse to the courts; those at private ones do not (183 n. 20). For the extent of desegregation in the South, see ibid., 169; and in the Deep South, see U.S. Commission on Civil Rights, *Equal Protection*, 69.

6. The State Advisory Committees (on Civil Rights), *The 50 States Report* (Washington: GPO, 1961), 600. In addition to Mack H. Hannah and William B. Bates, the Texas committee was comprised of Thomas B. Ramey of Tyler (chair), Jerome K. Crossman of Dallas (secretary), Robert Lee Bobbitt of San Antonio, J. S. Birdwell of Wichita Falls, Maurice R. Bullock of Fort Stockton, and Dr. M. E. Sadler of Fort Worth.

7. Quotation from Price Daniel to TSUN Board of Directors, 31 July 1948, II-B-205, NAACP Papers; see also "NAACP Youth Council Protests Exclusion of Whites from Texas State University," *HI*, 22 January 1949; "Resolution on Segregation in Education Adopted by the Youth Council, Houston Branch NAACP," 9 January 1949, PD Papers, Box 56; and Youth Council, Houston Branch NAACP to Daniel, 12 January 1949, PD Papers, Box 56. Note that Schachtel's name sometimes appears spelled as "Schachter."

8. "Applies for Admission to T.S.U.: Churches Should Have Taken Integration Lead, Cleric Says," *HC*, 8 September 1955.

9. On postponement of the board's vote, see "Showdown Due on Segregation in Negro School," *HC*, 8 September 1955, and "In the Colleges," *SSN*, October 1955, 14. On the opening of TSU, see "T.S.U. Desegregates Students and Faculty," *HC*, 11 January 1956; "TSU Board Votes 6–1 to Desegregate," *Houston Press*, 11 January 1956; and "In the Colleges," *SSN*, February 1956, p. 9; for quotations from Lee and the executive committee's recommendation, see "Integration for TSU Is Voted by Directors," *HP*, 11 January 1956. On whites who applied to TSU's 1956 fall term, see "T.S.U. Admits White Students," *HC*, 9 September 1956; and on Samuel M. Nabrit's "special counseling," see "No White Students Register at T.S.U.," *HC*, 18 September 1956.

10. "Segregationist White Pastor Enters T.S.U.," *HC*, 15 September 1958 (includes photograph); "White Pastor Finds Another on T.S.U. Rolls," *HC*, 18 September 1958 (includes photographs); "Preacher Vows Court Fight as Entry at TSU Challenged," *HP*, 18 September 1958. In the first of these articles TSU registrar E. O. Bell said that several white students had enrolled the previous year, but he refused to state how many and whether any remained or to identify them to the press.

11. First quote is in "Rev Munroe Enrolls at TSU; Tactics Hit by Bd Member," *HI*, 20 September 1958; second quote is in " 'Object Lesson,' " *SSN*, October 1958, 14; and the third, "Pastor Hopes His Example Will Help," *HC*, 18 September 1958.

Reacting to McMahill's enrollment, one of the board members of St. Thomas said: "This is a shock. I don't approve of it myself." My thanks to Berniece McBeth of Houston, past chair of the Archives and History Committee of the United Methodist Center (Texas Annual Conference), for helping me find out more about McMahill.

Carter Wesley said nothing about McMahill, but in his editorial "Anarchy Vs The Rule of Law," in *HI*, 20 September 1958, he wrote in his acidic manner that "when a Baptist preacher places placards in the hands of school children, attacking and defying the Constitution of the United States, as interpreted by the Supreme Court; and leads those children in a public demonstration against the law, we are witnessing one of the worst forms of [a] plea for anarchy."

After the initial news sensation, the issue of whites at TSU faded from public view. In small numbers they entered the school, especially its schools of pharmacy and law. As for faculty desegregation, TSU hired whites with unparalleled vigor. Five years after the board voted to drop the color line, whites made up fifteen percent of TSU's faculty; see "In the Colleges," *SSN*, April 1962, 17. No traditionally white university hired anywhere near that proportion of blacks as faculty then, nor has since.

12. For quotations, see "In the Colleges," *SSN*, March 1960, 10. Dooley's order opening WTSC went into effect on 31 May 1960. Blacks had attempted to enter state teachers colleges at least as early as 1956; see "In the Colleges," *SSN*, October 1956, 14. The last quotation is from Judge Joe Dooley's summary judgment in *Shipp* v. *White*, U.S.D.Ct., Northern District, Texas, Amarillo Division, 1 March 1960, Civil Action 2789, in *Race Relations Law Reporter* 5 (Fall 1960): 740.

Dooley's decision occurred just as a wave of sit-in protests swept the South after 1 February 1960. Sit-ins began to take place in Texas within a month of the lunch counter action at Greensboro, North Carolina. See the articles "Negroes Militant," "Protest at UT," "T.S.U. Students' 'Sit-Ins,'" and "Cox Vs. the 'Sit-Ins,'" in the *Texas Observer*, 11 March 1960, 1, 3, 7; and "S.A. Stores Integrate; White Held in Cutting," 18 March 1960, ibid., 1–2; "Sit-Ins Resumed," 25 March 1960, ibid., 3; and "Bold Sit-Ins in Marshall," 1 April 1960, ibid., 1–2.

13. Minutes of the Texas State College for Women Executive Committee meeting, 1 April 1952, Executive Committee Folder, Integration File. My thanks to special collections librarian Kim Grover-Haskin at TWU for her help. On TWU's history, see Whisenhunt, *Encyclopedia*, 156–57.

14. Excerpt from the Minutes of the Texas State College for Women Executive Committee meeting, 9 May 1955, in the "President's Report to the Board of Regents on a Recommendation of the Executive Committee on the Subject of Segregation," in the Minutes of the Board of Regents meeting, 14 January 1956, Integration File.

15. Minutes of the Texas State College for Women Executive Committee meeting, 14 May 1957, Executive Committee Folder, Integration File. See also Minutes of the Board of Regents meeting, 3 June 1957, for "Copy of Statement on Integration Policy," Integration File. On John A. Guinn, see Frank C. Rigler, "Texas College for Women Has a New President," *Texas Outlook*, August 1951, 17.

16. Minutes of the Board of Regents meeting, 24 August 1961, Integration File; on Dowells, see "Women's University Becomes Biracial," *SSN*, October 1961, 15,

and Yvonne Barlow, "Integration at Texas Women's University," *Daily Lasso*, 19 November 1991.

See also other installments on integration by Barlow: on Liz Williams-Johnson, see "Alumna Recalls Experiences at TWU," *Daily Lasso*, 25 April 1991; on, see Gloria Brannon Washington, "Black Alumna Met Opposition in School, Job Market," *Daily Lasso*, 20 November 1991; on Bettye Person Gabern, see "Alumna Found Racist Attitudes at Early TWU," *Daily Lasso*, 21 November 1991; and on Ruby Griffin House, see "Alumna Still Vocal on Educational Issues," *Daily Lasso*, 4 December 1991 (quotation).

See also the results of Richard Morehead's *Dallas Morning News* survey of desegregation in Texas colleges in Integration File. A. A. Smith, assistant to the president, completed Morehead's questionnaire, reporting that an estimated five blacks had attended TWU before the fall semester of 1962. Out of a total enrollment of 2,970 for the fall 1962 semester, he estimated there were 7 black students. He added a note asking that TWU "not be singled out for special notice of any kind."

17. "Negroes Enter Tech; Exact Number Unknown," *SSN*, August 1961, 9; for Merrell T. Reed as having little help from the local NAACP branch in opening Tech and other places (e.g., Woolworths, Walgreen, the bus station, and area motels), see Reed to Clarence A. Laws, 16 December 1961, NAACP Papers, and Julius Amin, "Black Lubbock: 1955 to the Present," *West Texas Historical Association Year Book* 65 (1989): 26.

On J. Evetts Haley, especially his role in firing several Tech professors, one for writing scholarly articles on college desegregation, see George Norris Green, *The Establishment in Texas Politics: The Primitive Years, 1938–1957* (Norman: University of Oklahoma Press, 1979), 174–75, 185 (note the year of the expiration of Haley's regency is erroneously printed as 1958; see 237 n. 23 and 282 n. 32); and on his role as a leading book censor via Texans for America and the Federation for Constitutional Government, see Numan V. Bartley, *The Rise of Massive Resistance: Race and Politics in the South during the 1950's* (Baton Rouge: Louisiana State University Press, 1969), 235. For Tech's legal origins and history, see Texas Laws 1923, 39th Legislature, ch. 20; Tex. Civ. Stat. (Vernon, 1950 Supp.) art. 2629; *Bulletin of Texas Tech University: Undergraduate Catalog, 1995–96*, June 1995, 72:2, 12; and Whisenhunt, *Encyclopedia*, 154.

Before Haley died, one of his friends said of the Canyon native that he was "possessed with the world view of a Texas plainsman," adding: "Writing and acting out his beliefs — sometimes extreme, intemperate, and just plain wrong; at other times poetic, sympathetic, and full of insight — J. Evetts Haley has never held back." Of course, the people whose lives he ruined, the many black students whom he denied the right of equal educational opportunity and the professors he fired for espousing ideas that differed from his probably prayed many a night that he might have "held back" and questioned his warped worldview. See Don Carleton, "From the Director," *The Center for American History* (Winter 1995), 2. Carleton quotes himself from his book *Who Shot the Bear? J. Evetts Haley and the Eugene C. Barker Texas History Center* (Austin: Wind River Press, 1984).

Tech's dismissal of Dr. Herbert Greenberg, the blind psychologist who lost his job in the summer of 1957, as an egregious violation of the principle of academic freedom helped put the college on the American Association of University Professors censured list. He was the lead author of an article that ran him afoul of the regents. See Greenberg, "Some Effects of Segregated Education on Various of the Personality of those Members of Disadvantaged Groups Experiencing This Form of Education," *Desegregation Abstracts* (1955): 1784; Greenberg, Arthur L. Chase, and Thomas M. Gannon Jr., "Attitudes of White and Negro Students in a West Texas Town toward School Integration," *Journal of Applied Psychology* (February 1957): 27–31; and "In the Colleges," *SSN*, August 1957, 8, where it is reported that the board, led by Haley, fired Greenberg because he stated publicly that he favored racial integration.

See also Wayne H. Holtzman, "Attitudes of College Men Toward Non-Segregation in Texas Schools," *Public Opinion Quarterly* (Fall 1956): 559–69. The author of this article was an associate professor of psychology and associate director of the Hogg Foundation for Mental Hygiene at UT. He too ran into trouble with UT regents, school officials, and unreasoning segregationists. See Murray Illson, "New Stimuli Asked for Military Duty," *NYT*, 9 September 1953; this article summarizes the proceedings of the sixty-first annual convention of the American Psychological Association, where Holtzman and a colleague, Ira Iscoe, presented the findings of their study of 539 male undergraduates at UT. Other infringements on academic freedom at Texas colleges occurred at Sam Houston State and West Texas State; see C. Vann Woodward, "The Unreported Crisis in the Southern Colleges," *Harper's Magazine*, October 1962, 82–83. It is plausible—judging from the names of the faculty members who came under fire for their research and their views on segregation (i.e., Greenberg, Holtzman, etc.)—that anti-Semitism may also have been a factor in the negative sanctions and hostile attention they received.

18. On the early experience of blacks at Texas Tech, see Robert L. Foster and Alwyn Barr, "Black Lubbock," *West Texas Historical Association Year Book* 54 (1978): 28–29, and Jane Gilmore Rushing and Kline A. Nall, *Evolution of a University: Texas Tech's First Fifty Years* (Austin: Eakin Press, 1975), 122–24.

On Tech's first black football player, see Richard Pennington, *Breaking the Ice: The Racial Integration of Southwest Conference Football* (Jefferson, N.C.: McFarland, 1987), 138–41; and on the school's decision to desegregate intercollegiate athletics, see "College Announces Desegregation of Varsity Sports," *SSN*, January 1964, 7.

19. "Summer News Capsules," *Daily Cougar* 29 (4 September 1962): 4.

20. Quoted in Meredith Trube, "Integrated over Summer: Ten Negro Students at UH—No Incidents," *Houston Press*, probably September 1962, in clippings file at UH Special Collections, M. D. Anderson Library, Houston, Texas; see also Trube, "U. of Houston Integration Going Well," *Houston Press*, 12 March 1963. For two small articles indicative of how editors gave desegregation as little attention as possible, see "Negroes Are in U.H. Classrooms," *HC*, 2 October 1962, and "UH Enrolls 10 Negro Students," *HP*, 3 October 1962.

21. Oral interview with Senator A. R. Schwartz (18 April 1985), part of the University of Houston Research Project, "The Campaign to Win Full State Support for the University of Houston, 1958–1963," University of Houston Archives, M. D. Anderson Library. On Schwartz, see Ruthe Winegarten and Cathy Schechter, *Deep in the Heart: The Lives and Legends of Texas Jews* (Austin: Eakin Press, 1990), 180–81.

Several months before they actually admitted blacks, the *HP* reported that UH and Rice University, also in Houston, had both made plans to move "towards desegregation in the near future" and that in both cases the move was "not entirely voluntarily." See "Rice and UH Expected to Desegregate," *HP*, 29 March 1962, and "Newspaper Reports Two Universities to Admit Negroes," *SSN*, April 1962, 17.

22. Quoted in Reinhard Friederich, "Integration Plans Indefinite as Yet," *Daily Cougar*, 1 November 1962, 3. Jerry Wizig, *Eat 'Em up, Cougars* (Huntsville, Ala.: Strode Publishers, 1977), is a popular read on UH athletic desegregation, especially on the activities of star players like Warren McVea, Paul Gipson, Riley Odoms, Jerry Drones, Elmo Wright, Robert Newhouse, Charlie Hall, Wilson Whitley, and others (see 165–66, 206–12, 264–71, 287–90, and 327–30).

See also the furor created by a *Cougar* editorial calling on President Hoffman and coach Bill Yeoman to cancel a scheduled football match between UH and the University of Mississippi following the outbreak of violence surrounding James Meredith's attempt to enter the school in the fall of 1962. A bevy of letters poured into the *Cougar*. The letters, published in the 4–16 October issues, mostly supported the stance that Ole Miss officials had taken against integration and in fully supported continuing with the game. The contest was held and the Rebels romped over the Cougars, 40–7.

23. See Jim McClellan, "Old Times There Are Not Forgotten," October 1968, in the Rebel Theme Controversy Collection, UTAL.

24. The first quote is from Marion T. Harrington to Members of the [A&M System] Board of Directors, 11 July 1962, in the Black at UTA File, UTAL; for second quote, see a verbatim copy of "Integration Success at Arlington State," *Shorthorn*, 21 September 1962, in ibid.; on the student center's Confederate decor, see "UTA Still Feels Effects of Negroes' Demand," *Fort Worth Press*, 18 January 1970; and on black numbers at ASC in 1961 and 1962, see "70 Per Cent More Negroes Attend Desegregated Colleges This Year," *SSN*, November 1963, 13. "In the Colleges," *SSN*, September 1963, 7, noted that four blacks tried out and became "the first members of their race on the squad" of ASC's football team in the fall semester of 1963.

For Phala Mae Price's recollection of UTA, see Caron Wong, "Unretiring Faith: Building Attendant Observed Social Change," *Shorthorn*, 31 August 1988. Her three children all went to UTA but none finished from the college. Her sons graduated from Dallas Baptist College and Wiley College, respectively, and her daughter graduated with second highest honors from the University of North Texas with a master's degree.

25. Quote is from Tom Milligan, "Negroes Enter A&M without Incidents," *DMN*, 5 June 1963. See also "A&M Enrolls Six Negroes," *Waco News-Tribune*, 16 July 1963; "3 Negroes Enroll at Texas A&M," *SSN*, July 1963, 3; and "6 Negroes Sign for Texas A&M Summer Session," *SSN*, August 1963, 17. For an estimate of the number of blacks at A&M in 1962 and 1963, see "70 Per Cent More Negroes Attend Desegregated Colleges this Year," *SSN*, November 1963, 13. For the names and backgrounds of the six students, see "6 Negroes, 2 of Them Women, Register at A&M," *HP*, 16 July 1963.

Chris Vaughn, in "First Black Enrollee Recalls College Days," *Battalion*, 6 February 1990, identifies Courtney James of Galveston as the first black A&M admitted and the third to graduate when he obtained his bachelor of science degree in 1967 and then a doctorate degree of veterinary medicine from the school in 1970. The article, although essentially a typical piece of Aggie boosterism, has some interesting reflections on desegregation from a black, firsthand point of view.

On A&M's gender "desegregation," see the summaries of the two cases *Heaton* v. *Bristol*, 317 S.W.2d 86, in *Race Relations Law Reporter* 4 (Texas Civil Appeal 1958): 302–5; *cert. denied*, 359 U.S. 999, in *Race Relations Law Reporter* 4 (1959): 12; and *Allred* v. *Heaton*, in *Race Relations Law Reporter* 4 (1960): 730–39; and "Texas A&M Could Lose Male Status," *SSN*, June 1960, 13.

26. See "Connally Cites 'Tremendous' Biracial Gains," *SSN*, August 1963, 17. On the Kennedy and Johnson administrations and civil rights, see Mark Stern, *Calculating Visions: Kennedy, Johnson, and Civil Rights* (New Brunswick, N.J.: Rutgers University Press, 1992). For a glimpse of the Kennedy-Johnson attack on racial barriers through a contemporaneous news source, see Robert E. Baskin, "Kennedy Asks Business Group to Help Break Down Barriers," *DMN*, 5 June 1963, and "Race Bars on Federal Work Hit," in ibid.

27. The quotes are from Abelardo Baeza, "*La Escuela Escondida*: History of the Morgan School in Alpine, Texas, 1929–1954," *Journal of Big Bend Studies* (January 1994): 96. See also Abelardo Baeza, "*La Escuela del Barrio*: A History of the Alpine Centennial School, 1939–1969," *Journal of Big Bend Studies* (January 1992): 134. Sul Ross's enabling act did not carry a "white students only" restriction. Certain general articles refer to the establishment of state normal schools for the training of "white teachers." See Texas Laws 1917, 35th Legislature, ch. 197, and Texas Civil Statutes (Vernon, 1950 Supp.) Art. 2645–2647g. I am grateful to my friend Mark Saka, assistant professor of history at Sul Ross State University, for bringing the Baeza articles to my attention and for other generous assistance he extended.

28. Baeza, "*La Escuela Escondida*," 94–95; Baeza, "*La Escuela del Barrio*," 137.

29. See *Dana Jean Smith, etc., et al.* v. *John Garland Flowers, etc., et al.* U.S.D.Ct., Western District, Texas, Austin Division, 4 February 1963, Civil Action No. 1305, in *Race Relations Law Reporter* 8 (1963): 117–20. Flowers is quoted in SWT's 1964 annual, no page numbers.

30. See "70 Per Cent More Negroes," 13; for Prairie View's announced desegregation and on the first whites to attend the college, see Edward Martin, dean of arts and sciences at Prairie View A&M University, conversation with author, 10 March 1994, Prairie View, Texas. Governor Connally pressured Tarleton to announce its desegregation policy; see Jim Mousner, "Connally: Our Colleges Open to All," *HP*, 10 June 1964, and "Last State College Drops Racial Bars," *DMN*, 10 June 1964. Prairie View's president, E. B. Evans, faced great student unrest on the campus in 1963 over what they felt was his accommodation of segregation and his extreme authoritarianism. On the student group Students for Equality, Liberty and Freedom (SELF), which challenged Evans, see "Texas," *SSN*, February 1964, 7.

31. State Teachers College Board of Regents, Minutes, Meeting of 12 August 1955, quoted in James Olson, ed., "Years of Anxiety and Change" (13 June 1991), part of an unpublished manuscript on the history of Sam Houston State University by a deceased member of the university faculty. I am thankful to Dr. Olson, chair of Sam Houston State University's Department of History for generously sharing with me a draft copy of this manuscript, which he is revising for publication.

32. Rupert Koeninger quote is from "Racial Integration Problems Discussed," *Houston Press*, 17 May 1955. For a local article that appeared around the time of the

meeting charging that the fund organizer, James Dombrowski, was a former member of the Communist Party, see "Integration Unit Aides under Fire of Senate Group," *HC*, 17 May 1955. On Koeninger's firing and its aftermath, see Woodward, "Unreported Crisis," 82; "Segregation Issue Involved in Board's Firing of Professor," *SSN*, June 1962, 2; "Dr. Koeninger Now Finds Academic Rights at TSU," *SSN*, January 1963; and Olson "Years of Anxiety and Change."

Another incident negatively spotlighting Sam Houston State's segregation occurred in March 1963, when the eleventh annual meeting of the Texas Association of German Students switched the site of its meeting scheduled for 26–27 April from the Huntsville college to the University of Houston. President Lowman had made it clear that black student delegates to the meeting would not be allowed on the campus. "We're not integrated," he said, "and the T.S.U. students will not be permitted to attend." See "Meet Shifts Here So Negroes May Attend," *HC*, 1 March 1963.

33. On the legal struggle with regents, see "2 Negroes Sue to Go to SHSTC," *HP*, 6 June 1964; "All State Teachers' Colleges," *SSN*, July 1964; and State Teachers Colleges Board of Regents, Minutes, Meeting of 5–6 June 1964, quoted in Olson, "Years of Anxiety and Change." On Connally's announcement, see Mousner, "Connally," *HP*, and Mousner, "Last State College," *DMN*. For an earlier example of Connally's attitude toward desegregation, see "Connally for Continued Voluntary Racial Effort," *HP*, 23 June 1963.

34. Quotes are from Gayle McNutt, "First Negro Is Enrolled at SHSTC," *HP*, 10 June 1964; and Olson, "Years of Anxiety and Change."

35. On Nacogdoches as a "hard core" area, see William Harlow Jr., "Ralph W. Steen, 1905–1980, and the Business of Twentieth Century Texas Education" (Ph.D. dissertation, Texas A&M University, 1990), 139; on the East Texas area, see the classic discussion by D. W. Meinig, *Imperial Texas: An Interpretive Essay in Cultural Geography* (Austin: University of Texas Press, 1969), 92–95.

UT's legendary historian (who shortly before he died in a car crash joined the faculty of UH) reprinted his famous "Ignore the Log" address in Walter P. Webb, *A Corner of the Old South* (Austin: Steck Company, 1959), 9. See also "Webb Says 'Ignore the Log,'" *Texas Observer*, 20 June 1959, 2.

36. The quote is from an interview with Edwin Gaston Jr. in Harlow, "Ralph W. Steen," 117. See also "All State Teachers' Colleges."

37. James Gee's quote and other material on East Texas is from Debra Wilkison, "Eyewitness to Social Change: The Desegregation of East Texas State College," (M.A. thesis, East Texas State University, 1990), 16, and "State Colleges Have Nonracial Policies," *SSN*, August 1964, 3. I am very grateful to Wilkison for sending me a copy of her thesis and for other ideas she shared at a conference where we presented papers together. Her interview with Waters, especially, gleaned an important side of the story of East Texas's transformation.

38. Wilkison, "Eyewitness to Social Change," 16–18. Gee retired in 1965 after eighteen years as president. His departure sped up East Texas State's adjustment to racial change. Enrollment at the college did not decline because of desegregation. In 1964 4,502 students were enrolled, and a year later that number increased to 5,330. See "At Least 51 Tax-Supported Colleges Are Desegregated," *SSN*, November 1964, 2.

Coda

1. James Baldwin, *The Fire Next Time* (New York: Vintage, 1993), 100. See also his "Faulkner and Desegregation," in *James Baldwin Collected Essays* (New York: Library of America, 1998), 209. Connecting Baldwin to the concerns of this book feels natural and is enriched by a reading of the work of Lawrie Balfour, *The Evidence of Things Not Said: James Baldwin and the Promise of American Democracy* (Ithaca: Cornell University Press, 2001).

2. Vernon McDaniel, *History of the Teachers State Association of Texas* (Washington: National Education Association, 1977), 77–87.

3. Alice Walker, *In Search of Our Mothers' Garden*, quoted in Constance Curry, *Silver Rights* (New York: Harcourt Brace, 1995), vii; see also Curry's coming to think about the goal of freedom as the oppressed did (xxvii). See also Orlando Patterson, *The Ordeal of Integration: Progress and Resentment in America's "Racial" Debate* (Washington: Civitas, 1997).

4. Ayi Kwei Armah, *Two Thousand Seasons* (Popenguine, Senegal: Per Ankh, 2000), 315.

5. Armah, *Two Thousand Seasons*, 317. My thanks to Rhoda Johnson for the gift of a copy of Armah's book from her trip to Senegal and to Asa G. Hilliard III–Nana Baffour Amankwatia II for recommending she get me this particular one. Without it I might not have finished my book in its right season.

Bibliography

Manuscript Sources

Arlington, Texas
    University of Texas at Arlington Libraries Special Collections Division
        Black at UTA File
        Rebel Theme Controversy Collection
Austin, Texas
    Center for American History, University of Texas
        Attorney General's Papers, *State of Texas* v. *NAACP*
        Juanita Craft Papers
        Jaybird Association Papers
        John A. Lomax Papers
        NAACP Papers
        Negro Scrapbook
        Homer P. Rainey Papers
        University of Texas President's Office Records
    Texas State Archives
        Governor Beauford R. Jester Papers
        Governor W. Lee O'Daniel Papers
        Governor Allan Shivers Papers
        Governor Coke R. Stevenson Papers
Beaumont, Texas
    Mary and John Gray Library, Lamar University
        Board of Regents Minutes and Resolutions
        President Floren Lee McDonald Papers
Denton, Texas
    Texas Woman's University Library, Special Collections
        Executive Committee Minutes
        Integration File
    Willis Library, University of North Texas
        James Carl Matthews Papers

Galveston, Texas
   Moody Medical Library, Blocker History of Medicine Collection, University of
      Texas Medical Branch
      Chauncey Leake Papers
   Rosenberg Library Archives Department
      Leon A. Morgan Papers
Houston, Texas
   M. D. Anderson Library, University of Houston
      Governor James V. Allred Papers
      University Clippings Scrapbooks
   Metropolitan Research Center, Houston Public Library
      Houston Press Clippings
      Texas Commission on Inter-racial Cooperation Papers
Kingsville, Texas
   James C. Jernigan Library, Texas A&M University
      South Texas Archives Black Community Project
Liberty, Texas
   Sam Houston Regional Library and Research Center
      Governor Price Daniel Papers
Washington, D.C.
   Library of Congress, Manuscript Division
      Thurgood Marshall Papers
      NAACP Papers

Government Documents

Blackstock, Graham. *Staff Monograph on Higher Education for Negroes in Texas.* Austin:
   Texas Legislative Council, 1950.
———. *Staff Monograph on Higher Education for Negroes in Texas.* Austin: Texas Legisla-
   tive Council, 1951.
Coffman, L. D., et al. *Texas Educational Survey Report: Higher Education.* Austin: Texas
   Educational Survey Commission, 1925.
Du Bois, W. E. B. *What the Negro Has Done for the United States and Texas.* Washington:
   GPO, 1936.
General and Special Laws of the State of Texas. Austin: Secretary of State, 1927.
Hall, Charles E. *Progress of the Negro in Texas.* Washington: GPO, 1936.
Klein, Arthur. *Survey of Negro Colleges and Universities,* Bulletin no. 7. Washington:
   GPO, 1929.
Montgomery, T. S. *The Senior Colleges for Negroes in Texas: A Study Made at the Direction
   of the Bi-Racial Conference on Education for Negroes in Texas.* N.p., April 1944.
State Advisory Committees (on Civil Rights). *The 50 States Report.* Washington:
   GPO, 1961.
Texas Department of Education. *Laws, Rules and Regulations Governing State Teachers
   Certificates.* Bulletin no. 289, 1923; and no. 299, 1932.
Texas Legislative Council. *Higher Education Survey.* Part 1. Austin: Texas Legislative
   Council, 1951.

———. *Public Higher Education in Texas*. Austin: 51st Legislature, 1950.

U.S. Bureau of the Census. *Special Reports: Occupations at the Twelfth Census*. Washington: GPO, 1904.

———. *Thirteenth Census of the U.S. Taken in the Year 1910*. Occupation Statistics. Washington: GPO, 1914.

———. *Fourteenth Census of the U.S. Taken in the Year 1920*. Occupations. Washington: GPO, 1923.

———. *Fifteenth Census of the U.S.: 1930*. Occupations, by States. Washington: GPO, 1933.

———. *Sixteenth Census of the U.S.: 1940*. The Labor Force, Part 5. Washington: GPO, 1943.

———. *Negro Population in the United States, 1790–1915*. 1918. Reprint, New York: Arno Press, 1968.

U.S. Commission on Civil Rights. *Equal Protection of the Laws in Public Higher Education, 1960*. Washington: GPO, 1961.

———. *Freedom to be Free: A Century of Emancipation, 1863–1963*. Washington: GPO, 1963.

———. *Fulfilling the Letter and the Spirit of the Law: Desegregation of the Nation's Public Schools*. Report. Washington: GPO, 1976.

———. *Racial Isolation in the Public Schools*. Washington: GPO, 1967.

Works, George A. *Texas Educational Survey Report*. Austin: Texas Educational Survey Commission, 1925.

Wright, Harry K. *"Texas." Civil Rights U.S.A., Public Schools in Southern States*. Washington: GPO, 1964.

Oral Histories and Interviews

Barnett, Wylma White. Interview by author. 16 July 1995.

Beal, Anthony Wayne. Interview by author. 18 August 1995.

Blasingame, F. J. L. Interview by Joe Tom Davis. 15 June 1993. ITVM Department, J. M. Hodges Library, Wharton County Junior College.

Briscoe, Edna. Interview by author. 3 August 1989.

Cecil, Mary. Telephone interview by author. 14 July 1989.

Chase, John. Interview by author. 1 March 1996.

Frank, Winona. Interview by author. 4 November 1990.

Johns, Theodore. Interview by author. 16 June 1989.

Johnson, Lola. Telephone interview by author. 29 November 1990.

Jones, Kirkland. Interview by author. 17 July 1990.

Poindexter, Zeb. Interview by author. 8 March 1996.

Randolph, Alvin. Interview by author. 22 June 1989.

Saint Julian, Grant. Interview by author. 25 February 1996.

Saint Julian, Leah. Interview by author. 3 August 1990.

Wooster, Ralph A. Interview by author. 23 June 1989.

Wyche, Sessia. Telephone interview by author. 24 July 1994.

Judicial Decisions

Brown v. *Board of Education of Topeka,* 347 U.S. 483 (1954).

Jackson v. *McDonald,* 93 S.W. (2d).

Gaines v. *Canada,* 305 U.S. 337 (1938).

"Memorandum Opinion." *Joe L. Atkins, A Minor, by his father and next friend, Willie Atkins,* v. *James Carl Matthews, President, North Texas State College, et al.,* U.S. District Court, Eastern District, Texas, Civ. No. 1104 (59th Dist.), 8 December 1955, pp. 5–6.

"Order Denying Plaintiff's Motion for a Preliminary Injunction," *Joe L. Atkins, A Minor, by his father and next friend, Willie Atkins,* v. *James Carl Matthews, President, North Texas State College, et al.,* U.S. District Court, Eastern District, Texas, Civ. No. 1104, 19 September 1955.

Plessy v. *Ferguson,* 163 U.S. 537 (1896).

Shipp v. *White,* Northern District, Texas, Amarillo Division, 1 March 1960, Civil Action No. 2789.

Smith v. *Flowers,* U.S.D.Ct., Western District, Texas, Austin Division, 4 February 1963, Civil Action No. 1305.

Sweatt v. *Painter,* 339 U.S. 629 (1950).

White v. *Smith,* United States District Court, Western District (Civ. No. 1616), 25 July 1955.

Newspapers and Periodicals

Baytown Sun
Beaumont Enterprise
Beaumont Journal
The Crisis
Daily Texan
Dallas Dispatch
Dallas Express
Dallas Morning News
Dallas Times Herald
Denton Record-Chronicle
Houston Chronicle
Houston Defender
Houston Informer
Houston NewsPages
Houston Post
Houston Press
Kingsville Record
Kountze News
New South
New York Times
Race Relations Law Reporter
San Antonio Register

Southern School News, 1954–65
Springfield New-Sun
Texas Observer
Texas Outlook
Wharton Spectator
Wichita Falls Daily Times
Wichita Falls Record News

College Yearbooks and Other University Publications

Bulletin of Texas Tech University: Undergraduate Catalog, 1995–96, June 1995.
Campus Chat. North Texas State College student newspaper.
The Cardinal. Lamar State College of Technology annual.
Daily Cougar. University of Houston student newspaper.
Daily Lasso. Texas Woman's University student newspaper.
Daily Texan. University of Texas student newspaper.
Houstonian. University of Houston annual.
Pioneer Log. Wharton County Junior College annual.
Redbird (*University Press*). Lamar University student newspaper.
The Trailblazer. Wharton County Junior College student newspaper.
Wai-Kun. Midwestern University annual.

Books

Adams, Effie Kay. *Tall Black Texans: Men of Courage*. Dubuque, Iowa: Kendall-Hunt, 1972.
Adler, Mortimer J. *Great Ideas from the Great Books*. New York: Washington Square Press, 1963.
Ames, Jessie Daniel. *Democratic Processes at Work in the South*. Atlanta: Commission on Inter-racial Cooperation, 1941.
Anderson, James D. *The Education of Blacks in the South, 1860–1935*. Chapel Hill: University of North Carolina Press, 1988.
Armah, Ayi Kwei. *Two Thousand Seasons*. Popenguine, Senegal: Per Ankh, 2000.
Asbury, Ray. *The South Park Story*. Fort Worth: Evans Press, 1972.
Babbidge, Homer, Jr., and Robert Rosenzweig. *The Federal Interest in Higher Education*. New York: McGraw-Hill, 1962.
Baldwin, James. *The Fire Next Time*. New York: Vintage, 1993.
———. *James Baldwin Collected Essays*. New York: Library of America, 1998.
Balfour, Lawrie. *The Evidence of Things Not Said: James Baldwin and the Promise of American Democracy*. Ithaca: Cornell University Press, 2001.
Barr, Alwyn. *Black Texans*. Austin: Jenkins, 1973.
Barr, Alwyn, and Robert A. Calvert, eds. *Black Leaders: Texans for Their Times*. Austin: Texas State Historical Association, 1981.
Bartley, Numan V. *The Rise of Massive Resistance: Race and Politics in the South during the 1950's*. Baton Rouge: Louisiana State University Press, 1969.

Berman, Daniel M. *It Is So Ordered: The Supreme Court Rules on School Segregation*. New York: Norton, 1966.

Berry, Mary Frances, and John Blassingame. *Long Memory: The Black Experience in America*. New York: Oxford University Press, 1982.

Blauner, Robert. *Racial Oppression in America*. New York: Harper & Row, 1972.

Brauer, Carl M. *John F. Kennedy and the Second Reconstruction*. New York: Columbia University Press, 1977.

Breed, Warren. *Beaumont, Texas: College Desegregation without Popular Support*. No. 2, Field Reports on Desegregation in the South. New York: B'nai B'rith, 1957[?]

Brewer, J. Mason. *Heralding Dawn*. Dallas: Mathis Publishing, 1936.

——. *Negro Legislators of Texas*. Austin: Pemberton, 1970.

Brooks, Charles. *The Official History and Manual of the Grand United Order of the Odd Fellows in America*. Freeport: Libraries Press, 1971.

Buhle, Mari Jo, Paul Buhle, and Dan Georgakas, eds. *Encyclopedia of the American Left*. Urbana: University of Illinois Press, 1992.

Bullock, Henry Allen. *A History of Negro Education in the South from 1619 to the Present*. Cambridge: Harvard University Press, 1967.

Brownell, Herbert. *Advising Ike: The Memoirs of Attorney General Herbert Brownell*. With John P. Burke. Lawrence: University Press of Kansas, 1993.

Burk, Robert F. *The Eisenhower Administration and Black Civil Rights*. Knoxville: University of Tennessee Press, 1984.

Carleton, Don. *Who Shot the Bear? J. Evetts Haley and the Eugene C. Barker Texas History Center*. Austin: Wind River Press, 1984.

Carnegie Commission on Higher Education. *From Isolation to Mainstream: Problems of the Colleges Founded for Negroes*. New York: McGraw-Hill, 1967.

Cash, W. J. *The Mind of the South*. New York: Knopf, 1941.

Chambers, M. M. *Colleges and the Courts, 1946–1950*. New York: Columbia University Press, 1952.

Clark, E. Culpepper. *The Schoolhouse Door: Segregation's Last Stand at the University of Alabama*. New York: Oxford University Press, 1993.

Committee on Higher Educational Opportunity in the South. *The Negro and Higher Education in the South*. Atlanta: Southern Regional Education Board, 1967.

Cruse, Harold. *The Crisis of the Negro Intellectual: From Its Origins to the Present*. New York: Morrow, 1967.

Curry, Constance. *Silver Rights*. New York: Harcourt Brace, 1995.

Davis, William Riley. *The Development and Present Status of Negro Education in East Texas*. 1934. Reprint, New York: AMS Press, 1972.

Dethloff, Henry C. *A Centennial History of Texas A&M University, 1876–1976*. Vol. 1. College Station: Texas A&M Press, 1975.

Dittmer, John, George C. Wright, and W. Marvin Dulaney. *Essays on the American Civil Rights Movement*. Edited by W. Marvin Dulaney and Kathleen Underwood. College Station: Texas A&M Press, 1993.

Duram, James. *A Moderate among Extremists: Dwight D. Eisenhower and the School Desegregation Crisis*. Chicago: Nelson-Hall, 1981.

Duren, Almetris. *Overcoming: A History of Black Integration at the University of Texas at Austin*. Austin: University of Texas, 1979.

Eagles, Charles W., ed. *The Civil Rights Movement in America*. Jackson: University Press of Mississippi, 1986.

Eby, Frederick. *The Development of Education in Texas*. New York: Macmillan, 1925.

———. *Education in Texas Source Materials*. Austin: University of Texas, 1918.

Evans, C. E. *The Story of Texas Schools*. Austin: Steck, 1955.

Fairclough, Adam. *Race & Democracy: The Civil Rights Struggle in Louisiana, 1915–1972*. Athens: University of Georgia Press, 1995.

Farmer, James. *Freedom — When?* New York: Random House, 1965.

Franklin, John Hope, and Alfred A. Moss Jr. *From Slavery to Freedom: A History of Negro Americans*. 6th ed. New York: McGraw-Hill, 1988.

Genovese, Eugene D. *Roll, Jordan, Roll: The World the Slaves Made*. New York: Vintage Books, 1976.

Goldfield, David R. *Black, White, and Southern: Race Relations and Southern Culture, 1940 to the Present*. Baton Rouge: Louisiana State University Press, 1990.

Guzman, Jessie P. *Twenty Years of Court Decisions Affecting Higher Education in the South, 1938–1958*. Tuskegee, Ala.: Tuskegee Institute, 1960.

Hall, Jacquelyn Dowd. *Revolt against Chivalry*. New York: Columbia University Press, 1979.

Hare, Maud Cuney. *Norris Wright Cuney: A Tribune of the Black People*. 1913. Reprint, Austin: Steck-Vaughn, 1968.

Heintze, Michael R. *Private Black Colleges in Texas, 1865–1954*. College Station: Texas A&M University Press, 1985.

Himmel, Richard, and Robert S. La Forte. *Down the Corridor of Years: A Centennial History of the University of Texas in Photographs, 1890–1990*. Denton: University of North Texas Press, 1990.

Hine, Darlene Clark. *Black Victory: The Rise and Fall of the White Primary in Texas*. Millwood: KTO Press, 1979.

Horne, Gerald. *Communist Front? The Civil Rights Congress, 1946–1956*. Rutherford: Fairleigh-Dickinson University Press, 1987.

Jackson, Andrew Webster. *A Sure Foundation*. Houston: A. W. Jackson, 1940.

Jackson, Gwendolyn. *The History of the Negro in Wichita Falls, Texas, 1880–1982*. Wichita Falls: Humphrey Printing, in press.

Jackson, Kenneth T. *The Ku Klux Klan in the City, 1915–1930*. New York: Oxford University Press, 1967.

Key, V. O., Jr. *Southern Politics*. New York: Vintage, 1949.

Kinch, Sam, and Stuart Long. *Allan Shivers: The Pied Piper of Texas Politics*. Austin: Shoal Creek, 1973.

Kirby, Jack Temple. *Darkness at the Dawning*. Philadelphia: Lippincott, 1972.

Kluger, Richard. *Simple Justice: The History of Brown v. Board of Education and Black America's Struggle for Equality*. New York: Vintage Books, 1977.

Marable, Manning. *Beyond Black and White: Transforming African-American Politics*. New York: Verso, 1995.

———. *Race, Reform, and Rebellion: The Second Reconstruction in Black America, 1945–1990*. Jackson: University of Mississippi, 1991.

Marcus, Laurence R., and Benjamin D. Stickney. *Race and Education: The Unending Controversy*. Springfield: Charles C. Thomas, 1981.

McDaniel, Vernon. *History of the Teachers State Association of Texas*. Washington: National Education Association, 1977.

McMillen, Neil R. *The Citizens' Council: Organized Resistance to the Second Reconstruction, 1954–1964*. Urbana: University of Illinois Press, 1971.

Meinig, D. W. *Imperial Texas: An Interpretive Essay in Cultural Geography*. Austin: University of Texas Press, 1969.

Morgan, Gordon D., and Izola Preston. *The Edge of Campus: A Journal of the Black Experience at the University of Arkansas*. Fayetteville: University of Arkansas Press, 1990.

Peltason, Jack W. *Fifty-Eight Lonely Men: Southern Federal Court Judges and School Desegregation*. New York: Harcourt, Brace and World, 1961.

Pennington, Richard. *Breaking the Ice: The Racial Integration of Southwest Conference Football*. Jefferson, N.C.: McFarland, 1987.

Pitre, Merline. *In Struggle against Jim Crow: Lula B. White and the NAACP, 1900–1957*. College Station: Texas A&M Press, 1999.

Proceedings of the First Annual Session of the Conference on Education for Negroes in Texas. Prairie View: Prairie View Standard, 1930.

Proceedings of the Eighth Educational Conference. Prairie View: Prairie View College State Normal and Industrial, November 1932.

Proceedings of the Eleventh Educational Conference. Hempstead: Prairie View College Press, November 1940.

Ramsdell, Charles W. *Reconstruction in Texas*. Gloucester, N.Y.: Peter Smith, 1910.

Rawick, George P., ed. *The American Slave: A Composite Autobiography*. Texas Narratives. Westport, Conn.: Greenwood Press, 1972.

Redfield, Margaret Park, ed. *The Social Uses of Social Science: The Papers of Robert Redfield*. Chicago: University of Chicago Press, 1963.

Reed, Linda. *Simple Decency and Common Sense: The Southern Conference Movement, 1938–1963*. Bloomington: Indiana University Press, 1991.

Rice, Lawrence D. *The Negro in Texas: 1874–1900*. Baton Rouge: Louisiana State University Press, 1971.

Richardson, Rupert N., Ernest Wallace, and Adrian Anderson. *Texas: The Lone Star State*. 5th ed. Englewood Cliffs: Prentice-Hall, 1981.

Rogers, James L. *The Story of North Texas: From Texas Normal College, 1890, to North Texas State University, 1965*. Denton: North Texas State University Press, 1965.

Rushing, Jane Gilmore, and Kline A. Nall. *Evolution of a University: Texas Tech's First Fifty Years*. Austin: Eakin Press, 1975.

San Miguel, Guadalupe, Jr. *"Let All of Them Take Heed": Mexican Americans and the Campaign for Educational Equality, 1910–1981*. Austin: University of Texas Press, 1987.

Seliger, Martin. *The Marxist Conception of Ideology: A Critical Essay*. Cambridge: Cambridge University Press, 1977.

Shabazz, Amilcar. *The Forty Acres Documents*. Baton Rouge: House of Songhay, 1994.

Shoemaker, Don, ed. *With All Deliberate Speed*. New York: Harper and Brothers, 1957.

Smallwood, James M. *Time of Hope, Time of Despair: Black Texans during Reconstruction*. Port Washington, N.Y.: Kennikat Press, 1981.

Stephan, Walter, and Joe Feagin, eds. *School Desegregation: Past, Present, and Future*. New York: Plenum, 1980.

Taylor, Joe F. *The AC Story: Journal of a College*. Canyon: Stacked Plains Press, 1979.

Tindall, George Brown. *South Carolina Negroes, 1877–1900*. 1952. Reprint, Baton Rouge: Louisiana State University Press, 1966.

Tushnet, Mark V. *Making Civil Rights Law: Thurgood Marshall and the Supreme Court, 1936–1961*. New York: Oxford University Press, 1994.

———. *The NAACP's Legal Strategy against Segregated Education, 1925–1950*. Chapel Hill: University of North Carolina Press, 1987.

Warren, Earl. *The Memoirs of Earl Warren*. Garden City: Doubleday, 1977.

Washington, Booker T. *Up from Slavery*. 1900. Reprint, New York: Bantam Books, 1963.

Watson, Levi. *Fighting Hard: The Alabama State Experience*. Tuscaloosa: University of Alabama Press, 1987.

Webb, Walter P. *A Corner of the Old South*. Austin: Steck Company, 1959.

Weinberg, Meyer. *A Chance to Learn: A History of Race and Education in the United States*. Cambridge: Cambridge University Press, 1977.

———. *Integrated Education: A Reader*. Beverly Hills: Glencoe Press, 1968.

———. *The Search for Quality Integrated Education: Policy and Research on Minority Students in School and College*. Westport, Conn.: Greenwood Press, 1983.

Wharton County Historical Commission. *Wharton County Pictorial History, 1846–1946*. Austin: Eakin Press, 1993.

Williams, Annie Lee. *A History of Wharton County, 1846–1961*. Austin: Von Boeckmann–Jones Press, 1964.

Williams, John B., ed. *Desegregating America's Colleges and Universities: Title VI Regulation of Higher Education*. New York: Teachers College Press, 1988.

Williamson, Joel. *After Slavery: The Negro in South Carolina during Reconstruction, 1861–1877*. Chapel Hill: University of North Carolina Press, 1965.

Willie, Charles V. "The Future of School Desegregation." In *State of Black America 1987*. Washington, D.C.: National Urban League, 1987.

———. *The Ivory and Ebony Towers: Race Relations and Higher Education*. Lexington, Mass.: LexingtonBooks, 1981.

Wilson, James Q. *Negro Politics*. New York: Free Press of Glencoe, 1965.

Wilson, William J. *The Declining Significance of Race: Blacks and Changing American Institutions*. 2d ed. Chicago: University of Chicago Press, 1980.

———. *Power, Racism, and Privilege: Race Relations in Theoretical and Sociohistorical Perspectives*. New York: Macmillan, 1973.

Winegarten, Ruthe, and Cathy Schechter. *Deep in the Heart: The Lives and Legends of Texas Jews*. Austin: Eakin Press, 1990.

Wizig, Jerry. *Eat 'Em up, Cougars*. Huntsville, Ala.: Strode Publishers, 1977.

Wolters, Raymond. *The Burden of Brown: Thirty Years of School Desegregation*. Knoxville: University of Tennessee Press, 1984.

Woolfolk, George Ruble. *The Free Negro in Texas, 1800–1860: A Study in Cultural Compromise*. Ann Arbor: University Microform, 1966.

———. *Prairie View: A Study in Public Conscience, 1878–1946*. New York: Pageant Press, 1962.

Yelderman, Pauline. *The Jay Birds of Fort Bend County: A White Man's Union*. Waco: Texian Press, 1979.

Journal Articles

Amin, Julius. "Black Lubbock: 1955 to the Present." *West Texas Historical Association Year Book* 65 (1989): 26.

Arline, Ralph, Jr. "Desegregation in the Beaumont Schools, 1954–1985." *Touchstone* 9 (1990): 47–54.

Baeza, Abelardo. "*La Escuela del Barrio*: A History of the Alpine Centennial School, 1939–1969." *Journal of Big Bend Studies* (January 1992).

———. "*La Escuela Escondida*: History of the Morgan School in Alpine, Texas, 1929–1954." *Journal of Big Bend Studies* (January 1994).

Becnel, Nia Dorian. "John S. Chase." *Texas Architect* (November/December 1989): 47.

Bell, Major T. "Lamar Cecil — The Days That Were His." *Texas Gulf Historical and Biographical Record* 12 (November 1976): 20–24.

Bullock, Henry Allen. "Negro Higher and Professional Education in Texas." *Journal of Negro Education* 18 (Summer 1948): 378–88.

Burran, James A. "Violence in an 'Arsenal of Democracy': The Beaumont Race Riot, 1943." *East Texas Historical Journal* 14 (Spring 1976): 39–52.

Dalfiume, Richard M. "The 'Forgotten Years' of the Negro Revolution." *Journal of American History* 55 (June 1968): 90–106.

Gillette, Michael L. "Blacks Challenge the White University." *Southwestern Historical Quarterly* 86 (October 1982): 321–44.

———. "The Rise of the NAACP in Texas." *Southwestern Historical Quarterly* 81 (April 1978): 371–92.

Foster, Robert L., and Alwyn Barr, "Black Lubbock." *West Texas Historical Association Year Book* 54 (1978): 25–32.

Greenberg, Herbert. "Some Effects of Segregated Education on Various of the Personality of those Members of Disadvantaged Groups Experiencing This Form of Education." *Desegregation Abstracts*, 1955.

Greenberg, Herbert, Arthur L. Chase, and Thomas M. Gannon Jr. "Attitudes of White and Negro Students in a West Texas Town toward School Integration." *Journal of Applied Psychology* (February 1957): 27–31.

Hill, Larry D., and Robert A. Calvert, "The University of Texas Extension Services and Progressivism." *Southwestern Historical Quarterly* 86 (October 1982): 231–54.

Hine, Darlene Clark. "The Elusive Ballot: The Black Struggle against the Texas Democratic White Primary, 1932–1945." *Southwestern Historical Quarterly* 81 (April 1978): 371–92.

Holtzman, Wayne H. "Attitudes of College Men toward Non-Segregation in Texas Schools." *Public Opinion Quarterly* (Fall 1956): 559–69.

Hornsby, Alton, Jr. "The 'Colored Branch University' Issue in Texas–Prelude to *Sweatt* vs. *Painter*." *Journal of Negro History* 76 (April 1973).

Jones, William H. "The Status of Educational Desegregation in Texas." *Journal of Negro Education* 25 (Summer 1956): 334–44.

Kemble, C. Robert. "Lamar in Perspective." *Texas Gulf Historical and Biographical Record* 19 (November 1983): 14–34.

Kirk, W. Astor, and John Q. Taylor King, "Desegregation of Higher Education in Texas." *Journal of Negro Education* 27 (Summer 1958).

Klarman, Michael J. "How *Brown* Changed Race Relations: The Backlash Thesis." *Journal of American History* 81 (June 1994): 81–118.

Marcello, Ronald E. "The Integration of Intercollegiate Athletics in Texas: North Texas State College as a Test Case, 1956." *Journal of Sport History* 14 (Winter 1987): 286–316.

McCaslin, Richard B. "Steadfast in His Intent: John W. Hargis and the Integration of the University of Texas at Austin." *Southwestern Historical Quarterly* 95 (July 1991): 20–41.

McWilliams, Alyce. "A Brief History of the Beaumont City Schools." *Texas Gulf Historical and Biographical Record* 2 (November 1966): 23–28.

Neal, Diane, and Thomas Kremm. "'What Shall We Do with the Negro?': The Freedmen's Bureau in Texas." *East Texas Historical Journal* 27 (Fall 1989): 29–39.

Olson, James, and Sharon Phair. "The Anatomy of a Race Riot: Beaumont, Texas, 1943." *Texana* 11 (Spring 1973): 64–72.

Pitre, Merline. "Black Houstonians and the 'Separate but Equal' Doctrine: Carter W. Wesley versus Lulu B. White." *Houston Review* 12 (1990): 23–36.

Scott, Alan. "Twenty-Five Years of Opinion on Integration in Texas." *Southwestern Social Science Quarterly* 48 (September 1967): 155–63.

Shabazz, Amilcar. "The African American Educational Legacy in Beaumont, Texas: A Preliminary Analysis." *Texas Gulf Historical and Biographical Record* 27 (1991): 56–76.

Sitkoff, Harvard. "Racial Militancy and Interracial Violence in the Second World War." *Journal of American History* 58 (December 1971): 661–81.

Sutherland, Thomas S. "I'm Proud of Texas." As told to Hart Stilwell. *Coronet* (February 1956): 50–58.

Valien, Preston. "Desegregation in Higher Education: A Critical Summary." *Journal of Negro Education* 27 (Summer 1958): 373–80.

Vincent, Joseph J. "A Brief History of the Jefferson County Schools." *Texas Gulf Historical and Biographical Record* 4 (November 1968): 28–34.

Vines, Kenneth N. "Federal District Judges and Race Relations Cases in the South." *Journal of Politics* 26 (1964): 337–57.

Woodward, C. Vann. "The Unreported Crisis in the Southern Colleges." *Harper's Magazine*, October 1962, 82–83.

Reference Works

Beaumont City Directory. Dallas: Morrison and Fourmy, 1910–60.

Buhle, Mari Jo, Paul Buhle, and Dan Georgakas, eds. *Encylopedia of the American Left.* Urbana: University of Illinois Press, 1992.

Dallas Morning News. *Texas Almanac.* Dallas: A. H. Belo, 1954–87.

Jackson, Juanita, and Jean Wallace. *A Directory of Black Businesses, Churches, Clubs, and Organizations in Beaumont, Texas.* Beaumont Public Library, 1981, n.p., in author's possession.

Webb, Walter Prescott, ed. *The Handbook of Texas.* Austin: Texas State Historical Association, 1952.

Whisenhunt, Donald W. *The Encyclopedia of Texas Colleges and Universities: An Historical Profile.* Austin: Eakin Press, 1986.

Dissertations, Theses, and Unpublished Documents

Adams, Claude R. "A Historical Development of Education for Negroes in Texas." M.A. thesis, Prairie View Agricultural and Mechanical College, 1949.

Adams, Howard. "Certain Characteristics of the Freshman Class Entering Lamar State College of Technology, 1957–1958." Ed.D. diss., University of Nebraska, 1958.

Banks, Melvin J. "The Pursuit of Equality: The Movement for First Class Citizenship among Negroes in Texas, 1920–1950." D.S.S. diss., Syracuse University, 1962.

Barchus, Gale L. "The Dynamics of Black Demands and White Responses for Negro Higher Education in the State of Texas, 1945–1950." M.A. thesis, University of Texas, 1970.

Bessent, Nancy Ruth Eckols. "The Publisher: A Biography of Carter Wesley." M.A. thesis, University of Texas, 1981.

Brophy, William Joseph. "The Black Texan, 1900–1950: A Quantitative History." Ph.D. diss., Vanderbilt University, 1974.

Dailey, Nancy. "History of the Beaumont, Texas, Chapter of the National Association for the Advancement of Colored People, 1918–1970." M.A. thesis, Lamar University, 1971.

Gillette, Michael L. "The NAACP in Texas, 1937–1957." Ph.D. diss., University of Texas, 1984.

Glasrud, Bruce. "Black Texans, 1900–1930: A History." Ph.D. diss., Texas Technological College, 1969.

Gray, Billy Richard. "The Growth and Development of Midwestern University, 1922–1957." M.A. thesis, University of Texas at Austin, 1959.

Head, Richard Henry. "Public School Desegregation in Beaumont, Texas, 1954–1969." M.A. thesis, Lamar State College of Technology, 1970.

Kroutter, Thomas E. "The Ku Klux Klan in Jefferson County, Texas, 1921–1924." M.A. thesis, Lamar University, 1972.

Lane, Harry B. "The Present Status of Secondary Education for Negroes in Texas." M.A. thesis, University of Southern California, 1932.

Linsley, Judith W. "A Social History of Beaumont, Texas, in the 1920's." M.A. thesis, Lamar University, 1971.

Masters, Basil Earl. "A History of Early Education in Northeast Texas." M.A. thesis, University of Texas at Austin, 1929.

McLaughlin, Marvin L. "Reflections of the Philosophy and Practices of Lamar State College of Technology as Shown through Its History." Ed.D. diss., University of Houston, 1955.

Meltzer, Mildred H. "Chapters in the Struggle for Negro Rights in Houston, 1944–1962." M.A. thesis, University of Houston, 1963.

Musslewhite, Lynn Ray. "Texas in the 1920's: A History of Social Change." Ph.D. diss., University of Texas, 1975.

O'Brien, Florence B. "Adequacy of Texas History Texts in Reporting Negro Achievements." M.A. thesis, Stephen F. Austin Teachers College, 1939.

Olson, James, ed. "Years of Anxiety and Change." Draft manuscript in author's possession.

Richter, William Lee. "The Army in Texas during Reconstruction, 1865–1870." Ph.D. diss., University of Texas, 1971.

Sapper, Neil Gary. "A Survey of the History of the Black People of Texas, 1930–1954." Ph.D. diss., Texas Tech University, 1972.

Shabazz, Amilcar. "The Desegregation of Lamar State College of Technology: An Analysis of Race and Education in Southeast Texas." M.A. thesis, Lamar University, 1990.

Tarrow, Willie A. "A University for Negroes of Texas — A Promise Unfulfilled." M.A. thesis, Prairie View Agricultural and Mechanical College, 1946.

Urquhart, George R. "The Status of Secondary and Higher Education of Negroes in Texas." M.A. thesis, University of Texas, 1931.

Wade, Michael G. "From Reform to Massive Resistance: The Desegregation of the Louisiana State Colleges, 1954–1964." Paper delivered at the Annual Meeting of the Southern History Association, New Orleans, La., October 1995; copy in author's possession.

Welch, Joe Ben. "A History of the Growth and Development of Lamar University from 1949 to 1973." Ed.D. diss., McNeese State University, 1974.

Wilkison, Debra. "Eyewitness to Social Change: The Desegregation of East Texas State College." M.A. thesis, East Texas State University, 1990.

Williams, David A. "The History of Higher Education for Black Texans, 1872–1977." Ed.D. diss., Baylor University, 1978.

White, Leslie J. "A Study of Recent Efforts to Equalize Educational Opportunities for Negroes in Texas." M.A. thesis, Fisk University, 1945.

Index

INDEX

Joseph, Lillie Mae, 175
Juneteenth, 8–10

Kappa Alpha Psi fraternity, 72
Kazen, Abraham, Jr., 193
Kennedy administration, 209
Kilgore Junior College, 145, 147
King, Leon, 166
King, Martin Luther, Jr., 218–19
Kirk, W. Astor, 72, 74–78, 904
Kirkwood, Carolyn Jean, 214–15
Kirkwood v. Sam Houston State Teachers College, 215
Klein, Arthur, 21
Knight, Rev. C. D., 67
Koeninger, Rupert, 213–14
Ku Klux Klan, 147, 169, 186; in Dallas, 106; and cross-burnings, 116, 166, 171–73

Lamar State College of Technology, 61, 168–80, 189, 216
Lambert, Ellen King, 168
Lanier, Ralph O'Hara, 46, 85, 90, 114, 115, 120, 187
League of United Latin American Citizens (LULAC), 122, 126
Leake, Chauncey Depew, 81, 85, 87–89, 187
Lee, H. E., 41
Lee, Dr. A. Julian, 71
Legal Defense and Educational Fund (LDF), 61, 188, 198
Lewis, Marion, 189
Liberal integrationism, 4–5. See also Civil libertarianism
Lightfoot, Frances, 173, 176–77
Lockeridge, S. M., 131
Lodge, Henry Cabot, Jr., 139
Lone Star State Medical and Pharmaceutical Association, 42, 83, 118
Lott, Trent, 221–22
Lucas, Rev. A. A., 194
Lucy, Autherine, 146, 165

Malone, Don, 155
Mandell, Arthur J., 65, 101
Marshall, Thurgood, 7–8, 34, 69, 74, 163, 186; in SNC-EEO, 46–48; on black schools as perpetuating segregation education, 49, 104–5; legal strategy for higher education equalization, 52–53, 100–101, 110; on black Texans, 54–56; Denison address, 62–63; on Brown, 138–39
Martin, Louis, 62
Massive resistance to desegregation, 94, 146, 186–87

Masters, Basil Earl, 144, 146–48, 176
Maston, Thomas Buford, 130–32
Matthews, E. J., 67–68
McBride, Carl, 148
McBride, Doris Ann, 149
McClennan, W. D., 111
McCown, Henry Y., 91–92
McKinnon, Rev. Snowden I., 129
McLaurin, G. W., 93
McLaurin v. Oklahoma, 101–11
McMillan, Mae Frances, 89
Mendez v. Westminster School District, 58
Menefee, Marilyn, 148–49, 195
Mexican Americans, 5, 141, 150, 153, 193, 199; as source for Sweatt legal strategy, 58; in Brownsville, 120–23; in Corpus Christi, 126–28; in Kingsville, 167; as filibusteros, 193–94; in Alpine, 210–11. See also American G. I. Forum; League of United Latin American Citizens
Midwestern University (MU), 141–42, 148–50, 166
Militant race consciousness, 57, 61
Military service, blacks in: as argument for desegregation, 36, 148–49, 153; Tuskegee airman experiment, 82–83; from Webb Air Force Base, 123; from Amarillo Air Force Base, 124; from Sheppard Air Force Base, 149; from Fort Bliss and Biggs Field, 161; Naval Auxiliary Air Station and Japan experience, 167
Miller, A. Tennyson, 162–63, 166
Miller, Dorie, 38
Miscegenation bugaboo, 112, 147
Mongrelization, 147
Montgomery, John L., 181, 185
Moon, Henry Lee, 84
Moore, Ophelia, 205
Morgan, Leon Augustus, 89, 159
Morton, James Hemanway, 71–73, 75, 83–84, 86, 111, 117
Murphy, Carl, 55, 64
Murphy, Samuel J., 31
Myers, Pollie Anne, 146

Nabrit, James, 54, 56
Nabrit, Dr. Samuel M., 201–2
National Association for the Advancement of Colored People (NAACP), 3–5, 7–8, 42–43, 84, 105, 141, 188, 198; red-baited, 50–52, 146; in LaGrange, 57, 147; in Hearne, 57–59, 63; in Texas, 66, 73–77, 123, 125–26, 180–82, 186, 192; Austin branch, 71–74; Freedom Movement, 72; Crisis, 73; Houston branch, 75, 193; in Wichita Falls, 141, 148; in Wharton, 150–51; Beaumont branch, 170,

298